PETER DRUCKER

SHAPING THE MANAGERIAL MIND

PETER DRUCKER

SHAPING THE MANAGERIAL MIND

JOHN E. FLAHERTY

JOSSEY-BASS
A Wiley Company
www.josseybass.com

Published by

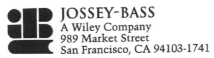

JOSSEY-BASS
A Wiley Company
989 Market Street
San Francisco, CA 94103-1741

www.josseybass.com

Copyright © 1999 by John Wiley & Sons, Inc.

Jossey-Bass is a registered trademark of John Wiley & Sons, Inc.

Jossey-Bass books and products are available through most bookstores. To contact Jossey-Bass
directly, call (888) 378-2537, fax to (800) 605-2665, or visit our website at www.josseybass.com.

Substantial discounts on bulk quantities of Jossey-Bass books are available to corporations,
professional associations, and other organizations. For details and discount information, contact the
special sales department at Jossey-Bass.

We at Jossey-Bass strive to use the most environmentally sensitive paper stocks available to us. Our
publications are printed on acid-free recycled stock whenever possible, and our paper always meets or
exceeds minimum GPO and EPA requirements.

All the quotations in this book from Peter Drucker's works are reprinted with the permission of Peter F. Drucker.

Library of Congress Cataloging-in-Publication Data

Flaherty, John E.
    Peter Drucker : shaping the managerial mind / John E. Flaherty.
  1st ed.
    p. cm.
  Includes bibliographical references and index.
  ISBN 0-7879-4764-4 (hardcover)
  ISBN 0-7879-6066-7 (paperback)
  1. Drucker, Peter Ferdinand, date. 2. Industrial management.
  I. Title.
  HD31 .F537 1999
  300'.92—dc21
  [B]
                            99-6371

FIRST EDITION

HB Printing 10 9 8 7 6 5 4 3 2
PB Printing 10 9 8 7 6 5 4 3 2 1

CONTENTS

PART THREE: ON EXECUTIVE EFFECTIVENESS

PREFACE

Peter Drucker has been variously labeled a journalist, novelist, economist, sociologist, political theorist, philosopher, and art critic. He has earned distinction in each of these professional roles, but he is most widely known as the father of modern management.

Since his popularization of modern management after World War II, countless books have been written on the subject. Because the overwhelming majority have focused on fads, gimmicks, and panaceas, they have passed into oblivion. Yet despite the explosive changes in society during Drucker's long career, his own managerial concepts and principles retain an astonishing vitality and utility. Testimonies to his continuing relevance and popularity are the reprinting of his major nonmanagement works by Transaction Publishers at Rutgers University and the publication in 1998 by Harvard University Press of a volume of his selected articles, titled *Peter Drucker on the Profession of Management*. And Harvard University Press intends to keep his main management books in print for seventeen years after his death.

It is ironic that Drucker did not start out with the goal of developing modern management, nor was he passionately interested in the field of business. His primary concern when he began his studies in the 1930s was understanding the contributions and justification of institutions to society. In examining the failure of totalitarian responses and the ineffectiveness of conventional capitalism, he hypothesized that the modern corporation, with its salaried cadre of professional managers as catalysts of change, was the most feasible hope for the future. Equally important, he found that the modern corporation was the one institution open to scholarly investigation on the issues of performance and legitimacy.

In this study I have attempted to show, first, how Drucker's early political thinking, as revealed in his writings, shaped his managerial mind; the imprint is indelible. Second, I have wanted to show that implicit in his main purpose of molding a managerial mentality was the concurrent emergence of the modern discipline of management. Under this intellectual rubric, I have concentrated on three major themes: (1) the transition from the traditional model of functional business specialties to a theoretical approach that integrated corporate survival objectives into an organic discipline; (2) the innovative concept of systematically managing corporate change, a task for which Drucker introduced organized strategic policies and entrepreneurial principles; and (3) the proposition that managerial activity is a systematic form of work that (if not literally teachable) is definitely learnable and improvable as a method for achieving greater productivity and results.

Audience

I perceive the book to have particular benefits, appeal, and relevance for three groups. First, for accountable executives of business and other social organizations it provides a compilation of principles and techniques for improved performance. Second, for academics it suggests an instructional tool for understanding the roots of management theory and the fundamentals of executive effectiveness. Third, for senior managers directly responsible for strategic planning it offers a frame of reference for meeting the challenges of tomorrow in a competitive environment of accelerated change.

Overview of the Contents

Following the essence of the three major themes, I have structured this book with three segments. Part One, Chapters Three through Six, addresses the quest for a theory in Drucker's early years. This segment covers the influences of his formative years and how his early writings depict his conceptual methodologies and form the design of his managerial philosophy. After a chronological discussion of his early books, I end this section with an examination of *The Practice of Management* (1954), the work that establishes the framework of his managerial theory and suggests guidelines for practitioners. Part Two, Chapters Seven through Eleven, treats Drucker's views on strategy and entrepreneurship. It focuses on what Drucker describes as the two central tasks of managerial operations: (1) "making work productive and the worker achieving" and (2) "moving capital from less to more productive areas." Part Three, Chapters Twelve through Seventeen, discusses executive effectiveness from multiple perspectives.

In 1970, I coedited *Peter Drucker: Contributions to Business Enterprise,* a collection of essays by twenty-three academic scholars and prominent business executives, on varied topics important in Drucker's work. Originally, I had thought about updating that project, using the title *Drucker Revisited.* I then changed my mind, however, deciding to undertake the challenge myself, with the aim of providing greater consistency and coherence in the matter of Drucker's influence on modern management and the shaping of his managerial views. This meant also giving up a plan to write separate chapters on other subjects of deep concern to Peter Drucker, topics such as education, economics, Japan, the not-for-profit sector, corporate governance, and comparative management (although I do discuss these topics in relation to Drucker's management views). However, coincidentally, Jack Beatty, senior editor at the *Atlantic Monthly,* has recently published a first-rate study on Drucker's political, economic, and social ideas, called *The World According to Peter Drucker* (1998).

Acknowledgments

No book emerges in a vacuum. This one owes a debt of gratitude to many people. First, to my wife, Christine, and my two old friends Richard Matthews and Thomas P. Robinson, for encouraging the project and nourishing it with their helpful suggestions. Second, to the staff of Pace University Lubin School of Business, Dean Arthur Centonze, Associate Dean Peter Hoefer, and John Dory, director of the doctoral program, for their scheduling support and administrative assistance; to Diana Ward, assistant director of applied research, for providing three competent graduate students to check on sources; and to those students themselves—Mindy Erlichman, Lei Wang, and Victoria Hottenrott—for their help. Third, to Margaret Jacques, for her infinite patience while deciphering my scribbled script and typing the manuscript. And finally, to my friend and mentor Peter Drucker, whose pioneering perceptual talents and analytical abilities were the genesis and inspiration of this book. Although the organization and interpretation of the material are my own, I have endeavored to present a digest of his concepts and ideas as I believe he depicted them. Of course the usual disclaimer is in order. I bear full responsibility for any mistakes of interpretation.

Convent Station, New Jersey   John E. Flaherty
July 1999

PETER DRUCKER

SHAPING THE MANAGERIAL MIND

To Marie and Martin

CHAPTER ONE

INTRODUCTION

Few people are accorded the rare distinction of establishing a modern academic discipline. Recognized as "the father of modern management"[1] and acknowledged as "the man who invented the corporate society,"[2] Peter Drucker merits this rare honor. For almost six decades his writings, lectures, and consulting activities have created a rich legacy of scholarship for students of management and have served as a fertile source of inspiration and relevant methodology for business practitioners.

Drucker is widely acclaimed as the doyen of management; literature over the past half-century documents that he is the most frequently cited author in the field. By consensus his works are considered landmarks in the discipline of management. According to John Micklethwait and Adrian Wooldridge, editors of the *Economist*, "So far, management theory has produced, at most, one 'great' thinker: Peter Drucker."[3] Kenneth Boulding, the noted economist, considers him a "foremost philosopher of American society."[4] Tom Peters, the celebrated management consultant, declares there was "no true discipline of management" before Drucker, and in the same passage Micklethwait and Wooldridge add that "like his biblical namesake, he is the rock on which the current church is founded, as the voices crying in the wilderness who preceded him will confirm."[5] G. S. Day, a marketing specialist, puts Drucker at the "head of the list" of the leading contributors to the marketing discipline; his "seminal writings on the nature and purpose of organizations and sheer mastery of the intricacies of a strategy and its execution remain a continuing inspiration to anyone trying to make sense out of a market."[6]

In addition, a number of specialized business scholars have paid tribute to him as a shining example of relevance in their respective fields: Robert Kaplan in accounting, Alan Lakein in time management, George Harris in psychology, Robert Heller in comparative management, Edward Hall in communications theory, George Odiorne in organizational theory, and Melvin Kranzberg in technology. Gary Hamel and C. K. Prahalad, currently regarded as the two most outstanding scholars on corporate strategy, have commented on his pioneering influence, saying, "He has also been an unfailing beacon, lighting the way toward the management issues of tomorrow."[7]

A list of business executives who have been directly influenced by him would take pages, but the following is a short sample of this list. Walter Wriston, former chairman of Citicorp, remarks: "Peter is an extraordinary person. He is able to look out the same window we do and see different things than we see."[8] Responding to the question of which management books influenced him the most, Bill Gates of Microsoft replies, "Well, Drucker, of course."[9] Jack Welch, CEO of General Electric, credits Drucker with his key entrepreneurial decision: "My first central idea for GE back in 1981 came from Peter Drucker. It was my decision to be either number one or number two in each of our businesses—or get out of them altogether."[10] Andrew Grove, Intel's chairman, remarks: "Drucker is a hero of mine. He writes and thinks with exquisite clarity—a standout among a bunch of muddled fad mongers."[11] Michael Kami, former director of research at IBM and Xerox, states that "Peter Drucker is without doubt the foremost management scholar in the world. Not only has he maintained that post for the past forty years; he continually adds new concepts and innovative ideas to keep ahead of the fast-changing social and economic environment."[12]

A poll of business managers, faculty, and consultants could easily extend this list of tributes, but we should consider some contrarian points of view. Agha Hasan Abedi, founder of BCCI, once boasted to his employees that he understood management far better than Peter Drucker, the highly acclaimed management guru, whom he dismissed as an apprentice.[13] Hasan Abedi of course was responsible for one of the biggest bank failures in history.

Most of the criticism of Drucker has a similar superficiality. For example, he has been called an armchair philosopher who has never met a payroll; a journalist rather than a scholar, who uses anecdotes as examples; a person who lacks academic credentials in management; and a poor researcher (because he refuses to bolster his arguments with footnotes, formulae, theorems, and models). There is a need, of course, for an in-depth critical analysis of his views; but up to now there has been no such study.

Lack of substantive criticism is, paradoxically, a proof of the enduring value of Drucker's work, as is the fact that even a perfunctory review of the management literature reveals an astonishing number of authors in the field who neglect to ascribe credit to Drucker for much of their material. Perhaps the reason for this failure was best explained by Theodore Levitt of Harvard University when he noted that "nobody is more qualified to attest to a man's genius than his plagiarizers. A man as productive, creative, and versatile as Drucker predictably has lots of them. I am proud to confess membership in the large and grateful body of Drucker plagiarizers. If imitation is the highest form of flattery, plagiarism must have God's social transcendental blessing. If He creates only an occasional genius He has no choice but to condone Drucker's plagiarizers—unless God is willing to have the truths spoken by His genius degraded into unprepossessing copies."[14]

It is ironic that Drucker has been said to lack formal education in the management field, yet books and articles in this same discipline have blatantly appropriated his ideas and insights. As he continued to ponder why so many writers have borrowed so liberally from Drucker, to the point of intellectual kleptomania, Levitt confessed that even he has been "a resolute, appreciative, but seldom footnoting Drucker plagiarizer . . . Drucker's literary style and agile mind are such that even the most profound observation seems so innocently commonplace that the reader is hardly aware of its profundity or of Drucker's authorship. That not only makes plagiarism highly probable; it also enables its perpetrator to feel little guilt."[15]

It is no exaggeration to say that Peter Drucker's name has become synonymous with the theory and practice of management. This means that a number of questions about Drucker's career can be profitably explored. Among them are the following: What were the influences that shaped his thinking? What forces and events in his life directed him toward the field of management? What impact did his early academic writings have on the future discipline of management? And what intellectual methodologies and thinking techniques formed the basis of his analysis? In this book, I explore these and related questions in considerable detail.

I do this in part out of a friendship and personal contact with Peter Drucker spanning forty years. Some of my special experiences in this relationship have been the following: coediting a book on his managerial contributions, auditing all his classes and seminars at New York University for more than a ten-year period covering the late 1950s and most of the 1960s, attending a great many of his public lectures over the past three decades, using many of his insights and techniques in my teaching career, applying his principles when consulting with clients and conducting seminars for business executives, and of course, benefiting from his knowledge and advice given in the course of innumerable conversations and correspondence over the years. This exposure has made me the recipient of an unusual intellectual osmosis concerning his work and, I believe, gives me a certain authenticity and degree of credibility as an interpreter of his work.

Perhaps of most importance as far as this book is concerned, it has enabled me to avoid a bland regurgitation of Drucker's thoughts and to punctuate the text with personal evaluations in order to illuminate the subject matter. A major illustration of this judgmental method is the *paradigm of change* model I have introduced in Chapter Seven. Of course this is highly un-Druckerian because he has always been uncomfortable with models. However, I trust I have not diluted the essence and spirit of his thought, because, in many ways, this approach serves to reflect his organic approach of combining fundamental management principles against the dynamic backdrop of interacting continuity and change. On other occasions I use such phrases as *Drucker argued* or *according to Drucker* to introduce syntheses and inferential judgments of his various analyses. In taking these liberties, I hope I have added to the lucidity and cogency of the content.

CHAPTER TWO

FORMATIVE YEARS

I t goes without saying, but better with saying, that early formative influences play an important role in shaping a life. Three main and interdependent roots helped mold Drucker's career: the impact of two elementary school teachers, the intellectual atmosphere of post–World War I Vienna, and an early attraction toward the classics and humanities.[1] Of course it is only in retrospect that these three factors make any sense as influences, but looking back, the first contributed the foundation of good work habits and writing skills; the second helped develop his pragmatic intelligence, which led him to blend concepts with reality; and the third established a basis for his holistic thinking, for a pattern of seeing the whole as greater than the sum of the parts.

Early Schooling

Drucker was disillusioned with his formal schooling, considering it a compulsory encounter with dullness and boredom. He described his distaste for the system in Dickensian terms: "It was not higher education (or education of any kind) when I spent eight years in the Austrian Gymnasium on Latin irregular verbs. There was no attempt to relate this study to any language, living or dead, to literature, culture and history. There was hardly a hint from any of the teachers that Horace and Tacitus, might be read except to find their grammatical mistakes. . . . Latin may well belong in higher education; but it must be taught as something other than mechanical memory drill to be education at all."[2]

His disenchantment with his teachers was cushioned by two exceptions; he had the good fortune to experience two master teachers in elementary school. In different ways each of these two spinster instructors had a profound effect on him. One, a pedagogical martinet, introduced him to the rudimentary skills of writing, and insisted that he convert potential into performance. The other, an affable and lovable woman, ignored the traditional emphasis on routine skills and the rigors of scholastic practice and through sheer force of personality inspired him in the direction of imaginative and conceptual thought. The taskmaster instructor indelibly impressed on him the need for constant drill and high performance standards in writing while the charismatic teacher appealed to the perceptive and imaginative side of his nature. In later years Drucker acknowledged his tremendous debt to the combined talents of these two teachers for instructing him in the craft of a terse and lucid writing style and inculcating in him the importance of gracefully expressing his perceptions.[3]

Outside Influences

Finding formal academic training unendurable and the normative methods of acquiring an education a hindrance, Drucker became, he reported, a living example of an indifferent and lackadaisical student who studied little and learned less but had a talent for scoring well on exams. However, he never allowed school to interfere with his education. He had no choice but to go through the motions of what he considered the stifling and oppressive atmosphere of high school training but found his real educational challenges outside the classroom. To a large extent his intellectual curiosity was stimulated by his highly cultured parents. But equally important in nourishing his insatiable intellectual appetite was his exposure to his family's network of friends, which included some of the leading professionals and intellectual luminaries of Vienna.

As he described their influence in *Adventures of a Bystander,* these contacts developed his practical intelligence by giving him the opportunity to see how professionals made their knowledge accountable. Whether they were musicians, doctors, lawyers, politicians, artists, economists, or experts in other fields, they concentrated on performance and results. Subconsciously, this cosmopolitan, informal education implanted the seeds of an insightful pragmatism that would flourish and blossom in later life. In his dialogues with his mentors the youthful Drucker also learned lessons impossible to absorb from conventional textbooks. For example, he gathered the rudiments of courtesy and civility, shaped a foundation of charm and confidence, and developed a penetrating wit and a robust sense of humor.

Additionally, during his teenage years, he was invited to several of the Viennese intellectual salons, many of which were informal lyceums. Treating him as a young adult, the conductors of these sessions made no distinction between senior and junior guests. Contribution and respect for learning were the only demands at these meetings. Papers on social problems and contemporary issues were presented, discussed, and critiqued. From these improvised seminars Drucker learned problem identification and the fundamentals of basic research, but most important of all, he "learned how to learn." At the age of eighteen, he produced his first published article, a statistical study on the economic impact of the Panama Canal on world trade. He demonstrated that even at such an early age he possessed the requisite cognitive capacities and personal motivation to do original work.[4]

Study of Humanities

Much has been written recently on the decline of the humanities in U.S. universities. The professional disciplines, particularly the study of business, have pushed the liberal arts into a secondary position. Despite the fact that Drucker helped elevate the status of management into a respectable professional discipline, he never ceased to consider liberal arts to be the heart and soul of the managerial process. His untutored exploration into the classics as a young man later convinced him that without the liberal arts, management would degenerate into a bloodless and inanimate subject. By using countless examples and anecdotes from the past in his writings and lectures, Drucker characteristically wove, wherever possible, the strands of the humanities into the fabric of business process.

As an act of filial obedience Drucker achieved satisfactory grades in school, but the real source of his academic learning was self-study. His taste for literature and sense of history made the readings of serious books an important part of his daily life. In endorsing a stress on the liberal arts Drucker contended that management was *liberal* because it dealt with conceptual and theoretical knowledge and was an *art* because it focused on results and the human relation skills needed to achieve them.

His interest in the classics and humanities contributed to his wide range of interests and the holistic thinking that laid the foundation for his future scholarship in management. This self-imposed liberal arts training was to form the core of his beliefs and mental attitudes and to support a philosophical approach to interpreting the broad spectrum of social issues. Moreover, study of the humanities helped him avoid the disillusionment that follows when a person allows fads and gimmicks to raise false expectations.

Drucker was particularly attracted to authors who were able to convert their research into scholarly configurations. Among the figures in the social sciences who influenced him directly in holistic thinking were Bernard de Jouvenal, Søren Kierkegaard, Ferdinand Toennies, Georg Simmel, Henry Adams, John R. Commons, Thorstein Veblen, and Walter Bagehot.[5]

Drucker's early capacity for mastering the craft of basic learning skills, his pragmatic intelligence, and his passion for the humanities would depend for their translation into relevant knowledge on unseen opportunities awaiting him in the field of management. Nevertheless, without the planting of these seeds and their continued nourishment in his youth, he would not have produced the organic philosophy and perceptual insights so characteristic of his later years.

Quest for a Career

As a youngster Drucker faced the typical problem of preparing for a career, which in his case was proof that nothing was so unpredictable as the trajectory of human life. After graduation from the gymnasium it would have pleased his parents had he chosen one of the traditional collegiate disciplines (law, political theory, sociology, economics, or history), each of which was considered suitable to his talents.

Drucker, however, found matriculation at Vienna University unacceptable for three reasons. First, post–World War I Austria, in Drucker's perception, had been unable to come to terms with modernity. He found the city obsessed with the past, an atmosphere reminding him of a fog that permeated every-thing, paralyzed everything, choked the imagination, and smothered thought. Even as a child he knew he had to seek a change of scenery. Second, he viewed full-time attendance at the university as a prolongation of adolescence. He later explained that unlike the fascination of today's world with collegiate cre-dentials, the outlook then was that it was appropriate and acceptable to join the workforce at an early age: "When I decided in 1926 not to go to college but to go to work after finishing secondary school, my father was quite dis-tressed; ours had long been a family of lawyers and doctors. But he did not call me a 'dropout.' He did not try to change my mind. And he did not even prophesy that I would never amount to anything. I was a responsible adult wanting to work as an adult."[6]

Third, Drucker's diverse intellectual interests temperamentally inhibited him from making a professional commitment to an academic specialization. Countless writers have expressed the opinion that Drucker's reputation as an authority in management has tended to overshadow the brilliance of his writ-ings in politics, history of economics, sociology, and philosophy.

Throughout his life the idea of holding fast to a single career has proved an enigma to Drucker. He has defied professional labels. At one time or an-other, book reviewers have classified him as a journalist, political scientist, economist, statistician, historian, philosopher, art critic, teacher, and business consultant. On one occasion, responding to a reporter's question about his actual field of specialization, he replied, "Here I am, 58, and I still don't know what I am going to do when I grow up."[7] His remark was less a reference to a career, which in Drucker's case had depended on accident and unforeseen cir-cumstances, than it was a comment on the need for continual learning in order to be prepared for new opportunities.

In 1926, with college out of the question and the choice of a career ambiguous, Drucker knew only that he had to seek a job that would give him the experience and opportunity for improvement and personal growth. Con-sequently, aided by his father's connections, at the age of seventeen he left Vienna and took a job as a trainee clerk in a Hamburg trading house.

This clerkship enabled him to enter the adult world and learn the rudi-ments of business practice. Drucker's next position, in 1928, was as a security analyst at a small Frankfurt bank. After the financial panic of 1929, he was dismissed on the grounds of a personnel policy of last in, first out. He was for-tunate, however, in quickly finding employment as a financial writer for the

Frankfurter General Anzeiger, a leading regional newspaper. Recognizing his writing talents, the publisher promoted him to senior editor with responsibility for both business and foreign news. His editorial experience from 1929 to 1933 not only expanded his knowledge of social and economic events but at the same time produced an opportunity to enter the corridors of higher education.

Academic Achievement

As mentioned earlier, after his graduation from the gymnasium Drucker repeatedly insisted that spending four full years in college was a waste of time because it had nothing to do with genuine learning. But this distaste for regimented education did not apply when he perceived a chance to take responsibility for his own intellectual development by enrolling in the law program at Frankfurt University.

This program allowed him to continue his editorial job while pursuing a higher academic credential. It especially appealed to him because it provided a large degree of autonomy for a student who wished to custom-tailor his coursework around his own needs and interests. Indeed, the culture, structure, and content of continental legal education differed substantially from the U.S. model in several ways. First, the chief objective of the German system was the training of civil servants rather than the preparation of professionals for formal law practice.

Second, as a result, the German course curriculum was far more flexible. For example, it was possible that a student registered on a full-time basis would not have to take a single requisite course, attend compulsory lectures, take periodic examinations, or prepare regular written assignments. The only major requirement for receiving the degree was passing a final examination at the end of program. Eligibility for sitting for the final exam entailed a number of procedural details such as paying a small monetary fee, registering for a certain number of courses, and maintaining matriculation over an eight-semester period. Studying and preparing for the exam, however, the student was entirely on his own.

Third, and most important for Drucker, was the provision for a full-time degree candidate to hold a full-time job. This commingling of work experience and the pursuit of an advanced academic degree was the path taken by several of his friends and relatives. For example, his father and his uncle by marriage (Hans Kelsen, one of the world's leading political philosophers) had chosen to have full-time jobs while achieving their law degrees. The combining of work and study left an indelible mark on Drucker. In his subsequent teaching career he confessed a partiality for part-time students with full-time jobs. He felt they brought into the classroom a maturity and a commitment to grasping theoretical concepts that were characteristically lacking in young full-time students without experience.

Fourth, not being a German citizen, Drucker could not take the law exam. He had to go all out for a Ph.D. degree in political science, writing a dissertation on the historical and philosophical foundation of international law. He got his Ph.D. in 1931, when he was not quite twenty-two years old. His professor urged him to become a privatdocent—the German equivalent to the assistant professor in U.S. schools, though the position was without a salary. Drucker's privatdocent dissertation had actually been accepted by the faculty, but he delayed accepting the appointment. Being a government appointee, a privatdocent automatically became a German citizen. And in early 1932, Drucker already anticipated Hitler's coming to power and had no desire to become Hitler's subject.[8]

An ancillary benefit of attending a German university was the privilege registered students had to audit classes and attend university lectures. Finding this informal avenue of education the most challenging and exciting feature of academic life, he encountered some of the most respected and formidable minds in the scholarly world. A brief list includes Eugene Altchul in statistics and quantitative methods, Richard Wilhelm in oriental studies, Franz Oppenheimer in sociology, Ernst Kantorowicz in medieval history, and Martin Buber in philosophy and theology.

Each of these distinguished scholars enjoyed an international reputation for scholarship, and even today they are well-known names in their respective disciplines. To use a popular sports metaphor, these scholars represented a faculty dream team; combined, they had an enormous impact on Drucker, stimulating his curiosity and fostering the multidisciplinary thinking he later applied to management and other fields. Of course in the late twenties and early thirties the term management had little meaning for him. It is largely in retrospect that the benefits of this informal education can be seen to have had real pertinence.[9]

Impact of Friedrich Julius Stahl

The worldwide economic Depression of the early thirties and the rise of Hitler dramatically altered Drucker's circumstances. Considering totalitarianism intolerable, he contemplated moving to a society where the value of freedom was esteemed. The episode that directly influenced his decision to migrate was his publication of a controversial scholarly monograph on Friedrich Julius Stahl (1802–1863), a converted Jew and prominent politician who succeeded Georg Hegel as professor of philosophy at the University of Berlin.

Drucker had intended to discuss Stahl in his inaugural lecture if he became a full-fledged Privat Docent. He selected Stahl as a topic of investigation because he thought that many elements of Stahl's philosophy provided a sensible alternative to Nazism's reactionary nationalism and Communism's promise of a secular Nirvana. Stahl's interpretation of history also impressed Drucker because Stahl rejected the ideological determinism of Marx and Hegel, the philosophical icons of interwar Germany. He viewed history as an organic interaction between continuity and change, which produced tensions and turbulence but also provided challenging opportunities for the astute and perceptive statesman. In essence Stahl's conservatism called for preserving the strengths of traditional society and at the same time recognizing the dynamics and the meanings of adjusting to novel conditions.

Stahl was dogmatic in his opposition to abstract absolutes as a vehicle for dealing with current economic and political problems. Making a distinction between the imaginative we wish for and the reality that is, he said, "We must keep in mind not only what should happen but also what will happen."[10] According to Stahl, the most pressing need of the post-Napoleonic epoch was to maintain the continuity and stability of the monarchy in light of the radical and irreversible changes brought about by the French Revolution. In his mind, patriarchal kingship and constitutional liberalism each contained elements of truth, but existing separately they were counterproductive and destructive. Conversely, political harmony was possible by combining both components into the synthesis known as a constitutional monarchy. As part of this union, Stahl also insisted that the old institutional infrastructure (crown, church, military, universities, cities, nobility) had to rejuvenate itself by making its power more legitimate and responsible.

Advocating a form of political pluralism in which the monarchial principle commingled with representative institutions, he stated, "The prince must heed the estates, just as they must heed the prince; they are two independent but different centres of power."[11] Central to Stahl's conservatism was a pivotal role for religion. Without the presence of a Christian worldview the secular ideologies of liberalism and socialism were sterile and shallow. In effect it was the allegiance to spiritual values that cemented the relationship between hereditary monarchy and society's new institutions. According to Drucker, Stahl is remembered today less as a politician or a political philosopher than as the person who revised the moribund Protestant theology of the nineteenth century.

Drucker also saw his study of Stahl as a chapter for a potential book on continuity and change, centered on the theme of the Rechsstaat in the nineteenth century. He especially wanted to focus on the careers of Wilhelm von Humbolt (1767–1865) and Joseph von Radowitz (1797–1853), the first an agnostic Protestant statesman and the second a Catholic general in the Prussian army, a prominent politician, and an activist journalist. Like Stahl, both men wrestled with the turbulence of the French Revolution in attempting to reconcile the tensions between continuity and change; each recognized that it was impossible to turn back the clock of history but also that it was impossible to control the universe through secular salvation. They hoped to avoid political extremes and strike a balance between unabashed liberalism and nostalgic conservatism. Because Nazism completely broke all continuity, the project was abandoned—the first of many books Drucker never completed.

It is difficult to establish how many of Stahl's political concepts Drucker subscribed to, but it is possible to infer that many of his basic political ideas were reinforced by his study of Stahl. Among the principles that are identifiable as part of his later political and corporate philosophy are the important role of discontinuity in the process of continuity and change, skepticism about social salvation through manmade absolutes, rejection of historical determinism, acceptance of spiritual values as a prime requisite for an harmonious society, and a belief that power needs to be responsible and accountable. Stahl's views implanted the seed of Drucker's personal political identity as a *conservative innovator.*

The Stahl monograph was accepted by the country's leading publisher in the discipline of political theory—a rare distinction because the usual policy was to reserve such publication for senior faculty members. Additional icing on the cake accrued to Drucker when the publisher selected the little book to be No. 100 in Germany's most distinguished series in political science and to be the book to celebrate its centennial anniversary edition. Yet because Drucker strongly indicated that Nazi Germany failed to meet the criteria of political legitimacy, the monograph was abruptly banned by the government. Apart from Drucker's personal copy, only one other copy has survived, hidden away in a German university library.[12] Convinced that remaining in Germany both endangered his life and violated his conscience, he departed in 1933 to England to take a position as executive secretary in a small merchant bank.

During his tenure at the London bank, Drucker not only learned the fundamentals of banking but developed a clearer understanding of the financial activities of the bank's clients, particularly in the realm of mergers and acquisitions. In 1936, though already a partner, he left. Banking, whatever its temporary pecuniary merits and advantages, failed to meet his expectations for an exciting and challenging career and did not fulfill his need for intellectual renewal.

During his stay in England, Japanese art, a field remote from business activities, attracted Drucker to a new intellectual commitment and a singular aesthetic preoccupation. Chance, as with so many things in his life, played a role in his selecting this unconventional discipline. Caught in a London rainstorm in 1934, he sought cover by ambling into a Japanese art exhibit. He was so stimulated by the experience that he was hooked on the subject for life. Subsequently he gained recognition as a noted connoisseur and has achieved considerable distinction as a collector, concentrating on Japanese paintings from the fourteenth to the nineteenth century.

Journey to the United States

The year 1937 was a pivotal one in Drucker's life for both personal and professional reasons. To begin with he married Doris Schmitz, who became the mother of his four children, a pillar of personal support, and his number one consultant for over sixty years. (Apropos of this relationship he once commented that he had made two great decisions in his life. The first was not to attend college on a full-time basis, which he felt would be a waste of time and contribute nothing to his growth. The second was that he refused to take the first no from his future wife.)[13] Then he decided to accept a position as a freelance correspondent for several British newspapers, writing essays on economic issues, political trends, social forces, and the condition of higher education in the United States. As a result of this decision, he chose to make the United States his permanent home and to become a U.S. citizen.

Given his innate curiosity, gregarious personality, and propensity to learn, Drucker had little difficulty adjusting to this new stage in his journalistic career. Moreover, it provided an opportunity for him to hone his writing skills, becoming in the process a talented essayist. Equally significant, professional reporting and analysis revealed his prescient power of identifying economic trends and social phenomena. This diagnostic talent, which allowed him to reconnoiter, interpret, and evaluate complicated issues and then simplify them for popular audiences, was apparent in his *Wall Street Journal* pieces and magazine articles. During the late thirties and early forties, his journalistic assignments carried him throughout the country and enabled him to interview or work with such personalities as Henry Luce, John L. Lewis, Henry Wallace, Harry Hopkins, Herbert Agar, Buckminster Fuller, and Marshall McLuhan, to cite a few.

Yet the choice of a permanent career remained tantalizingly elusive. It was becoming increasingly clear from Drucker's multifaceted interests and boundless enthusiasm that he was temperamentally unsuited for a single professional pursuit. It also seemed inevitable, however, that in any portfolio of potential careers, teaching would have to have a place. Teaching not only fulfilled his need for human contact but provided an audience for testing his many ideas. His appointment as adjunct faculty member at Sarah Lawrence College in 1939 helped fulfill this passionate need. Except for times when he has had an occasional research commitment or government consulting assignment, he has been teaching continually up to the present, holding full-time appointments at Bennington, New York University, and Claremont College.

Following the axiom that to teach is to learn twice, Drucker has viewed the classroom as an opportunity to explore in greater depth his many diverse intellectual interests. Over the years, he has taught a wide range of subjects, including economics, ethics, political theory, philosophy, literature, sociology, history, Japanese art, statistics, and international affairs. Though some have accordingly classified him as a dilettante, his scholarly and provocative articles in these varied fields have attested to both research and knowledge competence along with an ability to present complex ideas in readable and understandable prose.

A certain irony prevails in the perception of Drucker among the academic community. Despite his acknowledged recognition as the founder of the modern discipline of management, his prodigious scholarly output over many decades, and the offers of many teaching appointments from such prestigious universities as Harvard, Yale, Princeton, and Stanford, some people continue to look upon him as a journalist. Perhaps in an age of ultra academic specialization, it is understandable that individuals in the humanities and persons in the nonmanagement disciplines of business schools view him in this fashion. But it seems unpardonable that a small segment within the management discipline still considers him a journalist rather than a professional scholar.[14]

Each of the fields of professional endeavor Drucker had ventured into before reaching the age of thirty was a magnet offering personal attraction and growth, but none was powerful enough for him to make an exclusive commitment. The fact that in his twenties he had experienced a host of possible careers mirrored his multidisciplinary intellectual inclinations and multifaceted professional interests. Ultimately, the reconciliation of a career with his interests as a genuine polymath attained a degree of reality when he revolutionized the study of management.

Drucker's multidisciplinary versatility, however, was often a handicap in seeking a permanent collegiate position in the United States. Although he had previously taught philosophy, political theory, and history, academic department heads had difficulty placing him in their particular social science disciplines. Similarly, when the dean of Harvard's School of Business later offered Drucker a position, he turned it down because it amounted to teaching a technical business specialization. General education in business was a nonexistent discipline at the time, but Drucker was using the study of management as his intellectual fulcrum for functional integration and social inquiry: "I studied management not because I was interested in business but because I was interested in society, community, and organization."[15]

In retrospect, it appears that the 1939 publication of his first major book, *The End of Economic Man,* was the turning point that directed his intellectual compass toward the ocean of management thought. Having once set sail on that course, he has remained on it.

PART ONE

DISCOVERING MODERN MANAGEMENT

PETER DRUCKER

CHAPTER THREE

THE END OF ECONOMIC MAN

D rucker's writings from 1938 to the publication of *The Practice of Management* in 1954 were chiefly characterized by his intellectual search for a deeper understanding of the meaning, threats, and challenges of contemporary industrialism. In the course of his research he early posed the hypothesis that the large corporation was the single most powerful institution of modern society and that its cadre of professional managers had assumed the status of the major leadership group in society.

Drucker did not begin with a blueprint specifying the structural significance of the corporation and the putative importance of management as a unique discipline. The seeds of these ideas had to be cultivated before they could eventually grow into a theoretical model of the business corporation and the first codification of managerial principles and practices.

Because no predictive relationship exists between Drucker's initial scholarly interest in the social and political ramifications of industrialism and his later formulation of managerial configurations and precepts, it is only with the advantage of hindsight that we can deduce how his early writing shaped the making of his future managerial mentality.

Although in his early books Drucker was viewing events chiefly through the prism of a political philosopher, all these books served as special building blocks in his later managerial edifice. *The End of Economic Man* (1939), for example, explored the realities of the prewar economic landscape in the developed Western world. It focused on the inadequacies of all *isms* (capitalism, socialism, Fascism, and Communism) in coping with the challenges of advanced technological development. Drucker cited the superiority of capitalism's market mechanism over other contemporary ideologies but questioned its survival capacity unless it created imaginative structural responses to overcome its vulnerabilities to unemployment, class conflict, and social alienation.

The Future of Industrial Man (1942) specifically singled out the large corporation as the foundation of structural change for the new society. Drucker visualized the corporation as a partial antidote to the monopoly of the sovereign state with its antipathy toward autonomous institutions. He warned, however, that even if a large corporation met the challenge of superior economic performance, its management would still face the task of defining its social missions, justifying its legitimacy, and reconciling its frictional relationship with an adversarial workforce.

Concept of the Corporation (1946) was an unprecedented clinical investigation of General Motors, the world's leading manufacturer. Drucker spent a fruitful two years inspecting and studying how the company thought through and designed its business operations. He concluded the book with a compelling corporate analysis, looking at GM's purposes, policies, practices, and performance. In addition, he offered the novel insight that the business had a governmental dimension as well as an economic one.

The New Society (1950) was Drucker's effort both to evaluate and summarize his findings of the previous decade and to sketch an outline of the specifications and prerequisites for a viable theory of management. It was also important because it identified two major trends—the emergence of a society of organizations and the rise of the knowledge worker.

The Practice of Management (1954) was a culmination, bringing Drucker's early thought into a coherent synthesis. It concentrated on the managerial requirement of integrating the autonomous business functions into a relevant corporate purpose, indicating the ingredients of managerial effectiveness, and examining the challenge of managing change for future results. In studying how the essence of Drucker's model emerged, each of these major early works (with the exception of *The New Society*) merits deeper treatment. Each therefore will be examined separately. Chapter Four reviews the ideas and insights in *The Future of Industrial Man,* Chapter Five looks at *Concept of the Corporation,* and

Chapters Six and Seven examine in some detail *The Practice of Management.* The remainder of this chapter considers the ideas in *The End of Economic Man.*

Background

In the history of Western civilization, 1939 will go down as one of its bleakest and darkest years. Totalitarianism, whether in its Marxist, Nazi, or even Fascist form, appeared as the seemingly indisputable wave of the future. The traditional European values of freedom, reason, individualism, parliamentarianism, and so forth, seemed headed for the historical graveyard. Benito Mussolini was popularly acclaimed for bringing unprecedented stability and efficiency to Italy. The supporters of Adolf Hitler lauded him for creating the German "economic miracle," with its apparent solution of erstwhile intractable industrial problems. Joseph Stalin had an endless parade of visiting scholars and journalists who confidently echoed the words of journalist Lincoln Steffens: "I have been over into the future, and it works."[1] Prominent visitors also celebrated the magic tool of *central economic planning* as an economic innovation leading inexorably to a new and better world. Totalitarianism was being viewed in contrast to the Great Depression, which had devastated the decade of the thirties with more than 20 percent unemployment, paralyzed prospects for economic growth, and stubbornly resisted attempts to resolve a plethora of social and economic problems. A state of despair and despondency persisted in much of the democratic world.

In the realm of foreign policy the political security of the democratic states appeared equally problematic as the totalitarian states asserted that they were on the threshold of realizing their historical destiny and fulfilling their ideological invincibility, both of these ends proving mythical. Italy had completed its conquest of North Africa. Germany had forged its *Anschluss* with Austria and was ready to claim more living space at the expense of Eastern Europe. The aggressive policy of the Japanese military had established a puppet government in Manchuria, created a sphere of influence in China, and threatened Indochina and Southeast Asia. Meanwhile the Soviet Union viewed the imperialism of the democracies and the pseudo-socialism of the Fascist states as the last debilitating stage of capitalism. The imminent collapse of both of them, according to the historical laws of the Marxist dialectic, would inevitably mark the end of history by creating an earthly secular paradise.

In the midst of these ominous threats from the various manifestations of totalitarianism, the Western democracies relied on the toothless diplomatic instrument of collective security, accepted ultimatums meekly, ignored potent propaganda, or practiced, as in the case of the United States, a policy of *splendid isolation*. The turbulent domestic conditions and the destabilizing international issues were considered so perilous that a gloomy consensus existed among a host of European social observers, many of whom, even with a passionate hatred of totalitarianism, seriously questioned whether Western civilization could overcome its disintegrative disabilities.

Arguably, the year 1939, with its cauldron of nationalistic tensions and international turmoil, was not the most propitious time for a sober and detached study on how modern industrialism had contributed to the pessimistic human condition and the chaotic state of world affairs. Yet this is precisely the setting into which the young and hitherto unpublished Peter Drucker, quixotically or not, hoped to insert a voice of calm rationalism and a mild note of optimism with the publication of *The End of Economic Man*. Using a multidisciplinary approach that integrated economics, political theory, philosophy, and psychology, he introduced provocative configurations and commonsense observations in an original conceptual command of his subject matter. In paying tribute to Drucker's refreshing perceptual talents, H. N. Brailsford, a leading British social thinker, remarked:

> Men differ in their perceptive capacity chiefly in their ability to see movement. All of us can see what is static and at rest. It is the gifted eye that discerns the pattern and rhythm of the motions in a complex drama of forces. As a musician, listening to a fugue, can continue it in his imagination if the players suddenly stop, so a student of contemporary affairs, if he have instinct as well as training, should be able to divine the future course of a movement. His eye can read its springing curve, and trace in time the motions of parabola on ellipse. Peter Drucker has this rare gift and exercises it with some audacity.[2]

Content

The End of Economic Man is an analytical survey of the contemporary world immediately prior to World War II—a society that by general consensus was chaotically out of joint. Drucker's primary goal was to describe how modern industrialism, in failing to meet its basic challenges, had created a social, cultural, and economic malaise throughout the developed world. The inability of the capitalist democracies to cope with poverty, unemployment, class struggle, and economic growth had produced a widespread condition of despair, disenchantment, and disillusionment. He also pointed out that although the totalitarian cure was worse than the disease, it was the bankruptcy of nerve in the free world that made totalitarianism an attractive option.

Drucker at the outset candidly admitted that he had no specific solutions for the tantalizing problems of advanced technological society. He insisted, however, that future solutions for saving Western civilization would have to depend on a reaffirmation of spiritual values. Without this recovery of spiritual beliefs, the techniques of economics and the tools of politics would be of no avail in ameliorating the social condition.

The book's contextual material was woven around two main threads. First, Drucker evaluated capitalism's inability to satisfy the criteria of economic performance and its moral failure to provide labor with dignity, support autonomous institutions, and promote freedom throughout society. Second, he offered an explanation of the rise, practices, policies, and future prospects of the totalitarian phenomenon. Drucker viewed totalitarianism not as the beginning of a dynamic new order but as the end of the disintegrating old order. Because Nazism failed to fuse the two elements of *continuity* and *change* in a satisfactory fashion, he saw its imminent downfall and predicted that it would "dissolve as soon as a new order, a new concept of man" appeared.[3]

Capitalism

According to Drucker the foremost reason for the stagnancy of twentieth-century capitalism was capitalism's monistic allegiance to a single supreme, sublime, and supine integrating value of social and economic life—the secular doctrine of *economic man*. He forcefully contended that the credo of economic man, which rested on the premises of selfishness and greed, pursuit of economic salvation, and the apotheosis of materialistic expectations, was both inadequate and inappropriate as an approach to a meaningful and coherent industrial society. He deplored a philosophical concept that preached the following: "All social energies have to be concentrated upon the promotion of economic ends, because economic progress carries the promise of the social millennium."[4]

It was inconceivable to him that any creed that ignored the dignity of man, converted private vices into public virtues, dismissed the concept of freedom, violated the standards of a decent and just society, and contradicted the essential requirements of the human condition could receive philosophical acceptance and social endorsement.

The elevation of economics as the dominant value of capitalism divorced capitalism from ethics, making it inevitable that the centrifugal forces of narrow self-interest would produce wealth within the state only at the price of rupturing the centripetal social bonds that provided society with a cohesive sense of community. Instead of establishing a mundane Eden of materialistic fulfillment, the separation of economics from ethics produced a society in which the worst rather than the best aspects of human nature prevailed.

As Drucker saw society, Western civilization in the first half of the twentieth century was in a state of drift and decay because mindless institutional fragmentation had replaced meaningful organizational purpose, parochial and personal interests had been substituted for the needs of the commonweal, and the illegitimate norms of might over right had undermined the concepts of legitimate authority and personal responsibility.

José Ortega y Gasset, the astute Spanish philosopher, diagnosed the disintegrating social and political condition of the capitalist democracies as a prelude to the "revolt of the masses."[5] In Drucker's mind, Ortega y Gasset had drawn the wrong conclusion from his brilliant analysis. Describing the masses as being in a state of revolt implied that they had a conscious commitment to social and economic activism, no matter how misguided the program's agenda in others' views. Because Drucker saw a population immersed in passivity, indifference, and apathy, he took exception to Ortega y Gasset's revolt of the masses. Instead he saw a society entrenched in what he called the "despair of the masses."[6] Considering this apathetic and indifferent condition an escape from freedom and responsibility, he observed that "the masses, then, have become prepared to abandon freedom if this promises to reestablish the rationality of the world. If freedom is incompatible with equality, they will give up freedom. If it is incompatible with security, they will decide for security."[7]

It was, concluded Drucker, capitalism's failure to establish the legitimacy of the power of its key institutions and to engender a vitality of citizenship that enhanced the irrational appeal of demagogues, whether of the Communist, Nazi, or Fascist variety.

Drucker placed a considerable amount of blame for the social anomie on the Christian churches, claiming they failed in both their spiritual and pastoral missions. On the spiritual level, rather than emphasizing personal account-

ability to a supernatural Being in the afterlife and promulgating the importance of human dignity under natural law as a cushion against materialistic
expectations, the churches fostered an attitude in which church attendance
was a social event for parroting obtuse prayers and an exercise of empty ritu-
als. On the pastoral level church leaders were indifferent to the realities of
technological change. Suspicious of modernity, they took an unsympathetic
attitude toward trade unions, a hostile stance toward social reform, and a reactionary position toward social innovation. The failure of the churches to sym-
pathize with the vital needs and demands of the working classes fostered
support of the status quo and endorsed a neutrality on political issues that
made it easier for extremists on the right and the left to attract the apathetic
masses with simplistic blandishments.

Compared to the ideologies of Fascism, Communism, and socialism, capitalism received Drucker's firm support. Because of the strength of the market mechanism with its elements of freedom, he considered capitalism superior
to the state central planning with restrictive controls over individuals that was
the hallmark of totalitarianism. Given this position, he took pains to point out
that his severe criticism of democratic capitalism was not intended as a self-
righteous, patronizing indictment. On the contrary, he hoped that the structural
strengths of capitalism could be merged in a rejuvenating fashion with the core
traditional beliefs of Western civilization. In short, only a meaningful union of
the material and the spiritual could offer an antidote to the prevailing despair
and pessimism of contemporary society and could avoid totalitarianism.

Totalitarianism

In addressing his second major theme in *The End of Economic Man*, the rise of
European totalitarianism, Drucker took serious issue with the validity of the
conventional and popular explanations; at best he found them to explain
superficial manifestations of the totalitarian movements. He analyzed each of
the major current interpretations and found their rationales devoid of substance, particularly in the case of Nazi Germany.

Elaborating on their content and dissecting their weaknesses, he analyzed,
for example, the following specific explanations: the supposed primitive bar-
barity and intrinsically brutal character of the German people, the unique
personality and charismatic leadership traits of Hitler, the poisonous social
disease of anti-Semitism, the paranoiac fear of Bolshevism, the deterministic

Marxian dialectic that Fascism and Naziism were the final stages of capitalism, the exaggeration of the manipulative powers of mass propaganda, the factor of revenge for the humiliations incurred under the Treaty of Versailles, and the traditional imperatives of international power politics.

In light of the shortcomings of analysis he perceived in each of these explanations, he offered his own interpretation for the rise of National Socialism. First, each of the aforementioned hypotheses had a certain surface attraction, but each viewed the totalitarian phenomenon exclusively through the prism of nationalism rather than as a function of inability to cope with the impacts of modern technology. He concluded therefore that they all lacked depth and cogency in capturing the real challenge of the twentieth century, attempting to solve the problems of modern industrialism.

Second, modern industrialism in Germany and Italy did not emerge organically from below but was introduced from above with state guidance, resulting in weak ideological foundations and a deficient institutional infrastructure. In effect, because both Germany and Italy had achieved nationhood in the recent past, less than seventy years ago, they undertook the challenge of industrializing with a predominantly mercantile climate of opinion and with many obsolete mercantile institutions.

Third, under the guise of demonstrating the advantages of sagacious state direction, the Nazi leadership adroitly usurped control of the economy by appealing emotionally for popular support while promising an industrial utopia, substituting for avaricious aspects of capitalism a clever nonpecuniary reward system of titles and privileges, reducing unemployment with infrastructure contracts and military projects, avoiding the risks of nationalization by simultaneously milking and feeding the cow of big business, undermining the power of labor unions and regulating the leisure time of workers through the control of sports and recreational activities, coopting the independence of autonomous institutions, and neutralizing the influence of churches. Based on the amoral principle of might over right and a fundamental mistrust of the masses, all these policies were enforced by appropriate amounts of fear, discipline, coercion, and terror.

In Drucker's view, instead of creating a legitimate new society, totalitarianism was a weak effort to fill the vacuum caused by the failure of European capitalism. He declared: "The totalitarian revolution is clearly not the beginning of a new order but the result of the total collapse of the old. It is not a miracle, but a mirage which will dissolve as soon as a new order, a new concept of man, appear. Fascism can only deny the concept of Economic Man which has broken down. It cannot create the new concept which should take its place. But unless a new order and new concept based upon the European values of freedom and equality can be found, Europe and the Occident are doomed."[8]

Economic Performance. Drucker followed his detailed analysis of the roots of German totalitarianism with an evaluation of its economic achievements, exposing the popular myth of the economic miracle with the reality of the economic mirage.[9]

In his economic analysis he noted that the quantitative statistics of economic growth bore little relationship to qualitative measurements of the quality of life, pointing out that the increased economic power of the state was not synonymous with the welfare of the people. For example, he acknowledged that the Nazi regime solved the unemployment problem through military and public work programs, but he also suggested that the creation of such temporary jobs was counterproductive for long-term wealth creation.

Moreover, when he considered the accompanying loss of freedom, he thought this price for solving unemployment was socially and politically unacceptable. Consequently, efforts to build a viable industrial economy based on a nonmonetary reward system and the valuing of guns over butter represented more shadow than substance. He concluded therefore that the state-directed palliatives practiced by the Nazis were bound to fail in the long run because they rejected the market test and were indifferent to the cost factor in the allocation of resources, dependent on a stifling bureaucracy, and resistant to social and economic innovation.

Most important, Drucker stated that in the tradition of Western political philosophy, "the justification of power must be the central problem."[10] Because Nazi totalitarianism failed to legitimize its power with an acceptable form of consent, he predicted the demise of the system. He noted that the tombstones of history were filled with societies that substituted terror for consent, replaced spiritual values with false promises of secular redemption, and replaced autonomous institutions with leviathan bureaucracies. Despite its claims of creating a new economic and social order, Nazi totalitarianism had sown the seeds of its own destruction—in Drucker's mind, it was only a question of time.

Foreign Policy. Drucker's treatment of international relations in *The End of Economic Man* concentrated chiefly on the foreign policies of the totalitarian states of Nazi Germany and the Soviet Union. He covered the crusading ideological conflicts between the hostile states, which featured diplomats making threats of extinction, vitriolic propaganda battles, and subversive fifth-column activities. So ferocious and intense was the belligerency between Nazi Germany and Communist Russia that if there was one certainty almost universally endorsed by foreign policy experts at the time, it was that there were only two chances of reconciliation between these totalitarian powers—slim and none. Drucker took a dissenting position on this popular point of view. Almost a year before the ratification of the Nazi-Soviet Pact, he wrote, "From every angle the alliance between Germany and Russia seems to be almost unavoidable."[11]

Drucker was not a contrarian, but throughout his career he was more than slightly suspicious of those who asserted they knew things with certainty. His prediction of a marriage of convenience between the two enemies in the near future was a controversial one, but its forthcoming reality was a tribute to the acuteness of his political antennae.

His prognosis of an uneasy rapprochement was based only peripherally on the historical element of power politics, in which Poland traditionally served as a sacrificial lamb to satisfy the mutual appetites of German and Russian expansion. More appealing than the realpolitik argument for an alliance were these three factors: (1) the intrinsic totalitarian characteristics of the two regimes created a certain attraction between the nations, largely because human and civil rights were irrelevant to these nations' conduct of foreign policy; (2) the benefits derived from accommodation would overcome some of the nations' mutual economic difficulties; and (3) the ideological principle of renouncing any cooperation with the democratic and capitalist world fitted both these nations' immediate interests. It would be a masterpiece of overstatement to say that given the conditions of the era, foreign policy experts agreed with Drucker's projected rationale. Yet the speed with which the two countries formed the Nazi-Soviet Pact of 1939 was presumably startling even to Drucker, because it took place less than six months after the publication of his book.

A half century later there was a parallel instance of Drucker's perceptiveness in foreign policy. With the publication of *The New Realities* in 1989, in the heat of the apparently endless Cold War, he predicted the approaching demise of the Soviet Empire, commenting that "within twenty-five years, if not sooner, the Russian Empire too will have disappeared ... and will create totally new realities in international politics."[12] In August 1991, the dissolution of the Soviet Union was formally pronounced. Once again it was only the speed of the dissolution that surprised him. He equated the economic failure of Soviet Communism to build a viable industrial system and a legitimate society with the similar shortcomings he had analyzed in Nazi Germany fifty years earlier: the inability of central planning to develop a meaningful cost system, the absence of personal freedom, the onus of a bloated and corrupt bureaucracy, and the failure of the proletarian paradise to give dignity and goods to the workers.

Conclusion

The Future of Industrial Man, Drucker's second major work, was published during World War II. The book reiterates and reinforces most of the main points of his political and social philosophy found in *The End of Economic Man.* One difference in the new book is his effort to prescribe in some detail the type of economic policies and institutions needed to overcome the challenges and dilemmas of building a harmonious industrial society. Drucker essentially viewed the two books as continuous. Adopting this perspective, I have chosen to present in the next chapter a combined summary of the influences and impacts these two volumes had on his managerial philosophy.

CHAPTER FOUR

THE FUTURE OF INDUSTRIAL MAN

The laudatory reviews accorded *The End of Economic Man* elevated the young Drucker to front-rank stature as a social commentator. One result of his enhanced reputation was an invitation from Henry Luce, the famed publisher, to serve as an editorial consultant for the tenth anniversary issue of *Fortune* magazine. After completing the assignment Drucker turned down Luce's generous offer to him to join the permanent staff for *Time* and *Life* magazines. He resisted the temptation of an attractive corporate salary and accompanying perks because working in Luce's paternalistic culture would, he thought, destroy his intellectual independence.[1]

His enhanced reputation, however, also opened the door to teaching opportunities, and he accepted teaching posts at Sarah Lawrence and Bennington, two highly regarded small colleges. But a total, full-time commitment to academe was contrary to his temperament and uncongenial to his multifaceted professional activities.[2]

The outbreak of World War II disrupted any thought of long-term career planning. The hostilities, however, did not interfere with his varied activities; teaching, lecturing, and freelance writing continued to occupy most of his time. As if these three categories of professional activity were not enough,

Drucker also found time to act as a consultant to the military on several productivity studies and also completed, in 1942, his second major work, *The Future of Industrial Man*.

The new work echoed both the spiritual malaise of Western civilization and the failings of modern industrialism that were treated in *The End of Economic Man*. It disturbed Drucker that after two centuries of uninterrupted material progress, there was no similar advance in the social and political realm. It troubled him that despite all their technological progress, the developed nations had not created a genuinely functional society. This failure was the chief reason for the crisis they faced in the modern era. In *The Future of Industrial Man* he wrote: "Man in his social and political existence must have a functioning society just as he must have air to breathe in his biological existence. However, the fact that man has to have a society does not necessarily mean that he has it. Nobody calls the mass of unorganized, panicky, stampeding humanity in a shipwreck a society."[3]

Industrial performance existing alongside political regression is a mismatch, and Drucker attributed this mismatch to the fact that the leadership elites in the developed countries of the Western world were anchored to a mercantile ethos that was not only preindustrial in methodology but essentially anti-industrial in spirit. Because these elites tried to endorse the archaic concept of economic man and ignored the need for a new infrastructure to support contemporary industrial society, he accused them of poor leadership; they were attempting to place a brake on inexorable change by defending the status quo. He specifically singled out such national elites as the landed gentry in England, the petit bourgeoisie in France, the Junker landlords in Germany, and the Jeffersonian agrarians in the United States.

To illuminate this hypothesis, Drucker focused on how national states failed to blend the factors of continuity and change, a theme he would later apply to the business institution. In *The Future of Industrial Man* his focus was on what he found to be the two essential requirements for a functioning society: (1) recognition of the large autonomous corporation as society's representative social institution and (2) the need for corporate management to justify its legitimacy as an organ of government. In close connection with this requirement for establishing legitimacy, he addressed the theme of corporate responsibility for providing the status and function of the worker.

The Autonomous Enterprise

Drucker was not the first to identify the economic dominance and power ramifications of the large corporation. In considering it the centerpiece institution of modern industrialism, however, he was arguably the first to probe its intrinsic noneconomic characteristics and to examine how it related and contributed to the larger society. He viewed the modern large corporation as sui generis, an institutional phenomenon differing from any past social or political organization. One badge of its uniqueness was that over the past four hundred years it was the first autonomous institution to emerge that was powerful enough to dilute the absolute sovereignty of the national state.

The corporation's independence from total control by the central government was mirrored by its pivotal role in the allocation of economic resources, as a dominant source of employment, and as the economic base for a complementary infrastructure of small business enterprises. What Drucker found particularly striking in this recent growth of private economic power was that few people recognized the modern corporation as the most important institutional innovation of modern times and, equally startling, that virtually no one considered the examination of its constituent components as a respectable topic of scholarly research.

According to Drucker, the modern giant corporation was more than an ephemeral historical episode; it was the chief institutional symbol of a new social order. So crucial was the corporation for the vitality of contemporary society, he added, that if it did not exist in its present form, it would manifest itself in some other fashion. The technological complexities and sophisticated distribution needs in a developed economy required some type of independent organizational power divorced from bureaucratic interference and arbitrary state control.

The corporation's need for structural autonomy, with adequate power and appropriate knowledge to conduct its tasks, was an imperative, but this did not mean it should act as an institutional automaton. With its large size and complexity it also required an independent leadership cadre to direct and coordinate it. In effect this professional management, which has power without property, "has become the decisive and representative power in the industrial system."[4] Drucker considered the autonomous corporation to be the first major innovation of industrial civilization, and professional management, as its governing unit, is the second. In identifying and stressing the significance of corporate autonomy and a managerial elite, Drucker saw himself as a disinterested political theorist who was interested chiefly in the ramifications of cultural change. At the time, he did not contemplate an exploration into management theory or a description of executive practices.

The problem of corporate legitimacy and the provision of status and function for the worker were of particular concern to him as he was writing *The Future of Industrial Man.* He insisted that failing to address shortcomings in these constitutional and human organizational areas made corporations vulnerable and the quest for a free and integrated society unrealizable. To avoid the threat of managerial irresponsibility and to escape the abuse of corporate power, he designated these two areas as twilight zones of ambiguity needing philosophical illumination and sociological understanding.

In examining the subject of corporate management as an intellectual frontier rather than a potential academic discipline, Drucker felt it was important to discuss several defects of the corporation from a constitutional and structural point of view.

Corporate Legitimacy

The massive accumulation of power by giant enterprises in the twentieth century was Drucker's starting point in analyzing the topic of corporate legitimacy. In acknowledging the unprecedented impact of the economic strength of giant businesses, he implied that the leading businesses had greater financial assets than most political entities. However, he was more concerned with the more intangible and less obvious qualitative factors of corporate influence and control upon the social commonwealth.

Arguing from the premise that "no social power can endure unless it is legitimate power,"[5] Drucker raised a number of basic questions such as these: Was corporate power legitimate or was it power without an acceptable consensual societal authority? Was it a power devoid of cultural beliefs and values? Was it a power advocating that the ends justified the means? Was it a power that disregarded the ethical principle of right over might? Drucker found current responses to these and other questions unsatisfactory in terms of justifying the enormous power in the hands of the large industrial and financial institutions.

Corporate Governance

Approximately a decade before the publication of *The Future of Industrial Man,*
Calvin Coolidge confidently expressed the ideological conviction that "the
business of America is business."[6] The roots of the United States as a business
civilization are traceable to the Puritan ethic that deifies work, posits the classical economic doctrine of economic man, and advances the social Darwin-
ist notion of rugged individualism. All three concepts were regarded as articles
of faith by the political and the business establishments, thereby allowing little room for an analytical investigation of the business enterprise as a viable
social institution. Drucker attributed the lack of scholarly recognition of the
corporation to the political concept of national sovereignty; given that concept there was little reason to probe the authority of intermediate organizations of the state.

Drucker feared that the failure of corporate management to face the problem of legitimacy might lead to a totalitarian alternative in which the state was
the only agency of control. In addition, if managerial capitalism rejected the
philosophical challenge of justifying its corporate power, it was a tacit admission that business power was corrupt and tainted. In that case, instead of promoting a free, functioning industrial society, contemporary capitalism would
allow society to disintegrate into a Hobbesian world—a war of all against all—
which was almost as bad as totalitarianism.

Explanations of Power

Drucker approached the task of explaining corporate power from two basic
perspectives—traditional political theory and contemporary explanations.
With regard to traditional political theory, he argued that a central tenet of
Western civilization was that power could be justified by an acceptable form
of either sacred or secular consent.

From a sweeping historical survey he inferred a number of basic principles
and putative guidelines. First, power that was not derived from social consent
was illegitimate power. Second, illegitimate power was incapable of producing
wise and good rulers. Third, force and coercion were incapable of building a
free society. Fourth, creating a legitimate society depended on the acceptance
of core transcendental values. In the case of Western civilization, these values, or beliefs, were monotheism, individual accountability to a supreme super-

natural authority, and natural law. Fifth, it was chimerical to assume that legitimacy of power could be established in precise and absolute terms; in the world of practical affairs its meaning could only be approximated.

In addition to examining the relationship between power and legitimacy within the framework of political science, Drucker examined two leading contemporary explanations: (1) James Burnham's thesis of the *managerial revolution*[7] and (2) shareholder democracy, which asserted that stockholders, voting by proxy, delegated their property rights to professional managers.

The Managerial Revolution. Burnham's popular book *The Managerial Revolution* (1941) advanced the thesis that sophisticated technological and industrial change in the recent past created in all the world's developed countries a new ruling elite of *professional managers.* Burnham, a former Marxist, based his hypothesis on historical determinism. He saw the managerial revolution as a necessary stage in the economic evolutionary process. Because the large corporation and its ruling elite of professional managers were preordained by the inexorable dialectic forces of history, there was actually no need to investigate the roots of an organization's legitimacy and sources of authority.

In short Drucker saw Burnham's arguments as tantamount to supporting might over right, as saying "that actual rule successfully invents its own ideological justification."[8] Needless to say, this mechanistic explanation failed to meet his aforementioned criteria for legitimate power in Western philosophy.

Shareholder Democracy. The rationale of shareholder democracy, the delegation of power by stock owners' proxies to professional managers, was in Drucker's mind a weak argument in defense of corporate legitimacy. He conceded that there was some validity for property as a source of legitimacy when a single owner held the majority of the stock. But with the separation of ownership and control around the turn of the century, professional managers who owned a minuscule amount of stock could no longer claim property as a source of authority for their power.

According to Drucker, "The abdication of individual property rights as a basis of social power is the central institutional change of our times."[9] Moreover, the control managers received through proxies was a ritualistic exercise rather than a substantive case for legitimacy. In reality, the separation of ownership and control meant that shareholders had irreversibly abdicated their rights as property owners.

The election of the board of directors, moreover, was not a reflection of democratic consent because the stockholders were not interested in corporate operations—their prime interest was in dividends. Instead of acting like owners they were passive investors who sold their stock if they were dissatisfied with corporate profitability. Drucker reasoned that shareholder democracy was a myth because the shareholder had become "superfluous" as far as control was concerned. After throwing away shareholder rights it became impossible for the shareholder to resume these rights, "for to him they are nothing but burdens; they are entirely contrary to his purpose in becoming a stock owner."[10]

Corporate Illegitimacy

After surveying briefly the rudiments of the theoretical justification of power by Western political scientists and the popular explanations of contemporary analysts, Drucker reached the conclusion that "there is no absolute legitimacy."[11] One reason for the futility of establishing a universal test for the legitimacy of corporate power was that it was impossible to integrate the concept into the mores and customs of every society. Pointing out the relativity of absolute legitimacy, he wrote: "Power can be legitimate only in relation to a basic social belief. What constitutes 'legitimacy' is a question that must be answered in terms of a given society and its given political beliefs."[12]

Drucker asserted that because absolute legitimacy was an untenable philosophical position, there was no reason to dismiss the need to comprehend managerial power and authority. As he had asserted, illegitimate power was the root cause of the crises in industrial society. One step in understanding illegitimate power was to realize that it must adapt to the value system of society. In short, illegitimate power is that which "does not derive its claim from the basic beliefs of the society."[13] Adding that if power is designated as illegitimate, it cannot be accountable and responsible, he wrote: "Illegitimate power cannot be controlled; it is by its nature uncontrollable. It cannot be made responsible since there is no criterion of responsibility, no socially accepted final authority for its justification. And what is unjustifiable cannot be responsible."[14]

Drucker realized that the problem of ascertaining the legitimacy of power in the modern business enterprise became especially complex and confusing because that power had to be justified on three distinct levels—economic, political, and social. In order to perform its economic tasks of creating goods, jobs, and wealth, the corporation required economic power. Concomitantly, it also possessed political power in that it controlled employee livelihood and established the rules and regulations of employment. Finally, the corporation had social power by virtue of conferring social status upon the workers. Possessing the necessary power to operate in these three dimensions was one thing, but how an organization could find the proper focus and locus of consent for this power in all three areas was an enigma to Drucker. He also expressed skepticism about establishing consensual authority for such vast power when a society existed in a cultural vacuum: "Politically and socially, however, we have no industrial civilization, no industrial community life, no industrial order or organization."[15] He was not alone in his puzzlement over the legitimacy of corporate power. Robert Dahl, professor of government at Yale University, scolded his political science colleagues for failing to recognize the issue as a problem and leaving it to Drucker, a sociologist outside the profession, to grapple with the philosophical nuances.[16]

Drucker's conclusive test for the absence of corporate legitimacy was the virtual impossibility of removing management from control. He declared that under the circumstances of a separation of power and property, the only possible outcome was the structure of a self-perpetuating bureaucracy: "In the modern corporation the decisive power, that of the managers, is derived from no one but from the managers themselves, controlled by nobody and nothing and responsible to no one."[17]

Contending that a self-perpetuating bureaucracy was a violation of the democratic process, which demanded the political right of change for any institution, Drucker also rejected the argument that integrity in the managerial cadre would be a satisfactory response and would legitimate power. The most charitable outcome of such integrity was "enlightened despotism." Moreover, what appeared as benevolence to those in power was perceived by those under its dominance as naked tyranny. He stated tersely, "The answer to Machiavelli is not honest and enlightened despots, but legitimate rulers."[18]

Notwithstanding his strong indictment of corporate management as illegitimate, Drucker also noted that managerial control was not the result of a sinister coup or malicious conspiracy. "On the contrary," he stated, "there has never been a more efficient, a more honest, a more capable and conscientious group of rulers than the professional management of the great American corporations today."[19] Rather than usurpation, managerial exercise of power was a response to the ancient political axiom that nature abhors a vacuum—a condition created in this case by stockholder apathy, ignorance, and indifference. Moreover, when he considered options to the structure of the large corporation, he found no viable alternative.

Drucker candidly confessed that he had no pat solution to the problem of corporate legitimacy. He conceded that it was a thorny and sticky issue because, as mentioned, in practice the corporation had to seek its legitimacy on three levels—economic performance, political control over people, and the granting of social status to employees. He hoped that further study by political scientists would improve understanding of the power relationship on these three levels, but he also cautioned that it was not a question of searching for the ideal and utopian answer but for the tolerable and possible response.

The subject of corporate legitimacy along with its corollary aspect of social responsibility in the performance of noneconomic activities has been a tantalizing and troublesome one throughout Drucker's entire career. He was convinced that if a corporation was only a single-purpose economic institution, then it would have no compulsion to concern itself with progressive employee affairs and with the negative environmental impacts it imposed on society. Such a managerial approach was tantamount to having a healthy economic corporation in a sick society—a contradictory and intolerable position for any long-run survival.

Drucker implied that although the corporation's primary responsibility was economic performance, it was not solely limited to that task. However, when it came to the corporation's noneconomic activities dealing with employee affairs and quality of life, Drucker had difficulty in locating the precise authority for these activities without infringing on individual rights or usurping the authority of other institutions.

The fact that Drucker did not come up with a satisfactory answer to the problem of legitimacy should not detract from his pioneering effort in elevating the topic of corporate governance to a new intellectual level. He also deserves credit for raising the right questions on the dilemma of justifying power in a free, democratic industrial society. Perhaps the most important and elemental issues were these: If corporate management went beyond its economic function and tackled various social and political problems, from where did it derive its authority? If the corporation did nothing, could it be accused of greed and selfishness? If the corporation enlarged its power and did too much in the noneconomic realm, was there the danger of industrial feudalism? In *The Future of Industrial Man* and throughout his career Drucker wrestled with the dilemma of balancing the requirements of corporate economic performance with societal demands, recognizing that either alternative taken to an extreme could threaten the viability of both an autonomous corporation and a free society.

Given his position that current managerial power was basically illegitimate, Drucker was not optimistic about reconciling the dilemma of corporate self-interest with the needs of the commonwealth. Several years later in *The New Society* and *Concept of the Corporation*, he modified this extreme position by stating that the corporation was neither completely illegitimate nor totally legitimate but existed in a philosophical twilight zone of nonlegitimacy. The rationale of this new position was that if the corporation did not rule in the interests of its subjects, it did not follow that it ruled in its own interests.

It is difficult to assess whether Drucker's hypothesis of corporate nonlegitimacy is an intellectual cop-out or a reflection of the confusion in explaining the justification of corporate power. In future decades he addressed the problem in his major works, probing the subtle nuances and convoluted complexities of managerial power and responsibility. In the decade of the eighties, he argued that the hostile takeovers and leveraged buyouts of those years exposed the corporate failure to resolve the legitimacy of managerial capitalism. He pointed out once again that even sound financial companies that appeared to be competently managed had fallen prey to hostile raiders. They were left naked to their competition because their potential consensual constituents (labor, stockholders, suppliers, community members, and so on) failed to support them in the takeover crisis.

Status and Function of the Worker

The third major theme of *The Future of Industrial Man* addressed the problem of balancing corporate needs with human aspirations in the conversion of industrial society into a free society. "The central fact in the social crisis of our time is that the industrial plant has become the basic social unit, but that it is not yet a social institution."[20] The message conveyed by this statement was that despite the material achievements of industrialism, society was experiencing a psychological malaise because mutual trust and a community of interest had not developed between the corporation and its employees.

To avoid this spiritual malaise and worker alienation, managers had to assume responsibility for worker status and function. The realization of status and function was the employee's path toward industrial citizenship. Without genuine worker constitutional participation in the organizational life of the enterprise, Drucker warned, "there can be no society but only a mass of social atoms flying through space without aim or purpose."[21] Lack of recognized worker status and function was creating irrationality and unpredictability in the conduct of social affairs.

Drucker viewed harmonizing the political demands of any government with the needs of the members of the polity as one of the central dilemmas and challenges of Western political theory. It was his firm contention that the modern corporation should face the reality that it had to provide a form of citizenship for its members. Elaborating on this assumption, he criticized the academic community for its intellectual myopia. In emphasizing only economic performance, it neglected the institutional factors of purpose, coherence, and cohesiveness that should be the cementing factors of industrial life: "That the employed worker in modern mass-production industry has no social status and function is usually overlooked by modern writers who have been taught that nothing counts in social life except income and economic wealth."[22]

Maintaining that it was chimerical to seek absolute corporate legitimacy, he nevertheless argued it was necessary to reconcile the conflicts and contradictions between the needs of the group and the interests of the individual. He stated that the "social status and function of the individual is the equation of the relationship between the group and the individual member. It symbolizes the integration of the individual with the group and that of the group with the individual. It expresses the individual purpose in terms of the society, and the social purpose in terms of the individual. It thus makes comprehensible and rational individual existence from the point of the group, and group existence from that of the individual."[23]

Failure to harmonize the goals of the organization with workers' needs resulted in alienation and anomie, a certain prescription for the loss of employee allegiance to the enterprise and a dilution of society's spiritual cohesiveness. Divorcing his argument from the academic jargon of sociology, Drucker encouraged managers to use their organization's power by taking responsibility for enhancing the respect and dignity of the workers in the community and making jobs more fulfilling and meaningful.

Drucker reported that under present industrial conditions, work made no sense to the worker because the assembly line irreparably divorced the worker from the means of production and converted him into an engineering misfit.

As a result of the assembly line, he said, "what has become automatic and mechanical is the worker."[24] Alienated from any real sense of personal contribution to the product and deprived of personal esteem, the contemporary industrial worker presented a grim, Dickensian picture: "He is not a human being in society, but a freely replaceable cog in an inhumanely efficient machine."[25] Given his bleak estimate of industrial relations in the capitalist world, Drucker was not optimistic for any immediate solution of the intractable problem of achieving status and function for employees. However, considering job security to be the essential factor in meeting the challenge of status and function, he explored the two main responses of capitalism in responding to chronic unemployment: paternalism and unionization.

Paternalism

As instruments for fashioning an organizational environment compatible with corporate survival needs and employee expectations, paternalism and unionization were, in Drucker's view, little better than palliatives. They mitigated the symptoms but failed to attack the industrial diseases.

Drucker considered paternalism a praiseworthy and conscientious effort on the part of well-intentioned individual managers to alleviate the potential abuses in the industrial system, most notably the problem of unemployment. Although he considered job security a must for industrial harmony in a free society, by itself it failed to meet the criteria for ensuring status and function, on both economic and social grounds. Economic satisfaction and job security were more hygienic than therapeutic factors in employees' health and welfare.

Anticipating the postwar psychological studies on the relationship between job satisfaction and pecuniary rewards, Drucker argued that "economic satisfactions can be likened to vitamins; their absence creates deficiency diseases of a most serious nature, but they do not in themselves provide calories."[26] Another difficulty of ensuring job security was that the good intentions of the employer evaporated in the uncertainty of the business cycle with its periodic depressions. In short, the theoretical axiom of legitimate government was that it ruled in the interests of its subjects, but this adage did not apply to the business enterprise. In hard times management always placed the interests of the firm over those of the workers.

Drucker concluded that guaranteed job security carried an unacceptable price for the elimination of unemployment because it failed to pave a path toward industrial citizenship in a free society. In effect, it produced an environment of dependency in which the employee was treated as a child, it developed an atmosphere for manipulation rather than worker involvement, and it virtually guaranteed benevolent despotism. Finally, Drucker considered business paternalism, with its emphasis on the paycheck as a panacea, an admission of bankruptcy. The paternalistic doctrine encouraged the idea that work was inherently disagreeable and intrinsically meaningless, which completely ignored the prospects for a positive status and function relationship as the foundation for industrial citizenship.

Unionism

Idealists, intellectuals, liberals, and factory organizers, the main proponents of the trade union movement, visualized the union as the chief catalyst for the realization of employee status and function in the thirties. In the judgment of Drucker, however, unionism "is the greatest mirage of our times. It is certain to end not in a free but in a despotic society."[27]

He initially agreed with many of the good intentions of unionism but upon deeper analysis saw a deep chasm between its constitutional goals and operating practices. Serving as a countervailing institutional force for the illegitimate power of management, unions had an ephemeral merit in contemporary industrial society. At the same time, they were flawed in rendering genuine industrial citizenship for employees. Among the main reasons for unionism's constitutional inappropriateness were its mirage of democracy, negative characteristics, and bureaucratic tendencies.

Mirage of democracy. The facade of union democracy diluted its claim to legitimacy. According to Drucker, "The individual union member is like the individual stockholder; he neither wants to exercise his individual rights, nor would he know how to do it and for what purpose."[28] In actuality, the union member transferred responsibility to the union leader. In elaborating the comparison of the union member with the stockholder, Drucker saw that the former was in a more disadvantaged position because he lacked the factor of mobility: "The stockholder can always sell his shares, whereas the union member must remain a member on pain of losing his livelihood."[29]

Negative characteristics. Drucker characterized the union as "the negative to the corporation's positive."[30] Essentially, the union by its very nature was adversarial and indifferent to the interests of other corporate constituencies. The union's own narrow interest of "more and more" (higher wages, shorter hours, and increased benefits) fostered an irrational attitude toward profitability and innovation. In analyzing the countervailing plus and minus features of the union as an institution, Drucker stated: "The trade-union is beneficial and desirable today because it counterbalances some of the more obvious ills of our social body. It is an anti-organization, an antibody against social toxins. But it is not a constructive institution—nor designed as one."[31]

Bureaucratic tendencies. Drucker took the position that union leadership was doomed to play the role of the loyal opposition without any prospects of assuming the mantle of management. He predicted that as the union became stronger and more mature, its original idealistic objectives for worker welfare would diminish. Like corporate management, union leadership would disintegrate into an illegitimate, self-interested bureaucracy, more interested in its own power than in the needs and aspirations of its constituents: "As soon as a union or a corporation is strong and well established, management of necessity becomes self-perpetuating and absolute."[32] In the event that union leadership actually were to take control of the enterprise, it would still be exercising illegitimate power, with no real change in the structure of authority. Instead of the new corporate management's becoming the instrument of participative industrial citizenship, it would simply burden the workers with new masters. "The rulers would be changed, but not the rule."[33]

Arguing that both paternalism and unionism were countereffective, Drucker stated that the prescription for improved status and function for the worker was greater autonomy within the enterprise: "The plant must be made into a functioning self-governing social community."[34] His suggestion for this attitudinal shift from adversarial to more cooperative relationships did not envisage any dilution of management's strategic decision-making powers but called for greater employee participation in the social affairs and procedural working conditions within the factory.

He assumed workers' self-respect and esteem would increase if workers were given authority for work rules, safety conditions, vacation scheduling, and other issues that had a direct impact on improving the climate of general working conditions. Ideally, he hoped that sowing the seeds of industrial citizenship within the plant community would produce such results among workers as a firmer sense of group membership, improved morale and job satisfaction, greater understanding of company goals, and an opportunity for outstanding workers to join the management cadre. In essence Drucker was suggesting a form of corporate federalism based on one of his favorite documents—the U.S. Constitution. Under this arrangement, all the crucial powers not exclusively designated for management would revert to the workers. Drucker was under no illusion that a more democratic plant community provided the complete answer to workers' lack of power and alienation, but he felt it superior to the alternatives of trade unionism and paternalism.

In later years Drucker's writings made many allusions to the need for industrial citizenship, but the concept received a cool reception from managers, largely because they feared it represented an effort to usurp their authority. Union leadership, with its predominant concentration on enlargement of personal power and additional concentration on economic bread-and-butter issues, failed to give anything but token endorsement to Drucker's plant community proposals.

Although for five decades Drucker preached the value of industrial citizenship for the workers, the issue of corporate membership has now become significantly less important. This is because the technology of the information revolution has created a reversal in the structure of the workforce, from an emphasis on blue-collar workers to an emphasis on knowledge workers. Status and function, Drucker has noted, have become less relevant for knowledge workers because, by virtue of their unique skills and talents, they now own the means of production. This repositioning of the power relationship means that management has become more dependent on knowledge workers than the other way around. Consequently, in a world where knowledge equals authority, management has no choice but to recruit competitively for knowledge workers' services, cater to their allegiance, challenge their intellectual development, provide the tools for their performance, and allow for their participation in the strategic decision-making process.

Drucker was not only the first to question the relevance of the trade union as a constitutional vehicle for giving status and function to blue-collar workers, he was also among the first to recognize that the skills and crafts of manual and mechanical workers would disappear with the emergence of the concepts and ideas of the knowledge workers. But the increasing decline of manual workers in manufacturing has not eliminated the need for worker status and function completely. Drucker has seen this need shifting to the less educated service workers. At the same time, he has continued to advance his long-term position that there are no second-class jobs and second-class citizens; every job, no matter how menial, has dignity and deserves respect. The problem of status and function has shifted from the manual to the service sector, but its solution is almost as distant as ever.

Conclusion

The End of Economic Man and *The Future of Industrial Man* are more than period pieces; they are revealing sources on the origin of the modern discipline of management. The recently issued new editions of these works, published by the Transactional Press at Rutgers University, attest to their longevity, popularity, and current relevance. Although not generally placed in the genre of management literature, Drucker's first two major books played a significant role in his career for two basic reasons: first, they formed the foundation for many insights and ideas that have shaped his managerial mind-set, and second, they provided the framework for the conceptual analysis and structural methodology of many of the chief themes that permeated his future writings.

In his review of *The Future of Industrial Man,* Jacques Barzun, Columbia University's eminent cultural historian, was one of the first to capture Drucker's unique ability to combine analytical and perceptual talents and to recognize his future relevance with great prescience: "With some books, indeed, the single and simple idea they contain is fully expressed in the title, but with Mr. Drucker's work this simplification is deplorable. Here is a book of some 300 pages, which is so perfectly planned and so transparently written as to read with almost indifferent ease. But its substance was obviously not improvised to fit a title. Each page is the fruit of much learning and long reflection. It should accordingly be studied, pondered over, analyzed word by word, with the care that our scholars reserve for authors who have been dead a thousand years."[35]

Alan Kantrow of Harvard University has commented that Drucker's two earliest works are not concerned with "how to do" but do provide "a case study in how to think."[36] This emphasis on supplementing business techniques with a new dimension of thought that comes from converting concepts from political theory into concepts of management was also present in Drucker's early works, as the following insights from those works reveal:

- The large corporation has become the most representative institution in modern industrial society, and its corporate management cadre has become a new leadership elite.

- Economic performance and social responsibility must be considered in establishing business purpose.

- A challenge exists for management to narrow the gap between the ideals of society's moral values and the amoral realities of economic activities.

- The justification of corporate legitimacy is an issue of critical importance because illegitimate institutions are those that cannot justify their power and that are incapable of long-term survival in a free society.

- There are limits on the ability of reason to control human activities, and the idea that we can attain human and organizational perfection is a myth.

- The harmony and effectiveness of the business enterprise requires the introduction of industrial citizenship for employees.

- In the concept of economic man it is a fallacy that only pecuniary reward matters and that labor is simply another physical commodity; the proposition of one-dimensional man destroys the web of mutual trust and healthy human relationships in capitalistic society.

- The limitations of mindless rationality and the inherent flaws of structural designs based on manmade absolutes are two managerial lessons we can learn from the study of Nazi and Soviet totalitarianism.

- It is a mistake to view the corporation exclusively as an economic institution; it is also a social and political microcommunity.

- The enterprise system is superior to other organizing alternatives, yet it faces the dilemma of reconciling successful economic performance with societal accountability.

- Under present circumstances the trade union is a necessary countervailing force against management power, but its negative and adversarial characteristics along with its unaccountable bureaucratic leadership prevent its legitimacy.

- An inextricable relationship exists between the tools of technology and the nature, design, and bonds of work.

The topics and issues that flow from these insights and ideas are now taken for granted as part of the conceptual thinking in the process and teaching of management, but they were either unnoticed or virtually unaddressed before Drucker's innovative treatment of them. It is easy for cynics to state that his observations are obvious, but it was Drucker who made them obvious. As Kantrow puts it: "How remarkably familiar has become his vision of modern industrial society as constituted by large scale organizations. How obvious it now seems to regard business as the representative institution of that society, and how matter-of-fact an exercise it now is to apply to business the same modes of analysis appropriate to any social or political institution."[37]

Drucker's two earliest volumes also augured two organizational themes that would play an important part in the design of his future management philosophy: (1) the interaction between continuity and change and (2) the methodological concepts of *systems theory* and *social ecology*.

Continuity and Change

According to Drucker the two major theories describing change—the economist's model of equilibrium and the political scientist's paradigm of balance of power—failed to meet the test of dynamic reality. In his analysis he viewed both of these models as closed systems that endorsed static equilibrium and supported the status quo. Because major change was viewed from the vantage point of natural catastrophes, the disciplines of economics and political science were based on Cartesian mechanical formulations, allowing little room for human volition, dynamic interaction between organizations, and external complexities.

Drucker interpreted continuity and change from an organic historical perspective. He divided the process into three interconnected stages—the "what," the "why," and the "so what." Seeking patterns in each stage, he sought understanding of the what from his analysis of factual events. To understand the why, he related past to present realities, with an eye to identifying discontinuities or unique events that broke the linear patterns of continuity. To understand the so what, he interpreted the recent past through his study of the what and why, projecting the hopes and fears, threats and opportunities, and social problems and dilemmas that affected society.

Drucker emphasized that just as an individual is totally disoriented without memory, an institution exists in a dangerous, surrealistic twilight zone when deprived of a sense of continuity. In short, it is essential to recognize the inter-connections between major transitions in human expectations as well as the restraints of human responses. His concept of continuity and change ensured that the past had its claims, the present its relevance, and the future its potential opportunities. He was convinced that his open-ended approach had advantages over current theories because it focused on dynamic disequilibrium rather than the stagnant interpretation of a closed society.

Systems Theory and Social Ecology

In his approach to understanding reality and discovering meaningful patterns, Drucker also rejected the one-dimensional approach to knowledge, which he feared would force him into the quicksand of specialization. As a result he chose the path of being reasonably literate in all the social sciences.

His early works reflected this multidisciplinary approach, and that approach explains why at various times he has been labeled political scientist, philosopher, psychologist, historian, economist, and sociologist. Adam Smith, the media commentator and journalist, wrote recently that Drucker's refusal to become a professional economist had its downside because it eliminated any chance he had of receiving a Nobel Prize.[38] On the positive side, however, one advantage of his interdisciplinary approach revealed in his early writings is his ability to use the two diagnostic tools of systems theory and social ecology. These tools gave him a greater intellectual latitude for looking at reality and converting it into significant insights. It was not until later years that the concepts of systems theory and social ecology were labeled as such by Drucker, but the seeds were clearly planted in his early works.

Systems theory and social ecology shaped Drucker's efforts to devise sensible observations about the complex circumstances surrounding him. The institutional focus, for example, in *The End of Economic Man* was on the nation state, but as Drucker's interest in management became more pronounced, he shifted his concentration to the business corporation and nonprofit organizations. Unlike most academics, who as prisoners of their disciplines were unwilling to risk questioning and drawing upon knowledge from other fields, Drucker viewed no discipline as sublimely superior and all knowledge as potentially relevant.

His adoption of the methodologies of systems theory and social ecology not only provided Drucker with a frame of reference for his analysis but made him sui generis in the embryonic field of management theory. Whether he realized it fully or not, his approach marked a major innovation, moving abruptly away from viewing management traditionally, through the lens of accounting, marketing, engineering, industrial psychology, public relations, finance, or any other specialized discipline.

Because the terms *systems theory* and *social ecology* are not household concepts and have not received wide acceptance and endorsement in business and academic circles, a brief elaboration of their essence is in order.

Systems Theory. Systems theory originated as a result of an information overload in every academic discipline. Because research and discovery inexorably created more facts leading to increased fragmentation in all subjects, mastering a total discipline became increasingly untenable. Moreover, attempts to relate a particular discipline to others only heightened intellectual disorder. As facts outpaced understanding and confusion replaced efforts at synthesizing specialties, the need to distill a more cohesive, coherent, and integrative organization of knowledge became apparent in all academic disciplines. The search for greater clarity through the systems approach originated in the field of biology but rapidly spread to other subjects. Along with several others prior to World War II, Drucker was a votary of this approach in the discipline of political theory, and after the war he pioneered the concept in management theory.

Briefly stated, systems theory was an attempt to create a mental model of unity out of diversity, to view institutions from a holistic rather than a fragmented perspective, and to perceive organizational reality in terms of dynamic disequilibrium, whether the unit under consideration was a tribe, nation state, city, region, family, or corporation. Given the central proposition that the parts of any system (biological or social) had autonomy but only the whole had purpose, it followed that the components of any system made sense only in contemplation of its totality. A system, according to the theorists, had the following characteristics: interaction of parts or subsystems, transaction of external inputs into institution outputs, maintenance of a condition of dynamic disequilibrium through the mechanism of constant feedback, and (for human institutions) a need for purpose.

In his later writings, Drucker was to cite many examples of the interrelationship between the parts and the whole. One of his favorite illustrations has been the symphony orchestra, in which the musical functions are means that produce only noise unless the conductor blends the instruments into the holistic harmony of music.

Social Ecology. Many basic similarities exist between systems theory and social ecology. Each embraces the multidisciplinary approach, looks for the big picture, favors organic interaction over isolated fragmentation, and seeks patterns of probability rather than responds to repetitive rules and rigid formulas. The two conceptual insights differ chiefly in their emphasis on the internal and the external. Systems theory concentrates mainly on the internal dimensions and operations of the social unit being examined. Social ecology is chiefly concerned with making sense of the impact of outside forces and trends encountered by organizations.

The concept of social ecology was initially applied by Drucker in *The End of Economic Man,* but he did not coin the term until almost fifty years later. However, he did note that the methodology had a lineage traceable to the ancient Greeks. Among the prominent thinkers historically associated with this line of analysis were Herodotus, Thucydides, Aristotle, Edmund Burke, Alexis de Tocqueville, Hippolyte Taine, and Walter Bagehot, to cite a few. What attracted Drucker to these thinkers was their ability to transcend the artificial boundaries of subject matter, to recognize that interacting elements must be studied as a unit, to establish novel patterns of relevance, and to relate timeless topics to the temper of their times. Drucker's current academic title at Claremont Graduate School is professor of social science. Titles have never had much effect on Drucker, but I am sure he would prefer the position to be called professor of social ecology. If the trustees and faculty decided to introduce such an innovative label, it would be the first in academic history.

In applying the term *social ecology* to these thinkers of the past, Drucker hoped to give the phrase greater currency in modern times by introducing the techniques of the scientific ecologist to social issues. Correlating the intellectual activity of the scientific ecologist with that of the social ecologist, he noted how the former analyzes his subject matter. In his search for relevant patterns the scientific ecologist selects a natural entity for investigation (ocean, swamp, desert, river, mountain, and so on). He then incorporates the ancillary disciplines (biology, botany, geology, zoology, ornithology, and so on) for their specialized contributions to understanding the broader topic. In a similar vein the social ecologist pursues meaningful synergy and looks for configurations in the artificial environment of the organization by using the social sciences (history, economics, sociology, and philosophy).

To distinguish the qualitative difference between the physical and the social ecologist further, Drucker observed that "the physical ecologist believes, must believe, in the sanctity of natural creation. The social ecologist believes, must believe, in the sanctity of spiritual creation."[39] A major premise of the social ecologist in doing research was that the outside environment did not adapt itself to the institution, whether it was a national state or a corporation, but that the institution must adapt itself to its outside surroundings. In this process of adjustment and renewal the organization had to come to terms with changing times, and it was the task of the manager to identify those issues and trends that had an impact on the survival of the enterprise. To illustrate, Drucker argued in *The End of Economic Man* and *The Future of Industrial Man* that European society was frozen in its attempt to adjust to the new industrial order. The result in the case of Germany and Italy was an aggressive war and for Britain and France an ill-prepared war.

Drucker was under no illusion that systems theory and social ecology constituted a Rosetta stone of understanding. To the contrary, he was acutely aware that like all tools, they had vulnerabilities. The most glaring limitations were their inability to establish meaningful boundaries of knowledge in investigating a topic and the resistance to satisfactory verification. Moreover, Drucker frequently warned that tools, whether of the hardware or conceptual variety, were only means. Deriving larger insights and understandings from the tools of systems theory and social ecology depended in the final analysis on the user. In short, the user's capability of discerning pertinent threads in the social fabric depends on how the user has reflected on experience and applied perceptual talents. Despite these limitations, Drucker felt that the dual concepts of systems theory and social ecology, which viewed reality through the prism of pattern and configuration, were superior to current Cartesian specializations, which were devoid of a meaningful comprehensive focus.[40]

In any event, their advantages notwithstanding, Drucker did not consider systems theory and social ecology the last word but only a temporary interpretation of reality, to be used until something more adequate emerged. As significant as the problem of organizing knowledge was, he considered the *organization of ignorance* an even more formidable challenge. He filed away the title *Organizing Ignorance* under a long list of his intended but unwritten books.

CHAPTER FIVE

CONCEPT OF THE CORPORATION

The favorable reviews accorded to *The Future of Industrial Man* had both an uplifting and disconcerting effect on Drucker. On the one hand the provocative treatment and significance of his twin hypotheses—the unique institutional importance of the large corporation and the unprecedented leadership role of professional management—added to his stature as a social commentator. On the other hand he realized his insights were intellectual abstractions devoid of empirical confirmation. More important, given his limited exposure to the operating environment of big business, he was aware that he was in no position to tackle the job of probing the complex relationship between theory and practice in a systematic fashion. He was, he thought, in the situation of "studying anatomy without a skeleton."[1]

Background

Of all Drucker's books, *Concept of the Corporation* has the most fascinating history. The underlying research was conceived (or misconceived) as a sponsored sociological study that would test his hypotheses of corporate government. It was unique in that it was his only book for which he accepted private corporate sponsorship or any kind of a grant at all. And the study was filled from start to finish with many surprises and unexpected circumstances.

To go beyond his intellectual postulates and overcome his ignorance of the management process, Drucker decided in 1943 to conduct an epistolary campaign in order to obtain entry into the corridors of many corporate executive suites. He wrote scores of letters to the chief executives of many large manufacturing plants requesting permission to conduct a study of their organizational structure, corporate governance, operating procedures, and management policies. The responses ranged from polite negatives to accusations that Drucker was almost certainly a subversive for suggesting such an egregious invasion of corporate privilege and executive privacy.

Concept of the Corporation, the result of the first analytical study of a major big business enterprise, was a product of coincidence. Because the prospects of obtaining a sponsor appeared hopeless, Drucker was ready to abandon his research project when an unexpected and fortuitous event occurred that ultimately turned his life around. That surprise incident was a phone call from Paul Garrett, vice president of public relations of General Motors, inviting him to undertake a detailed scholarly investigation of General Motors's corporate governance and administrative operations.

General Motors was so huge and powerful a corporation, with arguably the most esteemed and respected top management team in American business, that Drucker had been too intimidated to include it in his original project list of companies. Moreover, unknown to Drucker at the time, the top managers of General Motors, including its chairman, the famed Alfred Sloan, were far from enthusiastic about the proposed study. They had been reluctantly persuaded to endorse the project by Donaldson Brown, vice president of finance, who was particularly impressed by Drucker's previous writings and was convinced of the merit of an analytical business study by an outsider.

Unknown to the top management of the firm, Drucker also had his own agenda. He had no interest in General Motors in particular or the automobile industry in general; his ulterior goal was to use the company as a means to understand the conflict between industrial efficiency and social harmony. For example, his major concern was with the dignity and status of the individual employee and the role of the corporation in satisfying this end of industrial citizenship and social community.[2]

Drucker hoped that studying one representative company in depth would enhance his understanding of corporate reality by raising such specific questions as these: How does a free enterprise economy function and what are its strengths and weaknesses? What are the crucial components of the corporation's mission, and what are the activities that are irrelevant? What are the things that management can do to contribute to society's improvement, and what are the things it should avoid?

Needless to say, Drucker accepted the invitation with enthusiastic alacrity because it not only provided him the opportunity to conduct an unprecedented management study of a major business but also came from the world's largest and most successful manufacturing corporation. Privately, Drucker saw the General Motors experience as a once-in-a-lifetime learning opportunity because of the way it would combine research with practice.

According to the terms of the contract the study was to take two years of full-time research, with Drucker being paid his regular academic salary. Early on in the project, however, Drucker found that many of the executives he interviewed were less than candid. He discovered that people thought the revelations of a private in-house study might affect their future careers. In order to remove this obstacle, Drucker requested that the original stipulation that he would perform a private study be changed to allow him to write a commercially published book. General Motors graciously approved the proposal, with only one restriction—it insisted that there be no mention of any military projects the company was conducting for the war effort. Under the title *Concept of the Corporation*, the study was published in 1946.[3]

In *Concept of the Corporation*, positioning himself in the wings of the ongoing corporate drama, Drucker viewed the events at General Motors from the perspective of a bystander. This role was not that of an indifferent and passive spectator but of an interested and reflective observer of the shifting scenes and a critical commentator on the collective performance of the cast. On one occasion he elaborated on this perspective, remarking that "bystanders have no history of their own. They are on the stage but are not part of the action. They are not even audience. The fortunes of the play and of every actor in it depend on the audience whereas the reaction of the bystander has no effect except on himself. But standing in the wings—much like the fireman in the theater—the bystander sees things neither actor nor audience notices. Above all, he sees differently from the way actors or audience see. Bystanders reflect—and reflection is a prism rather than a mirror; it refracts."[4]

Drucker did not start his book by tracing the history or describing the operations of General Motors. Instead he sketched the characteristics and common denominators of organizations in general. Painting with a broad brush, he analyzed such institutional features as the justification of corporate existence in terms of purpose and contribution to society, the dynamic interaction between the corporate entity and society, the harmonization of organizational needs with the requirements of the state and the values of society, alternative structural designs, the predicament of reconciling meritocracy with equality of opportunity in the workforce, the problems surrounding top management succession for entities designed in perpetuity, human resources as the institution's most important asset, one-man rule and reliance on geniuses as unacceptable guidelines for survival, and need for continual training and development of the organization's membership. By not focusing on the personalities of the executives and by not explaining their daily operations, Drucker showed he was more interested in the process of management than in the daily activities of the company per se.

In his treatment of these topics, Drucker drew on the axioms of political theory and illustrations from such widely diverse organizations as the church, army, university, civil service, and religious orders. In effect, he demonstrated that the principles discussed in these nonbusiness organizations also have a direct relevance to business.

Drucker turned next to delineating some of the unique features of the modern business enterprise: the crucial role of corporate purpose, the conflict between the demands of long-run and short-term strategies, the role of markets and questions of monopoly and size, the main survival functions (a cursory exploration of marketing, profitability, human relations, and social responsibility), the tensions between specialist skills and generalist attitudes, the pattern of top management decision making, the nature of work and standards of productivity, the profit motive, and rivalry between the bureaucrats who support the status quo and the mavericks who want to do things differently, to cite a few of the diverse factors encountered by modern management.

Corporate Strengths

General Motors's outstanding achievements in the areas of corporate profits, engineering skills, and financial methodologies were singled out by Drucker as factors enabling the company to become the world's most admired and largest manufacturer. Of course these were by consensus the accepted competencies, acknowledged and substantiated by countless business journals. Drucker, however, probed the corporation's success more deeply, suggesting that General Motors apparently had, in addition to the conventional competencies found also in many successfully competitive businesses, two unique excellencies—federal decentralization and an outstanding top management team.

Federal Decentralization

From the standpoint of structural design, General Motors adopted the principle of federal decentralization. This concept assumed that top management would establish corporate vision and objectives. A number of local subsidiaries with their own autonomous managements would be responsible for contributing to total business results. This combination of central command and control with local authority and participative decision making had several advantages. First, federal decentralization enabled the company to transcend the limitations of size by maintaining autonomous operating divisions without sacrificing the benefits of bigness. In theory, as in the U.S. Constitution, all powers not specifically granted to central top management were considered the responsibilities of the large operating units. Second, federal decentralization developed a functioning form of corporate government that tamed naked power by making management the servant of corporate purpose rather than its master. Third, federal decentralization was especially feasible for General Motors because its technological base was relatively simple and concentrated. Drucker implied that its concentrated knowledge of motors was the centripetal force synthesizing and synergizing almost all the company's activities. For example, instead of becoming diverse, it could focus intensively by selling its own knowledge of motors over and over again in such products as cars, trucks, buses, vans, and railroad trains as well as in the countless components that composed the manufacture of the many varieties of motors.

Outstanding Top Management Team

When Alfred Sloan became the chief executive of General Motors shortly after World War I, the company was in disarray. Its top management was made up of a motley group of divisional mavericks, many of them former race car drivers. Sloan created a central cabinet of five key members, each a distinctly different personality and each outstanding in his own business specialty. However, regardless of the collegial atmosphere and the individual strengths of group members, there was no question that it was Sloan who sat at the head of the table and had the final say in all critical decisions.

In addition to authoring the decentralization plan in the company, Sloan was generally credited with the marketing strategy of a car for every purse. Because it met the upward middle-class mobility of the American dream, this policy replaced the Ford mass-production strategy of allowing the customer to have any color as long as it was black and quickly moved General Motors into the number one position of the nation's largest industry.[5]

Drucker was aware of other highlights of General Motors's corporate performance under the guidance of Sloan and his top management team, most notably its sophisticated method of cost accounting, technological improvements, and contributions to the war effort. But aside from his unimpeachable integrity, what impressed Drucker most about Sloan were two special ingredients of his decision-making process. One was his talent for selecting people. When Drucker once asked him why he spent so much time on personnel decisions, he replied that it was imperative to calculate the strengths and weaknesses of the candidate slowly because a wrong decision was extremely difficult to reverse and could do incalculable harm to the company. In his screening process Sloan paid little attention to personality traits and educational credentials, which he considered cosmetic, and instead concentrated on whether or not the person had the appropriate skills, knowledge competencies, and a responsible commitment to the designated task.

Sloan's other unusual talent when making decisions was to demand alternatives for any proposal on the table. Drucker reported that Sloan believed that a mindless consensus, achieved without considering options, was not a substantive decision. If serious disagreements were not presented, he postponed discussion until alternatives were suggested and evaluated at a later meeting. Unless this approach was taken, according to Sloan, there could be no understanding of what the decision was all about; alternatives were the most critical antecedent for any risk-taking judgment.

What particularly impressed Drucker about Sloan was the fact that he was managing without benefit of any codified theory, little realizing he was laying the foundation for the managerial discipline. (Drucker later made a similar point with respect to the management consultant. "There is no precedent for him and no parallel. The management consultant is not only a part of the practice of management. He has been, above all, central to the development of the theory, the discipline, and the profession of management.")[6]

Critique

Despite General Motors's sponsorship of Drucker's project, playing the role of corporate apologist would have amounted to a betrayal of his scholarly and journalistic standards. At the same time, it would have been uncharacteristic of his temperament and personality if he had conducted a critique based on polemics and personalities. His criticism was couched therefore in a cool and detached style, shifting between an evaluation of big business deficiencies in general to the defects of General Motors in particular. Throughout his critique he especially stressed that a free and healthy enterprise system depended on how management overcame these weaknesses. Among the major shortcomings at General Motors were (1) the conflict between continuity and change, (2) the flaws of federal decentralization, (3) the problems of industrial citizenship, and (4) the issue of social responsibility.

Conflict Between Continuity and Change

Drucker faulted the management of General Motors for its failure to comprehend conceptually the dynamic interaction between the claims of the past and the needs of the future. Mesmerized by the company's brilliant economic success, top management operated under a monopolistic assumption that this corporate success would last forever. Drucker stressed that "General Motors is a functioning and moving organization of human beings and not a static blueprint."[7] He warned that the failure to cope with change more systematically meant that the corporation was on a collision course with tomorrow's realities. "Change," he said, "rather than faithful continuity was what GM needed."[8]

Moreover, General Motors was unaware that its very success was largely instrumental in shaping the new set of circumstances that could not be ignored. Insisting that it was a strategic mistake to expect that tomorrow's business would be a clone of today's business, Drucker urged that management adopt a realistic policy attuned to the dynamics of a new environment rather than expect the environment automatically to adjust to the enterprise.

Federal Decentralization

Drucker conceded that federal decentralization was a valuable design structure but also thought it was far from the omnipotent tool that General Motors's executives contended it was. He had serious reservations about federal decentralization on three counts. First, it was a poor substitute for corporate mission and identity; second, as it was constituted at General Motors it did not deliver on management development; and third, it failed to establish adequate guidelines for the balancing of operational authority and responsibility throughout the system.

On the one hand, General Motors subscribed to the proposition that structure determined strategy. On the other hand, Drucker believed that "organization is a means to an end rather than an end itself."[9] He recognized the important role that the structural design of federalism played in performance, but form without function is barren and sterile. It does not replace the significance of a strong statement of mission and purpose. Moreover, "decentralization, being concerned with organization, cannot, by its very nature, provide something as unorganizable as imagination and understanding."[10]

Drucker cited the relationship between a large-scale manufacturing division and small-scale dealerships as an example of General Motors's failure to distinguish between structure and strategy. Under the premise of decentralization, executives viewed both profit segments as having the same purpose, but Drucker argued they were two different businesses. For example, the manufacturing parent saw the customer exclusively in terms of the purchase of new cars whereas the dealer subsidiaries, with their small business mentality, saw economic performance revolving around the purchase of used cars. These differing realities of profitability meant that instead of the rhetorical harmony preached through the decentralization formula, the two sectors had competing businesses strategies.

According to Drucker, the incongruities of this economic arrangement resulted in the used car determining the price of the new car. His argument rested on the fact that the new car was subsequently resold several times over, establishing an extended life cycle for the product and giving poorer segments of the population access to cheap transportation. Therefore new cars might determine the short-term profit for General Motors, but used cars were also important to its long-term survival goals. (Drucker also maintained that the economic process of continually turning over used cars to less affluent buyers was one of the greatest marketing devices ever devised because it promoted wide distribution of ownership without any government interference.)

Because the corporate culture of General Motors considered structure more significant than strategy, Drucker concluded that federal decentralization had clouded the role of defining the business. He urged the company to recognize that it had two distinct customers—the new car purchaser and the distribution stream of small dealerships with a small business mentality. In order to make decentralization a more effective tool, General Motors had to reconcile the requirements of the two segments by clarifying its identity.

Another disturbing feature of decentralization was General Motors's neglect of managerial development. Because of its partiality toward specialists over generalists, the company favored product efficiency over people effectiveness. Contending these priorities needed a reversal, Drucker wrote that "the ability of an institution to produce leaders is more important than its ability to produce efficiently and cheaply."[11] For example, the rigidity of the corporation promotion system at General Motors denied workers an opportunity to advance into the managerial ranks, whereas Drucker argued for meritocracy, saying it was "imperative for the corporation to make it possible for men of ability to gain preferment regardless of the formal education they were able to acquire before going to work in industry."[12] Apropos of this remark on the current loss of brainpower, Drucker had in mind United Automobile Workers head Walter Reuther. He later said Reuther was perhaps the most competent leader at General Motors but was denied a managerial position because of his trade union and educational background.[13]

Decentralization was supposed to control size, but Drucker was troubled by the growth of Chevrolet, which, if independent, would have been one of the largest firms in the country. Consequently, he found it paradoxical that the head of the potent Chevrolet division was not part of General Motors's top management cabinet. Of even greater concern to him was that at Chevrolet, as at other key divisions, the operating policy contained in practice less flexibility in autonomous decision making than the corporate rhetoric indicated. The gap between the theory of decentralization and its operating practice compelled Drucker to assert that no attention was being rendered to the problem of top management succession, of replacing the team that Sloan had assembled.

Drucker concluded that decentralization at General Motors had many strengths, but that the company was so enamored with the strengths it failed to recognize the company weaknesses decentralization produced, such as taking the strategic mission for granted, failing to provide for adequate management development, and allowing size imbalances among the operating divisions that threatened the stability of the system.

Industrial Citizenship

It was no accident that the automobile industry had the worst labor relations in U.S. industry. With regard to worker status and function, Drucker conceded that the industry had achieved substantial results by advancing the workers onto the path of the middle class. However, this was not accompanied by instilling in the workers a sense of institutional belonging, producing a spirit of corporate allegiance and loyalty, ensuring reasonable job security, recognizing human dignity, and integrating individual effort into common achievement. Moreover, little attention was devoted to industrial citizenship as long as the company viewed workers not as human resources but as economic commodities and socially as a cadre of proletarian mercenaries.[14]

Drucker detected on the part of General Motors executives a sense of superiority and smugness toward the workers; they seemed to be considered engineering misfits who performed mindless jobs. This element of condescension was apparent throughout the company; Drucker observed that "the labor-relations expert of a large corporation who said that 'nobody with an I.Q. above moron should be allowed to work on the assembly line' was fairly representative."[15]

In pointing out the major characteristics of the assembly line—numbing boredom and meaningless repetitive work, absence of pride in producing a product, response to the rhythm of the machine (rather than work with a machine that adjusted to human rhythm)—Drucker declared that the management of General Motors saw these issues as intractable problems rather than as opportunities to grant the workers some degree of industrial citizenship. Therefore, it logically followed, according to the conventional wisdom of the era, that no suitable alternatives existed for the assembly line. When this assumption was combined with the short-term pressures for economic performance, constructing the foundation for a new era of labor relations appeared utopian.

In discussing how to ease worker disenchantment, gain the loyalty of the employees, and establish greater self-esteem and trust for the emerging middle-class workforce, Drucker returned to the concept of the plant community he had presented in his previous work, *The Future of Industrial Man*. He realized that the assembly line was hardly a suitable vehicle for improving the quality of the worker's life for the better, but what especially troubled him was the failure of management to recognize the gravity of the problem and that it was in the long-term self-interest of the corporation to seek a solution. Calling for enlightened self-interest, he remarked "that a solution of the problems of equal opportunities and of citizenship in industrial society is in the interest of the large corporation itself."[16]

Drucker mentioned that relying on managerial enlightened despotism, psychological gimmickry, and union paternalism for solutions was counterproductive and resulted only in reinforcing the proposition that adults should be treated like children. Among the steps for initiating a policy of industrial citizenship, he recommended the following: improved training, increased mobility for foreman and middle-management positions, and greater employee participation in the noneconomic affairs of the company (job safety, cafeterias, vacation scheduling, and health services). The exact list of participative activities, he contended, was less important than was the necessity to recognize that the worker was not simply a cost but an asset.

Drucker perceived the task of promoting industrial citizenship as one in which the corporation assumed the role of governing but not of government. For this task it required power, but it must never be allowed to become an end in itself and treat the individual as a means.

Social Responsibility

Drucker addressed the issue of corporate social responsibility at General Motors on two levels: the question of the source of corporate legitimacy and the parochial managerial attitude toward outside events.

General Motors justified the legitimacy of its enormous power chiefly by its contribution to society of outstanding economic performance. Drucker contended that this one-dimensional outlook failed to provide sufficient authentication and consent for society's major autonomous institution, the modern corporation. As he saw it, the modern corporation had to justify its power on a tridimensional basis—economic, social, and political. He granted that the dominant corporate responsibility was economic—the delivery of goods and services and the creation of jobs—but that was not the only corporate responsibility.

The corporation also had an accountability for its actions in the political and social realms. In the first realm, it was influential as a player in the political arena and had control over the job security of the worker. In the second, it was responsible for the status the worker received from his corporate employment and any specific negative impacts that the business might inflict on the environment. Because it was impossible to have a healthy economic institution operating in a potentially sick society, Drucker stressed it was mandatory for the firm to have obligations beyond the economic sphere of profitability. Arguing this point forcefully, he wrote: "This [economic purpose] does not mean that the corporation should be free from social obligations. On the contrary it should be so organized as to fulfill automatically its social obligations in the very act of seeking its own best self-interest."[17]

The conventional wisdom of corporate America at the time was based on laissez-faire economics and social Darwinism. According to classical economics, if the corporation pursued its economic self-interest, it would automatically act in the public interest, thereby relieving itself from any extra-curricular social accountability. And the ideology of the survival of fittest[18] declared that any business or human failure was, on moral grounds, a fully deserved outcome. At General Motors, moreover, the executives specifically argued cogently and logically that they lacked the authority and knowledge to confront political and social issues, which were best left in the hands of other, more appropriate societal institutions so that the company would not be liable to indictments of industrial feudalism and usurpation of political and social functions. Drucker conceded these arguments possessed a high degree of logical rigor, but they nevertheless failed to meet the realities that the corporation encountered beyond its economic mission and that showed self-interest alone was an inadequate response.

The public relations department was normally responsible for General Motors's external relations, but Drucker pointed out that it took a limited view of its task. Viewing the world outside the corporation should be a corporate survival function, but to corporate public relations departments it was an adjunct of marketing. Drucker commented that "to the general public *public relations* means publicity—essentially an extension of advertising from advertising a product to advertising its producer."[19] However, in Drucker's mind, publicity seemed the least important job of the public relations department. Its main role should be identifying the new trends that would affect the corporation's future survival.

Such was not the case at General Motors, which performed so effectively and obtained such outstanding results from applying business techniques that this success blinded the company's management to the important realities of outside business forces. As a result Drucker considered General Motors a success as a business but a failure as a social institution.[20] Complaining that the typical U.S. executive was divorced from outside interests and activities, he wrote that an executive "affects society by every one of his moves and is affected by it. Yet he inevitably lives in an artificial environment and almost as isolated as if he were in a monastery."[21] Further elaborating on the one-dimensional financial outlook of the managerial mentality and corporate indifference toward the quality of life, he said, "Hence executive life not only breeds a parochialism of the imagination comparable to the 'military mind' but places a considerable premium on it."[22]

Drucker portrayed General Motors's attention to outside factors as ritualistic and cosmetic, viewing consumer demands, dealer relationships, community affairs, and public relations in general as intrusions on the real, internal business concerns of productivity and profitability. He questioned whether this focus on short-term economic gains would continue to serve as an obstacle to long-term institutional policies of survival. Urging a change from a passive to an active stance on corporate responsibility, he suggested that management adopt a policy that he would later describe as "stakeholder responsibility":[23] "the question is how can the corporation give its management the imagination, the understanding of the outside point of view, of the public's (consumers, workers, voters, government) imagination and of the limits thereof."[24]

Sloan and Drucker

Throughout Drucker's long career the business community was considerably more enthusiastic in its praise of his books than was academe. In the case of *Concept of the Corporation*, by adroitly blending theoretical principles with managerial practices, he received almost unanimous approval in reviews from both segments. There was, however, one political scientist who praised the book but still considered the business corporation unworthy of future scholarly investigation. He cynically remarked, "It is to be hoped that the author will soon apply his considerable talents to a more respectable topic."[25] Fortunately, Drucker refused to accept this well-meaning professorial advice.

Perhaps the single strongest endorsement from the business community came from Ernest Breech, CEO of the Ford Motor Company, who, in the midst of restructuring the company after the egregious mismanagement of the senile Henry Ford I, insisted that every executive read *Concept of the Corporation*.[26] It also became compulsory reading for Henry Ford II, the young inexperienced president and grandson of the founder, who looked upon it as a primer in his management development.[27]

In one corner of the business world, however, there was no adulation: the executive suites of General Motors. Senior executives were so offended that for many years the book was unmentionable in the company. Despite the fact that *Concept of the Corporation* was widely considered a probusiness book, it received a hostile reception from its financial patron. It was resoundingly criticized within the organization for portraying as vulnerabilities what General Motors considered strengths. Considering the book unfair in its criticism and decidedly antibusiness in tone, the company's official policy was to treat its publication as a nonevent—ignoring its accompanying publicity, prohibiting its purchase as a gift for suppliers, dissociating the company from its opinions, and censoring any internal or external discussion of its merits.

Little doubt existed that the pariah status stamped on the book emanated from the CEO, Alfred Sloan. If General Motors was widely regarded as the quintessential symbol of industrial might, Sloan was esteemed throughout the country as the icon of the professional management revolution. His inimical attitude toward Drucker's study, however, was philosophical and not personal.

Sloan's intellectual disagreement with Drucker stemmed from his different angle of vision in interpreting the issue of corporate governance. According to Sloan the essence of the management function was the role of the professional practitioner, which emphasized character, leadership, moral suasion, and integrity. Drucker fully acknowledged these professional aspects of managerial leadership, but where he differed with Sloan was on questions of emphasis and application.

According to Drucker, Sloan was chiefly concerned with internal operations and viewed external conditions as factors outside his managerial concern.[28] Describing how Sloan was able to draw the curtain between internal corporate performance and outside business impacts, Drucker wrote: "A 'professional' for him was not a man without interests, without convictions, without a personal life. He was a man who separated his interests, his convictions, and his personal life from the task. Anything that to Sloan was personally important was by that very fact professionally suspect."[29]

Sloan maintained that he could find no source of authority warranting him to assume responsibility in such areas as education, health, and politics. Even if the company had special competence in an area of social responsibility and it was in the interest of the company, the concept of such responsibility was professionally unacceptable to him. Considering it a form of managerial ego to indulge in extraneous endeavors, he equated it with senseless gamesmanship: "A surgeon . . . does not take out an appendix because he is good at appendectomies or because he likes the operation. He takes it out because the patient's diagnosis calls for it."[30]

In adopting a more comprehensive interpretation of corporate responsibility, Drucker argued it was irrelevant that Sloan was as a professional executive, personally disinterested in getting the corporation involved in outside activities. The increasing complexities and accelerating changes in the environment made it a survival necessity for the company to respond to its own negative impacts. The amount and type of participation and commitment were subjects of debate, but it was no longer professionally feasible to view external factors as one would a spectator sport. Drucker maintained that Sloan saw the primary role of the professional manager as that of the technocrat whose major task was economic performance. He argued that fulfilling the economic task was the corporation's dominant social responsibility but not the sole one. Whether management liked it or not, there was an inescapable accountability to the quality of life.

Of course Sloan's strict constructionist approach to corporate responsibility propelled General Motors to the heights of economic success. The failure to adopt Drucker's broader approach, however, explained why the company failed to gain the public's esteem by meeting the expectations of society. In the years following the publication of *Concept of the Corporation,* Sloan and Drucker maintained a cool but cordial personal relationship. Their intellectual disagreement then surfaced again in 1964 when Sloan published his corporate memoirs, *My Years with General Motors.*

Prior to his book's publication, Sloan showed Drucker the draft, requesting suggestions. Drucker's main point of criticism was directed to the narrow and impersonal role Sloan saw for the professional manager. He also mentioned that Sloan did not take credit for such substantial innovations as revolutionizing the role of pricing in the used car market (that is, it was the car's retail value in the secondary market that determined the price of the new car), developing the acquisition formula of buying mature businesses and turning them into world-class subsidiaries, founding the General Motors vocational training center, and improving the performance of the research lab. Sloan politely rejected the suggestions, but because the book was antidotal to Drucker's *Concept of the Corporation,* he must have found a certain solace and satisfaction from the fact that it immediately became a best-seller—an unprecedented episode in publishing history for a book on business.

In his appraisal of Sloan's book Drucker visualized Sloan as playing the part of a paragon, the quintessential professional manager who had replaced the old robber baron tycoon. In describing how he served his corporate client unselfishly and idealistically, Sloan did not present himself in the role of hero; instead General Motors became the hero, which was tantamount to staging *Hamlet* without the prince. Because it presented a bloodless leader who over-rationalized the managerial process, Drucker felt the book should have been titled *General Motors While I Was There.*

Considering Sloan one of the "great organizers" of modern U.S. business, Drucker felt he was anything but the cold, imperial chief executive he portrayed himself to be in his book. In failing to chronicle his achievements and interests, Drucker felt Sloan did himself and his colleagues an injustice and did not depict the divergent personalities and human strengths of General Motors's top management. In elevating the institution to central stage, Sloan also omitted his personal compassion for friends and employees and his charitable concerns, sense of trust, ability to motivate and inspire, political activities, and interest in worker and auto safety—all of which he dismissed because he considered them personal interests and irrelevant to his professional role.

To illuminate his philosophical differences with Sloan, Drucker cited the two basic streams of thought on governance in the Western political tradition. The first originated with Plato and Aristotle and concentrated on guidelines for the preservation of order, the problem of succession, and safeguards against tyranny. The best illustration of the second approach was *Education of a Christian Prince,* by Erasmus, which concerned itself with the qualities and character required by a ruler as the first servant of the state. Drucker considered both schools of thought essential in the management process—the systematic codification of governing principles and the personal role of the ruler. Sloan was a votary of the latter, as Drucker observed: "But to Sloan the discipline of management came second—and a very distant second—to the profession of the manager."[31]

Despite their differing views on social responsibility and corporate governance, Drucker and Sloan formally continued their friendship and mutual self-
respect. Sloan solicited Drucker's input in establishing the Sloan School of
Management at MIT, and Drucker served on several of Sloan's management
study committees as well as other charitable concerns.

In recent years General Motors has been studied in business schools as a
case study in classic mismanagement. Of course many of the problems the
company encountered had been foreshadowed by Drucker. He subsequently
wondered if he should have been more outspoken in his criticism of the company. In addition to the points in his critique, he felt he should have mentioned
General Motors's failure to spin off Chevrolet as a separate entity and its
attempts to freeze market share in the industry. He attributed his less forceful
critique in *Concept of the Corporation* to his inexperience, possible intimidation
before the leading corporate titans, and the friendships he developed within
the company. In any event, it was a tribute to Sloan's original vision that his
legacy of success continued for several decades. After his passing, it was difficult to detect a single new strategic decision. It was not Sloan's fault that in
the recent past the company was undermanaged and overadministered.

Conclusion: Impact of *Concept of the Corporation*

Drucker had every reason to be grateful for the favorable public reception of
Concept of the Corporation. Perhaps more than any other of his books it has
enhanced and sustained its popularity over the years; after forty years it was
still selling 20,000 copies a year. Even more significant, it had pivotal impact
in shaping Drucker's professional career.

After Drucker's study of General Motors, the corporation was no longer
a subject of benign intellectual neglect. *Concept of the Corporation* elevated it to a
respectable topic of research. Drucker's pioneering study was a catalyst for the
publication in the 1950s of an unprecedented number of books dealing with
big business. Moreover, he not only confirmed his hypothesis that the large
corporation was the dominant institution of industrial society but also broke
intellectual ground in asserting that management as a universal organ of governance was conducive to systematic study as a distinct form of work.

As a result of his study of General Motors, in addition to these two major
insights, Drucker was formulating an as-yet inchoate managerial theory of the

business firm based on the specifications of management practice.[32] And it is possible to infer from *Concept of the Corporation* a number of principles that will fuse into the matrix of his later philosophical system. At this earlier stage, Drucker might not have been certain about the criteria of good management, but in his diagnosis of the large corporation, he was reasonably sure what constituted poor management. C. N. Parkinson, the British political scientist and author of *Parkinson's Law*, astutely observed that the coming years would be a questioning period for Drucker in his codification of management theory, commenting that Drucker "would not claim to know what all these principles are but he is groping towards them, convinced from the outset that they exist."[33]

A number of managerial principles can be inferred from Concept of the Corporation *and Drucker's other early writings:*

- The channel of distribution is as much a customer as is the ultimate consumer.

- The corporation is a social and political system as well as an economic organization.

- Bigness does not confer distinction, only performance does.

- One great advantage of size is that it can often survive major blunders.

- Success creates euphoria and hubris; businesses come to think they are excellent in all corporate functions, but along with notable institutional strengths come major concomitant organizational weaknesses.

- Each incremental tier of organization increases the noise level but decreases effective communication.

- Organizational charts are poor barometers of contribution because they are incapable of defining tasks.

- People respect the doer, the business practitioner who, unlike the academic, deals with reality and uncertainty.

- Organization is a means, not an end.

- Strategy follows structure.

- Perfection is not a trait given to human beings, nor is it a characteristic of organizations.

- Paternalism and enlightened despotism run counter to an axiom of organizational experience: namely, that a person should have a private life of his or her own.

- Corporations mold the environment, but the environment also molds them.

- Organizations, like individuals, cannot be excellent at everything.

- Unlike past organizations that tried to prevent change, the modern business enterprise is designed to produce change.

- Corporations must allocate resources for today's and tomorrow's businesses simultaneously.

- Without recognizing it, the practitioner is the forerunner of the theoretical discipline.

- Publicity is the least important function of public relations; more important is serving as a sensing device for critical trends affecting the corporation's survival.

- Profitability is the result, not the cause, of business performance.

- The profit motive is a myth. If archangels operated businesses, profitability "would have to be the first law of action."

- Succession is a crucial problem for any institution organized for perpetuity.

- A human relations policy that does not enhance the bonds of work is a useless policy.

- Workers are assets and resources, not costs and expenses.

- Economic contribution is the main responsibility of the business but not the only one.

- There is no single correct organizational design.

- Performance, not charisma, determines leadership.

- Top management is the brain function of the business.

- Illegitimate institutions are incapable of producing wise and decent rulers.

- Authority without responsibility is illegitimate, but so is responsibility without authority. Both lead to tyranny.

Most of the management principles inferred from *Concept of the Corporation* (see the box) have been accepted into the lore of management. Younger students take them for granted or believe they have discovered them. But most of them were formally introduced for the first time more than fifty years ago.

His experiential exposure at General Motors was the springboard for Drucker's future consulting career, which would eventually run into several thousand clients. The book that came from it had a major effect on his teaching focus. No longer did he instruct philosophy, history, ethics, sociology, and economics as isolated academic subjects but was now able to teach them all by incorporating relevant material extracted from them into a synthesized body of knowledge about management. As mentioned earlier, as an educational experience the General Motors study was for Drucker a university without walls, one that improved his self-knowledge, deepened his powers of perception, liberated him from the vacuum of academic abstraction, and heightened his respect for executives operating among the harsh realities of power and results.

As a result of *Concept of the Corporation,* Drucker was finally able to integrate a career choice around the intellectual common denominator of the business enterprise and the work of the manager. This did not mean Drucker admired the business organization over other organizations but considered its study a means to the larger end of understanding community and society. In committing himself to probe the organizational design of the corporation and research the nature of managerial work, his goal was to integrate the disciplines of teaching, consulting, journalism, and lecturing into a coherent multiprofessional pattern and concentrated intellectual purpose. As noted earlier, he was temperamentally unsuited to pursue a single professional career, but he found satisfaction in the fact that he now had "a calling"—the study of the theory and practice of management.

CHAPTER SIX

ESTABLISHING THE FUNDAMENTALS

Once Drucker crossed an intellectual Rubicon by selecting the modern corporation's operations as the central core of his future scholarly attention, he contemplated the construction of a theoretical model of the enterprise and its managerial practices. The publication of *The Practice of Management* fifteen years later, in 1954, was to be the culmination of his conjectures over that previous decade and a half on the significance of the large corporation and its generic organ of management. It has become a seminal book in that it was the first attempt to codify managerial principles, prescribe basic skills for managerial effectiveness, and establish a foundation for the inchoate discipline of management. Drucker's thinking during the years preceding publication of *The Practice of Management* bears investigating in detail.

Background

In order to obtain a firmer grasp of the subject matter, Drucker decided to explore what is currently known about the topic of management. In surveying the status and condition of the field, he chose the following areas for investigation: the prototypical manager, international business, the university curriculum, business literature, great organizers, and intellectual pioneers.

Prototypical Manager

The professional norm for most American business executives immediately after World War II was managerial illiteracy, a situation in which specialists within the corporation viewed reality from the vantage point of their particular function. Corporations' failure to define themselves as interactive entities fostered a condition in which each specialization interpreted a business identity in its own fashion and proceeded to do its own thing according to the mandates of its discipline.

A Tower of Babel resulted from this multitude of parochial perceptions, and Drucker described this communications gridlock with a heavy dose of satire. The accounting and financial departments were mesmerized by the bottom line of profits in their evaluation of business performance while failing to recognize its shortcomings as a measurement of the firm's future costs and risks. Marketing professionals were obsessed with sales volume as the magic bullet of business success while neglecting such crucial criteria as industrial growth and total customer satisfaction. Describing the interaction between accounting and marketing executives, Drucker portrayed the former as so beguiled by the theology of numbers that they confined their reading exclusively to income statements, whereas the latter proudly and pompously proclaimed that they would not be caught dead reading a balance sheet.

Drucker found a similar myopia all across the functional landscape of the business world. Production engineers, for example, blatantly indifferent to cost, elevated quality and design to the highest rank among company objectives while naively believing that the stork actually delivered customers. Research scientists were passionately concerned with advancing the frontiers of knowledge and enthusiastically welcomed the approbation of their professional peers for their research achievements while being indifferent to product features of immediate business relevance and application. Personnel psychologists conducted questionable tests and proposed untested theories to improve worker motivation while seriously suspicious of the humanity and sanity of their subjects. Public relations technicians visualized their task as distributing to the press inconsequential publicity releases while remaining blind to the social and economic forces that were determining the future of the enterprise. Business economists favored abstract techniques over concrete applications and adopted the premises of static equilibrium theory while ignoring the entrepreneurial dynamics of using business disequilibrium in meeting the challenges of tomorrow.

Corporate lawyers, with their penchant for focusing on *what not to do*, had such an averseness to risk that they unconsciously paralyzed the crucial pursuit of opportunities. Statisticians were so enthralled with the beauty of their mathematical models, the precision of their formulas, and the validity of their measurements that they considered it an infringement of professional privilege if someone raised the question of results.

In puncturing the pride and exposing the arrogance of technocrats, Drucker acknowledged that there were many exceptional examples of managerial competence, particularly in a minority of excellent companies. Yet he forcefully contended that his hyperbolic hypothesis of managerial illiteracy was not an exaggeration when applied generally to business executives.

Moreover, he asserted that a myopic corporate vision was hardly surprising when executive training and experience were considered. He attributed the absence of a generalist mind-set chiefly to a business education that emphasized functional training and to a promotion-and-reward system that focused on specialized performance. Departmental conflicts were a natural characteristic of organizational life, but such tensions became a threat to corporate survival when they caused people to disregard the common vision of the enterprise. As long as managerial illiteracy with its internal perspectives on business identity dominated the culture of organizational life, there ensued a built-in prescription to defend the status quo. In short, the technocrat's angle of vision precluded paying attention to innovation or purposefully planned change; such change was possible only through an organic or systems approach that developed a broader vision of business objectives.

International Business

In exploring the field of international business, Drucker found in every country cultural restraints that inhibited the realization of a free autonomous enterprise and a systematic methodology of management. For example, in Britain the "muddling through" amateur was esteemed but the sophisticated and competent manager was viewed with snobbish disdain. In Germany the management model for big business was predicated on hereditary privilege. In many instances the company director (manager was an unapproved term) actually performed the top management job, but he was considered a hired hand. Everybody knew that real authority derived from birthright, from possessing the proper genes and chromosomes. In France the stamping of the passport for passing through the portals of the managerial elite depended on graduation from one of the exclusive *grands écoles.* This meritocracy of technical experts, however, had as its prime objective resistance to change and dilution of the entrepreneurial spirit in order to sustain the economic power of the oligarchy of the celebrated "two hundred families." In Italy the power of management was equated with paternalistic authority and an insider network of political connections. In Japan management control was vested in the *zaibatsu,* a family-dominated and government-sponsored conglomerate of six major business cartels.

In the Marxist countries, management was concerned with one major function—the meeting of the productivity targets dictated by the government. The concept of viewing management as a unique activity embracing the synthesis of many knowledge functions was an unthinkable abstraction. According to Vladimir Lenin, the Bolshevik dictator, after the nationalization of production the economic function of managing could be handled by a cook or a tailor. Drucker considered that Soviet central planning was a method for avoiding real management decisions, because the handful of policy planners could place the failure for economic results on the backs of a multitude of technical administrators.[1]

Drucker concluded that the concept of management held outside the United States had convoluted definitions and pejorative connotations. It was intellectually barren and sterile as a source of insights for the putative discipline of organic management. Even though there were some outstanding business success stories, nobody appeared interested in chronicling these achievements from a managerial perspective and helping to develop an organized body of knowledge.

University Curriculum

The reviews of *Concept of the Corporation* confirmed in Drucker's mind that management had no status as a respectable academic discipline. In the liberal arts colleges, political scientists considered it a branch of economics, economists categorized it as an adjunct of political theory, and sociologists had banished it to the limbo of nonexistence. It might be expected that management would have intellectual respectability in the business curriculum, but such was not the case.

As far as the study and development of management was concerned, the university mirrored corporate practice, offering simply a smorgasbord of specialized courses—sales management, financial management, production management, and engineering management, to cite a few. In essence the typical college bulletin recognized management only as an afterthought, something to be tacked onto the various business functions. Because management had no established central core of knowledge, it was chimerical to hope that nuggets of managerial relevance would be mined from collegiate teaching and research. Certain faculty members were undoubtedly aware of the need to bridge the gap between the business disciplines by introducing a unified focus, but that need never became a program to be implemented.

College bulletins used the title "school of business administration" to describe the institution's business education philosophy, but Drucker pointed out that this broad intellectual scope was a myth—in practice these schools were nothing more than programs of business techniques. Their transfer of managerial insights and ideas was even more infrequent and accidental than such learning was in business. Drucker noted that people in a business may be specialized but the problems never are. Therefore, regardless of their refusal to openly integrate with other functional departments, business specialists have no choice in reality but to interact in one fashion or another with specialists from other areas in the decision-making process. But this was not the case in academe. Departments might be artificial constructs, but professors protected their turf with all the combative intensity of feudal barons. At the time, multidisciplinary teaching methodologies were rare. And indeed, five decades later Drucker has confessed that he has observed little change over the years in faculty attitudes—specializations and techniques are still the lodestones of business curriculum. He also criticized the educational establishment for its lack of accountability in terms of results, its indifference to blending theory with practice, and the inability of professional specialists to make their knowledge relevant to other professionals.[2]

Business Literature

Drucker also explored the voluminous business literature, concentrating particularly on the categories of individual success stories and company histories. The former described the initial entrepreneurial exploits of the founding fathers of many of the most prominent national enterprises but were less instructive in revealing the common denominators of the management process after the business was firmly established. Moreover, each of these early tycoons

looked upon his business as a reflection of his individual genius or an extension of his unique personality, assumptions unlikely to produce meaningful
managerial principles. Henry Ford, a classic example of a mogul who saw his
company as a lengthening shadow of himself, was responsible for one of the
greatest entrepreneurial insights in U.S. history—the idea of producing an
affordable automobile for the average working man. As Ford failed to sustain
this vision and ignored the need for the fundamentals of management, his
career not only quickly became a record of gross mismanagement but also a
clinical study in nonmanagement.

From his research into official business histories of the day, Drucker discovered they were predominantly corporate-sponsored litanies of praise cel-
ebrating the highlights of corporate success. Drawn from dusty corporate
archives, they consisted chiefly of a parade of dull chronological events, vapid
descriptions of routine decisions, and a host of anecdotes from corporate folk-
lore but were silent when it came to furnishing guidelines for the nuts and bolts
of executive work, not to mention offering any criteria-based evaluation of
managerial performance and relevant theory.

Great Organizers

The managerial revolution around the turn of the twentieth century, triggered
by the separation of ownership and control, shifted the actual running of the
large corporation from the original founders into the hands of salaried professional managers. The basic rationale for this power transition was that theoretically the professionals possessed the authority of knowledge. As mentioned
earlier, however, Drucker viewed the achievements of Sloan and the other
great corporate leaders of the first half of the twentieth century to be more
models of successful technical performance than examples of management
according to a bundle of systematic principles.

The common feature of all these outstanding professional managers
was a guiding vision that they were able to translate into specific innovations
in financial methodology, structural design, market strategy, and personnel
training—many of which were to become the building blocks of Drucker's
theory. It seemed paradoxical that although these great organizers were trail-
blazers in systematically managing for results, they had no idea that their practices were transferable to others through learning or that they were laying the
foundation for a codified discipline. Drucker attributed this phenomenon to

a principle in political theory that institutional practice precedes the codification of the relevant theory.

A specific lesson that Drucker drew from his study of such dominant corporate giants as Theodore Vail of AT&T, Walter Teague of Standard Oil, Gerald Swope of General Electric, Julius Rosenwald and Robert Wood of Sears Roebuck, Simon Marks of Marks and Spencer, George Siemens of Deutsche Bank, and Thomas Watson of IBM was that one learns chiefly from excellence. From the performance of mediocre companies, he asserted, one learns only the pedestrian and the routine, which are hardly worth the effort because they produce only marginal results. And from failures one learns only what not to do.

Intellectual Pioneers

Another source that had an organizing impact on Drucker's thought was the research done by a host of individuals evaluating the critical survival functions of businesses. This scholarly legacy confirmed in his mind the importance of these specialized functions as the infrastructure for corporate performance. He subsequently synthesized the management tasks required by these essential autonomous subsystems into the celebrated tool of management by objectives. To those intellectual pioneers who were addressing business issues prior to World War I, Drucker also acknowledged a debt of gratitude for contributing to his understanding.

Among the most prominent individuals he singled out for their important breakthroughs in specialized segments of business activity were these. Frederick Taylor, the father of *scientific management,* was an innovator in understanding the neglected phenomenon of work, the actual job itself, and the methodology for objectively measuring worker productivity. Elton Mayo, an Australian sociologist, was noted for his unprecedented studies at Western Electric's Hawthorne plant, which documented that the concept of economic man was a myth, demonstrated the significance of informal work groups, and distinguished the differences between work and working for human behavior (a distinction discussed further in Chapter Twelve). Henri Fayol, a French executive, recognized the role of top management and the significance of such major organizational functions as direction, coordination, and control. Joseph Schumpeter, an Austrian economist, introduced the concept of *creative destruction,* which emphasized consumer demand and economic disequilibrium, precursors of the marketing concept and the research and development function. Eugen Schmalenbach developed the financial tool of cost accounting, enabling management practitioners to allocate capital assets more effectively. Walter Rathenau, a German industrialist, and Eiichi Shibusawa, a Japanese entrepreneur, were unique in viewing profit as a result rather than a cause of business activity and for their analysis of social responsibility.

Drucker later admitted his intellectual debt to these professionals for setting the table with the major ingredients for the concoction of his theory. Of special importance to him was Frederick Taylor. He believed Taylor's philosophical ideas defeated Marxism, because instead of becoming revolution conscious, the U.S. workforce became job and productivity conscious. At the same time, Drucker exposed some of the myths that had grown up around Taylor's work and thought.

> Everybody "knows" the following facts about Frederick Winslow Taylor: His aim was "efficiency," which meant reducing costs and increasing profits. He believed that workers responded primarily to economic incentives. He invented the "speed-up" and the assembly line. He saw only the individual worker, and not the work group. He considered workers to be machines and to be used as machines. He wanted to put all power and control into the hands of management, while he had deep contempt for the workingman. And he was the father of "classical organization theory," with its hierarchical pyramids, its concepts of the span of control, its functions, and so on. . . . [E]very one of these "well-known facts" is pure myth.[3]

Aside from their great specific breakthroughs, Drucker was impressed by the fact that these individuals were not simply thinkers but doers; all of them at one time or another had responsibility for institutional performance. He was also especially struck by the international character of these early pioneers who investigated the strands in the management fabric. It confirmed in his own mind the significance of the corporation as society's key institution for developed countries throughout the world.

At the same time, he observed that although all these outstanding individuals were contemporaries, each concentrated his research exclusively within the boundaries of his particular discipline. They apparently gave no thought to exchanging their intellectual linen among themselves. Meanwhile, in the period after World War I, academic work continued in the direction of increased specialization, building on the original insights of the aforementioned pioneers. As a result a rich legacy of information about component business parts existed, but the notion of totality and interaction attracted little attention. Consequently when Drucker, in the late 1930s and early 1940s, perceived the corporation as society's most crucial organization, he recognized that the foundation and the beams for the theoretical house of management had already been assembled. He accepted the challenge for drawing up the blueprint for an architectonic whole.

Drucker did list one U.S. exception to the functional approach that predominated prior to World War II. This was Mary Parker Follett, whom he called the "prophet" of the discipline of management theory. Despite her vision and contributions, however, he also confessed that she is scarcely remembered today. Follett had been the brightest star in the management firmament. And—to change the metaphor—she had struck every single chord in what now constitutes the management symphony. Ten years later not even her memory remained, at least in the United States. In the annals of management she had become a nonperson.[4]

Nevertheless, although Drucker's consuming insight on the phenomenon of corporate management was shared by few contemporaries and was viewed in Europe as a counterculture manifesto, he was later able to remark: "The emergence of management may be the pivotal event of our time, far more important than all the events that make the headlines. Rarely, if ever, has a new basic institution, a new leading group, a new central function, emerged as fast as has management since the turn of the century. Rarely in human history has a new institution proven indispensable so quickly. Even less often has a new institution arrived with so little opposition, so little disturbance, so little controversy."[5]

Thinking of Victor Hugo's dictum that it is impossible to stop an idea whose time had come, Drucker confessed that if he had not formulated an interdisciplinary model of management, it was inevitable that somebody would have done so in the near future. His pioneering role resulted from his perceiving the importance of corporate management as a leadership group more quickly than others did. As he commented: "When I talked about business organizations the timing was right, just five seconds before the public became receptive. That's the definition of a successful pioneer; one who is just a single subway stop ahead."[6]

Reception

Drucker's reputation as the father of modern management was largely attributable to the immediate popular acclaim and enduring recognition of *The Practice of Management*. Both at home and abroad, *The Practice of Management* was especially well received in the business community chiefly because it filled an immediate need. It offered a thoughtful guide to a new generation of business professionals who were navigating the uncharted waters of the post–World War II unprecedented prosperity. According to the testimony of many consultants of the period, *The Practice of Management* was, without exception, the one book found in every office of corporate America. It also became the leading textbook for businesses in the nascent field of in-house management training programs.

Drucker might have become an instantaneous household word in the corporate corridors, but this was not to be repeated in the halls of academe. Most educators were uncomfortable with the book because it failed to adhere to conventional scholarly methodology accompanied by intensive footnoting, impressive graphs, and intimidating formulas. Drucker rejected this provincial view of academic worth, arguing it was the obligation of a professional school to provide knowledge in a popular form for the practitioner.

Another reason Drucker did not receive the enthusiastic endorsement of the academic community was its inability to categorize him in any of the traditional collegiate departments. He responded to the criticisms of failing to embrace a single specialty by stating: "I know absolutely nothing technical. My product is organized thinking."[7] Actually he always maintained that his writings were basically commonsense musings. However, he also contended that this principle of common sense was more preached than practiced by most executives.

Drucker had, however, a substantial body of admirers in urban business schools, whose students and faculty were more attuned to pragmatic practices. And it was no accident that he had chosen the word *practice* for the book's title, over such intellectual words as *process, pattern,* or *principles of management.* Concepts, tasks, principles, patterns, and theory—all played an important role in Drucker's writings, but they were incidental to his pragmatic goal of making "common people achieve uncommon performance."[8] He added that if a professional discipline was not contributing to the performance of the practitioner, it was barren exercise in mental gymnastics.

Content

Realizing that scholarly exposition would only bore his main audience, Drucker did not offer a litany of abstractions. Without being dull and pedantic and without sacrificing substance for trendy remedies, *The Practice of Management* offered executives a lucid and readable treatment of the interrelationship between principles and practices, delineated concepts with concrete applications, interwove examples of individual success stories, interspersed relevant corporate case studies, and presented invigorating anecdotes and vignettes on the personalities, techniques, and styles of business leaders.

The specific contents of *The Practice of Management* reiterated many of the topics touched on in his earlier writings, but also placed greater focus on organized learning. Among the main issues addressed were these familiar ones: the superiority of the market over centralized planning, recognition of management as a distinct form of work, the ingredients of the decision-making process, corporate legitimacy and responsibility, the significance of leadership, corporate governance, models of organizational design, training and development, communication skills, professional commitment, labor relations, personnel policies, the role of the plant community in removing the hostility between management and labor, and employee training.

In treating these topics, Drucker avoided prescribing normative rules and regulations. A distinguishing characteristic of *The Practice of Management* was that the material was handled analytically and pragmatically against the background of three major premises—the recognition of management as a conceptual discipline, the need for executives to develop a "holistic mind-set," and the importance of corporate purpose.

Drucker assumed throughout his analysis that to make sense of the how-to-do of specialized business activities, executives also had to apply the how-to-think aspects of the job, based on a coherent body of managerial knowledge. He made no pretense that he had invented the discipline of management, which had been around in various administrative forms since the dawn of civilization. It is, however, fair to conclude that he was the first to discover how the tools, techniques, and principles of executive work were subject to systematic application and improvement.

According to Drucker a fundamental requirement of the management discipline for professional executives was a generalized executive mind-set.

This managerial mentality demanded a comprehensive vision of ends rather than emphasis on the instrumental features of means, a perception of social and economic forces affecting corporations, and use of the humanities to improve human relations. Philosophically, Drucker was discarding the prevailing Cartesian premise that the whole is equal to the sum of the parts and substituting the systems approach that the whole is greater than the sum of its parts. In effect Drucker invented nothing specifically new in the way of business functions, but his contribution in *The Practice of Management* was to blend the existing functions into a pattern of dynamic integration.

Drucker generally believed that more often than not definitions obscured more than they illuminated. But having attacked the legal, economic, social, and other parochial, functional definitions of the firm, he was compelled to propose a more realistic substitute. From his writings I have inferred the following general definition: a business is a human institution organized in perpetuity, having as its purpose the creation and satisfaction of a customer, requiring an adequate profit for future risk, identifying and implementing new opportunities to combat inevitable obsolescence, and recognizing the factor of corporate social responsibility to improve the quality of life.

The Practice of Management set the agenda for management over the next two decades. Particularly controversial and contentious, arousing the most discussion and debate, were these three major themes: (1) the function of profit, (2) management by objectives, and (3) the systematic management of change. (Although *The Practice of Management* is the fulcrum of analysis in this chapter and the next, I also use excerpts from later works to reinforce these Druckerian themes.) The first two are discussed in the remainder of this chapter. Managing change is the subject of Chapter Seven.

Drucker had a deep respect for competent performers in their specialized fields but at the same time argued that a person who has mastered only the skills and techniques of a function was a technician and not a manager. Because knowledge of a specialized function could not provide vision, he ruled it out as an approach for understanding from a managerial perspective. He believed that the prototypical technician was inclined to concentrate on means above ends, neglect interactive business tasks, ignore unmet customer needs, and express an indifference to outside events and trends.

Using the metaphor of a symphony orchestra, he stressed that the isolated instrumental parts could produce only noise, never music, and he wrote about distinguishing the manager who created joint performance by conducting from the member who simply contributed: "The task of creating a genuine whole also requires that the manager in every one of his acts consider simultaneously the performance and results of the enterprise as a whole and the diverse activities needed to achieve synchronized performance. It is here, perhaps, that the comparison with the orchestra conductor fits best. A conductor must always hear both the whole orchestra and, say, the second oboe."[9]

Function of Profit

According to popular surveys conducted inside and outside of businesses, the majority of respondents believed profit was the main purpose of corporate existence. Drucker took serious exception to such an interpretation, considering it an illusion, more veneer than reality. He thought it understandable for the average citizen to have such a simplistic understanding of the enterprise but considered it unpardonable for the average executive to possess so little sophistication about the rationale of corporate existence. It also troubled him that the conventional notion of profitability had such a tenacious hold on the business community; for Drucker, organized stupidity was still stupidity.[10]

In analyzing the conventional explanations of profit, Drucker found that they distorted rather than illuminated its essential meaning. Questioning the validity of the bloodless bottom line as a useful standard of measurement, he wrote: "What is the measurement of performance in a business? The bottom line is the standard answer. But how does one truly measure the bottom line? Everyone talks of profit—for some it is the executive's Holy Grail, for others, it is a dirty word. But what is profit really? How does any business, its executives, its investors, its employees, know whether the company's reported profit is good or inadequate?"[11]

In examining what he considered a misdiagnosis of the function of corporate profit, he attacked four specific misconceptions: classical economic theory, reward for the risk taker, the profit motive, and profit maximization. He found classical economic theory basically flawed because its assumption of equilibrium prevented it from offering a satisfactory definition of the role of profit. Once the business environment was assumed to possess open-ended dynamic disequilibrium, the economists' argument that profit was simply the revenue that remained after costs were deducted made no sense. Drucker thought it more feasible to assert that profit was future investment in the creation of tomorrow's jobs.

Drucker objected on both moral and economic grounds to the proposition that profit was a reward for the risk taker. Such an explanation, he asserted, elevated greed and bribery as the driving forces of the capitalist system. He thought it the height of sophistry to make private vice a public virtue. According to Drucker, the hostility of the public toward the concept of profit could be largely attributed to this crass explanation of reward for risk. Moreover, businessmen did themselves a disservice by endorsing this position. Instead of exploitation, profit and personal savings were the two indispensable features in the creation of wealth under the enterprise system.

Drucker thought he had slain the dragon of the concept of economic man in his first book, *The End of Economic Man* (1939). He was mistaken; its ghost was still manifest. He never ceased to be surprised by the number of people who sustained this myth despite the lack of empirical evidence that the avaricious pursuit of profit is an inherent human trait. Granting the necessity of profitability as a condition of business survival, he added that this fact also had nothing to do with human nature. Even if a corporation were run by saints, profit would still be a reality. If an individual manager exhibited an obsessive personal drive in the pursuit of amassing profit, this was a private matter having nothing to do with the corporate imperative for making a profit. Profit, Drucker concluded, had no more to do with promoting corporate behavior than breathing air had to do with the goals of human life. Both were necessary conditions of sustenance, but they were redundant with regard to purpose.

As a business goal and a financial measurement, the maximization of profit, Drucker argued, was ill-conceived because it threatened the foundation of the corporation's economic assets. The public and Wall Street too often misdiagnosed flashy and seductive financial numbers as solid economic performance and corporate eminence. Excellence in the so-called bottom line financial performance, for example, was not always an indicator of achieving the best total results for the business. Drucker noted that in today's economy it did not require a management consultant to identify many businesses with outstanding economic results, but it was also highly improbable that these firms would be around a few years later, because of their neglect of other survival functions.

As a measurement, Drucker pointed out, the financial bottom line could be metaphorically compared to a sundial, which reveals the time of day only when the sun shines and gives no information on a cloudy day or at night. For example, maximization of profit does not measure such unquantifiable factors as the failure to identify and implement new opportunities, the development of human assets, and the recognition of negative externalities threatening the firm. Drucker's often-repeated opinions on the limitations of quantitative measurement are reflected, for example, by this comment:

> I do not believe that one can manage a business by reports. I am a figures man, and a quantifier, and one of those people to whom figures talk. I also know that reports are abstractions, and that they can only tell us what we have determined to ask. They are high-level abstractions. That is all right if we have the understanding, the meaning, and the perception. One must spend a great deal of time outside, where the results are. Inside a business one only has costs. One looks at markets, at customers, at society, and at knowledge, all of which are outside the business, to see what is really happening. That reports will never tell you.[12]

The conventional interpretations of corporate profit were severely criticized by Drucker for being too one dimensional, too abstract, too simplistic, and too internally focused. More important, they lacked a managerial perspective, compelling Drucker to provide his own interpretation. His analysis from a managerial standpoint included such elements as industrial aggregates, measurement options, and the factors of risk and future costs.

Just as no criminal planned to end up in jail, it was axiomatic that no individual business wanted failure. But what was true in the particular might not be true in the aggregate. According to Drucker, business failure, or "profit loss," was equally important in an enterprise economy as "profit gain." Without the periodic failure of certain business firms, capital would be directed to the defense of yesterday's products rather than toward the encouragement of tomorrow's opportunities. For example, if the buggy whip manufacturers had had their way, they would have opposed technological change in the form of the automobile and opted for routine and stability in the form of the horse and carriage. However, the reality of dynamic competition will shatter any dream of an economy characterized by static equilibrium.

Drucker suggested that the concept of profit loss versus profit gain was analogous to oil industry practices predicated on the assumption that the drilling of dry wells was as much a part of the system as discovering productive gushers. However, in order to have a prosperous industry, the producing wells had to outnumber the failed ones. Similarly, from an aggregate economic point of view, profit losses were just as crucial to the enterprise system as profit gains, providing that they did not outnumber the profitable business performers. Moreover, the market test was the vehicle that provided for the economic elimination of failed businesses, without which the competitive system would disintegrate into inertia and stagnancy. In short, a reasonable proportion of business failures was a healthy symptom in a dynamic enterprise economy and a feature totally lacking in a totalitarian economy.

Relevant measurement of business costs in the evaluation of financial performance was also one of the great strengths of capitalism over totalitarian systems. Drucker singled out profitability as the feedback mechanism for identifying financial results. For calculating performance he cited several applicable measurements (return on assets, return on sales, cash flow, and stockholder equity). At the same time, he cautioned that these financial measurements had weaknesses as well as strengths. For example, none of these financial tools was able to provide total information for evaluating results. Given the uncertainty of quantifying crucial qualitative factors—production of an excellent product, satisfaction of a customer, and the passion of management—with precise assessment, Drucker did not advocate the acceptance of a single measurement of economic performance. He did suggest, however, it was the obligation of any competent financial officer to examine all the financial measurement alternatives and then select the one that had the most appropriate validity for the individual business.

Regardless of the financial indicator selected, Drucker reemphasized that it was futile to equate any financial performance measurement with purpose. He argued strenuously that there were no results inside the business, only costs; the outside factors of the customer and innovation were the crucial keys to performance, but no business had control of them.

Viewing financial analysis from a managerial standpoint, Drucker offered two general guidelines. First, to avoid the rule of profit maximization, he applied the principle of *profit optimization,* that is, ascertaining the most compatible ratio between risks on the one hand and opportunities on the other. Second, rather than looking at profit as a reward for risk, managers could, Drucker recommended, view profit as future cost, that is, the costs to cover today's unintended operating crises and tomorrow's uncertain innovative decisions.

The principle of profit as future costs exposed a fundamental weakness of the accounting model. Drucker viewed traditional cost accounting as a liquidation model; its time frame was the past, and therefore it could measure only past business costs with any degree of accuracy. This model was an unconvincing yardstick for determining the time factor and information needed for handling the challenge of future costs. And it was the estimation of these future costs that mirrored the chief role of profits in a business.

Another significant Druckerian insight in *The Practice of Management* was that profit was not cause but result. For example, if corporate management performed satisfactorily in basic nonfinancial survival areas of the business (marketing, human relations, innovation, and corporate responsibility), then, because of these areas' synergistic contribution, profit became essentially a question of appropriate measurement. Profit was therefore the ending rather than the beginning. Moreover, Drucker considered it culturally dangerous for management to render allegiance to a single value, such as economics, to the exclusion of all other social values.

A corollary of Drucker's proposition that from a managerial perspective it was a mistake to equate profit with cause was that this latter view ran contrary to one of his prime organizational tenets—institutional purpose is related to the institution's contribution to society. He further stressed that no matter how proficient the experience, knowledge, skills, and techniques of management, they were meaningless if corporate purpose was misdiagnosed. From this he repeated that the source of purpose had to be external, rather than an internal function such as finance. He further maintained again that inside a business were only costs, efforts, problems, frictions, and crises but never results. In seeking the source of business purpose, Drucker concluded it was the creation and satisfaction of the customer—in essence what has come to be known in the managerial textbooks as the *marketing concept*.

In the broadest sense, only marketing produced results; everything else in the business was cost. Drucker stressed that no product had any value until it found a customer. Customers were totally indifferent to the internal efforts corporations made in providing a product or service; they had only one concern—did the product or service give them utility? For example, according to Drucker, quality was not determined by how difficult or expensive it was to make a product. He equated excessive difficulties in the allocation of corporate cost with managerial incompetency. The factor of pricing a product or service was evaluated from an internal financial approach rather than from an external market perspective. Value constituted only one thing—how much the consumer was willing to pay for the product.

Recapitulating the analysis of profit from a managerial perspective, Drucker concluded that it was a vital survival condition for achieving results, a method for measuring performance, and a critical source of revenue to cover future costs and risks, but it was the result of and not the cause of corporate purpose.

Management by Objectives

For more than a decade, Drucker had been concerned with the failure of academic specialists to develop a meaningful vision of the enterprise and to create a conceptual tool for integrating their functional specialities into the corporate whole. His proposed remedy in *The Practice of Management* for this corporate challenge was the innovative concept of *management by objectives*. The idea originated as he combined his consulting experience and his study of systems theory.

Consulting experience had brought Drucker into contact with such highly esteemed managers as Alfred Sloan of General Motors and Ralph Cordiner of General Electric, leaders who in shaping corporate mission had a rare ability to interconnect individual business units in a synergistic fashion. Drucker observed that Sloan and Cordiner considered this talent of creating unity from diversity to be little more than a pragmatic technique. Instead he looked upon this concept for creating unity out of diversity as a valid management principle suitable for all organizations. Drucker himself, however, applied the lesson mentioned previously that he learned from political theory: namely that practice precedes theory, which means that it is the doer who initiates a concept but it is the scholar who translates it into a theoretical principle.

Systems theory, the second source for the organizing principle of management by objectives, was (as discussed earlier) considered an appropriate holistic approach to avoiding the atomization of information into isolated knowledge disciplines.

The large business organization, faced with pressures to cope with change and adjust to an increasingly complex environment, was in a state of confusion, poorly prepared to handle its information overload. The result was typically a misdiagnosis of mission and a gridlock in the relationships among the interlocking functions, with every department inclined to do its own thing. As also mentioned earlier, in function after function there was a tendency for knowledge to breed new bundles of specialization, which then acted as independent units within the enterprise. Citing the corporate legal affairs department as an example, Drucker depicted Cartesian segmentation with a vengeance. The department included a variety of legal subdisciplines, concerned with such matters as contracts, liability, antitrust issues, regulations, labor relations, compensation, securities, bankruptcy, real estate, patent copyrights, and compensation—to name a few.

Operating under the mandate bestowed by the authority of knowledge, every department viewed itself as an independent center of expertise. According to Drucker, the systems concept, based on the premise that all functions that interact should be studied together in a synthesized fashion, was the exception rather than the rule in corporate America. He added that tools and techniques were abundant but little was being done to promote the fusion and cross-fertilization of information.

Thus, because it was evident to Drucker that managers were not automatically directed toward common goals, he introduced the diagnostic tool of management by objectives. It was a first step in defining the survival functions of the business in an organized managerial fashion. Reflecting on his innovative insight into the need to convert centrifugal forces into a centripetal configuration, he later wrote: "When I came into management, a lot of it came out of engineering. And a lot of it came out of accounting. And some of it came out of psychology. And some more came out of labor relations. Each of those was considered separate, and each of them, by itself, was ineffectual. You can't do carpentry, you know, if you only have a saw, or only a hammer, or you never heard of a pair of pliers. It's when you put all those tools into one kit that you invent."[13]

Survival Objectives. The specific survival objectives of any business were not an automatic given. Drucker identified as key activities those that required at least minimum performance in order to ensure continued corporate vitality. In *The Practice of Management,* he chose eight critical areas in which objectives were mandatory: market standing, productivity, physical and financial resources, innovation, profitability, worker contribution, managerial performance, and public responsibility. Without diluting his basic conceptual framework, in an article published four years later in the *Chicago Journal of Business,* he compressed the eight categories into five basic survival objectives—marketing, human resources, innovation, profitability, and social responsibility.

Again, according to Drucker, these survival objectives were fundamental characteristics of all businesses—large or small.[14]

Drucker separated his analysis of the rationale of management by objectives into two major segments—institutional and individual. Under the organizational rubric, two major topics were addressed: (1) eradicating the myth of a single dominant business objective, and (2) emphasizing the importance of minimum performance for all vital functions. For the individual aspect of management by objectives, Drucker concentrated on the importance of executives' improving their relationships with colleagues in other functions and developing a managerial mentality.

The Myth of a Single Perspective. Insisting that there was nothing more dangerous than a single overriding business objective, Drucker rejected the notion that it was possible to categorize survival objectives into a hierarchy by importance. To consider profitability or any other single objective as predominant would create a fractional corporate identity, dilute the importance of the other crucial objectives, and lead inevitably to the demise of the enterprise.

In his examination of the decision-making process within the enterprise, Drucker argued that there was no such thing as an isolated functional decision. In effect, it was meaningless to talk about individual financial, marketing, research, personnel, or public relations decisions. Because of the interdependence and interaction of all the vital corporate subsystems in a single business configuration, there was *one and only one* decision and that was a managerial decision.[15]

In short, when the enterprise was viewed as a system rather than as a single component, separate functions, theoretically, did not exist. For example, once the customer was posited as the purpose of the business, the notion of departmental customers was a senseless concept. Once the business accepted this principle of the customer as the business purpose, there were only business profits, business risks, business investments, and business customers. Consequently, profitability or any other function was irrelevant in determining business reality.

Apropos of balancing the survival objectives of the business, systems theory assumed that if any vital function failed then the entire enterprise would collapse. Drucker maintained, therefore, that each function had to operate at a minimum performance level to maintain a healthy balance. He further warned that if one vital function drastically overperformed to such a degree of excellence that it upset its balance with other functions within the system, there was also a danger that it could threaten the stability of the entire system. Using the analogy of the human body, for example, he noted that transplanting the heart of a twenty-year-old person into the body of a sixty-year-old could cause an adverse reaction because the weaker biological condition of the elderly person would be often incapable of adjusting to the outstanding performance of the stronger transplanted organ.

A similar imbalance could occur in a business if one function were performing far beyond its normal competence. For example, the Studebaker automobile company committed so much effort and resources to harmonious labor relations that it failed to pay attention to other survival objectives and wound up in bankruptcy. Illustrations of companies obsessively pursuing the bottom line of profitability have already been suggested. The electrical utility industry did such a brilliant job in marketing new products that it then had to modify its marketing expansion and adopt the strategy of "save a watt." Bell Laboratories, the research arm of AT&T, devoted excessive efforts to innovation, without any thought of economic results—the invention of the transistor, for instance, is a classic example of the company's being driven by technology rather than by the market. William Norris of Control Data, in his efforts to solve social problems, was removed by the company's board of directors because he gave priority to the good intentions of social responsibility at the expense of total business performance. Under the assumption that they could manage diverse types of businesses with equal competency, the conglomerates of the sixties failed to achieve minimum performance in many of their individual business units, thereby exposing the fragile imbalance of the entire system. According to Drucker, these examples were only a small portion of the many that confirmed the proposition that business performance was endangered when management endorsed a single, dominant corporate objective.

The Importance of Minimum Performance. Management by objectives lived up to its substantive meaning when professionals allowed their skills and competencies to penetrate, percolate through, and permeate the entire decision-making process. And Drucker continued to make a distinction between technical competencies and broad-gauged managerial work: "This means, above all, that managers practice management. They do not practice economics. They do not practice quantification. They do not practice behavioral science. These are tools for the manager. But he no more practices economics than a physician practices blood testing. He no more practices behavioral sciences than a biologist practices the microscope. He no more practices quantification than a lawyer practices precedents. He practices management."[16]

Drucker pointed out it was the task of the chief executive officer to determine and communicate the general mission of the business, but those managers with operating accountability were responsible for implementation and results. In effect, each department spelled out its own objectives for performance based on the general mission statement and with the approval of top management. But the development of these objectives is part of a manager's responsibility; indeed, it is his first responsibility.

Drucker also offered a practical suggestion that he labeled *the management letter.* It was a way of removing executive illiteracy, promoting increased professional involvement, monitoring the results of previous corporate decisions and departmental objectives, and improving the communication relationships among senior executives and their subordinate colleagues.

> This [setting of objectives] is so important that some of the most effective managers I know go one step further. They have each of their subordinates write a "manager's letter" twice a year. In this letter to his superior, each manager first defines the objectives of his superior's job and of his own job as he sees them. He then sets down the performance standards which he believes are being applied to him. Next, he lists the things he must do himself to attain these goals—and the things within his own unit he considers the major obstacles. He lists the things his superior and the company do that help him and the things that hamper him. Finally, he outlines what he proposes to do during the next year to reach his goals. If his superior accepts this statement, the "manager's letter" becomes the charter under which the manager operates.[17]

Advantages and Disadvantages. In implementing the tool of management by objectives Drucker was aware of the gap between the ideal and reality. Rhetorically subscribing to the concept was not the same as altering executive behavior for joint organizational performance. Never underestimating the problem of implementing a substantive change, he recognized that like the movement of marbles in a bag that touch without adhering, moving from a mechanistic framework of technical thinking to an organic process of human interaction was fraught with resistance. To operate effectively, management by objectives had to curb corporate power struggles without thwarting ambition, distinguish between useless and relevant information in the communication process, avoid the danger of rigid rationalization and paralyzing analysis at the cost of imagination and spontaneity, recognize the difference between healthy tensions and subversive conflict in departmental relationships, and identify the managers who talk the game of cooperation but continue to act as soloists in pursuing personal objectives. All these demands and many more confirm the challenge of converting a theoretical principle, no matter how outwardly appealing, into an organizational operating reality. As a result, Drucker noted the distinct possibility that management by objectives could degenerate into a bureaucratic charge rather than a practical tool for improving performance.

Appraisal. Of all Drucker's innumerable insights and concepts, perhaps none has received more individual attention than management by objectives. Not only did it find its way into every management textbook, but hundreds of specific books have been written on the subject. Shortly after the publication of *The Practice of Management* in 1954, management literature became replete with books and articles emphasizing the importance of establishing detailed objectives for all the survival functions of the enterprise. Scores of books, for example, were written on marketing objectives, personnel objectives, public policy objectives, research objectives, and financial objectives. In becoming a buzzword for publishers, management by objectives also became a cottage industry. Books and articles appeared calling for objectives on virtually every facet of business life—advertising, brands, inventory, purchasing, distributions, career planning, training, and shareholder relationships, to mention a few.

Drucker believed that whatever merit the concept had for integrating the major survival functions, the whole focus disintegrated when the tool was truncated into another version of Cartesianism. He admonished, therefore, that management by objectives was far short of being an omnipotent tool; it was beneficial only to the extent that executives carefully thought through the crucial areas requiring objectives and then made sure they understood the essence of these objectives.

Finally, it is possible to draw another kind of major conclusion from Drucker's management by objectives. Every practice evolved from a theory, even if the practitioner was unaware of it. Prior to Drucker's innovation, there was no organizing principle for tackling managerial tasks. The tool might have been imperfect by general consensus, but it was an improvement on what preceded it. In the future, it was no longer possible to consider management a functional technique, no longer possible to confine decision making to a particular corporate geographical area, no longer possible to consider top management omniscient, and no longer possible to ignore the vital role of middle managers. As a result of their exposure to management by objectives, a generation of executives saw themselves as professional managers and not as administrative technocrats.

PETER DRUCKER

PART TWO

ON STRATEGY
AND
ENTREPRENEURSHIP

CHAPTER SEVEN

MANAGING CHANGE

Concern with the systematic management of change was the third major theme in *The Practice of Management*. Drucker expressed the position that the business enterprise was unique because it "was designed to produce change," whereas past social institutions were structured to preserve continuity. "Throughout most of history," he later observed, "change was considered catastrophe, and immutability the goal of organized human efforts. All social institutions of man for thousands of years had as their first purpose to prevent, or at least slow down, the onrush of change."[1]

As I have been discussing, a prime concern of Drucker's early books was the political theme of organizational rejuvenation—the reconciliation of the claims of the past with the social forces dictating a different institutional future. He applied the same principle to the modern corporation, recognizing that the competencies originally needed to attain success would no longer be adequate in the future. Any management, therefore, that wanted to survive was compelled to operate simultaneously in today's state of being and tomorrow's state of becoming. If this process of systematic change in adjusting to outside trends was to be successful, it would have to develop a new set of commitments, competencies, and organizational forms.

Because of the market test, which presupposed that the customer wanted his unfilled needs satisfied, the corporation had no choice but to be future oriented. Despite the imperative of change, there was, Drucker pointed out, a paradox in the enterprise system. On the one hand, businessmen were the silent revolutionaries of social change, altering the environment through the creation of new products, services, and jobs. On the other hand, in business, nothing failed like success. Those who were once business revolutionaries often became reactionaries, acting as though their early achievements were set permanently in cement.

It was easy to point out the importance of coping with change systematically; it was far more difficult to develop a program of implementation. Drucker was acutely aware of the difficulties the corporation faced in encountering the future, an area devoid of facts but ripe with expectations. In weathering the seas of change, managers were compelled to navigate their corporate ships through the uncharted waters of uncertainty. In their journey they could expect such obstacles as the gales of competition, the hazards of predicting consumer demand, the unexpected arrival of economic and social squalls, the need to maneuver through the misty fog of technological innovation, and the challenge of training the crew for stormy weather emergencies.

In *The Practice of Management* Drucker captured the essence of this entrepreneurial process long before the term *entrepreneur* became fashionable in the textbooks and collegiate courses in recent decades. He never, however, prescribed a rigorous methodology for the systematic management of change, but by elucidating his insights and raising the right questions, it is possible to frame a paradigm on the topic.

Paradigm of Change

Model building was an activity for which Drucker expressed little affection. Nevertheless, there is an irresistible temptation for this writer to interpret Drucker's ideas on the management of change and synthesize them into a paradigm. I share Drucker's reservation about paradigms. They are usually too rigid and circumscribed. But in the instance of formulating, interpreting, and understanding his thoughts on managing change, a paradigm has merit as a mental road map.

From *The Practice of Management* it is possible to deduce the specific outlines of a model for managing change in an organized fashion. According to Drucker the business enterprise existed contemporaneously in three interacting but different time zones—past, present, and future. To clarify this structural trinity, I have labeled these three business dimensions, respectively, *traditional, transitional,* and *transformational.* (See Figure 7.1 for a graphic description of the paradigm. The proposed structural skeleton is of course mine, yet the spirit and insights are Drucker's.)

In addition to the tridimensional structural framework of the enterprise, Drucker saw three other main features that I have added to the paradigm described here. First, there was the reality of constant tension among the dimensions caused by fighting over budget priorities, an internecine struggle between those wishing to defend the present within the traditional business and those seeking to do new things by pursuing opportunities within the framework of the transitional and transformational businesses.

FIGURE 7.1. PARADIGM OF CHANGE.

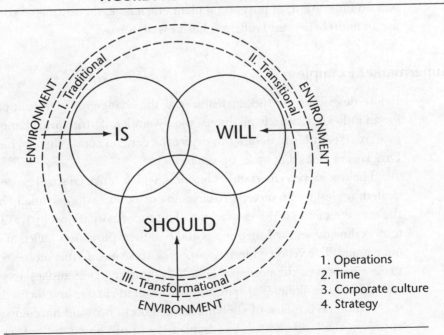

1. Operations
2. Time
3. Corporate culture
4. Strategy

Second, based on the assumption that the environment was in a state of constant flux as a result of competition, technology, and successful marketing, Drucker emphasized again that the outside boundaries of the business were the only sources of opportunities for future growth—inside any business there were only costs, efforts, and problems. A corollary of this assumption was that during the process of change the business was concurrently shaping the environment and being shaped by it.

The third characteristic Drucker observed concerned decision making. In the overlapping past, present, and future businesses operating under the same umbrella, he asserted that there was no such thing as a future decision, only the futurity of a present one. He made it clear that because all three of these business segments had to be managed simultaneously, the starting point in planning for tomorrow was today.

The characteristic differences among the three segments were best defined by the direction of what each was supposed to accomplish. For example, the focus for managing the traditional business was on improving current operations; the emphasis for the transitional business was adapting to new opportunities in the environment; and the thrust of the transformational business was on innovation, or purposeful planned change, the sowing of seeds today for an entirely new and different business tomorrow.

Supermarket Example

Before describing the specific features of the change management paradigm for an individual firm, I will discuss the dynamics of structural change for the supermarket industry in order to depict the general comprehensiveness of the Druckerian ideas that make up the model.

The traditional supermarket business, which replaced small grocery stores staffed by clerks who served groceries to customers, was essentially based on the concept of the vending machine. The supermarket novelty was that customers directly selected their items and had their purchases tallied at a checkout counter. The vending machine aspect of today's supermarket has continued to occupy most of the store space but has contributed less and less to store revenues. If the traditional supermarket had resisted change and focused only on the traditional business of shelving staple goods, it would have encountered entropy—the tendency for an organization to run down unless that trend is countered by new inputs.

The innovative input that created the transitional phase of the supermarket business was to add specialty boutiques such as delicatessens, custom cut and packaged meat, floral departments, bakeries, and pharmacies to meet the perceived unmet needs of the customer. Possessing greater profit margins than the traditional grocery items, boutique products yielded proportionately greater income. The new transitional business phase also created qualitative changes in the supermarket workforce. In addition to manual employees who used their muscle to stock the shelves, stores began employing more sophisticated employees who provided personal attention and services for the boutique customers.

The transformational phase of the supermarket industry, the shift to a new and different business, still has to be written. As a result of the new real-time information technologies, a number of potential scenarios have emerged that may revolutionize supermarket retailing. In the process of experimentation are on-site branch banking, portable scanners, debit cards, warehouse stores, and video purchasing, to cite a few. The common denominator of all these and other innovations is that the new tools of the information revolution are eliminating much of the need for handling goods within the store, devising new methods for improved inventory and removing now redundant warehouses, and attacking the vulnerability to gridlock of the checkout counter.

To sum up, the present-day supermarket still contains elements of muscle work in its traditional business. The transitional business focuses more on specialized products and service. The transformational business is being nourished by a host of information-based innovations. The only certainty is that with muscle work diminishing and service becoming more sophisticated, the supermarket of today is transforming itself qualitatively into a new and different retailing institution.

Company Paradigm

The supermarket illustration captures the pattern of structural change for an industry. Drucker, however, was more concerned with the practical understanding and management of change for individual corporations, and he spelled out in great detail how the traditional, transitional, and transformational types of business were specifically to be managed. He cited four essential features that must be managed simultaneously for all three units but that each had to be managed differently. These four were operations, the time factor, the corporate culture, and the business strategy.

Operations. According to Drucker, managing today's traditional business entailed more from executives than frozen rigidity, passive procedures, and defense of the status quo. At the same time, he made the assumption that all businesses were cluttered with myriad inefficiencies resulting from past decisions and hampering change. In order to liberate resources for tomorrow's opportunities and create an atmosphere for encouraging change, the operational focus consisted of moving resources from less productive to more productive results. By applying known skills, techniques, and principles achieved by successful corporations in making capital work harder and people work smarter, managers could convert their present-day knowledge into improved allocation of resources, abandonment of unproductive activities, and concentration on company strengths and excellencies.

Drucker emphasized that managing for today might not be exciting but it was important systematized work, without which receptivity toward change would be nonexistent. Moreover, if management did not organize itself for the undramatic task of improving today's operations, then the company would not have the vision and energy to do the right things for tomorrow. Tactically, this required a frank recognition by management that the present business was not performing competently and would not improve itself if left to its own devices. The immediate task, therefore, was the removal of the unproductive activities before speculating on a better tomorrow.

The operational code of the transitional business was adaptation to new opportunities. In essence this involved satisfying unmet customer needs and attracting new customers. Because managers were beginning to deal with the future in the transitional business, there were fewer principles and techniques than in the traditional business. (A fuller treatment of these principles is offered in Chapter Eight.)

Drucker was particularly circumspect in detailing the operational characteristics of the transformational business. If the information for the transitional business was thin and sketchy, the information for operating the transformational business was virtually nonexistent. He pointed out, for example, that there was no way to market research a genuinely new product or service. To achieve purposefully planned change based on innovation, on an entirely novel and different product or service, the methodology required was not organizing knowledge but organizing ignorance. Essentially the businessman had to devise some imaginable future and from that vision work backward into the present.

Because the operational basis of innovation transcended mere improvement, as in the transitional business, success in the transformational business depended on recognizing the significance of a discontinuity, or break, in the linear trends in the environment. In addition to perception of the unique event that was obvious to all but that nobody was doing anything about, success in the transformational business required that the innovating individual possess a monomaniacal commitment to his or her vision. In short, when everybody said a thing couldn't be done, he or she would go ahead and do it. And when the breakthrough succeeded, it usually resulted in the creation of a new industry, as it had in the case of plastics, antibiotics, computers, lasers, transistors, biogenetics, space exploration, microprocessors, and high-tech hospital equipment, to name a few.

The Time Factor. Drucker defined the time element in managing change in reference to the moment when tangible economic results were recorded. Economic revenues for the traditional business were tabulated in the immediate present because they were actually the benefits of past corporate decision making. The earnings from the current product line provided the capital for future risks. Drucker contended that there was risk in everything the business did, but the greatest risk of all was doing nothing. Consequently, the transitional business had to be concerned with new projects based on opportunities in the changing environment. The time span for these new projects of the transitional business depended on an anticipated date in the future when they would actually contribute to economic performance; until that day arrived, these projects only incurred costs. Typically, a large company's budget would reflect scores of new products and services in its business pipeline, but each would have a different time span in relation to anticipated future costs and results.

Given the rationale that genuine innovative breakthroughs demanded extended periods of risk, the time span for the transformational business could be long—an extended period of costs without any certainty of results. Nevertheless, despite the fact that a breakthrough decision could not be precisely quantified, it had to be made not in the future but today, or else the business would be overwhelmed by the competition in the future.

Concrete examples of the time factor could be derived from any business. I think, however, that AT&T provides appropriate illustrations of the cost duration before achieving performance. In AT&T's traditional business, for example, the generator of earnings for decades was the concept of universal telephone service, devised by Theodore Vail around the turn of the century. In its transitional business, AT&T turned out scores of different products and services, but two clearly mirrored the range of new marketing activities. First, in order to fill telephone network downtime, the company introduced the dial-a-joke service. This undramatic marketing venture required a small amount of financial resources but produced economic results in a few months. Second, as part of its product line AT&T also introduced a technologically superior PBX (telephone exchange center). In this instance the company expected to incur five years of costs before it generated any income. Both were examples of successful adaptation for improved performance of two products with widely different time spans within the transitional phase of the business, but neither radically altered the business identity.

The transformational direction of AT&T, the Baby Bells, and countless other telecommunication companies is clear, but the final shape of these enterprises is still a question for conjecture. The merging of the media has meant a convergence in the methodologies for transmitting and recording voice, picture, and print into a unified technological configuration. As a result of the inventions of the transistor and microprocessor, the telecommunication industry is shifting from a relatively stable mechanical and electronic knowledge base to a complex and scientific one, composed of many sophisticated theoretical disciplines. And every competitor is aware that if it does not make substantial innovative investments today, it will not have any future tomorrow. This technological shift has already produced a host of spectacular devices for residential communication and "the office of the future," such as cellular phones, fax machines, e-mail systems, and smart phones. Yet these are but portents; the transformation is in its embryonic stage, and nobody can predict with certainty the shape and time of the transformational outcome.

The Corporate Culture. The third major component of the paradigm is corporate culture, which Drucker defined as the system of values and beliefs practiced by a company. He pointed out that as a business underwent alterations in its customer base and knowledge foundation, it would have to hire outsiders to accomplish the different things it had to do. As noted earlier, when the supermarket industry adapted to changing circumstances, each individual chain moved from a muscle, to a service, and then to a knowledge mutation of the business. Each phase required different types of employees with different skills, values, and commitments.

According to Drucker the reward-and-promotion pattern was often the most revealing clue to company values. For example, it was who got promoted that told most about what a company stood for. At IBM the path to top management was sales; for Du Pont and AT&T it was chemical engineering and electrical engineering, respectively. Other companies had other privileged functions (such as law, finance, or marketing) that were considered for one reason or another as the passport to advancement. Of course, altered circumstances could change such patterns. For example, at Du Pont the legacy of chemical engineering as the path to promotion was broken when the company faced antitrust problems and decided to hire a lawyer for the CEO post. Recently, however, it has given renewed status to chemical engineering.

The compensation pattern in the corporate culture was also a reflection of the tensions between the traditional, transitional, and transformational sectors, between those managers who wanted to improve things in today's business and the more entrepreneurial types who wanted to create a new tomorrow. A cultural dilemma existed in determining how to compensate those whose results were benefiting from past decisions compared to those who were operating under a veil of uncertainty and whose measurable results were in the future. The danger to corporate culture arrives when either extreme is endorsed by top management. RCA, for example, had one chief executive who focused predominantly on tomorrow's products and neglected the fundamentals of managing today. He was replaced by a person who went to the other extreme by concentrating only on today and rejecting tomorrow—he was also ousted by the board of directors. Drucker concluded that a sound corporate culture demanded a judgmental balance in pay between those executives devoting their time to implementing past decisions and those working on innovation. There was no easy solution to compensation; the best that could be hoped for was a policy based on fairness.

The Business Strategy. Managing change systematically demanded a form of strategic planning that amalgamated performing competently today with preparing for tomorrow's opportunities. For Drucker, strategic thinking was not a mechanistic set of rules but a process of thinking through the company's purpose and objectives. In this process each of the paradigm's segments raised a different strategic question and response regarding corporate direction and identity. In the traditional phase the question was, What is the business? in the transitional phase, What will the business be? and in the transformational phase, What should the business be?

Traditional. Drucker argued that the main reason for business failures was the inability to answer, with reasonable precision, the question, What is the business? He also described how successful businesses assigned the question a high priority in their decision-making process. The majority of managements, however, considered the question unworthy of attention because they believed the answer was pointless and obvious. Taking serious exception to the notion that the question was unimportant, Drucker wrote:

> Nothing may seem simpler or more obvious than to answer what a company's business is. A steel mill makes steel, a railroad runs trains to carry freight and passengers, an insurance company underwrites fire risks. Indeed, the question looks so simple that it is seldom raised, the answer seems so obvious that it is seldom given.
>   Actually "what is our business" is almost always a difficult question which can be answered only after hard thinking and studying. And the right answer is usually anything but obvious.[2]

As mentioned earlier, for Drucker, corporate purpose was synonymous with the enterprise's identity. In diagnosing mission, Drucker ruled out the approach in which managers stated that their company was in retailing, steel, transportation, computers, and so on as unsatisfactory because the resulting generic definition revealed only the tip of a business's iceberg. Products were the vehicles, but they neither identified the customer's values nor expressed the beliefs management stood for. In short, what a business thought it produced had only superficial internal significance; it was the customer, located at the end of the business stream, and not the producer who was the source of corporate vision. Elaborating on this proposition, Drucker maintained that the business's identity focus must combine internal knowledge strengths with external stimuli: "What is our business is not determined by the producer but by the consumer. It is not defined by the company's name, statutes, or articles of incorporation but by the want the customer satisfies when he buys a product or a service. The question can therefore only be answered by looking at the business from the outside, from the point of view of the customer and the market."[3]

In answering the question, What is the business? the focus is on the distinction between competencies of a business and its excellencies, that is, the difference between doing things well and doing things superbly. In every industry there are a few leaders who demonstrate excellence, as opposed to the vast majority of firms who display only average competence. Drucker argued that any business that was profitable was also competent, but if it was only competent, it was also mediocre and marginal. Such a marginal company would be unable to weather competitive forces and business cycles. Moreover, instead of concentrating on a few knowledge strengths, mediocre companies aimlessly attempted to establish countless excellencies in multiple functions by trying to be all things to all people. In contrast, all outstanding businesses recognized they must perform competently in the vital survival functions (such as marketing, finance, innovation, human resources, and public relations), but they also realized they must go beyond competence in the business fundamentals by achieving outstanding performance in one or two areas that contributed qualitatively to customer satisfaction.

Outstanding corporate achievement, which emphasized doing something unique, usually centered on a concentration of activities related to customer offerings and customer values. For example, IBM billed for computers but trained its salesforce to know more than the customers about customer information needs. Anheuser-Busch converted entertainment and tourism into ancillary businesses in order to franchise its beer. McDonald's produced only an average hamburger but introduced a systems engineering approach using recent technology to improve the productivity and customer service of its unskilled and inexperienced workforce. Kmart and Wal-Mart developed sophisticated real-time information tools by introducing innovations in discounting and warehousing. Nordstrom stressed extraordinary sales service that went beyond the call of duty for its customers. Sears Roebuck developed a unique ability to act as the purchasing agent for the middle-class family. Maytag's singular talent was its obsession with quality control. AT&T centered its activities on universal telephone service. Bic's product line and decision making rotated around the concept of disposability; a product built to last would not become part of Bic's business vision. Estée Lauder's perfumes and cosmetics were elegantly packaged to sell hopes and dreams. Johnson & Johnson's unique strength was marketing therapeutic consumable products for mothers and nurses. Service Master distinguished itself by training the least skilled and educated people and converting them into competent performers. General Motors displayed a special ability to acquire mature firms and then turn them into star performers. General Electric created a core of technological excellence around its many profit centers. Procter & Gamble was able to sell its own marketing knowledge over and over again through its strong distribution system handling scores of diverse products. General Foods was distinctive in segmenting similar products with varied brand names. Marks & Spencer aimed at providing a middle-class wardrobe to accelerate the social mobility of poor British women. Nabisco was able to control shelf space by using its own salesforce to stock its supermarket shelves. 3M was able to program its technological innovation by projecting a large percentage of new products every five years. Sony focused on the miniaturization of its electronic technology. Rubbermaid put out an annual profusion of new products, hampering imitation by its competitiveness. Intel developed systematic improvement for each new generation of computer chips. Federal Express pioneered logistical and systems management.

Drucker also argued that maintaining excellence was precarious; in time every excellence inevitably became obsolete. It was never possible, therefore, to give a final answer to the question, What is the business? Instead the question must be subject to periodic reexamination in light of altered external circumstances and changing customer values. The tombstones in the business graveyard gave testimony to the validity of the proposition that in the event a corporate excellence evaporated, management had to redefine the corporation around some other unique strength or it would be unlikely to continue to perform in a first-rate fashion.

Transitional. A transitional business strategy was needed if management was to avoid being misled by the euphoria of success in the traditional business. Drucker feared that success often had a mesmerizing effect and fostered the illusion of institutional immortality. To deflate this simplistic delusion he urged management to take bearings on its present position, identify competitive perils, and scan the horizon for radically new social and economic trends. Central to Drucker's managerial philosophy of change was the proposition that a business could remain in its traditional phase and face stagnation or it could reinvigorate itself and continue to be successful. In selecting growth as an option, it had to respond to the question, What will the business be? This meant, for the transitional business, a commitment to adaptive innovation in order to rejuvenate the company's strengths and discover opportunities for old ones.

In essence, the managerial task was not just to meet demand but to create it. To implement this objective of constant renewal, managers had to satisfy the changing needs of current consumers, ascertain the composition of noncustomers, evaluate what could be borrowed from successful competitors, abandon obsolete products, devise new accounting methods for pricing and distribution, convert social problems into opportunities, and encourage an entrepreneurial corporate culture. Assuming that successes outweighed failures in pursuing these policies, managers had also to diagnose whether the improvements were complementary to the traditional business or whether the changes were so substantive that they constituted a new definition of business purpose. For example, if Procter & Gamble added another conventional household product to its wide distribution stream, it would experience an incremental business change that involved no radical alteration of its mission. However, if it entered the pharmaceutical field, it would have to redefine its identity to adjust to a new customer and knowledge base.

Transformational. Drucker candidly confessed that no systematic methodology existed for responding to the question, What should the business be? Because he did not have a clear and comprehensive concept for organizing ignorance, he asked managers to imagine a possible ideal future for a radically different business. As part of the process of coming to grips with the potential transformational business, he also suggested that managers should spell out what social and technological forces they were afraid of, the external threats to and internal vulnerabilities of the business, and the circumstances or products that would enable the customer to do without the envisioned product or service.

According to Drucker the main reason managers needed to be concerned with an entrepreneurial strategy for guiding the company through a metamorphosis was that even the most successful business would sooner or later become obsolete as a result of either the competition or new technology. It would be much wiser for managers to recognize this reality and then for them to do the obsoleting. For example, if any company had a chance to defy the iron law of obsolescence it was AT&T. For over a century it was the most successful monopoly in U.S. business history. But it had to alter its stable and secure identity because of its own technological innovation of the transistor, which undermined its monopoly of knowledge and gave rise to many new competitors who used the transistor to devise new communication products and services for the customer. Once these events occurred, AT&T had to undergo a major business transformation whose final form is still to be determined.

Conclusion

The popular reception accorded to *The Practice of Management*, particularly in the business community, provided substantial credence for the subsequent recognition of Drucker as the father of modern management. This book was the first analytical answer to the question, What is management? It presented management as a crucial function for attaining economic progress and social harmony and described managers as the catalytic agents of change in implementing those goals.

As a pioneering, comprehensive rationale of management as an organized discipline and as a separate form of work, *The Practice of Management* filled an intellectual vacuum; it synthesized the best of current practice into codified principles, integrated the specialized business functions into an organic whole, established the groundwork for the implementation of managerial tasks, and suggested guidelines for the improvement of executive skills.

For Drucker, the vision he advanced and the basic skills, techniques, concepts, and ideas he enumerated in the midfifties struck him as the epitome of common sense rather than an intellectual milestone. With the publication of *Concept of the Corporation* in 1946 and *The Practice of Management* in 1954, he codified, organized, and systematized the subject of management. As he said later, "I sat down and made a discipline of it."[4] His immediate goal had been to evaluate and investigate what was actually known about the topic. He didn't invent a single new managerial function; instead his originality consisted in merging the key specialties into a holistic perspective. As late as the time of World War II, it was possible to view a business as a cluster of mechanical functions; by 1958, such a position was untenable. In that year Drucker stated: "Today we know that, when we talk of a 'business,' the 'functions' simply do not exist. There is only business profit, business risk, business product, business investment, and business customer. The functions are irrelevant to any one of them. And yet it is equally obvious, if we look at the business, that the work has to be done by people who specialize, because nobody can know

enough even to know all there is to be known about one of the major functions today—they are growing too fast."[5]

Because Drucker viewed management as a distinct form of work applicable to all industrial societies, it was not surprising that *The Practice of Management* had international appeal. Although some critics in Europe described the
book as a counterculture manifesto, that did not diminish its acceptance in the
business community. Drucker's influence on Japan has been incalculable.

Another unconventional feature of *The Practice of Management* was that
Drucker never subscribed to the tenet that business was solely a commercial
subject. He found it incomprehensible that a person could be interested only
in business and remain purely specialized in his interests. Because business
depended on human resources for results, the practitioner could not avoid
being conversant with the insights derived from the liberal arts. Commencing
with *The Practice of Management,* Drucker was to insist that thinking about the
lessons of history and literature was the underlying foundation of doing. In
his writings he practiced what he preached by favoring the qualitative side of
management over the quantitative, by probing the intellectual rather than the
technical framework of decision making, by understanding the nonlogical
aspects of power and personality struggles within the organization, by examining the factor of continual learning as the key to personal development, by
examining the significance of social and demographic outside forces on corporate survival, by showing a concern for ethical values, and by familiarizing
himself with foreign cultures.

Three areas deserve special attention in any follow-up of what Drucker
started with *Concept of the Corporation* and *The Practice of Management:* (1) the management boom, (2) the status of management as a discipline, and (3) updating
Drucker.

The Management Boom

Drucker considered management theory an "unfinished business," always in
need of constant repair and rejuvenation. Shortly after the publication of *The
Practice of Management,* in order to meet the heightened demand and interest
of the executive community, a host of scholars contributed to a voluminous
boom in management literature. Among the most prominent of the new concepts and techniques were Theory X and Theory Y, management grids, program evaluation review technique (PERT), decision-making trees, contingency

theory, brainstorming techniques, transcendental meditation, and encounter groups. Drucker's attitude toward these techniques was that as long as they worked they constituted a valid addition to the body theory.

In his writings after *The Practice of Management,* Drucker adhered steadfastly to the fundamentals of managerial work, to bringing together people of diverse knowledge and skills for joint performance. One of Drucker's later insights, however, was to view management as a central organ for all institutions (military, scholastic, religious, labor, and hospital) and not exclusively for businesses. He turned down chairs at Harvard and Stanford Universities because they wanted him to concentrate solely on business.[6]

Over the years Drucker was the single leading contributor to the management boom. A major portion of his research appeared in specialized journals and demonstrated how the functional areas of business related to the whole. A mark of this productivity was his record-setting achievement of publishing thirty-one articles in the *Harvard Business Review.*

In conducting his research on internal business functions Drucker did not neglect the external factors impinging on corporate survival. He contended that when a corporation ignored its institutional purpose of justifying its contribution to society and became exclusively absorbed with internal issues and bureaucratic procedures, it was a sure sign that the company was on its decline. In order to capture the velocity of societal change resulting from the interplay of the corporation and its environment, almost half of Drucker's writings addressed the economic, political, and social issues of the contemporary corporation. Among some of the topics he treated as "the business of business" were education, ethics, economics, pluralism, technology, comparative international management, labor, demographics, the youth revolution, and political ideologies.

Management as a Discipline

Tom Peters contended that prior to Drucker "a true discipline of management" was nonexistent.[7] Harold Koontz, professor of management at University of California at Los Angeles, commented, "He is certainly the greatest management philosopher of any time."[8] These and similar tributes implied that Drucker had formulated a generally accepted theoretical consensus for the discipline of management. Drucker, however, denied any such achievement, insisting that his model was "an" analysis but not "the" analysis. He indicated that it was premature to elevate the discipline of management to the status of a testable theory because the core knowledge was grossly incomplete, the methodology highly unreliable, and the difficulties confronted in the integration of changing circumstances into a conceptual framework daunting.

In considering the title for his book, Drucker had rejected the word *art* because the title "must be practical and focused on the actual experience of managing."[9] He maintained that if an art ever became popular, it ceased to be an art. At the same time, he admitted that both *theory* and *art* played intrinsic roles in the pattern of management, but that they were polar roles. Art is private and subjective; theory is a set of impersonal rules and prescriptions. Art entails experience; theory subscribes to concepts. Art is basically ambiguous; theory aims at precision. Art is instinctual; theory is logical. Art breeds innovators; theory produces technicians. Art is an unteachable gift; theory assumes a learnable body of knowledge. In short, the theoretician follows the book of conventional wisdom; the artist, through a feat of personal mastery and originality, writes his or her own book. Thus theory and art are separate managerial currents; it is only when united by the practitioner into meaningful performance that they produce synergy.

In one of his books, Drucker, making the distinction between theory and practice, gave the following advice to his readers: "A management text that is purely 'concept' and 'theory' may enable the student to acquire information, but it will not enable him or her to become a successful practitioner. On the other hand, a book that is purely 'practice' will not enable a student who has no or little experience as a manager—and probably not even experience as an employee in managed institutions—to learn."[10]

Drucker opted for the title *The Practice of Management* because *practice* was a more realistic term than either management theory or art. Practice concentrated on application over information, action over passive behavior, and results over scholarship. As mentioned earlier, Drucker viewed the practitioner as the pathfinder and the scholar as the codifier. It was only through this fusion of improved theoretical codification and personal professional commitment that ordinary people were capable of doing extraordinary things.

Because managerial work was primarily a doer's job in which the practitioner was responsible for results, educators had to avoid the danger of fossilized pedantry and had to assume accountability for communicating knowledge clearly and understandably to those who had to apply it. Drucker's intellectual rationale became more concrete when he compared the practice of management with the practice of medicine: "No book will ever make a wise man out of a donkey or a genius out of an incompetent. The foundation in a discipline, however, gives to today's competent physician a capacity to perform well beyond that of the ablest doctor of a century ago, and enables the outstanding physician of today to do what the medical genius of yesterday could hardly have dreamt of. No discipline can lengthen a man's arm. But it can lengthen his reach by hoisting him on the shoulders of his predecessors."[11]

Attempts to Update Drucker

In a 1992 article in *Business Week,* John Byrne discussed the current condition of management theory and listed the five major schools of thought considered by executives and academics as models for management in the twenty-first century: empowerment, learning organization, reengineering, organizational architecture, and core competencies. All five of these reigning methodologies had grown from seeds first planted and cultivated in the soil of Drucker's early writings. Consider for a moment how each of these popular buzzwords can be conceptually traced to Drucker—empowerment (management by objectives), learning organization (the knowledge worker), reengineering (the identification of the traditional, transitional, and transformational phases of the corporation), organizational architecture (the idea that structural design follows strategic purpose), and core competencies (central knowledge excellencies).

Nobody could accuse the proponents of these new approaches of simply rehashing and regurgitating Drucker; in fact he would applaud them for refining these older concepts in elegant ways to meet the needs of contemporary management. He would also endorse their efforts to take responsibility for conducting performance tests of their theories through their consulting endeavors with leading corporations, rather than letting their ideas stagnate in the dusty journals of academe. However, in discussing the interrelationship of Drucker's early writings with the avant-garde of today's managerial thinkers, and the role of the longevity of his thought, Byrne makes a most compelling point: "The new gurus aren't rewriting Drucker, the most enduring management thinker of our time. More often than not, they're updating him by adding new ideas and tools to what Drucker has called 'the practice of management.'"[12]

Charles Handy, a British scholar, supported Byrne's contention, when he stated that "virtually everything can be traced back to Drucker."[13] As pointed out in Chapter One, in their recent investigation into the history of management thought, Micklethwait and Wooldridge concluded, "So far, management theory has produced, at most, one 'great' thinker: Peter Drucker."[14] In a subsequent interview one of these authors reasserted this position: "Drucker is the one management thinker whom all other management thinkers kowtow to. Above all, he is one of the few thinkers from any discipline who can reasonably claim to have changed the world."[15]

According to the eminent British philosopher Alfred North Whitehead, all Western philosophy has been a footnote to Plato. In the opinion of Theodore Levitt, the same might be arguably said of Drucker with respect to the discipline of management. In his review of Drucker's *Management: Tasks, Responsibilities, Practices,* an updated version of *The Practice of Management,* Levitt lavished praise on Drucker's singular imagination, comprehensive understanding, and insightful contributions in creating the subject of management. Comparing Drucker's work to that of the seminal thinkers in the Western intellectual tradition, he wrote: "Like the styles of Newton, Smith, Marx, Freud, Darwin, and the others, Drucker's encyclopedic explication of the managerial tasks, responsibilities, and practices provides a meaning and casts an illumination on its subject that transcends the subject itself."[16]

CHAPTER EIGHT

THE ENTREPRENEURIAL PROCESS

A constant background theme in all of Drucker's business writings was the importance of entrepreneurship for managing change systematically. In viewing the business from the vantage point of today and tomorrow he focused his analysis of the process around the three corporate businesses outlined in the previous chapter: the traditional or existing business, the transitional or adaptive business, and the transformational or innovative business. The entrepreneurial strategies and tactics for each of these businesses will be treated separately in greater depth over Chapters Nine, Ten, and Eleven, but first it is illuminating to explore how Drucker saw understanding the nature of stability and flux as the foundation of the entrepreneurial process.

Continuity and Change

As noted earlier the theme of continuity and change has been perhaps the most consistent feature of Drucker's writings. He thought it axiomatic that to perceive the future, one had to understand the role of the past. Addressing the claims of the past as part of the entrepreneurial process, he listed five interacting features: (1) entropy, (2) permanence versus discontinuity, (3) the illusion of uninterrupted success, (4) dual time dimensions, and (5) corporate inertia. All five characteristics of continuity dictate the unfeasibility of mindlessly supporting the status quo and at the same time must be considered realities and restraints in preparing for the future.

Entropy

Entropy is a certain prescription for inhibiting future change. Uncertainty and risk are common denominators of entrepreneurship, but Drucker asserted that the greatest risk of all is doing nothing. Entropy is, in effect, an invitation to accept stagnancy because all physical processes have an inevitable tendency to disintegrate unless they receive new inputs. This phenomenon is particularly applicable to the corporation and other artificial institutions. According to Drucker the corporation operates in a social and not a physical universe. As a result, unlike the human body, which has normal restorative tendencies, the corporation, as an artificial body, is prone to degeneration.

Maintaining that a condition of stability is impossible in a dynamic economy, Drucker implied that the challenge of overcoming *the entropy trap* is central to understanding entrepreneurial decision making and business identity. Regardless of its knowledge skills and operating efficiencies, a company whose mission fails to meet the test of competition and technology is ready for the business graveyard. Moreover, he indicated that the failure of any individual nonperforming business would not be catastrophic in an entrepreneurial society. "If you have too many problems maybe you should go out of business. There is no law that says a company must last forever."[1]

Permanence Versus Discontinuity

The reality of the corporation shaping the environment and also being shaped by it in a competitive and technological society means that management cannot rely on the relevance of previous trends. Discontinuity, the rupturing of past social patterns from their linear environmental moorings, means that management must respond to new conditions. "The only things that evolve by themselves in an organization," Drucker observed, "are disorder, friction and malperformance."[2] In short, external realities do not adjust themselves to the corporation, management must adapt to the environment.

In the more placid past, continuity was a feasible guide in encountering the future, but it was increasingly improbable in a world of accelerating change because every major change has a destabilizing effect, upsetting the element of continuity. Drucker observed that the dynamics of accelerated change heighten the role of discontinuity and dictate managerial decisions of frightening complexity, turbulent uncertainty, and irrevocable commitments.[3]

Drucker noted that most businessmen, if given a choice, prefer to embrace the doctrine of permanence advocated by the Greek philosopher Parmenides. But he pointed out that Parmenides' intellectual opponent, Heraclitus, the philosopher of incessant flux, has far greater relevance for the dynamics of modern business. Drucker stressed that change was a categorical imperative for an entrepreneurial system, stating: "Earlier economic activity was based on the assumption that there would be no change, which assumption was institutionally guarded and defended. Altogether up to the seventeenth century it was the purpose of all human institutions to prevent change. The business enterprise is a significant and rather amazing novelty in that it is the first human institution having the purpose of bringing about change."[4]

The Illusion of Uninterrupted Success

According to Drucker, institutions outlive themselves when they fail to achieve their objectives or when they achieve them. Paradoxically, the latter part of this view implies that nothing fails like success. That is, he warned that business excellence is a temporary condition. Because outstanding performance eventually succumbs to the realities of competition and technology, it is only a question of time before every right product becomes the wrong product and the right business philosophy becomes the wrong one. Describing the specific impact of success on managerial activities, he thought it should be viewed as the end of a business's beginning stage, not the end of change in the corporate biography. "Success always obsoletes the very behavior that achieved it. It always creates new realities. It always creates, above all, its own and different problems. Only the fairy story ends They lived happily ever after."[5]

Drucker was convinced that the most dangerous period in a company's history was when it was applauded by the business press for achieving a reputation for outstanding business performance. Instead of questioning its strategic decisions and operations, it then developed the tendency to become imaginatively comatose, to look upon the reasons for past success as part of a "holy writ" emblazoned in stone.

It is rare for a company's management to comprehend the reality of dynamic disequilibrium when it is at the height of its triumph. This failure to see the company objectively means its successes blind management to the necessity of performing an entrepreneurial encore. "When it is all fair weather, and not a cloud on the horizon, that's the time a company should be making changes. But I have yet to have someone come to me and say, 'Everything we do is coming up roses, and we are worried about it.'. . . Although it's difficult to argue with success, management certainly doesn't wait until it is faced with extinction."[6]

Drucker maintained that good answers do not last forever, because there are no absolute good answers. It is a delusion to believe that excellence is eternal, simply because there is no absolute excellence. In rejecting perfection, he argued that all products are obsolete from the day of their inception. It is only a question of time before their original form will be changed by the producing firms themselves or by their competitors.

He cited the case of IBM and its failure to recognize that no business excellence will continue to make sense without major modifications. He chiefly criticized its top management for failing to see that the computer was a form of hardware that basically had become a commodity, and that software would be the driving force dominating the industry in the future. If IBM suffered the myopic affliction of being technologically driven rather than market driven, then the current super successes Wal-Mart and Microsoft might find it appropriate to examine the vulnerabilities that were part of their success. Unexamined and unquestioned success meant that a company would inevitably become a prisoner of continuity.[7]

For example, Wal-Mart "has [in 1994] 14 percent of the U.S. consumer-goods market," a magnificent success story in retailing. Yet this figure also indicates that the other 86 percent is not part of Wal-Mart's market share.[8] Drucker conjectured that despite its extraordinary success, Wal-Mart should concern itself with, among other current challenges, community pressures against opening up new stores; industry saturation, which increased costs for new outlets; its need to obtain core competencies in the grocery and international market segment; store managers' need for executive as well as logistical training; excessive stress on personnel due to long hours and productivity pressures, with a corresponding negative effect on family and private life; increased trade union opposition, and maintenance of the corporate culture inspired by Sam Walton, with its aggressive acquisition policy.

Dual Time Dimensions

The factor of time was another reminder of how past decision making affected the future. Warning that executives who focused on short-term results based on yesterday's decisions, mortgaged their future, Drucker observed that "all institutions live and perform in two time periods: that of today and that of tomorrow. Tomorrow is being made today, irrevocably in most cases."[9] Arguing that no solutions can be devised with information about the future and that decisions made today in anticipation of tomorrow had to be based to a large extent on past perceptions, Drucker said of the time interconnection of continuity and change: "The future will not just happen if one wishes hard enough. It requires decision—now. It imposes risk—now. It requires action—now. It demands allocation of resources, and above all, of human resources—now. It requires work—now."[10] Despite all the uncertainties in predicting tomorrow, he paradoxically emphasized that "Long-range planning is necessary precisely because we cannot forecast."[11]

Corporate Inertia

Drucker contended it was axiomatic for institutions to move from dynamism to drift. Because change is disturbing and disjointing, most executives have a partiality for the steady state mind-set of the status quo. As a result they tend to favor allocation of resources to the past over the future.

As described earlier, Drucker had observed that when a business loses its spirit of entrepreneurship, the business revolutionaries of yesterday often become the reactionaries of today's business. Among the symptoms of this stagnant condition are the conflicts between those who want to improve on the present rather than focus on new and different things, the tendency to feed problems and starve opportunities, and the concentration on resolving crises rather than practicing innovation. The claims of the past have a certain legitimacy but only to the extent that they restore normalcy. Inertia is not the way to manage change systematically and effectively.

Considerations of the Future

In examining the aforementioned vulnerabilities of the stationary state under conditions of dynamic disequilibrium, Drucker was dogmatic on the inevitability of change. Moreover, given the reality of the market test, which makes the business institution unique, he thought it quixotic to try to sustain permanence.

The opposite side of continuity's coin is change. Because change is synonymous with the future, echoing the words of Charles Kettering, the technological genius of General Motors, Drucker asserted that management of change was the subject on which managers should be spending most of their time. Given this operating premise, he thought it appropriate that business scholars synthesize what is actually known about the topic.

Without going into detail, it is in order, from an entrepreneurial standpoint, to review the highlights of Drucker's discussion of decision making in respect to the future. First, he stated the future is unpredictable; all we know for sure is that it will be different from the past. In alluding to the sardonic speciousness of prognostication, he was reminded of Girolamo Cardano, a sixteenth-century astrologer who constructed a horoscope that predicted his death. When the fateful day occurred, he was feeling fine. But rather than have his science falsified, he committed suicide. Pointing out the pitfalls of predicting the nonexistent, Drucker reiterated that the vision of the unexpected is uniquely different for every individual.

Second, there are no facts about the future; there are only expectations. In making the comparison between tangible present events and future expectations, Drucker contended that the planning process forces managers to deal with future events but not observable ones. They are never facts and therefore are incapable of measurement. With respect to market planning, he insisted that nobody could ever imagine the outcomes from the genuinely new.

Third, as discussed in relation to the dual time dimensions, there is no such thing as a future decision, only the futurity of a present one. Observing that solving problems involves risk-taking judgments, Drucker argued that there are no solutions with respect to the future. There are only riskful, imperfect, and uncertain choices, each demanding different efforts and costs.

Drucker also commented on the possible use of futurology and categorization as methodologies for comprehending the future. He described how the post–World War II winds of change were so turbulent and rapid that they produced a new cottage industry—the futurologists. These are the social and economic observers who work in think tanks, such as the Hudson Institute, Rand Corporation, and Institute for the Future, and whose main objective is composing future scenarios for society. Among the prominent individuals in this new genre are Alvin Toffler, Marshall McLuhan, and Herman Kahn.

Drucker pointed out that deciphering the future was hardly new. Many novelists in the nineteenth and early twentieth century, for example, were involved in technological prognostication. Despite the brilliance of their efforts, their predictions were diminished because of the historical circumstances under which they were rendered. Arguing that the environment had to be culturally receptive to new technology, Drucker noted that Jules Verne and H. G. Wells were futurologists before the term became fashionable. Although imaginative in their attempted foresight, they saw their technologies through the filters of Victorian and Edwardian social reality. They neglected to spell out the conditions that would have to be fulfilled for their predictions to be effective.

Although Drucker admired the imaginative insights of the modern futurologists, he questioned their utility. He concluded that these futurologists often revealed more about themselves and their beliefs and ideologies than about the future. He examined their track records, and the batting average was abysmally low. It was evident to him that their few successful guesses did not compare with their many failures of prediction.

With regard to categorization, Drucker adopted a circumspect stance, offering specific methods of categorization that he considered a useful approach to dealing with the future. He suggested thinking about the future in three classifications: (1) projection, (2) anticipation, and (3) innovation. Projection, which he labeled the soundest of the three approaches, is the future that has already happened. It is in such embryonic form, however, that only a few people can perceive that it has become reality. As will be examined later, still fewer people are able to convert this incipient development into an economic opportunity.

Anticipation is the future that one expects to happen. Because it is based on hunch and intuition, making decisions on the basis of anticipation is a chancy entrepreneurial exercise. Despite the low degree of probability, there are many examples of unconventional individuals who have been willing to bet on their different perception of reality and who have had the courage of their convictions to make a commitment to it.

Innovation is "purposefully planned change." In effect it is a systematic methodology for inventing the future. Because there are no meaningful trends within conventional wisdom, the practitioner has to take the paradoxical action of organizing his or her ignorance. Drucker saw this as a conceptual leap into the future—creating something new and then returning to the present to work on it. A successful innovation has such a qualitative impact on the future environment that it usually creates a new industry.[12]

Drucker frankly confessed that the mysteries of the unknown would not be uncovered by a mindless leap into the future. Nevertheless, he thought it possible to devise a configurative methodology for organizing ignorance for a project by writing new expectations about the innovation, working back to the present, and finally checking results through feedback. He included in this systems approach such successful examples as the conquest of polio, the discovery of the DNA molecule and the table of chemical elements, and the invention of the transistor and the atomic bomb.

He reached the conclusion that it was the impossibility of prediction and the lack of facts in the future that made entrepreneurial planning an indispensable executive task. He believed, therefore, that it is possible to manage change systematically by applying what is known about the topic. The framework Drucker outlined for this entrepreneurial task focused on characteristics and on strategies and tactics for managing the present, transitional, and transformational phases of the business.

Characteristics

The popular version of entrepreneurship, which depicted an independent operator opening a small business, was perhaps its least interesting aspect in Drucker's analysis. It was not that he viewed the opening of small businesses as unimportant. They were the source of a great deal of job creation, and many of them might become the giants of tomorrow. He considered, however, that the prototypical little business firm already in existence was incapable of contributing to the base of entrepreneurial knowledge. Because most of these new ventures did not devise novel structural configurations or innovative ways of meeting consumer demand, they did not attract his analytical attention. For example, opening a small family hamburger shop or hardware store, common models of commercial start-ups throughout the economy, did not qualify in Drucker's mind as an entrepreneurial endeavor. Conversely, founding a McDonald's or a Home Depot was entrepreneurial because of the innovative impact it had on business structure and consumer value. "Admittedly," he said, "all new small businesses have many factors in common. But to be entrepreneurial, an enterprise has to have special characteristics over and above being new and small. Indeed, entrepreneurs are a minority among new businesses. They create something new, something different; they change or transmute values."[13]

More surprising perhaps was Drucker's reservation about classifying all high-tech businesses as entrepreneurial ventures. "Indeed, high tech is the one sector that is not part of this new 'technology,' this 'entrepreneurial management.' The Silicon Valley high-tech entrepreneurs still operate mainly in the nineteenth-century mold. They still believe in Benjamin Franklin's dictum: 'If you invent a better mousetrap the world will beat a path to your door.' It does not yet occur to them to ask what makes a mousetrap 'better' or for whom?"[14] These businesses might have a sophisticated technological veneer, but their business strategies are often mired in a view of the product and not the customer as the determining business factor.

If Drucker found small business and high tech wanting in entrepreneurial insights, he derived considerable inspiration from the not-for-profit sector. His writings are replete with examples of colleges, churches, hospitals, and other social institutions that have enriched their constituents and society with major innovations by pursuing entrepreneurial principles and tactics.

Drucker's only book on the entrepreneurial process was *Innovation and Entrepreneurship* (1985), but his comments on these two themes were not confined to this single volume. Entrepreneurship was a topic that pervaded and penetrated through almost all of his writings on business strategy. Indeed, entrepreneurship was the conceptual core and intellectual foundation for what he labeled the systematic management of change.

Drucker treated the characteristics of entrepreneurship in a most expansive fashion. In weaving a meaningful fabric of entrepreneurship, he drew heavily upon the many technical strands he had witnessed during his consulting experience. Here are some of his most insightful ideas about entrepreneurship:

- It creates a business atmosphere that encourages constant change.

- It converts problems into opportunities.

- It manages resources in such a way that they will increase productive capacities.

- It focuses not on tomorrow but on what has to be done today in order to have a tomorrow.

- It satisfies the unmet needs of the customer.

- It concentrates on the creation of jobs and societal wealth.

- It emphasizes results and performance.

- It analyzes the risk factor as a precondition of survival but not as a guarantee of it.

- It recognizes that the task encompasses an artistic attitude, a monomaniacal mission, and a passionate commitment.

- It realizes that the autonomous nature of entrepreneurship transcends business specialization.

- It fuses internal corporate strengths with external stimuli.

- It understands that the challenge is not just to meet demand but to create demand.

- It knows risk avoidance is an escape from entrepreneurship (remember, executives are rarely penalized for neglecting opportunities).

According to Drucker, systematic work is the catalyst for translating the concepts and skills of entrepreneurship (such as those shown in the accompanying box) into reality. At the same time, he deplored concepts that are merely gimmicks and questioned the role of genius. "Entrepreneurship is not 'natural'; it is not 'creative.' It is work. . . . They [entrepreneurship and innovation] can be learned, but it requires effort."[15] In a matrix for developing a systematic approach to the entrepreneurial process, he included the following considerations and prerequisites: results over activities, output over input, performance over methodology, effectiveness over efficiency, and responsibilities over procedures.

It was the contention of Drucker that through experience and inference a substantive practice of entrepreneurial management currently existed, but its secrets would not reveal themselves automatically; it required study and commitment. "We have reached the point in [entrepreneurial management] where we know what the practice is, and it's not in waiting around for the muse to kiss you. The muse is very, very choosy, not only in whom she kisses but in where she kisses them. And so one can't wait."[16]

He cautioned that on the surface the principles and tools of entrepreneurship were deceptively simple in terms of intellectual comprehension but that translating them into practical results was another matter. As in all professional disciplines, raw talent and clever brilliance are irrelevant unless they are tightly forged into a practice based on a sense of personal persistence and a commitment to habitual improvement. He observed that entrepreneurship "is simple, but not easy. What you have to do and how you do it are incredibly simple. Are you willing to do it? That is another matter."[17] Elaborating on the difference between talking about a practice and actually achieving tangible results, he expressed the notion that the former always looked simple but the latter was never easy.

The Existing Business

Managing properly the fundamentals of the existing business is the foundation of the entrepreneurial process. A sine qua non of this task is a clear statement of corporate identity. Drucker especially emphasized that the mission statement should avoid broad ambiguous pronouncements and a compilation of good intentions—neither of which is conducive to relevant performance and meaningful feedback.

He stated bluntly that on the one hand, companies without a reasonably clear definition of themselves are not likely to achieve excellence. On the other hand, the great benefit of a lucid and understandable business commitment is that it focuses on what is needed, not what is wanted; provides a sense of employee understanding; reduces uncertainty; minimizes ambiguity; mitigates surprises by indicating what the business is not; shapes the pattern of systematic decision making; nourishes achievement by energizing motivation; determines corporate culture; and establishes a frame of reference for what the business is, will be, and should be (see Figure 7.1).

Drucker admitted that businesses with crystal-clear identity statements, such as Johnson & Johnson, were exceptions rather than the rule. Nevertheless a company that went through the studious exercise would illuminate such key operating questions as: Where are you? What are you? Who is your competition? and, How can you get a sense that things will be different?

In insisting on the importance of managing the existing business effectively, he also cautioned against any exclusive concern with current identity. Businesses require a sense of perspective. For example, if a company opts for putting resources only into the present business, it is tantamount to preempting the market of the dinosaur. Conversely, a concern with the chimerical future can also have disastrous consequences.

Drucker remarked there were many companies, such as RCA in the 1970s and 1980s, that at different times had followed a strategy that singularly emphasized the present or the future. Recognizing the dilemma and pointing out the ceaseless battle for resources between present and future, he asserted a judgmental balance was required: if a business, for example, does not provide for its immediate needs, there will be no long-range future. But if it sacrifices its long-range needs, there will also be no business fairly soon.[18]

It was partly because the conventional literature on entrepreneurship concentrated on the future as the dominant concern that Drucker insisted on giving proper perspective to the present. He saw solid performance in operating the existing business as a form of preventive medicine to combat the wasteful and degenerative effects of entropy, pointing out that nothing improves by itself and that neglect only invites confusion and chaos.

In short, Drucker maintained that in an entrepreneurial sense, managing the existing business does not require frozen rigidity or passive adaptation. Instead, it involves improving the productivity of resources through systematic study and application so that the organization will be in a stronger position and have a more receptive attitude as it meets the uncertainties of tomorrow. To those who argued that this was common sense and belaboring the obvious, Drucker partially agreed. He added, however, that typically fundamentals are thoughtlessly taken for granted simply because they are so obvious.

Drucker asserted not only that it is a mistake to take current operations for granted but that it is prudent to assume that today's business is being administered inefficiently. Because of inertia, even so-called excellent companies have an identifiable share of waste and misallocation. The removal of even some of those inefficiencies by management can foster a spirit of change and a focus on opportunities.

Misallocation of Resources

According to Drucker, the misallocation of resources is a common trait of all businesses—large and small, successful and marginal. The exact factor of misallocation on a company-to-company basis is dependent on such features as the number of disgruntled customers, the profitability profile, the lower level of productivity of its corporate assets compared to the competition, and the degree of weak morale. Because poor distribution of resources in the existing business is a handicap to the entrepreneurial process, Drucker identified four major elements accounting for the bulk of resource misdirection: (1) incompetency, (2) probability patterns, (3) a predilection for defending yesterday, and (4) an outdated information reporting system.

Incompetency. In the planning process for the shaping of tomorrow, most firms operate under the premise that today's business is managed competently. Drucker asserted that this premise is false. To cite one example, he observed that there is a strong organizational probability that the majority of efforts will allocate themselves to the events or people that produce a small minority of the most desirable results. Although he questioned whether this or other statistical laws were repealable, he thought it was possible to change ratios in favor of better results.

Probability patterns. Managers constantly fight probability rather than having it work for them. As a result there is a statistical diversion of resources away from results. Drucker ascribed this to the fact that organizations are imperfect entities; despite noble intentions they are inherently programmed for deficiencies. Because institutions are run by human beings, malfunctioning is axiomatic. This reality cannot be eliminated, but it can be moderated.

A predilection for defending yesterday. A major managerial mistake "is slaughtering tomorrow's opportunity on the altar of yesterday."[19] That is, the prime cause of waste and dissipation of resources is not concern with the competition but the inability of managers to abandon yesterday. Defending yesterday's activities means that outstanding people are distracted from opportunities. In favoring a policy of stability over growth, managers are opting for the market of the buggy whip. Equally important, Drucker considered the defense of yesterday's marginal breadwinners the deadliest foe of tomorrow's innovative products. Unfortunately, few managements can resist the temptation to rejuvenate their unhealthy performers.

An outdated information reporting system. Drucker attributed the paucity of relevant data for making entrepreneurial decisions in the existing business to the outdated model of standardized cost accounting. He conceded it was a major innovation seventy years ago but that it had failed in the interim to meet the complex economic and technological demands of modern business. Citing as one example the gap between theory and practice in the traditional cost accounting model, he observed that "most managements spend an enormous amount of time on capital appropriation decisions, but few pay much attention to what happens after a capital investment decision has been approved."[20] Among his additional criticisms of the accounting model were its concern with liquidity rather than with future results, neglect of the service industries, failure to identify contributions of business functions, and inattention to the factor of *mental capital*.

Drucker cautioned that obtaining the appropriate information for improved productivity of assets is a major challenge that does not lend itself to quick fixes and gimmicks. He suggested that managers pay attention to the techniques and concepts practiced by a handful of excellent companies for modifying misallocation of resources. In the long run he thought that the model of *activity accounting* might be the best approach to entrepreneurial management. (The status of this discipline will be addressed in the next chapter.)

Drucker asserted that it was possible to improve performance in the existing business by using the entrepreneurial approach of converting problems into opportunities and thus neutralizing resource misallocation and modifying vulnerabilities. He proposed three major operating devices: (1) the marketing concept, (2) managing capital assets, and (3) systematic abandonment. The first is introduced here, and the latter two are discussed in Chapter Nine.

The Marketing Concept

"There is only one valid definition of business purpose: to create a customer."[21] This remarkably terse comment is quintessential Drucker in that it conveys in a few words the incisive insight popularly known as the *marketing concept*. He never included the marketing concept in his coverage of entrepreneurship, but because it is such a vital ingredient for improving the existing business it deserves more than casual consideration.

In his treatment of the marketing concept, Drucker analyzed six major segments: (1) consumer sovereignty, (2) consumer rationality, (3) the utility function, (4) the distinction between sales and marketing, (5) the systems approach, and (6) the demand factor.

Consumer Sovereignty. In giving priority to the consumer, Drucker broke with the conventional wisdom of defining the business based on what is produced, and replaced it by looking at the business from the customer's point of view. He claimed he derived this insight from Mitsui, the sixteenth-century Japanese retailer, and Cyrus McCormick, the American inventor of the mechanical harvester. Without codifying their methods into textbook form, they practiced many of the attributes of modern marketing.

Implicit in the idea of consumer sovereignty was the assumption that no business has control of the customer, because that consumer can deny his or her purchasing power. Once the dynamic premise of consumer power was raised, it pointed up the challenge of meeting the unmet needs of the customer which in turn suggested such entrepreneurial questions as: How would I see this product if I were the customer? If I had to install it? If I had to service it? If I had to dispose of it? Who is the person who will make the buying decision? (This decision maker, not the person who pays, is the customer.) Successful answers to these questions stimulate change, ensure results, increase profits, and contribute to job creation.

Consumer Rationality. "There are no irrational customers,"[22] only lazy merchants and manufacturers. Drucker never retreated from this conviction. He considered it a form of arrogance for managers to believe that customers did not realize what was value and what was good for them. Customers are entirely rational but rational "in terms of their own realities." It is therefore the task of management to determine the answers to two key questions: What is in the customer's behavior that appears to be totally irrational? And what is there in his or her reality that I fail to see?

Drucker warned that on those occasions when executives portrayed themselves as being more expert than customers in assessing value, they faced the concomitant risk, based on the laws of probability, of being brilliantly wrong. He found it curious that everybody in a company would claim to know more about what the customer wanted than the consumer. Because this provincial approach to consumer wants was largely guesswork, the commonsense approach was to ask the consumer directly how he or she defined value. Drucker advised that it made little difference whether the product was a simple bar of soap, a complicated turbine, or a sophisticated piece of software; managers should stop trying to educate consumers. They should interview them to determine how they define satisfaction and value.

The Utility Function. According to Drucker, every product is a worthless combination of physical properties and every service a hollow claim of meaningless rhetoric until a customer makes a purchase. "The business enterprise produces neither things nor ideas but humanly determined values. The most beautifully designed machine is still only so much scrap metal until it has utility for a customer."[23] His analysis of the marketing concept reveals a particularly interesting insight, namely, that the perspectives of the producer and the consumer vary substantively. And what the former thinks is of secondary importance because "no customer ever perceives himself as buying what the producer or supplier delivers."[24] That is, the customer never buys a product, he or she purchases a satisfaction. In short, what matters is not what the producer puts in, it is what the customer gets out of the product or service.

Drucker further argued that quality was not what was difficult to make; failure to provide it was simply incompetence. But utility was what the customer was willing to pay for. Being technology driven, for example, was not the real test of a product. It not only had to work but had to work economically.

The Distinction Between Sales and Marketing. A pervasive theme in Drucker's marketing writings was that it is a mistake to equate selling and marketing. One of the strengths of the marketing concept was that it helped to expose this delusion. The attitude of U.S. businessmen, for example, might be that "the sales department will sell whatever the plant produces." The marketing concept, in contrast, emphasized producing what the market needed.[25]

In clarifying the difference between the components of marketing and selling, Drucker offered the hypothesis that in the event that marketing were done perfectly then selling would become redundant: "Indeed, selling and marketing are antithetical rather than synonymous or even complementary. There will always, one can assume, be need for some selling. But the aim of marketing is to make selling superfluous. The aim of marketing is to know and understand the customer so well that the product or service fits him and sells itself. Ideally, marketing should result in a customer who is ready to buy. All that should be needed then is to make the product or service available, i.e., logistics rather than salesmanship, and statistical distribution rather than promotion."[26]

Drucker had mixed feelings about the contribution of the sales function in the business. He looked, for example, upon advertising as a form of pre-selling, which, if done perfectly, would leave no need for salespeople. Of course, except in the minds of Madison Avenue pundits, it was never done ideally; that was why a nucleus of a salesforce was always necessary. In recognizing the reality of the need for a salesforce, he insisted, however, that it should be productive but small. He likened this small cadre of brilliant performers to the medieval knights who fearlessly set out to slay dragons in mortal combat. Similarly, a chief characteristic of excellent salespeople is their passionate confidence that they will make a sale. Believing that great salespeople are born rather than made, he declared: "Most sales training is totally unjustified. At best it makes an incompetent salesman out of a moron."[27]

If a salesforce is a requirement for a business, it should be one of quality and not quantity. Because maintaining a salesforce is a highly expensive use of resources, the focus should be on star performers who attain outstanding results. It was a constant puzzle to Drucker why companies budgeted such vast sums on sales education without any discernible results. Except for providing individuals with a sense of pride and confidence in the product, it seemed to him a waste of time, money, and effort. He remarked, "There are great differences in selling ability between salesmen which no amount of training seems to be able to overcome, or even significantly to narrow."[28] There is little evidence that sales training improves productivity other than giving the salesman confidence in the product.

Drucker also had misgivings about the computer as a tool for improved sales performance. Too frequently it seemed a distraction that prevented salespeople from doing what they were paid for: "In the department store they now spend so much time serving the computer that they have little time serving the customer."[29] It is noteworthy that with the technological advances of the information revolution, Drucker's contentious point of the marginal impact of selling on productivity has been further confirmed: "For traditional merchants, service means salespeople who personally take care of an individual customer. But the new retailers employ very few salespeople. Service to them means that customers do not need a salesperson, do not have to spend time trying to find one, do not have to ask, do not have to wait. It means that the customers know where goods are the moment they enter the store, in what colors and sizes, and at what price. It means providing information. But service for the new retailers also means getting customers out of the store as fast as possible."[30]

The Systems Approach. One of the beneficial insights of the marketing concept has been that it is the one function that transcends other business functions. Because Drucker found that there were "no departmental customers," marketing became the corporate catalyst that integrates all comparative strengths and core competencies in the pursuit of results.

Viewing marketing from the systems angle of vision makes it impossible to perceive it as an independent function. Marketing is so basic that it cannot be considered a separate function. It is the whole business seen from the point of view of its final result, that is, from the customer's point of view. Because marketing is result and not cost oriented, Drucker designated it as the one business function that is the direct concern of all employees and most especially those workers who have direct contact with the customer.

Drucker visualized that the holistic approach of the marketing concept could provide a conceptual understanding of the customer for everybody in the organization, regardless of his or her discipline. This would be especially true when the company's philosophy of marketing became synonymous with the firm's identity. In effect, this competency concept could serve as a cynosure for results. Amplifying this point, Drucker offered these illustrations. Sony's focus was a concerted concentration on the miniaturization of its product line. Gillette built its business strategy around the premise that "the customer buys a shave and not a thing." Herman Miller billed for office furniture but sold productivity and work atmosphere. JCPenney developed programs and policies for monitoring and measuring the results of shelf space. Johnson & Johnson learned skills for servicing mothers, nurses, and doctors with short-term disposal pharmaceutical products. Boeing overcame intractable engineering problems of tremendous complexity through team-based management. Stew Leonard's offered a variety of entertainment and day-care activities to sell its dairy and grocery products. Home Depot trained its employees to provide home repair solutions for its customers. Merck educated its salesforce to provide doctors with the contents and dosages of its drugs. Melville Shoes captured the demographic reality of the youth market by satisfying adolescents' demand for style. Intel proclaimed a concentrated commitment to obsoleting one generation of computer chips in order to innovate a radically different generation.

The list represented only a sample of the ways excellent companies focus on at least one marketing knowledge excellence. Of course it is possible to have two or three core competencies, as long as the real purpose of unique excellencies is not public relations rhetoric or *feel good* intentions but the finding of a path to customer satisfaction. Drucker proposed two major steps for identifying core competencies. First, make a list of customer purchasing patterns and unmet needs. Second, select the areas of strength that customers consider most critical in their purchasing decision.

The Demand Factor. According to Drucker's version of economic theory, a market is created by demand, which in turn determines the opportunities, needs, and other characteristics of a particular industry. He noted, however, that this essential factor of marketing is often misunderstood by management. The fact that markets are not natural phenomena supplied one reason for the miscomprehension of demand: "Markets are not created by God, nature, or economic forces but by businessmen."[31]

Drucker criticized businessmen for failing to grasp the scope of demand and focusing only on "our customers." He thought this a gross mistake because even firms that have leadership positions in their industry rarely have a genuine majority market share. Consequently, he suggested, the great reservoir of potential demand lies in the category of noncustomers. In short, even the most dominant market leader in an industry knows that a greater number of people are buying elsewhere than are buying from the dominant firm—these are potential new customers.

Drucker specifically singled out the U.S. department store for its failure to broaden its horizon by going beyond the satisfaction of its original customer base. It had done an excellent job of market research by collecting data on its current consumers but had neglected to visualize those who did not shop in department stores. Lacking this information, these stores could not identify growth opportunities. Explaining in part the crisis of the department stores, he pointed out that "their noncustomers were increasingly the young, affluent, double earner family who were the growth market of the 1980s."[32] Drucker concluded that this failure to research the noncustomer spectrum of marketing was a major gap between theory and practice.

The consumer movement provides an interesting innovative insight in Drucker's analysis of the marketing concept. Considering it a threat to the enterprise system, management, however, viewed it with fear and hostility. Drucker thought that corporate management, as the leader of the dominant economic institution in a diverse pluralistic society, would be mistaken to reject unfriendly criticisms from other societal associations. He argued, "We have an interest in maintaining this freedom, and therefore, we have an interest in a strong and active consumer movement. Don't make the mistake of thinking this is an enemy."[33] Attacking Ralph Nader as an intractable populist and an uncompromising ideologue missed the point of the movement. Management failed to recognize that Nader, as the father of the consumer movement, was not simply an angry crackpot but the pioneer of a new social force. Moreover,

Drucker argued that Nader's criticism of modern marketing should be converted into an opportunity, because he was actually doing the best market research in the country.[34]

Arnold Corbin, former professor of marketing at New York University, was the first to recognize the insight in Drucker's demonstration of the importance of marketing to entrepreneurship. Quoting Drucker's "marketing is innovation,"[35] he emphasized that businessmen would have to expand the traditional marketing concept by practicing this innovative marketing. The main message of innovative marketing is to remember that the customer has absolutely no interest in business profits nor in how hard managers work. The only consumer concern is this: What are you going to do for me as an encore? This topic will be covered further in the discussion of transitional and transformational strategies in Chapters Ten and Eleven.

CHAPTER NINE

INVESTING IN CHANGE

Singling out people and capital as the only two intrinsic corporate assets, Drucker emphasized that management's main task, and what it was actually paid for, was to make these basic resources productive in creating economic results. And he made this broad distinction between managing people and capital. In the case of people, the focus is on development that encourages them to work smarter. In the case of capital, which is dumb and stupid, with no objections to working overtime, the task is to exploit it by making it work harder.[1] People are discussed in Part Three, "On Executive Effectiveness," while this chapter concentrates on what is also the second dimension of the entrepreneurial approach to improving the effectiveness of the existing business: managing capital assets. This chapter also discusses the third element in the entrepreneurial approach, systematic abandonment.

Management of Capital Assets

Karl Marx was credited by Drucker with being the first economist to recognize the deleterious impact on an economy when capital ceases to be productive. Marx predicted an inevitable demise for the capitalist system because he assumed that capitalism was incapable of renewing its resources. Drucker acknowledged the originality of Marx's insight about the productivity of capital, but faulted him on his prognostication that it was incapable of improved productivity.

Although Drucker rejected Marx's interpretation, he thought it a useful frame of reference for analyzing the wealth-producing vitality of the corporation. In order to avoid the disease of economic anemia and corporate stagnation, management must recognize that no company can survive if the productivity of capital goes down.[2] He noted that the bourgeois system defied the predicted collapse largely because Marx was unable to foresee certain events such as entrepreneurial and innovative achievements, technological breakthroughs, Frederick Taylor's studies on worker productivity, the rise of professional management as a discipline, and the rejection by labor of revolutionary consciousness in favor of union membership.

Drucker advanced the principle that the ability to manage money productively was a key entrepreneurial task for today's business. He noted that competent corporate financial managers were able to get improved productivity of capital by applying a number of tested techniques, and he mentioned General Electric in the 1980s as one example of a firm having several times the productivity of capital as its competitor (in GE's case, Westinghouse). Cryptically commenting that this gap was too big to be a statistical error, he reported that mediocre firms actually worked harder in exploiting their physical and capital assets, but they worked on the wrong things.[3] What particularly astonished Drucker about this performance gap between excellent and marginal companies was that the same theoretical knowledge about revenue management was available to all but that too few executives perceived it as an opportunity for improvement.

Guidelines for Wealth Creation

Looking at excellent companies on the premise that it is possible to learn from them, Drucker concluded their one common denominator was the focus on results in improving financial assets. Always paying attention to qualitative performance, excellent companies were not deluded by quantitative gymnastics and misdirected activities. For example, no matter how cheap and efficient an effort, it is waste rather than cost if it is devoid of results. Drucker suggested four guidelines, or prescriptions, for wealth creation: (1) define investment, (2) evaluate cost of capital, (3) analyze aggregates versus components, and (4) engage in transactional analysis.

Define Investment. Because Drucker objected to using a single standardized benchmark, such as return on equity or percentage of sales, to capture the productivity of capital, he advised a more comprehensive financial strategy, starting with a clear understanding of the firm's investment pattern.[4]

As a substitute for being fascinated by some single magic figure of measurement, Drucker indicated that the firm needs to address two fundamental questions: How is investment defined? and, Where is the money and what does it do? He postulated that in a competitive environment the cost of labor would be roughly similar throughout an industry, allowing for little financial advantage. Therefore the investment pattern was determined by the type of industry in which the firm was engaged. To illustrate, the dominant segment of investment allocation in manufacturing was physical machinery, in retailing it was store and shelf space, for banks and brokerage houses it was office and high-tech equipment, and for businesses with very small fixed capital assets it was receivables. Although these were the key industrial and commercial components, Drucker stated it was also necessary to include the productivity of the total business investment, regardless of the origin of that capital. Again criticizing any popular narrow measurement, he said: "The conventional *earnings per share* figure not only doesn't measure corporate performance but it rarely measures true *earnings per share*. The term is a misnomer. What it really represents is *taxable earnings*."[5]

Drucker's assessment of the total investment picture included, in addition to money, the productivity factors of people, physical resources, and innovative efforts. In short, the appropriate yardstick was a return on all employed capital assets. Most important, he noted that capital per se was basically sterile and frequently a liability. He never considered it a substitute for thinking! For example, it was not money that produced results. It was the hard work of dedicated people who would also be in short supply.[6]

Define Cost of Capital. According to Drucker, "The minimum cost of staying in business . . . is the cost of capital."[7] Amplifying this principle he stated that any rate of profit that failed to equal the cost of capital was not wealth at all, it was a loss to both the company and the national economy.[8] In analyzing the financing of a corporation's future growth, Drucker divided the cost of capital into three overlapping segments: (1) the interest rate cost of capital, (2) the cost of current operational activities, and (3) the capital needs of the future.

Contending that management, in order to assure survival and healthy growth, had to focus on return of all assets employed and had to account for future costs, Drucker asserted that the proper question for any business was not, " 'What is the maximum profit this business can yield?' It is: 'What is the minimum profitability needed to cover future risks of this business?' "[9] The need to consider the relevance of the future to the cost of capital compelled him to reiterate his objection to the Wall Street guideline of earnings per share: "the stock market increasingly values companies according to their liquidity rather than by their earnings."[10] In short, Drucker did not view liquidity by itself as a corporate objective but as a restraint.

To illustrate the meaning of the cost of capital, Drucker used a basic formula found in any standard economics textbook: Earnings = Margin × Turnover. If a company's margin, for a simple example, was 6 percent and the money turned over once a year, then the resulting profit was 6 percent. Ideally, if margin (income divided by sales) and turnover (sales divided by net operating income) were simultaneously increased, then the company was in an enviable financial position. However, in a fiercely competitive environment, working on improved margin presented major competitive difficulties. The same was not true of working on turnover of capital (increasing the accumulation on each trip of the dollar) for money, receivables, and product line. Drucker indicated that by using tested techniques of revenue management, it was possible to increase turnover by 20 percent, thereby increasing the profit picture from 6 to 7.2 percent in his theoretical example.[11]

Analyze Aggregates Versus Components. Invoking the theoretical validity of the Earnings = Margin × Turnover formula was one thing, but it did not address the implementation of techniques for obtaining increased productivity from capital and other corporate assets. One reason for this failure was the inadequacy of the accounting model to properly process relevant information. Drucker particularly criticized the traditional cost accounting model for being past oriented, focusing on yesterday's costs rather than entrepreneurial opportunities, favoring overhead at the expense of utility, visualizing the business from a "fire sale" rather than an information system vantage point, and treating the budget process as a methodology of spending plans, or money allocation, while keeping silent on the results expected from the money.

Particularly confusing to Drucker was that the cost accounting model focused exclusively on the visible factors of production (land, labor, and capital) and was silent on the corporation's invisible but dominant resource—knowledge, or mental capital. It also astonished him, therefore, that the most highly trained and educated employees were allocated to efforts that produced the least results and were viewed as expenses rather than assets. Drucker described a condition in which accountants provided management with detailed data on the aggregate cost of knowledge work but were unable to evaluate individual knowledge elements and to measure specific results. As a result, he estimated that almost 75 percent of a firm's expensive knowledge resource was neither identified nor controlled.

Drucker's experience as a financial analyst in London before World War I taught him to beware of the precise figures of accountants and of statistics in general. Such numbers were particularly invalid when they were based on misleading assumptions. Echoing the common bromide that what accountants do not understand they label miscellaneous, he chided any reliance on the numerical exactitude of statistics: "no one has ever failed to find the facts he is looking for. Good statisticians know this and distrust all figures—they either know the fellow who found them or they do not know him; in either case they are suspicious."[12] To cite one example, as early as 1964, in *Managing for Results*, Drucker argued that the traditional method of figuring costs per unit for a product was bound to provide the wrong quantitative conclusions. He advised substituting for it the proposition that "*cost* should be defined as what the customer pays to obtain certain goods or services and to derive full utility from them."[13] At the very least, this had the advantage of demonstrating that costs included external distribution factors as well as internal productivity elements.

Drucker also bordered on the paranoid, however, when it came to the traditional cost accounting treatment of aggregate statistics. He felt that most of the distorted impressions and misguided conclusions in standardized accounting and comprehensive statistical reports were the result of misinterpreting figures in the form of the combined whole or a collection of particulars. For example, the aggregate inclusion of countless production line items in a report revealed little and explained less about the contribution to results from each individual unit. The same might be said with respect to a general review of the performing and nonperforming sectors in branch banking or in a supermarket or department store chain.

In attempting to make informational sense of the relationship between the whole and the parts, Drucker adopted a philosophical approach. He cited Plato's doctrine of the universal as one key to understanding knowledge. In his treatment of business activities, he used an aggregate as the starting point for his statistical analysis, but he found it had limitations when he needed to probe beyond the surface of a financial investment pattern. He used specific terms within aggregates and components to describe the relationship between the whole and the parts. In explaining the former usage, which determines how one looks at things, he wrote: " 'Aggregates,' to use the terms of the psychologist, are 'configurations.' Their reality is in the eye of the beholder. They depend not on definition but on perception."[14] If an analysis is anchored to the aggregate figures, however, the pattern becomes cloudy and loses its relevance. In short, if it tries to explain everything, it explains nothing. Drucker granted that one has to start an analysis with the aggregate figure, but he added, "one cannot manage an aggregate. One always has to manage—and therefore to measure first—major components separately."[15]

The restricted value of Plato's concept of the universal directed Drucker toward Aristotle's method of knowledge, understanding through particulars. This focus on components enabled the practitioner to identify the costs and contributions of parts of the whole in order to obtain a truer picture of the corporation's financial investment pattern. As opposed to the abstract aggregate, Drucker wanted to convey the message that components were concrete realities, capable of being organized for results or the lack of them. In order to fulfill this goal, he introduced the technique of *transactional analysis.*

Engage in Transactional Analysis. Drucker looked upon the pattern of business transactions as the final clue for improving asset productivity in the existing business. Transactional analysis typically revealed a business profile in which a small minority of products contributed the bulk of the revenue and a vast majority of products accounted for the dominant share of costs. "Most large companies typically end up with thousands of items in their product line—and all too frequently fewer than 20 really *sell*. However, these 20 items or less contribute revenues to carry the costs of the 9,999 non-sellers."[16]

Critical to understanding the format of transactional analysis is the proposition that a business has two basic financial flows—a cost stream and a revenue stream. Drucker expressed the relationship between these two streams with the following formula: revenue is roughly proportionate to volume, and cost is roughly proportionate to the number of transactions minus the fixed physical and raw material costs.[17] As a case in point he used this example: "$1 million in volume produced in one order—or in one product—carries the same cost as $1 million in volume produced by 1 million individual orders or by 50 different production runs."[18] Translated into layman's terms, the hypothesis behind this example of the interrelationship between the two business streams is that it costs approximately the same (minus fixed costs such as plant, advertising, clerical and office equipment) to obtain a large million-dollar order as it does to secure a small thousand-dollar one. Drucker considered it intolerable that so many managers were ignorant of how some of the key business segments and products contributed to total revenue results, and were unaware of the cost burdens of those parts of the business that were making little or no contribution to results. The implication of his findings was that the business should devote increased resources to the segments producing the greater revenue.

An examination of individual customer revenue flows in supermarket retailing offered another illustration of transactional analysis. The reasoning was that it cost the store approximately the same amount in support expenses to service a one-hundred-dollar-weekly customer as it did to service a ten-dollar account. The annual contribution to the revenue stream, however, from the one-hundred-dollar customer was over five thousand dollars as compared to five hundred dollars from the ten-dollar-weekly customer. And for each family spending two hundred to three hundred dollars on a weekly basis, a small segment of select customers, the supermarket received an annual revenue of ten thousand to fifteen thousand dollars.

Of course, Drucker was not suggesting that merchants ignore their smaller spending customers. The strategic goal was to raise their level of spending by providing good service for the store's customers. He was, however, indicating that the vending machine mentality of supermarket managers obscured the reality of separate cost and revenue streams. Also, because these managers rarely knew their big-ticket customers personally, it was impossible for them to attend particularly to key contributors to the revenue stream. In an atmosphere in which the store manager was usually invisible, there was a tendency to see all customers alike. Not only did this blind the manager to opportunities to give added value to a key customer, but it risked the possible loss of a major customer through employee discourtesy or some other failed activity that might cost the store thousands in annual revenue. Drucker thought it inexcusable that corporate financial managers were not educating their operating employees on the transactional formula so that with this knowledge they could assume responsibility for improved capital performance in the existing business: "It is high time that American business managers, in the great majority, learn and accept that managements are paid for managing productivity, especially the productivity of capital, on which, in the last analysis, all other productivities depend; that the productivity of capital can be managed, and that the productivity of capital *must* be managed."[19]

The cost-revenue stream of transactional analysis displayed an affinity to Pareto's law of social distribution: the statistical probability that a "vital few components" contribute substantially more to results than the "trivial many," which produce the bulk of the costs: "While 90 per cent of the results are being produced by the first 10 per cent of events, 90 per cent of the costs are incurred by the remaining and resultless 90 per cent of events."[20]

Essentially Drucker viewed Pareto's principle of probability as a statistical reinforcement, supplementing transactional analysis for improving the allocation of resources. He also considered it a reminder to accountants that it was a myth if they thought the auditing process offered 100 percent control of costs. With this in mind, it was feasible to apply transactional analysis as a managerial tool.[21]

In addition, Drucker saw transactional analysis as a way to improve resource allocation in such segments of business turnover as receivables, inventory control, use of shelf space per unit of time, and salesforce performance, to cite a few applications.

In the case of receivables, or the credit given to the firm's customers, Drucker did not see receivables exclusively as a financial tool that stressed low monetary loss as its key measurement. Emphasizing that the typical firm, a manufacturing business for example, was not in the banking business, he said receivables should be made to earn their keep. He raised the issue of credit policy purpose and concluded a business should not be financing the customers who provide it with the least revenue. In short, receivables should be viewed as a marketing tool to improve sales from key customers, to attract new customers, and to stimulate the introduction of innovative products.

With respect to inventory control, Drucker perceived in many instances an inflated warehouse system with excessive handling. He visualized the relocation or abandonment of existing locations as a relatively simple example of making capital work harder and support a larger volume of sales.

Drucker considered the movement of goods on the shelf over unit of time as perhaps the most reliable measurement of successful retailing. Through the technique of transactional analysis, it was possible to trace precisely what each product was contributing in revenue to economic results. For those products that were only performing marginally, management had to decide whether to continue to devote resources to them or abandon them. Drucker considered the former course of resuscitation an exercise in futility that defied the laws of probability.

As noted earlier, Drucker had serious doubts about the efficacy of sales training. He thought the time and cost too big a price to pay for instilling, at best, product confidence in salespeople. He also hypothesized that there were great and substantive differences in the selling ability of the individuals in a salesforce that no amount of training could overcome or significantly narrow. Applying transactional analysis and the Pareto formula, he found that frequently 10 percent of a salesforce produced 90 percent of the results. His observations also revealed that the single most critical resource of a salesperson was time, yet his studies convinced him that most of a salesperson's time was allocated to nonselling activities. It followed logically, he thought, that if the number of sales calls was increased, there would be concomitant improvement for both mediocre and star performers in the salesforce. In short, he urged that all nonselling activities (training, paperwork, mindless travel, meetings) be removed from the routine of the salesforce, so that these sales professionals could do more effectively what they were being paid for in the first place.

Drucker also visualized applying the techniques of transactional analysis to increase results in a broad array of business activities, such as reducing defects in the manufacturing process, improving the handling of telephone calls to avoid wasting time, reducing employee absenteeism and alcoholism, making suggestion systems functional, and evaluating research and development projects. Of course Drucker did not see probability analyses and financial tools as physical laws with absolute verity. These techniques would, however, enable management to understand the pattern of results versus nonresults arising from their management of assets in the existing business.

The Challenge of Activity Accounting

Drucker was a long-term proponent of activity accounting as a viable methodology for ameliorating the vulnerabilities of standardized cost accounting. Two prominent scholars of the discipline, Robert Kaplan and H. Thomas Johnson, credited him in 1983 for his pioneering contribution of transactional analysis almost thirty years earlier in *Managing for Results*. They lauded as one of the key building blocks in the field of activity accounting his ability to dissect the dangers of the traditional cost system that failed to trace accurately the costs of the individual products in a company's line. They wrote that Drucker's was a "brilliant insight" that was "extraordinarily prescient."[22]

Over the years Drucker praised the efforts of scholars who introduced new tools and techniques for solidifying the foundations of activity accounting. Nevertheless, he thought that these contributions were inadequate in meeting the overall needs for improved measurement of assets—a condition of "unaccountable accounting" still prevailed. He felt activity accounting failed to meet the dynamic demands of entrepreneurship for two major reasons.

First, as an informational tool, it continued to conceal the crucial data needed by corporate management for making innovative decisions. He likened the present costing system to a sundial, which tells the time only when the sun is out, because it correctly reported the visible but failed to reveal crucial covert costs and unseen opportunities.

Drucker turned to a medical metaphor to amplify the distinction between two categories of information. The first was the abundance of data accumulated from routine examinations. The second was the paucity of information emanating from perceptual diagnosis. On the first level, for example, were the basic tests (measuring blood pressure, weight, pulse, and temperature and taking X rays, and so forth) that were indispensable for detecting physical abnormalities. But there were no simple testing techniques for making a diagnosis of Parkinson's or of cardiac diseases. Drucker likened the routine physical readings to a "foundation of information," implying they were similar to the data of standardized cost accounting. He included in this category such quantitative accounting techniques as cash flow reports, profit-and-loss statements, budgetary projections, and cost allocations, adding recently that with the proper software these were easily attainable with a laptop computer. All this information was indispensable, but what troubled Drucker was the entrepreneurial information that management was not getting, particularly with regard to such intangibles as corporate vulnerabilities, innovative opportunities, and the identification of crucial external trends.

The second reason activity accounting failed to meet the dynamic demands of entrepreneurship was that the activity accounting model was structurally restrictive because of its obsessive efforts to control malfeasance, fraud, and deception. Drucker was uncomfortable with this obsession because it engendered an atmosphere of distrust and suspicion that percolated throughout the organization's corporate culture. Drucker conceded the requirement for this "policeman" role, but when that role was given such exclusive priority, it hampered the free flow of information so crucial in the management of change.[23]

Without claiming any intellectual authority to provide a solution to the protracted problems of activity accounting, Drucker nevertheless felt it was important to understand the dilemmas and complexities of the accounting challenge, and the accompanying box outlines some of his specific suggestions. Drucker realized that these specifications would give new meaning to the discipline of accounting. He also recognized that assessment of organizational issues defied numerical precision. Because he was trying to escape pseudo-exactitude, this lack of precision was not too troublesome to him. In fact, for certain types of measurement, he was satisfied if the statistics were "more or less" valid.

Reasserting that incremental analysis was cosmetic and assuming the role of a management strategist rather than a professional specialist in accounting, Drucker proposed the following specific actions and guidelines for a better comprehension of the realities of the accounting challenge:

- Accept the economic shift from making and moving things to formulating ideas and concepts as the dominant business condition.

- Estimate the assets required to attain a leadership position in one's industry.

- Provide in the budgetary process a way to ascertain the segments in the business that performed better than expected.

- Prepare two separate budgets: a detailed one consisting of expenses and a concise one focusing on opportunities.

- Evaluate the quantitative and qualitative costs of "not doing" (the costliest corporate waste) throughout the operations in the organization.

- Focus on results based on an understanding of the relationship between the revenue and the cost streams of the business.

- Calculate the cost of knowledge and service workers and their contribution to performance.

- Measure the costs of the entire system based on what the customer pays.

- Identify the key areas of investment, and measure results for specific business segments.

- Assess appropriate information on trends affecting the survival of the corporation and the costs involved in converting them into opportunities.

COMPASS BOOKS
S.F. INTERNATIONAL AIRPORT
NORTH TERMINAL
(650) 244-0616

170566 Reg 3 ID 19 9:08 pm 06/25/02

```
S PETER DRUCKER SHA   1 @ 18.00    18.00
SUBTOTAL                           18.00
SALES TAX - 8.25%                   1.49
TOTAL                              19.49
VISA PAYMENT                       19.49
Account# XXXXXXXXXXXX3904 Exp Date 1103
Authorization# 025936      Clerk 19
```

I agree to pay the above total amount
according to the card issuer agreement.

Thank you for shopping at Compass Books
OPEN EVERY DAY 5:30am to 10:00pm
Returns with receipt within 14 days

Perhaps the biggest obstacle to combining rigorous numerical analysis with a diagnosis of the perceived configurations of corporate strategy was the corporation's lack of a purpose containing a coherent philosophy. Moreover, no such systematic methodology was possible until there was some integration, or at least compatibility, between two distinct disciplines—financial accounting and a computer science that applied the techniques of data processing in a meaningful manner in executive decision making. Drucker predicted that in the future, corporate accounting departments would have to adjust their traditional attitudes of strict control and instead adopt policies conducive to a freer flow of relevant information. As for computer science departments, in the future they would be likely to remain cost centers, rather than become the result centers they could be.[24]

Drucker reasoned that the most appropriate place for the start of a merger of the two disciplines was in the academic curriculum. He was far from optimistic about the realization of such a structural and intellectual innovation in the immediate future. Nevertheless he did see one ray of hope for a genuine system of activity accounting. Because the right questions were being raised, progress would inevitably emerge, even though it was likely to be at a snail's pace. "It may take many years, decades perhaps, until we have the measurements we need in all these areas. But at least we know now that we need new measurements, and we know what they have to be. Slowly, and still gropingly, we are moving from counting to measuring."[25]

Systematic Abandonment

If the effective management of capital resources was the first test for improving corporate productivity, systematic abandonment was his first law of implementation. It was the central trend in the fabric for the improved allocation of capital resources in the existing business. He considered the one great advantage of an entrepreneurial economy its capacity for eliminating its mistakes through the market mechanism: "The failures . . . rarely are a real problem as they tend to liquidate themselves."[26]

According to Drucker the market is an infallible criterion for abandonment. If the customer does not buy the product, it is discarded. Despite this truism of economic theory, the market is less than omnipotent when applied to normal business operations. Because of institutional inertia, most organizations are encumbered with yesterday's promises, overburdened with a superabundance of superfluous activities, cluttered with redundant products, saturated with a surplus of outdated suppliers, saddled with swollen inventories, and smothered with needless levels of bureaucracy. In short, in the usual state of affairs, the typical company has a plethora of activities that contribute nothing to the customer or the business.

Drucker observed that as long as activities produce results a company cannot have enough of them. These positive assets need constant nourishment, but for the misallocated resources, probably incapable of renewal, a policy of systematic abandonment is required. Failure to develop a strategy for managing change effectively will mean that executives will be overwhelmed by external events and will choke from the pressure of internal stagnancy. To illuminate the need for an organized process of elimination, he applied a biological metaphor. "If you stop feeding the cow she stops giving milk. In old age she eats forty pounds of hay but doesn't give any milk."[27] For Drucker, systematic abandonment was a dogmatic principle involving economic and moral imperatives in the management of change. In emphasizing this principle, he asserted: "There is only one way to make innovation attractive to managers: a systematic policy of abandoning whatever is outworn, obsolete, no longer productive, as well as the mistakes, failures, and misdirections of effort."[28]

Viewing abandonment as the indispensable key to managing change, Drucker deemed it a futile exercise to resurrect marginal products and a sin to defend the unproductive products of yesterday. He insisted, therefore, that new investment is not the starting point of entrepreneurial activity; it is the elimination of nonproductive activities in the existing business. The starting point in a growth strategy is not to decide on how and where to grow but how to decide on what to abandon. "The first step in planning is to ask of any activity, any product, any process or market, *If we were not committed to this today would we go into it?*"[29]

Conducting a strategy of investing only in new products is often taken to imply that today's business is being run competently; Drucker disagreed, insisting that all the evidence pointed to a rampant misallocation of resources. Because all activities tend to outlive their usefulness, he questioned everything done today. "In the knowledge society, management must prepare to abandon everything they know."[30]

Drucker did not limit the principle of systematic abandonment to products and services; he stated that the principle of inevitable obsolescence also applied to a company's mission. He also hinted that it was only the most exceptional institutions that were capable of reinventing themselves by diagnosing their identity: "They accept that a theory's obsolescence is a degenerative and, indeed, life-threatening disease. And they know and accept the surgeon's time-tested principle, the oldest principle of effective decision making: A degenerative disease will not be cured by procrastination. It requires decisive action."[31]

Entrenched Opposition

Systematic abandonment of nonperforming activities contained such an irrefutable logic that it appeared incongruous for anyone to oppose its prescription for implementation. Drucker observed, however, that the realities of executive work and managerial frailties made the proposition of abandonment less simplistic and more sobering (see the accompanying box). It is very hard to stop doing the unproductive.

Among the organizational foes of abandonment, Drucker mentioned the following:

- The passion to rescue those products that are getting old and getting into trouble

- The proclivity to do effectively what should not be done at all

- The support of things that were not worth doing in the first place

- The failure to recognize that there is nothing worse than doing the wrong thing well

- The tendency to believe that everything will succeed (nobody wants to admit failure)

- The propensity of functional specialists to take a one-dimensional view of the business and to protect activities related to their function

---

According to Drucker, all these resistance arguments were human rationalizations for postponing the inevitable or excuses for doing nothing. Once managers adopted a formal policy of systematic abandonment that aimed at performance, however, then much of the former resistance to change evaporated.

Then people wondered why the support of the status quo had been pursued so tenaciously. "Abandoning anything is thus difficult—but only for a fairly short spell. Six months after such efforts have been abandoned, everybody wonders: *Why did it take us so long?*"[32]

Responses

Drucker argued that given the aforementioned obstacles to managing change effectively, it was a delusion to imagine that there was a magic wand for eliminating the unproductive. Although the concept of systematic abandonment was a simple idea, implementing it was another matter. Ruling out any reflex action response to a set of formulas, Drucker saw such implementation as a conscious commitment to diligent work. The aspect of responsibility in this view also ruled out the use of clever fads and gimmicks. In essence, the focus on improved productivity should not be on doing the dramatic elegantly but on doing the routine effectively.

Drucker used two main methodologies for diagnosis and removal of those things that were no longer productive—transactional analysis and the Bernoulli theorem. As discussed earlier, transactional analysis treated the relationship between the corporation's cost and revenue streams. The prime purpose of this diagnostic technique was to identify marginally successful products and outright clinkers. Drucker claimed that these were candidates for immediate extinction because regardless of the time, effort, and money invested in them, they were usually fortunate if they broke even.

Drucker believed a focus on results enabled the corporation to avert the arguments of functional specialists to retain unproductive products and services. For example, despite the hard evidence and commonsense conclusions provided by transactional analysis that nonperforming products required immediate elimination, specialists would offer rationales for retention. In practice, financial people would claim the product absorbed overhead, the salesforce would scream that a full product line was needed, engineers would argue that quality had been sacrificed, and finally, everyone involved in the creation of the product would feel that his managerial ego had been assaulted. Instead of recognizing the need for economic euthanasia, all these functional parties enter a common plea in the defense of yesterday, hoping to postpone abandonment until another fruitless study is conducted.

Drucker asserted that further study to revive a marginal product was an exercise in futility, and he offered the Bernoulli theorem, a principle of statistical probability, to support his contention. It stated that in any series of endeavors, the chances of succeeding were reduced 50 percent with each new effort. In practice, therefore, the better part of wisdom was to make one or two major undertakings and, if results were not forthcoming, drop the project. Drucker admitted that there were rare exceptions to the Bernoulli theorem, such as the mathematical probability of breaking the bank at a Las Vegas casino. In business, however, he pointed out that it was highly improbable one would have a best-seller after six months of exposure or that a supermarket product that did not sell in six months would ever become an outstanding performer.

Actually Drucker looked upon the Bernoulli theorem as the equivalent of the credo of a good medical diagnostician. For example, if things do not turn out as expected, the good diagnostician does not redouble initial efforts nor question results. "A good diagnostician thinks through what he expects to happen, he goes back and starts from scratch. He does not wait for his original diagnosis to be confirmed. He begins with his second diagnosis immediately. He does not argue with results."[33]

The major implication of diagnostic tools like the Bernoulli theorem is the entrepreneurial maxim that it is folly for managers to fight probability on those things that do not turn out or are unlikely to succeed as expected. In stressing the advantage of having probability work for them, managers have a confirmation that abandonment comes first or else nothing gets accomplished. It also enables them to dismiss the false compromises offered when functional specialists argue that a project is worth "one more try."

Drucker was careful in applying the principle of systematic abandonment to people. A policy of ruthless downsizing might be good for the bottom line, but he thought it doubtful that the emphasis on financial "quarteritis" was good for society. It violated standards of conscience, disavowed the moral contract with employees, and created a corporate culture of fear and trembling. He thought that it was an act of obscenity for top managements to downsize mindlessly while rewarding themselves with salary raises, bonuses, and stock options. He reminded executives that "in many if not most cases, downsizing has turned out to be something that surgeons for centuries have warned against: 'amputation before diagnosis.' The result is always a casualty."[34]

He did not, however, completely rule out using the Bernoulli theorem as a principle of abandonment in the staffing of a specific position. For example, he thought it justified in those instances where a series of competent individuals had failed in a given job. To continue to appoint more able people to the job was an invitation to future failures. He advised that the most sensible thing to do was to redesign the position so that it allowed for performance.

In addition to the diagnostic tools of transactional analysis and the Bernoulli theorem, Drucker suggested a number of questions and recommendations for implementing systematic abandonment (see the accompanying box). In his recommendations, Drucker often provided concrete examples of systematic abandonment. And he also reminded executives that aphorisms might illuminate but they do not implement. At the base of successful execution is the emotional anguish of wrestling with the basic abandonment decision. These decisions have one great common denominator: they all entail pain and risk. Finally, they all call for commitment and courage, but the executive job is no sinecure. These are the tasks that managers are paid for.[35]

Here is a two-part agenda for substituting fat for muscle in the organizational culture. The first part consists of questions. The second part offers actions.

- What are the things that did not turn out successfully?

- Would I undertake the project today if I were not already involved in it?

- What risk would I take if I did nothing at all?

- Am I a victim of the delusion that those things that have always failed will eventually succeed?

- Have I recognized that in-house support and service activities are de facto monopolies?

- Am I aware that doing things that one does not understand paradoxically contributes to their continuance?

- Am I excessively worried about what will happen tomorrow instead of being concerned with what was spoiled yesterday?

- Am I putting in dollar time on penny jobs that should not be done at all?

- Weed out the product garden; it's as important for the business as it is for the farm.

- Don't defend the things that are not worth doing.

- Before engaging in a new venture consider dropping an old one.

- Admit that the things you are postponing you are actually abandoning.

- Divest as many as possible of the nonperforming support assets that are remote from the company's basic strengths and core competencies.

- Avoid any proclivity to allocate good people and resources to the old.

- If you have to support a marginal product, make sure additional resources are not poured into it.

- Every three years question the company's continuation of every product and service with respect to contribution to results.

- If demand drops precipitously remember that the worst thing management can do is modernize. Occasionally, doing nothing is the best thing to do.

- Recognize that not everything worth doing is worth doing well.

- Identify products and services in which even if you perform heroically you only break even.

- Beware of reforming malfunctioning policies without knowing why they do not work. The best thing to do with such programs is to abolish them.

- Eliminate projects that research shows have engendered only minor improvements and after years of effort have provoked only interesting discussions.

Concentration Not Diversification

"Diversification," Drucker wrote, "destroys the performance capacity of an organization."[36] He never subscribed to the conglomerate movement of the 1960s, which, in adopting the philosophy of mindless diversification, contended it was possible for an executive knowledgeable in management to manage all types of businesses. Because every business demanded a unique knowledge and a distinct managerial temperament, he thought it was arrogant to maintain that any one executive could achieve first-rate performance in all varieties of business. In addition, to assume that there were "easy businesses" was a form of unwarranted hubris.

Creativity was another factor that was highly overrated in Drucker's mind. He confessed that he never encountered a business or an executive that did not have more ideas than could be used. A person with average imagination was capable of having an abundance of ideas. However, like jugglers, most of these people kept each idea in the air for only a few seconds. Instead of juggling a host of ideas simultaneously, Drucker insisted, executives should achieve results through concentration. They should determine what the things are that should be done first and what the things are that should be done not at all.

Arguing that it was futile for a business to be all things for all people, Drucker saw that the challenge of concentration was in emphasizing not priorities (new ideas) but posteriorities (the ideas to be left out). In promoting concentration, he applied a military axiom: the attempt to defend everything results in defending nothing. To reinforce the principle of concentration further, he drew on the medieval philosophical concept called Occam's razor, which states that it serves no purpose to achieve a result with many assumptions rather than with few. Finally he educed the law of scientific parsimony, which states that if there is one explanation of a phenomenon there is no need to ask for a second explanation.

In addition to these theoretical rationales for concentration, he considered concentration in a pragmatic business sense, seeing it as the opposite side of the shield of abandonment. In short, the more things management routinely eliminated from the existing business the more resources became available for the opportunities of tomorrow. Concentration therefore allowed executives to focus on corporate strengths (the things the business could do well) rather than mindlessly speculating on irrelevant activities.

Consequently, concentration synchronized positive action with the rhetoric of the company mission, called attention to those few key products and substantive activities that were supporting the vast array of specialties and nonrevenue producing activities, and compelled the company to allocate its resources to those few products and activities that were producing meaningful results. Such a focus on two or three distinct core competencies was what distinguished excellent companies from their mediocre counterparts. The average company, which was marginally profitable, had mediocre competencies but no excellencies.

A peculiar trait of a leader's excellence was that it was usually recognized by competitors, but these competitors were unable, for a variety of reasons, to imitate what the outstanding company found relatively easy to do. Because no business could possibly be excellent in everything, Drucker pointed out that a leader in a particular industry could never achieve a monopolistic position. Instead, it was typical for an industry to have two or three leaders, with each focusing on different concentrations of excellence because there was no single way to serve a mass market. Drucker also indicated that clues for discovering outstanding instances of concentration were usually found in a company's mission statement, providing of course that the focus was on strengths and not on good intentions. (A sampling of the corporate excellencies of specific companies, that is, their responses to the challenges of defining the business, was supplied in Chapter Seven.)

As a general rule, Drucker was reluctant to discuss the rationale of failures, maintaining that we learn only from things done successfully. He did, however, make an exception in exploring the failure of businesses to establish a meaningful concentration. He found the common denominator of failed concentration was twofold. First, there was the arrogance of corporate management in believing it could be equally excellent in carrying out a combination of diverse business strategies. Second, there was the inability of management to recognize that a process of elimination was required for the removal of the unproductive. As for the first reason, he argued that it was futile to believe that organizations could accomplish more than their resources allowed. As for the second, he offered some examples: the product line that became ossified because of a reluctance to drop the initial products that created the company's success; the supermarket chain that refused to drop its original store even though that outlet had not produced results in years; and the research lab that clung to projects that were going nowhere because of executive egos.

Conversely, the recent history of General Electric exemplified a concentrated quest for revitalized "single mindedness." Reginald Jones, General Electric's CEO in the early 1980s, received many accolades from the business journals as the most effective and esteemed top manager in the United States. He earned his reputation by concentrating on capital asset management and productivity of resources. In the 1990s, his successor, Jack Welch, raised the bar of corporate excellence with his decision to combine the concepts of systematic abandonment and concentration, and he later reported: "My first central idea for G.E. back in 1981 came from Peter Drucker: It was my decision to be either number one or number two in each of our businesses—or get out of them altogether."[37] Given the fact that GE had scores of profit centers, the move of selling off units that did not have a dominant market share and concentrating only on excellent performers was an audacious strategy. It turned out to be a remarkably successful decision for Welch, and one that rejuvenated the corporation and successfully shaped its future.

In short, Drucker found that the central factor in failures was the sacrifice of focused strengths for diffused diversity in the goals of the corporation. Reminding managers that an organization is a tool, and like any other tool (for example a multifaceted knife), it is incapable of performing efficiently if it is required to do too many different things, he wrote: "The organization must be single-minded or its members will become confused. They will follow their own specialty rather than apply it to the common task. They will define 'results' in terms of their own specialty and impose its values on the organizations. Only a focused and common mission will hold the organization together and enable it to produce."[38]

Conclusion

An apparent consensus existed among most businessmen immediately after World War II that normalcy meant a preference for continuity or at best a toleration of moderate change. Drucker took exception to this belief, arguing that what managers preferred was irrelevant; they had no choice other than to cope successfully with accelerated change. The starting point for meeting the challenge of change was in managing the basics of the existing business for results. In short, knowledge of such management fundamentals as the marketing concept, productivity of capital assets, and systematic abandonment and its corollary principle of concentration was the foundation of entrepreneurship and the key to future planning.

Drucker did not envisage successful performance in the existing business as producing an entirely new business phase. The main importance of managing for results today was that it triggered confidence and stimulated energy for future change in the corporate culture. He viewed the entrepreneurial approach as a seamless process in which the interrelationship between today and tomorrow produced a new business configuration that had its own unique "rhyme, rhythm, and reason." Amid the continuous convulsions of change in which the past, present, and future intersected, corporate management had to respond with a pattern of transition.

CHAPTER TEN

STRATEGIES FOR THE TRANSITIONAL BUSINESS

Drucker based his rationale for viewing the enterprise as an organic entity consisting of unique stages (traditional, transitional, and transformational) on a dynamic process. He described his idea of that dynamic process this way:

> A process knows neither beginning nor end. It may have stages but it does not divide into parts as such. From the ultimate consumer back to the first supplier of raw materials it has to be seamless, so to speak, yet at the same time conform to the second principle: that of *pattern, order, or form* behind the seemingly random and unpredictable flux of economic phenomena. If a business is to be considered a continuous process, instead of a series of disjointed stop-and-go events, then the economic universe in which a business operates—and all the major events within it—must have rhyme, rhythm, or reason.[1]

In the organizational tension of managing change, Drucker saw the improvement of current operations as the heart of the traditional business, but the projects dealing with new commitments and opportunities as the soul of the transitional enterprise. Rather than picturing this structural confrontation between stabilization and destabilization in a negative light, he made a distinction between managers and entrepreneurs. The former were synthesizers who by managing for results accumulated the risk capital for tomorrow. The latter were zealots who were focusing on and implementing new opportunities. He argued that the failure to innovate was the chief reason for the decline of an existing organization. But the inability to manage was the major reason for the demise of innovative organizations.

Structural Mutation

Drucker insisted that a mutation away from the steady state of the present business toward a new form was necessary because, unlike the human system, an artificial organization has no regenerative tendencies to restore itself. Consequently, the transitional business has no choice but to act contrary to the assumptions of the present business. It does so by formulating such new tasks as questioning rigorously past successes, devising strategies for doing things better and differently, and revising the corporate culture in light of new realities.

In going against the grain of the traditional business so it would undergo a metamorphosis into the transitional business, Drucker asserted that a reevaluation of corporate purpose was necessary. In short, the successful introduction of new products and the improvement in the wealth-creating resources of the corporation as a result of identifying new realities also forced management to shift its strategic focus from asking, What is the business?—the key concern of the traditional business—to asking, What will the business be?—the concern of the transitional business. To cite one example, the outstanding economic performance at 3M, built on such adaptive innovations as Scotch tape and Post-It pads, required a new look at the company's business mission. These and 3M's other consumer successes demanded a redefinition of adhesive technology (the linchpin of 3M's knowledge excellence) and a reevaluation of 3M's distribution system.

In describing innovation as a change in the wealth-producing capacity of existing resources, Drucker also cited the celebrated examples of oil and penicillin, which in effect produced entirely new industries. In each instance, he noted, these two products were virtually useless until some entrepreneur endowed them with economic value. For centuries, oil had marginal commercial use, and penicillin was, for decades, regarded as a nuisance that interfered with biochemical research work. Because of dramatic shifts in resource conversion in both instances, new commercial realities for these products created new forms of wealth and economic structures.

Drucker constantly warned executives that because managerial work and entrepreneurial work were qualitatively different, the innovative organization could not escape developing a split personality. Once managers recognized the increased importance of innovation, the orderly and predictable decision making of the traditional business was irrevocably undermined. Because the transitional business was characterized by imagination, inspiration, and good fortune, decision making became inextricably unpredictable and disorderly.

Need for Receptivity

Drucker was dogmatic in considering innovation, or the management of change, as a categorical imperative for the large corporation. He cautioned, however, that it was critical to understand the countervailing forces impeding the implementation of innovation. The conflicting goals between the existing and transitional businesses would not be reconciled by sermonizing on the need for adjusting perceptual differences. Issuing a managerial edict compelling people to manage concurrently both today and tomorrow was a futile exercise.

Drucker insisted that rhetoric divorced from reality was insufficient for two basic reasons. First, defenders of the steady state were acutely aware that innovation looked simple in theory but was difficult in practice because it required systematic work. In an atmosphere where memories were exalted and the past eulogized as ideal, raising the disturbing features of risk and uncertainty was not a popular executive position.

Second, because the attributes of bewilderment and anxiety in the corporate culture were inherently stronger than the elements promoting the momentum of change, there was a normal tendency to allocate resources to problems and crises, a temptation to support yesterday and ignore tomorrow, to reward on the basis of yesterday's easily measurable standards. All these organizational restraints on innovation often resulted in a cooptation of the innovators by the traditionalists. Arguing that fear was the most intrinsic factor in heightening hostility toward innovation, Drucker thought it futile for management to dwell on the obstacles to change whether perceived as real or superficial. That was the wrong approach. The proper approach was for management to adopt an innovative attitude in order to make the organization receptive to new business strategies.[2]

Drucker regarded the conventional textbook explanations for the opposition to change as superficial rationalizations. Viewing them as smoke screens, excuses for seeing innovation in unfriendly terms, he stated the fundamental reason for anti-innovation attitudes was resistance to change and that such resistance is grounded in ignorance and fear of the unknown. In this vein, he urged corporate adoption of the Latin motto *rerum novarum cupidus* ("greedy for new things").[3] According to Drucker, a major task of top management is to infuse the corporate culture with a spirit of change so that fear of change vanishes. Once change was welcomed as an opportunity rather than a threat, adapting to the challenge of innovation became much easier. "To be able to take advantage of change, enterprises have to welcome change. They have to consider change as normal rather than as an exception to be feared and to be avoided if at all possible."[4]

Once the only certainty was uncertainty, the modus operandi of the entrepreneur, then whining and complaining about the obstacles to change amounted to a senseless and fruitless exercise. Because the innovation function was replete with disarray and disappointment, managers had to accept the reality that the new was always "messy and untidy." Their only choice, therefore, was to either encourage it or discourage it.[5]

Once the commitment was made to innovation, Drucker stated that all the talk of resisting change should be discouraged and that management should promote talk about change as an indispensable mantra of the corporate culture. Enthusiastic encouragement, endorsement, and extolment of change were crucial for intensifying the corporate spirit of entrepreneurship. Because he considered entrepreneurship an embryonic discipline, capable of being learned and improved through systematic effort, Drucker believed the spirit of change had to be reduced to habit and routine: "The innovating organization requires a learning atmosphere throughout the entire business. It creates and maintains continuous learning."[6] He also insisted that it was the entrepreneurial job of managers to move all corporate members in the direction of growth: "Training and development must be built into . . . [the organization] on all levels—training and development that never stop."[7]

It is worth mentioning that Drucker saw two exceptions to the organizational need to innovate—the small business and any institution with a *mental set* impervious to change. Except in the rarest of cases, the small business was so concerned with immediate survival on a daily basis that it lacked the human resources, the time, and the energy for becoming a transitional business, for thinking through in a systematic way the answer to, What the business will be? What works best for a mature enterprise would overwhelm an infant, Drucker bluntly said. "The great majority of small businesses are incapable of innovation, partly because they don't have the resources, but a lot more because they don't have the time and they don't have the ambition. I'm not even talking about the corner cigar store. Look at the typical small business. It's grotesquely understaffed. It doesn't have the resources and the cash flow. Maybe the boss doesn't sweep the store anymore, but he's not that far away. He's basically fighting the daily battle. He doesn't have, by and large, the discipline. He doesn't have the background.[8]

Drucker also considered it a waste of time and effort to court innovation in an atmosphere where the function was ridiculed, rejected, and disrespected. "When innovation is perceived by the organization as something that goes against the grain, as swimming against the current, if not as a heroic achievement, there will be no innovation."[9] Declaring it an undeemable form of self-sacrifice, he said: "If you work in an organization that doesn't want innovation, let alone that penalizes anybody who rocks the boat, don't innovate. Your rewards are probably not even in heaven—they're certainly not here on earth."[10]

The Pattern of Innovation

In introducing the function of innovation as a concept of purposefully organized change, Drucker wrestled with the question of whether it was possible to have a discipline where there were no facts and no recognized empirical investigation. He synthesized the essential tasks of innovation as follows: "Innovation is the specific tool of entrepreneurs, the means by which they exploit change as an opportunity for a different business or a different service. It is capable of being presented as a discipline, capable of being learned, capable of being practiced. Entrepreneurs need to search purposefully for the sources of innovation, the changes and their symptoms that indicate opportunities for successful innovation. And they need to know and to apply the principles of successful innovation."[11]

In interpreting Drucker's analysis of innovation, I have separated it into two categories—*adaptive innovation* for the transitional business and *breakthrough innovation* for the transformational business. These business strategies share the common denominator of focusing on opportunities in meeting unmet consumer needs, but they differ in the degree of risk involved and the time required before they produce results.

Adaptive innovation looks at the current mix of products and services to determine the ways the corporation is not satisfying the customers. It is based on the proposition that in order to survive, the firm has to be different in order to be better. Taking an adaptive perspective in order to satisfy the unmet needs of the customer is, in effect, the methodology for answering the question, What will the business be? Although adaptive innovation rejects the notion that the company's mission is one of immutable permanence, in most instances the successful innovations Drucker saw were incremental. As a result they supplemented but did not usually radically alter business purpose.

Drucker cautioned, however, that in innovative planning, practice did not always follow his theory. A breakthrough proposal might result in a minor improvement, and a venture viewed as an incremental adaptation could have a dramatic and irrevocable impact on a company. For example, there was nothing technologically or scientifically sophisticated about moving a truck "off its wheels and putting it on a ship," but the concept of containerization revolutionized the marine transport industry.[12]

Breakthrough innovation, which is characteristic of the transformational business, is chiefly a response to the question, What should the business be? The implication is that if the putative breakthrough innovation is indeed a breakthrough, the old business will be totally transformed into an entirely new type of enterprise with a different set of core knowledge competencies, novel ways of giving value to the customer, new forms of competition, and a revised corporate structure and culture.

One feature, according to Drucker, that adaptive and breakthrough innovations have in common is that managers should see the innovation process as an identifiable practice with workable principles and guidelines that are capable of being learned through systematic effort. Drucker was adamant in insisting that the entrepreneurial process of managing change in an organized fashion is not dependent on geniuses or miracle workers. At the same time, he stated, paradoxically, that it is unlike any other discipline because the innovative process is so utterly dependent on the variables of imagination, inspiration, and luck. Because in my judgment the successful breakthrough innovation has a substantially different business impact from the adaptive innovation, I will discuss it in Chapter Eleven, along with the other features of the transformational business.

Adaptive Innovation

To establish a suitable foundation for the practice of adaptive innovation for the transitional business, Drucker listed a number of fundamental principles that he had drawn from entrepreneurial successes.

Simplicity

Simplicity was essential for a satisfactory innovative design. A venture whose framework was complicated with too many "ifs, ands, and buts" required an unwarranted amount of luck and a resolution of far too many premises for probable fulfillment. "Bright ideas are the riskiest and least successful source of innovative opportunities," Drucker observed. "The casualty rate is enormous. No more than one out of every hundred patents for an innovation of this kind earns enough to pay back development costs and patent fees. A far smaller proportion, perhaps as low as one in five hundred, makes any money above its out-of-pocket costs."[13] One way for management to avoid complexity was to concentrate on the firm's core excellencies. Nonentrepreneurial companies did not have the capacity for implementing this principle, however: "They see strengths where none exist and weaknesses where there are none."[14]

Autonomy

The effective management of change demanded a high degree of corporate decentralization. Unless autonomy was factored into the design of the innovative venture, new projects would be suffocated from lack of necessary independent space and deenergized for want of commitment.

Overcommitment

Large enterprises had a predilection to overfund new ventures with financial and human resources. Drucker felt huge investments of money and people at the initial stage of innovation were unnecessary. Arguing that everything new started small and that money was no substitute for proper thinking, he stated it was a mistake to believe "that money can be used in lieu of good people. . . . That is the quickest way to kill something—the combination of poor people and a generous budget. It's a guarantee of failure. It is the biggest mistake of all large organizations from the Pentagon on down."[15]

Leadership

An essential ingredient of the innovative process was that its target should be the leadership position at the head of the competitive parade. A window of opportunity should have projected results that mirror a real market niche or that promise a substantial impact on the economy by creating new values and different customer satisfactions. To satisfy these demands, it was necessary to raise the question, What innovative performance is needed to achieve a distinct leadership position?

Staffing Choices

According to Drucker, "Smart companies know that money does not produce innovation; people do."[16] The innovation process required that the people involved have a commitment to view it as a compulsory avenue to business growth and not as a destabilizing threat to corporate survival. Because talented individuals with this attitude would always be in short supply, the rule in staffing for new ventures was that mediocre people should not apply. Implementing innovation required the best human strengths available. The task would be impossible if people were exclusively committed to keeping yesterday alive. He parenthetically added that it was essential on both economic and moral grounds that a fair system of rewards and compensation be established for successful innovative performance.

Key Knowledge Strengths

The innovative focus fused unique corporate strengths (those things the corporation did easily and its competitors found difficult) with external stimuli that induced opportunities. This combination of matching internal knowledge strengths with outside forces was not just a robotic reaction but a calculated plan of action in which the business makes results happen by putting excellence into the marketplace. In essence this plan was the foundation of the mission statement, for without a managerial understanding of this vision there would be no organized innovation.

Walking Around Management

According to Drucker, the concept of *walking around management*, originally a device to improve human relations and communications with manufacturing employees, had become increasingly irrelevant in a knowledge society. However, he did see walking around management as a useful diagnostic tool for staying attuned to broad trends, gaining confidence in detecting opportunities, and recognizing that innovation was not something that took place within the organization but resided in the outside environment, which was the source of results.

Whereas an organization that insulated itself from the outside was inviting stagnancy, a company that took a panoramic view of the outside, with a selective eye for appropriate opportunities, was declaring an offensive in the competitive wars. Arguing that a defensive strategy at best limited losses, Drucker said that "seizing the offensive" was the only suitable strategy in a global competitive economy.[17]

Technological Tools

Considering the innovation function a practice rather than a science, Drucker found little relevance and no reliability in the techniques of simulated decision making for the entire entrepreneurial process. Another reason for his skepticism was the incapacity of computing techniques to divorce the uncertainties of daily operations and to remove inevitable crises in the planning models. He equated sophisticated models for innovation programming with guesswork, believing for example that projects with a duration of three to five years were not predictable. And the further out in time, the murkier the innovative project became: "In the expectations and anticipations of a business, the old rule of statistics usually applies that anything beyond twenty years equals infinity; and since expectations more than twenty years hence have normally a present value of zero, they should receive only a minimal allocation of present efforts and resources."[18]

Except for its ability to provide alternate scenarios for strategic decisions, Drucker was suspicious of mathematical modeling. Contending that the price of precise measurement was prohibitive, he thought it was prudent to be approximately right rather than exactly wrong. He was perfectly content, therefore, to rely on approximate measurement, because he had so far seen no evidence of a successfully simulated, major strategic decision. The computer could not handle all the variables that needed to be considered; it could handle only the quantifiable data. The most important information could not be analyzed; it could only be perceived.

In considering the all-important role of purpose in relation to technology, Drucker reiterated one of his original concepts, the priority of being market driven over product driven: "Innovative organizations know what 'innovation' means. They know that innovation is not science or technology, but value. They know it is not something that takes place within an organization but a change outside. The measure of innovation is the impact on the environment. Innovation in a business enterprise must therefore always be market focused. Innovation that is product focused is likely to produce 'miracles of technology' but disappointing rewards."[19]

Perception

Innovation contained both conceptual and perceptual characteristics. It was taken for granted that concepts were accompanied by information, but because innovation planning deals with expectations and not observable events, "today perception is more important than analysis. You need to be able to recognize patterns to see what is there rather than what you expect to see. You need the invaluable listener who says, *'I hear us all trying to kill the new product to protect the old one.'*"[20]

In the tension between the familiar and unfamiliar, an absence of imagination would force the practitioner to see only those things that had an engineering or measurable context. Drucker observed that "people see what is presented to them; what is not presented tends to be overlooked. And what is presented to most managers are 'problems'—especially in the areas where performance falls below expectations—which means that managers tend not to see opportunities. They are simply not being presented with them."[21]

Drucker once defined perception as seeing what everybody else had seen but ignored and thinking through what nobody else had thought through. He saw it as going beyond targeted guesswork, calling it a *mood* rather than a substantive collection of facts. He argued that a perceptual configuration defied quantification, but it was not abstract and intangible. It had a concrete reality capable of being tested and exploited as an innovative opportunity.

In the analogy of the glass seen as half empty or as half full, the former view reflected a mood of pessimism, an unacceptable position for an entrepreneur, whereas the latter mirrored optimism, enabling the practitioner to detect a trend invisible to others. This was illustrated by Drucker in the story of the two shoe salesmen who visited an underdeveloped country. One reported back that there was no demand there because the people did not wear shoes; the other perceived a major opportunity precisely because the people did not wear shoes.

Monomania

According to Drucker, every successful innovation revealed a unique story, and it was usually a tale written by a monomaniac consumed by the challenge. These fearless individuals were zealous iconoclasts who had no respect for bureaucrats and little reverence for administrative policies. They possessed traits of passion and perseverance and were not intimidated by the reality that new things rarely make sense and are easily shot down by cynical critics.

Instead, they adopted the position that even if everybody said a thing could not be done, they would still insist on doing it. Nine out of ten times the bureaucrats defending the status quo would probably be right and the innovating monomaniacs wrong. Nevertheless, if the organization failed to have an atmosphere congenial to the maverick, the innovation function would become moribund.

Size

For a considerable time the conventional view existed that the corporate culture of a big business was inherently inhospitable to the innovation function. The evidence that innovation was inversely proportionate to the size of a business was largely based on examples of industry leaders who had missed the boat on such major opportunities as motels, mini steel mills, frozen cakes, copiers, personal computers, supermarkets, and television entertainment, to name just a few.

Drucker did admit that many of the aforementioned obstacles to innovation were more pronounced in the large corporation. Mesmerized by the huge success of the earlier ventures that had transformed the business into a corporate giant, management subsequently found itself uncomfortable with small projects. The attitude was that "the new always looks so small, so puny, so unpromising next to the size and performance of maturity."[22] At the same time, he never accepted the proposition that large size was an automatic barrier to innovation. There were large companies that viewed innovation as the essence of corporate culture and as capable of being organized as a unique form of work, and Drucker cited many examples of brilliant innovative performance in such companies as Intel, Wal-Mart, Rubbermaid, 3M, Disney, and General Electric.

According to Drucker, size did not confer distinction. "A company is not necessarily better because it is bigger, any more than the elephant is better because it is bigger than the honeybee."[23] At the same time, a big corporation particularly needed innovation as a springboard for transition. "The large corporation has to learn to innovate, or it won't survive. For some companies that means reinventing themselves."[24]

In conjunction with the experiential principles for improved innovative performance, Drucker also listed the following caveats, or don'ts, based on the mistakes that inevitably led to failed ventures:

- Don't try to be clever. When entrepreneurs attempt to be brilliant, the odds are that they will be brilliantly wrong.

- Don't innovate for some "big bang" spectacular that you envision existing only for the distant future. There must be a recognizable need in the present environment and receptivity for your solution.

- Don't introduce a strategy that is impossible to implement because of inadequate human and financial resources.

- Don't diversify mindlessly. It is a form of hubris to believe that an organization can understand everything and manage anything.

- Don't propose new entrepreneurial ventures in organizations that look upon innovation as a heroic and insurmountable effort. "Even the Catholic Church does not encourage martyrdom."

- Don't assume that innovation is confined only to products. "Social innovation" is equally important and often more important than scientific or business innovation.

- Don't subscribe to the contention that innovation can be achieved through committees.

- Don't undertake a new venture without an appropriate study of the interaction between risk and opportunity.

Risk and Opportunity

Drucker placed the concepts of risk and opportunity at the center of the innovative decision-making process. Viewing risk and opportunity as an encounter with the unfamiliar rather than with the known, he roughly compared innovative decision making with medical diagnosis. For example, the doctor is constantly faced with examining a pattern of uncertainties in which he or she has to formulate hypotheses and then test them against the reality of results. The business practitioner similarly follows the diagnostic pattern when he or she analyzes the interaction of risk and opportunity for any new venture by identifying its relevance, evaluating cost-benefit dimensions, screening the various alternatives, determining information requirements, and exploring the methodology and tactics of implementation. Because Drucker considered risk as the starting point for thinking through a new project and looked upon opportunity as the springboard for subsequent action, I will follow this line of demarcation by first treating what he had to say about risk.

Focus on Risk

According to Drucker, risk was unquestionably a dynamic of the economics of the enterprise system. Riskless entrepreneurship was an oxymoron for two reasons. First, risk is inescapable; there is risk in everything we do. Second, there is the economic law that risk escalates in degree with successful performance.

In his effort throughout the compendium of his writings to clarify the concept of risk and remove misconceptions, Drucker offered these insights:

- The attempt to eliminate risks, even the attempts to minimize them, can only make them irrational and unbearable. It can only result in the greatest risk of all: the rigidity of doing nothing.

- To eliminate risk in business is futile. Risk is inherent in the commitment of present resources to future expectations.

- Short-term risk does not produce long-term results.

- Too frequently the corporate goal is minimum risk rather than maximum opportunity.

- There is no riskless action or even riskless nonaction.

- Entrepreneurship is risky because most people believe it is strictly a matter of hunch, intuition, and luck.

- There is an all-too-common belief that planning is a substitute for risk. This is a fallacy because planning is risk creating and risk taking.

■ The greater the opportunity the greater the risk.

■ The greatest risk of all is undertaking what one does not understand; the loss can be tremendous.

■ A common mistake in undertaking new ventures is the endless study of how to reduce the risk instead of dealing with it directly.

■ Entrepreneurship is risky but mainly because so few entrepreneurs know what they are doing.

■ The riskiest and least successful source of opportunities is the bright idea. Only one in a hundred such ideas pays back its development and patent fees.

Drucker viewed risk analysis not as an attempt to control but an effort to translate today's commitments in contemplation of tomorrow's results. He also realized that risk assessment was an all-inclusive process, covering the assumption of new projects, the continuation or abandonment of old activities, and the rationale for determining affordable and nonaffordable new ventures. Assessment of risk did not lend itself to precise quantification; this was because businesses could measure inside but not outside costs. The insurance decision in a business was perhaps the only area where the use of statistical probability was valid. Drucker, as shown earlier, contended that in an entrepreneurial decision the most important information was unmeasurable.

Because measuring that information with precision was useless, Drucker suggested classification as the most suitable concept of analysis for understanding risk. He perceived three categories of risk—the affordable, the nonaffordable, and the compulsory.

First, there was the risk a business could afford to take. If it succeeded at the innovation, it would not achieve major results, and if it failed, it would not do great corporate damage. Second, there was the risk a business could not afford to take. This risk usually involved an innovation that the company lacked the knowledge to implement, and usually wound up building the competition's business. Third, there was the risk a business could not afford not to take. Failure to undertake this innovation meant there might not be a business several years hence.[25]

Each classification of risk was usually associated with a similar category of opportunity. Accompanying the affordable risk was the additive opportunity. For example, if Procter & Gamble took an affordable risk in introducing a new product into its distribution stream, even if successful it would probably produce only marginal results and would not change the character of the business. And if the new product failed, it would not do irreparable harm to the business's financial resources reservoir.

The unaffordable risk displayed a complementary opportunity. In this situation, the new venture had the appearance of being similar to the strengths of the existing business, but in reality it called for new knowledge competencies within the business. Specifically, Drucker cited the failure of drug companies to succeed in perfumes. He called this innovation an unaffordable risk because the knowledge and corporate cultures required for marketing pharmaceuticals and marketing perfumes were radically different. The complementary opportunity, a misdiagnosis, was an open invitation for others to take advantage of the innovator's insight in meeting unmet consumer needs.

Finally, in the risk that a business could not afford not to take, the opportunity had to be one of qualitative innovation. If a company failed to risk involvement in this type of opportunity and another competitor succeeded with it in the marketplace, the odds were that the business that ignored the risk would become extinct.[26] Among some of the illustrations suggested by Drucker of correlating a radical risk with a necessary opportunity were AT&T's shift from analog into digital technology; P. W. Grace's transformation from a shipping to a chemical company; General Electric's decision to enter atomic energy; IBM's venture into personal computers; Sears Roebuck's extension of its retail operations into financial services; and Johnson & Johnson's decision to add high-tech medical products to its product line that had up to then consisted of simple consumables.

Focus on Opportunity

Drucker looked at risk as a restraint but viewed opportunity as the lubricant that fueled the entrepreneurial process. "Successful innovators are conservatives. They have to be. They are not 'risk-focused'; they are 'opportunity-focused.'"[27]

He also pointed out that the two biggest obstacles to obtaining an opportunity focus were excessive concern with problems and the intimidating factor of fear. Problems obscured attention to opportunities, because as long as the emphasis was on the comfortable retreat to regular routines and the concern was with daily crises, necessary change was postponed or even abandoned. Drucker insisted that a damage-control policy of giving dominant attention to problems was counterproductive on two counts. First, problems consumed just as much time as opportunities, and second, their solutions only restored normality and were barren of genuine results.

Mention was made earlier of how incessant talk and discussion could remove the factor of fear. Drucker also counseled that this encouraging rhetoric needed the corollary of positive economic performance. Because there was no way of conducting conventional market research for a nonexistent product, the usual collecting of market intelligence was an impossible methodology: "Everybody knows—or should know—that one cannot *market research* a truly new product."[28]

In effect Drucker looked on the opportunity focus as an entrepreneurial absolute; it organized for uncertainty and removed the fear of the unknown. To illuminate this hypothesis he offered these ideas:

- Change is opportunity.

- Results are obtained by converting problems into opportunities.

- A dedicated focus on opportunity analysis will provide a company with more ideas than it has competent people to implement them.

- Feed opportunities and starve problems.

- Opportunity knocks only at the door of those who deserve it.

- Opportunity is not a question of divine inspiration but is earned by systematic perception.

- Concentrating resources on opportunities is the best way of controlling costs.

- An old proverb states that opportunity is where you find it. It does not say it finds you. That is luck, and luck never built a business.

To conduct a survey for the right opportunities, each management must identify the key trends and forces affecting the survival of its institution. As touched on briefly in discussing Drucker's view of the future, he approached the challenges of tomorrow's complexity and uncertainty from three dimensions: (1) anticipation, (2) innovation, and (3) projection.

Anticipation. Drucker equated the examination of external trends with looking at expectations. Anticipation was a way of performing an entrepreneurial encore, and it was predicated on what the practitioner expected to happen with regard to an opportunity. Because the anticipation of success for a new venture was largely based on hunch and intuition, he thought it so risky that it assumed a true fortuneteller's skill in picking winners.

Despite its visceral and emotional characteristics, Drucker did not entirely rule out the possibility that nonrational thinking could select the right opportunities. For example, he compared the probability of success of nonlogical anticipatory thinking with the probability of producing one frog from a thousand frog eggs. Despite such odds, he witnessed over the years many entrepreneurial success stories, particularly in small businesses.

Innovation. Drucker defined innovation of course as purposefully planned change. In effect, it was a response in which the practitioner, without benefit of any market research, imposed himself on the environment by inventing something entirely new through a circular process of organizing ignorance. In this process the entrepreneur visualized an outside image of opportunity and then returned to the inside to assess the effort and resources needed for implementation. In a systematic way, the process was repeated and tested until the successful innovation was realized. When the opportunity was qualitatively innovative, the outcome resulted in an entirely new industry, as in the case of the laser, the transistor, the copier, antibiotics, the computer, biogenetics, and software. A more detailed treatment of innovation as purposeful change appears in Chapter Eleven.

Projection. Projection was labeled by Drucker as the recent past, the future that has already happened. Although major events have irrevocably occurred, no one has yet taken commercial advantage of these nascent circumstances. Drucker distinguished the diagnostic tool of projection from traditional statistical forecasting by noting that forecasting asks the question, What is likely to happen? Projection asks, instead, What has already happened that will create the future? The application of projection, or taking advantage of the recent past, was considered the most fertile and practical approach for identifying opportunities.[29] The discussion in Chapter Eleven on entrepreneurial tactics will reinforce this contention.

The Vital Outside

One feature that distinguished Drucker from his colleagues in the management discipline was his talent for combining inside analysis with outside relevance. Arguably this perceptual virtuosity did not always enhance his reputation. A segment of academe, particularly in the social sciences, believed he had sold out to the establishment because of his mundane interest in squalid commercial affairs. He was well suited for this role of external interpretation; from the 1930s on, he had been a highly regarded social observer in academe and journalism. After World War II he followed a pattern of alternating his books between examination of internal management principles and exploration of the social forces affecting the corporation. Actually, Drucker perceived his role as that of a bridge between intellectual theory and the pragmatic practitioner.

Similarly a cynical group in the business community considered his cultural writings as a redundant departure from the sole managerial concern of improving shareholder interest. Because Drucker considered himself a loner, he was indifferent to the opinions of any alleged establishment. More important, however, than any personal predilections, his main concern in validating the interaction of the internal and external sectors was to confirm that external circumstances were the real sources of innovation. In short it was impossible to understand the entrepreneurial process through the parochial prism of internal business functions.

In retrospect, writing in 1995, Drucker considered the previous four decades as a period in which social and cultural forces played a passive role in managerial decision making. The marketing emphasis was on the improvement of the existing product line rather than a search for revolutionary products and services. The corporate information system reflected an almost total concern with internal events. This emphasis on continuity over change was reflected in the priority of information technologists. Because of their reluctance to make an effort at quantifying external events in any meaningful way, "computer information tends to focus too much on inside information, not the outside sources and customers that count."[30] Feeling more comfortable with stability than disequilibrium, the provincial attitude of management was that the environment had to adjust to them rather than the other way around.

In discussing activity accounting (see Chapter Nine), Drucker noted that a major defect of the accounting system, also, was its inability to provide relevant data on outside trends. Its one-dimensional bias was the equivalent of "flying on one wing." He found it astonishing that information hardware was applauded for its technical virtuosity but so little attention was given to its utility and application for both market and nonmarket forces. Because the emphasis had been on computing speed, bigger memory storage, and sophisticated databanks, executives had given priority to "reporting over doing." As a result managers knew how to get data, but most still had to learn how to use the data.

According to Drucker, a sense of urgency was needed to replace the managerial sense of complacency with regard to external forces. Although there was a feeling that the present generation of managers was experiencing one of the most turbulent transformations in history, the phenomenon was seen as one of traumatic confusion rather than one in which information could be systematically organized and problems converted into opportunities. Claiming that the world in the last decade of the twentieth century had been turned upside down, Drucker asserted that the old assumption of meeting demand through traditional marketing techniques would no longer suffice for a dynamic business. In the tumultuous and disruptive world of today, the entrepreneurial task was to create demand. He visualized the modern executive straddling two time zones. The first offered a delusionary perspective of comfort and familiarity, encrusted with old habits and values. The other was a world where "today's certainties always become tomorrow's absurdities"[31] and where everybody was an inexperienced immigrant in time.

Corporate compartmentalization of information, the frenetic complexity of the pace of change, and managerial neglect of the opportunity focus compelled Drucker to suggest that executives view information from an ecological rather than a fragmented standpoint. A holistic analysis of information would force executives to recognize that there were only two managerial strategies— evolution or extinction. Because the ecological approach visualized the enterprise interacting and integrating itself through continuous transactions with the outside world, Drucker hoped that executives would realize that change was the basis for opportunities. He also hoped that this holistic way of understanding information perceptually would enable them to undertake opportunities more skillfully.

Drucker suggested that several unprecedented business patterns were already discernible, such as former customers emerging as rivals, previous enemies becoming allies, a surprisingly different cast of competitive actors on the global stage, a new set of customers arising in the global emporium, and the formation of unprecedented types of business alliances and partnerships.

Of course executives were cognizant of these changes, because they were making routine pragmatic decisions within the framework of these new business practices. However, they saw them only as symptoms and were only dimly aware of the underlying forces that were creating these new business realities. Moreover, executives tended to look upon the changed business landscape from the perspective of problems, and as Drucker repeatedly stressed, sacrificing opportunities for the allure of solving problems was perhaps the biggest mistake of management in failing to practice entrepreneurship.

Drucker never believed that any outsider, much less "an old school master" like himself, had any responsibility in the selection and implementation of opportunities. Management was paid for these tasks. He did contend that a consultant could help in framing the proper entrepreneurial questions, provided that executives concentrated not on what they wanted to do but on what they had to do in order to perform in a competitive enterprise economy.

Drucker stressed that each firm was sui generis; therefore management had to determine how major trends were specifically affecting the survival of the organization and the things it must do differently in reacting to them. The fact that each firm was a unique institution meant it had to view the prospects of innovation from the standpoint of whether the opportunity was negligible, whether it was manageable, or whether it was unacceptable. Drucker suggested that businesspeople assess how outside circumstances generally affected the firm; evaluate them specifically in terms of opportunities and threats; decide the actual impact on products, goods, and services; and develop an action agenda.

New Realities

Drucker scorned the pretense that the future could be foreseen. In fact, he considered What would tomorrow look like? to be the wrong question. People, however, could take advantage of trends if they asked instead, What do we have to tackle today to make a tomorrow?[32]

Drucker has perspicaciously explored the context of nonmarket forces in his two latest books, *Post-Capitalist Society* (1993) and *Managing in a Time of Great Change* (1995). In both these works he explained how nonmarket forces shaped new social and economic dynamics. Using a broad brush on a huge social canvas, Drucker sketched scores of problems and issues, which he highlighted from four major perspectives: (1) information technology, (2) decline of the corporate titans, (3) social challenges, and (4) global forces. He was careful to point out that the selection of these particular four categories was less important than recognizing the discontinuities and the changes in trends within the categories.

Information Technology

According to Drucker, a transition was taking place in which the old industrial form of manufacturing, which was characterized by the tangible process of "making and moving" things, was becoming increasingly inappropriate. The reality of the postcapitalist society was that intangible concepts and ideas were the driving force of the manufacturing process.[33] For the first time in history, information had become abundant rather than scarce, open rather than covert, and cheap rather than expensive; mobility of jobs was based on choice rather than birth; a network of knowledge relationships was more important than hierarchical command and control; and validity of data was emphasized over simply searching for "more and more" information.

In addition, in the information-poor societies of the past, there was little need for specialized disciplines and still less emphasis on knowledge as responsible for producing results. Drucker characterized the new reality as one in which what we called knowledge now had to have application and utility or it would be considered useless. Moreover, the information explosion would move toward more rather than less specialization in the years ahead. He labeled this phenomenon "the shift from knowledge to knowledges."[34] Implicit in this statement was the contention that given dependence on application, it was impossible to declare the predominance of any single type of knowledge over another: "No knowledge ranks higher than another; each is judged by its contribution to the common task rather than any inherent superiority or inferiority."[35] For example, if a person had a painful toenail, a brain surgeon could not help.

Decline of the Corporate Titans

Drucker made the point that too much early success could be corruptive and destructive for the individual.[36] He felt this was especially pertinent to the managers of many giant corporations during the post–World War II years, who discovered that their successful economic performance modified or obsoleted the behavior that created it. He observed that sooner or later every core knowledge excellence would become inappropriate, owing to radical social and economic transformations in the environment. At the same time, he also implied that in the future it would be possible to outsource all activities that were not core competencies. As a result, the conventional wisdom no longer held; namely, that the great virtue of size was its capacity for longevity. The cascading winds of change had wilted this belief in organizational permanence. "Corporations once built to last like pyramids are now more like tents."[37]

Not only did massive size no longer confer distinctive performance, but the large corporations often resembled dinosaurs, unable to fit the demands of modern competition. Because knowledge was becoming more accountable, there was less need for the hierarchical strictures of the command-and-control organization whose many levels were producing more noise than results. Drucker conceded of course that there would always be room for a few titans, but the large corporations had lost their dominance to more flexible smaller and medium-sized firms who had outperformed them in economic growth and job creation.

Social Challenges

In scanning the complex social challenges encountered by all institutions, Drucker used the discipline of social ecology to decipher the contemporary cultural pattern, covering such issues as education, political reform, ethics, social responsibility, meritocracy, health care, technology, and labor relations. Because a detailed explanation would require a separate volume, I will confine my survey to three interacting societal challenges that cry out for social innovations by responsible organizations. They are the "civilizing of the city," the widening gap between rich and poor, and a dependency ratio in which increasingly more entitlement recipients have fewer producers to pay for them.

First, in diagnosing the intractable problem of civilizing the modern city in order to achieve a satisfactory quality of urban life, Drucker viewed it from an historical perspective, reporting that a functioning and livable city had always been more myth than reality. He observed that such renowned cities as London, Paris, Florence, and Vienna were not fit places to live except for a small minority of their citizens. He believed that the modern city would continue to disintegrate unless there was a concerted effort by government, education, business, and the not-for-profit sector to take a fresh approach to social innovation by converting the problems of crime, drugs, pollution, prostitution, and transportation into opportunities for making the city more habitable.

Second, he feared that the deepening estrangement and widening isolation between the affluent and the impoverished was producing a society in which contacts between the two groups were becoming casual rather than substantive. Particularly disturbing was that this loss of community and the dilution of responsible citizenship denied the keys of political participation and economic security to a growing, disenfranchised underclass. He doubted the continued viability of society if a near majority of the population lacked medical insurance and pension funds.

Another moral threat to the American dream and a contradiction for an affluent and knowledge society was the societal division between the educated and the uneducated. Drucker feared the presence of twenty-five million functional illiterates, and those without college degrees suffered a paralyzing loss of self-esteem and were viewed by many in society as losers.

Third, Drucker was alarmed that having three and one-half employed workers for each nonproducing recipient in the nation would promote intense generational friction between the younger and older segments of the population. Further aggravating the problem in this ratio was the factor of early retirement and the demographic rise in life expectancy. Drucker could understand the desire for early retirement of unskilled manual workers but argued it was the failure of management to make work meaningful and attractive when knowledge workers opted to leave the workforce, particularly when they were still healthy. Unless the retirement age was extended to seventy, he foresaw the ratio of producers versus nonproducers reaching the figure of two to one in the next generation. If nothing was done about this challenge of maintaining a sounder dependency ratio, he believed that breaking the bonds of the generational social contract would result in a moral and economic bankruptcy of society. Addressing this aspect of middle-class entitlements, he argued that the elderly must continue working because the younger generation would refuse to hand over half their salaries for knowledge people who were physically fit.

Drucker did not underestimate the gravity of these domestic challenges, but he did not despair either. He based his hope on two features of U.S. society. First, the essence of entrepreneurship was to visualize all problems as opportunities, and second, the volunteerism of the nonprofit third sector was a progressive way of rejuvenating community and citizenship.

Global Forces

Drucker declared that the external forces producing unprecedented opportunities in the new society were in the global arena. Because of the scope and diversity of recent globalization, space does not permit a detailed commentary, but many trends are clearly visible and are having a profound effect in reshaping the environment (see the accompanying box).

Drucker observed that these external forces are rapidly changing the environment in which businesses operate:

- The same forces that destroyed Marxism as an ideology and communism as a social system are also rapidly making capitalism as a social order increasingly irrelevant.

- The movement of ideas and information is, for example, threatening the validity of national boundaries.

- Harmonious and distinct markets operating within the confined national boundaries of conventional capitalism are being replaced by complex and diverse global markets.

- Distribution channels and customer needs are changing globally far faster than technological innovations.

- There is no evidence that governmental trade and industrial policies based on economic engineering will produce the results they promise for the global economy.

- Major regional blocs such as Europe, North America, and the Pacific Rim are becoming the key structural units of the global economy.

- Productivity is the new "wealth of nations."

- Increasingly faceless rather than face-to-face exchanges will dominate global communications.

- Western societies are no longer the centers of economic, political, and cultural gravity.

- Money and information know no fatherland; they transcend geographical units.

- The rise of transnational corporations, international regionalism, and supra-national agencies have substantively and qualitatively diminished the concept of national sovereignty.

- Competent management, investment, and education are the main keys to economic development.

- The increasing number of new national states is a reaction to the rise of ethnic tribalism throughout the globe. This trend further reflects the superficial geographical demarcations of a world without accepted borders.

- Cross-border alliances, both formal and informal, are the strongest integrating forces of the world economy.

- Uncoupling of money, raw materials, and employment from the domestic economy will increase.

- Investment abroad creates jobs at home.

- The distinction between the domestic and international economy has ceased to be a reality; however, political, cultural, and psychological elements tenaciously cling to the idea.

- Money flows are economic destabilizers, unlike information flows, which have benign economic impacts.

- A business that wants to do well will have to be competitive internationally. Even if it is not in foreign operations, it must have a global mind-set.

- Money has slipped its leash; it has gone transnational. It cannot be controlled any longer by national states, not even when they act in concert.

- Pollution knows no boundaries any more than information and money do.

- In every developed country, traditional workers making and moving things will account for only one-sixth to one-eighth of the workforce in the coming generation.

Following the holistic aspects of the ecological approach, the combination of these four nonmarket forces formed Drucker's framework of the postcapitalist society. As mentioned earlier, these new realities constituted the basis of entrepreneurial opportunities. For example, the information revolution will establish the foundation for the new systems industries of biogenetics, biotechnology, information processing, health care, financial markets, social and educational innovations, and consumer globalization.

Methodology and Tactics

Drucker frequently expressed the opinion that innovation demanded an artistic attitude but rejected the notion that it depended on a creative genius or particular personality type. Contrary to the popular belief in the romance of invention, the "flash of genius" that converted the brilliant idea into a successful innovation was pure myth. In practice, the creative idea was likely to remain an empty idea. Drucker dismissed, therefore, the idea that entrepreneurial successes were simply a question of applying the macho, gunslinging mentality of cowboy economics. Contrary to what the popular press advanced, entrepreneurship was more than a grab bag of knee-jerk robotic responses.

Drucker admitted that entrepreneurship was deceptive on the surface: "It is simple, but not easy. What you have to do and how you do it are incredibly simple. Are you willing to do it? That is another matter. You have to ask the question."[38] What made it difficult was that it comprised a systematic form of work that was based on a personal conviction and commitment to implementation. Like any practice, it entailed some average artistic imagination, but it did not rely on divine inspiration in the development of routine habits and the application of learnable skills.

Of course, with innovation as with all practices, knowing the fundamentals was no guarantee of selecting and implementing the right opportunities, but it increased the probability of success. Drucker asserted that the great benefit of systematization was that it promoted good habits for improving the practice of innovation. Not that you get best performance, because there is only so much you can do. However, as with any other skill, greater knowledge reduced uncertainty and increased confidence.

In dealing specifically with methodology as a preparation for innovation, Drucker addressed two topics: opportunity meetings and dual budgets.

Opportunity Meetings

According to Drucker, the prototypical business meeting was concerned with the care and feeding of problems; successes were usually ignored. For example, in reading monthly reports most executives became alarmed when they went over their budget projections. But too few refused to focus on being ahead of their budget. Without this information they become fixated on problems to the neglect of opportunities.[39]

Of course problems had to be taken care of, but when crises received all the attention, management would be congratulating itself that it had done well simply when things did not get worse. More important, struggling with problems at the expense of opportunities would quickly produce a famine in resources. In effect, when problems were the only things discussed by management in its regular meetings, it was a sure sign that a business had passed its golden age. In contrast, a definite sign of displaying confidence in the future was to have opportunity meetings structured into the organizational routine.

Under the heading of opportunity meetings, Drucker suggested the following types: (1) show and tell, (2) subordinate-senior relationship, (3) review and monitoring, and (4) social demand. By no means did he consider the list exhaustive nor did he assign greater importance to one type of meeting over another. They all had a common purpose: to encourage change and ensure that a proportionate amount of time, effort, and resources was devoted to sessions on opportunities.

Show and tell. For a show-and-tell meeting Drucker took a page out of the elementary school pedagogy. The session involved having three or four outstanding performers describe how they identified an opportunity and how they translated it into successful performance. The great advantage of this success-structured technique was that it confirmed a focus on accomplishment over failure. The only beneficial lesson of failure was its instruction on what not to do, and it was barren with respect to innovative achievement.

Subordinate-senior relationship. Drucker argued that it was often the people who were closest to the customer who had the greatest knowledge and perspective on opportunities. He maintained that some of the most important innovative ideas were generated at a considerable distance from executive suite power centers. These people included salespeople, repair technicians, clerks, and others who had direct contact with customers. More often than not, these people were concerned with thinking about new ways of doing things, but usually their ideas were screened out of the flow of upward communications.

One method of tapping these opportunities was to use the mentor relationship between a junior and a senior. Not only was this relationship an excellent vehicle for upward communications, but it allowed the junior to express opinions on the threats and opportunities to the company and spell out his or her ideas on innovation. To avoid having such meetings dissolve into procedural rap sessions, Drucker imposed one agenda requirement. The new ideas should be put down in writing, and with mutual agreement, work was to begin immediately on at least one of the agreed-upon opportunities.

Review and monitoring. To keep costs under control and to evaluate efforts against results, Drucker felt it was imperative that a company have a periodic review for monitoring innovative ventures. Too often structured feedback in the assessment of outcome was conspicuous by its absence. Such reviews every two to three years helped pinpoint results and identified more clearly those projects that were candidates for abandonment and those that required additional resources. This exercise enabled management to identify those opportunities that had contributed to results and to set the financial targets for the next couple of years. Finally, management could also examine the innovative efforts of the competition as accurately as possible.

Social demand. Drucker urged corporate managements to view their critics, such as consumer and environmental groups, as opportunities rather than threats. He welcomed meetings between participants from these hostile groups and members of the corporation to explore ways in which business might contribute to solutions for improving the quality of life. Converting social problems into opportunities was the soundest approach to social responsibility.[40]

Dual Budgets

The *information glut* and the even less elegant *information garbage* were terms that reflected, Drucker suggested, the "age of quantification" among business practitioners. The passion for numbers was most evident in the appraisal of short-term results. This monitoring of economic performance was charted daily with the measurement of shareholder value, which Drucker viewed as an oversimplified X ray of only one part of the corporate skeleton. He rejected the maximizing of shareholder wealth as the single corporate goal and saw that it did not serve the long-term interests of the shareholders of the corporation. He maintained that the shareholder interests and the interests of the enterprise were best served when there was a judicious balance of profitability in meeting both long- and short-run objectives.

To obtain a more relevant focus on both the short- and long-term corporate wealth-producing capacities, some form of entrepreneurial accounting was needed to get a handle on out-of-control costs. Drucker specified that the entire cost chain of business activity, including the ultimate costs the consumer paid for a product or service, should be part of the financial information process. Therefore, in order to shift from an enumerated litany of expenses to cost effectiveness and to move from standardized computing to meaningful measurement of resources, Drucker prescribed the remedy of dual budgets. Although traditional data collection captured the surface impact of corporate economic health, it failed to illuminate the long-term threats to corporate survival such as the loss of competitive standing and failure to diagnose opportunities. Consequently, management needed a budget to identify present expenditures, but it also required a budget that provided information on promised and future results. Drucker labeled the former the *operational budget* and the latter the *opportunity budget*.[41]

In explaining the different characteristics of two budgets, he was in effect suggesting the foundation blocks for entrepreneurial accounting. For example, the operational budget was voluminous and contained everything that was being done. The opportunity budget, which was lean and sparse, included things that were being done differently and the new things to be worked on. The operational budget followed the ground rules of accepted accounting and financial principles. The opportunity budget did not start off with a fixed calculated expenditure; it ended up with a feasible approximation. The operational budget applied the concept of *satisficing;* that is, it estimated the minimum expenditures needed to get by without the business collapsing. The opportunity budget was the appropriate place for defining the time frame of innovative projects and spelling out the expenses contained in the risk and opportunity analysis. Because it was based on the highest rate of return, it *optimized* rather then *satisficed.*

Because Drucker thought it a mistake to mix operational work with entrepreneurial work, he assumed that the opportunity budget was autonomous. This concept of budgetary independence meant that new products could not be measured by a traditional return-on-investment analysis. A new product had to be on the market for at least two or three years before it contributed significant performance revenues and its financial viability and contribution could be ascertained. Explaining why it was senseless to carry the expenses of new products under the umbrella of the operational budget, Drucker compared the new product to a baby's having different needs than an adult. To consider that a fledgling could assume the ordinary burden of an ongoing business was like trying to assume an infant was self-sufficient. What proved best for an established business would kill an infant. "But the new project is an infant and will remain one for the foreseeable future, and infants belong in the nursery."[42]

Because the expenditures in the opportunity budget did not lend themselves to precise quantification, Drucker indicated that they should be structured on the basis of estimated projections and relevant probabilities. This was important in order to avoid paralysis by analysis as a result of trying to document everything to the tenth decimal place. Insisting that the operational and opportunity budgets were of equal importance even though one was massive and the other puny in comparison, he felt management should pay the same amount of attention and time to each budget.

Though recognizing that each budget posed different issues, he wrote:

The questions management asks of these two budgets are quite different. For the operational budget, one asks: "Is this effort and expenditure truly necessary? If not, how do we get out of it?" But if the answer is "Yes," one asks: "What is the *minimum* needed to prevent serious malfunction?" For the opportunities budget, the first question is: "Is this the right opportunity for us?" And if the answer is "Yes," one asks: "What is the optimum of efforts and resources this opportunity can absorb and put to productive use? And who is the right person to work on it?" The operational budget should always be funded on the lowest basis to get by. It should be "satisficed" rather than "optimized," to use the terms of formal decision theory.[43]

CHAPTER ELEVEN

TACTICS AND TRANSFORMATION

Drucker built his structural theory of entrepreneurship around the traditional, transitional, and transformational phases of the business. For the traditional business the emphasis was on extending what was already being done well. For the transitional business it was improving to a higher incremental level what was already being done well. For the transformational business, the focus was on designing a new and different business. Although all three businesses were conducted simultaneously within the corporation, each required different practices and skills.[1]

The skillful application of selected tactics was another way for managers of the transitional business to secure the future and develop a new business. It was Drucker's contention that a tactical approach to opportunities did not require managerial genius or technical skills. More often than not the opportunities were right under the noses of managers if they only took the trouble to visualize them. In this chapter I examine, first, the use of selected tactics and, second, the transformational business and the breakthrough innovation.

Practical Tactics

Drucker provided us with an array of practical tactics for identifying entrepreneurial opportunities. A list of his most significant includes (1) the unexpected,

(2) incongruities, (3) demographics, (4) industry and market structure, (5) creative imitation, (6) entrepreneurial judo, and (7) the ecological niche.

The Unexpected

In examining the phenomenon of the unexpected, Drucker discussed three categories: success, failure, and the outside event.

Unexpected Success. "No other area," wrote Drucker, "offers richer opportunities for successful innovation than the unexpected success."[2] He viewed the unexpected success as a product or service embedded within the business that was not recognized immediately for its true value. For example, department stores did not realize the potential of big-ticket appliances because these appliances did not fit their conventional merchandising mix. Banks were slow to see profits from fees for the new services that computer technology was creating. Although specialty items such as pharmaceuticals, delicatessen foods, and flowers produced substantially higher margins, supermarkets were hesitant in supplying the financial resources and training to develop them. It was not until competitive deregulation occurred that the telephone companies recognized the Yellow Pages as a major source of profitability.

Wondering why so many managements neglected to see the unexpected success as an opportunity, Drucker attributed it partially to "managerial ego." Frequently the allure and excitement of pet new ideas blinded them to opportunities embedded in their current strengths. He conceded it was important to have the big egos that could fuel entrepreneurship but also that managers were not being paid for being intellectually bright and right but for producing economic results. So successful managers had to have big egos, but there were times in which those big egos needed restraints, because "the unexpected presents an opportunity if you are willing to subordinate your ego."[3]

Another reason why the quest to follow through on the unexpected success was not routinely undertaken was that the business reporting system had a natural, structural proclivity to highlight existing products with a track record of longevity. This situation prompted some in the managerial cadre to consider the traditional as normal, as something that, implicitly, would last forever. Anything new was then looked upon as suspicious, because "anything that contradicts what we have come to consider a law of nature is then rejected as unsound, unhealthy and obviously abnormal."[4]

Rather than dismiss the unexpected as an "exception," some firms, however, are receptive to the unusual and not suspicious of it. In perceiving it as an opportunity, they also realized it required patience and special attention. "When it's a new venture, whether it's outside or inside and outside the business, it's a child. And you don't put a 40-pound pack on a 6-year-old's back when you take her hiking."[5]

In short, Drucker suggests that myopic managements view the unexpected as abnormal, whereas perceptive ones consider it a part of their corporate culture. For example, innovative companies consistently take advantage of the unexpected in their entrepreneurial practices.

IBM, for example, refused to confine the marketing of the early computers to a select scientific clientele but saw a more extensive computer applicability for handling the information needs of business.

3M transcended the original but restrictive use of Scotch tape as a binding material for library books by researching the needs of mothers, who discovered hundreds of household uses.

Du Pont took ten years to develop its surprising discovery of nylon into a successful commercial practice. Starting with women's hosiery, management followed up the unexpected success of nylon by introducing the polymer product to other manufacturers. This resulted in a wide variety of product uses, such as parachutes, warp knits, tire cords, textured yarn, and carpet yarn.

McDonald's got its start as one of the greatest entrepreneurial success stories in business history after Ray Kroc, a milkshake machine salesman, noticed the unexpected success one of his customers had by systematizing the fast-food business. The original McDonald's was a small hamburger outlet run by two brothers who purchased a large, unanticipated number of Kroc's milkshake machines. He quickly recognized that the small McDonald's operation was a manifestation of a larger phenomenon that had the potential for revolutionizing the fast-food business. Kroc bought the company and turned the innovation of the original McDonald's into a multibillion-dollar business.

Chrysler registered a totally unexpected success when it shifted its marketing strategy to minivans and light trucks, which had always been classified as commercial vehicles rather than passenger cars.

To neutralize managers' inhibitions against and resistance to the unexpected success and encourage the practice of doing better than initially intended, Drucker offered the following prescription for greater entrepreneurial alertness: "Managements must look at every unexpected success with the questions: (1) What would it mean to us if we exploited it? (2) Where could it lead us? (3) What would we have to do to convert it into an opportunity? and (4) How do we go about it? This means, first, that managements need to set aside specific time in which to discuss unexpected successes; and second, that someone should always be designated to analyze an unexpected success and to think through how it could be exploited."[6]

Unexpected Failure. One of the great strengths of the enterprise economy has been its capacity to purge losers out of the system when consumers refused to buy a company's product. When this happened to management, the typical response to an unanticipated failure in the marketplace was to stoically accept the defeat. Counseling against this negative spirit of resignation and calling for a more sophisticated understanding of failure, Drucker stressed that innovative managements could deflate the unpleasant surprise element of the unexpected failure by converting that failure into an economic opportunity. Neatly summarizing his position on this tactic, he stated that "failures, unlike successes, cannot be rejected and rarely go unnoticed. But they are seldom seen as symptoms of opportunity. A good many failures are, of course, nothing but mistakes, the results of greed, stupidity, thoughtless bandwagon climbing, or incompetence whether in design or execution. Yet if something fails despite being carefully planned, carefully designed, and conscientiously executed, that failure often bespeaks underlying change and, with it, opportunity."[7]

Elaborating on *symptom* as the operative word in this summary, Drucker used the Edsel as an illustration of turning a negative into a positive. Of course he did not attempt to rationalize the initial half-billion-dollar mistake that marketing textbooks have cited as the biggest marketing disaster in business history. His aim was to show how the Ford management reflected on this monumental mistake. He pointed out how top management recouped from its marketing loss by making two key decisions. First, instead of calling for another study in the hope of rejuvenating the Edsel, top management subordinated its managerial ego and promptly abandoned the project, despite the fact that the car was the most costly researched in automotive history.

Second, Ford looked upon the unexpected failure of the Edsel as an entrepreneurial learning experience. It reasoned that the original concept was sound in that the car had been seen as a response to the apparently archaic marketing formula of General Motors—"a car for every purse." Ford's market research was correct in detecting that the market need for this economic segmentation had passed its peak. Although the Edsel failed to fit the new marketing reality of youthful style, personal affluence, and psychological status, Ford was able to fulfill these perceived customer needs with the Mustang and Thunderbird.

Drucker also cited the examples of Novocain and the picture phone. The former was originally aimed at doctors, but upon review it found a market with dentists. The original market for the latter centered on women, but when they rejected it as an everyday household product, AT&T successfully shifted the emphasis to teleconferencing for business. The Coca-Cola company is another outstanding example of the unexpected failure being converted into an opportunity. After four years of intense market research, its management decided to challenge the assumption that Coca-Cola was not simply a drink but a religion in some parts of the country. However, the introduction of a new product turned out to be a monumental failure. Management, however, did not allow its arrogance to interfere with reality. Instead of saying "we were right," Coca-Cola executives said "there is an opportunity" in staying with an accepted strength, and that strength was restored and renamed Classic Coke. "Listening to the unexpected can hurt—and that must have hurt Coke quite a bit. But the pain was not to the pocket-book but the ego."[8]

Unexpected Outside Event. In further exploring the nuances of the unanticipated, Drucker discovered particular significance in the unexpected outside event as an advantageous tactic of innovation. Two of the illustrations he used were corporate responses to the personal computer and to television. In the 1960s and 1970s, IBM assumed that the unchallenged superiority of the mainframe computer was the foundation of its technological future. The company envisaged giant supercomputers, which would establish data banks for specialized business functions and create industrial informational utilities.

The outside event that according to projections augured poorly for the publishing industry, threatening a decline in book sales, was the arrival of television. The basis for these predictions was not only that after World War II television would capture the disposable time formerly allotted to reading but that Americans would increasingly rely on public libraries rather than purchase books in large numbers. However, instead of a precipitous decline in book sales, there was an unprecedented record-breaking rise. According to

Drucker, this unpredictable increase had nothing to do with the sales efforts of traditional bookstore owners or the marketing strategies of the publishers. He attributed this upsurge to the discounting of mass merchandisers, a group entirely outside the industry. The new popularity of books in the television era virtually eliminated the avuncular small store merchants who were noted for their love of books and familiarity with customer tastes. The employees of the mass merchandisers were chiefly, he said, composed of former cosmetic salespersons. This group of retailers did not treat books as literature but as items for generating larger sales through improved use of shelf space. Drucker caustically remarked: "The standing joke among them is that any salesperson who wants to read anything besides the price tag on the book is hopelessly overqualified."[9]

Anticipating the unexpected, whether in its manifestation of success, failure, or the outside event, is a sound tactic for avoiding unpleasant surprises from the original entrepreneurial decisions and for recognizing the significance of unintended results. One reason why such anticipation is difficult to implement is that everybody suffers from amnesia; people forget their expectation of an innovative venture six months after it started. Because memories are fragile, Drucker suggested that there would be less possibility of missing opportunities if at the outset managers used the diagnostic approach of writing down their expectations with respect to all new ventures. Such monitoring of the unexpected might not be quantifiable, but it was a qualitative way of not mindlessly taking things for granted.

Incongruities

Drucker defined a business incongruity as "a dissonance, between what is and what 'ought' to be."[10] Instead of recognizing that there was a way of narrowing the gap between the ideal and reality, most businesses took for granted the flaw or fault in their operations, as a natural part of the industry's design. Drucker lamented this indifference to incongruity because it riveted management to a diagnosis of incompetency instead of an attempt to convert the problem into an opportunity. He suggested the use of a vulnerability analysis to determine where the business system was operating below standards. To do this systematically, management had to identify the key pressure point, the point where the business paid a peak cost in the conduct of the business (see the accompanying box).

Rather than accept the presence of an incongruity as an article of faith, said Drucker, companies should take the first step in a vulnerability analysis and identify the point at which they paid a disproportionate price within the business system. To illuminate this point, he offered a variety of illustrations of industries' key pressure points:

- Transportation: the cost of the carrier at rest

- Steel: the heavy cost of energy resulting from the continual process of heating and cooling

- Lumber: the cost of paying for the entire tree but obtaining limited economic results because of the waste accrued in preparing the finished lumber for the mill

- Soft drinks: the weight of the water content considerably increasing the cost of distribution and handling

- Paper products: the high break-even point and the high air content in finished products

- Pharmaceuticals: the prohibitively high cost of product testing along with the inevitable dangers of side effects

- Cameras: the cumbersome difficulties in taking pictures and developing film

- Health and hospital care: the exponential rise in the cost of services without a concurrent improvement in performance

- Telephones: the extremely high cost to maintain and sustain an embedded transmission network of copper wire

- Brokerage services: the heavy expenses incurred from backroom paper handling

- Automobiles: the inflexible design of the assembly line and high marketing costs associated with a single product dealership system

- Retailing: the lack of real-time information within the system

- Supermarkets: the waste from frequent handling of goods throughout the store, particularly at the checkout counter

Drucker emphasized that the business incongruity contributed excessively to costs but nothing to results. He added that the customer was not concerned with the difficulties management encountered with problems of handling, waste, and delivery. The customer perceived value only when these peak cost problems were overcome by management and converted into a meaningful value (see the accompanying box).

Drucker described how several managements had correctly diagnosed costly pressure points and either modified or eliminated them in the process of producing improved economic results:

- The remedy for marine transportation was containerization, which reduced the port downtime from twelve days to twelve hours.

- Integrated unit trains and computer programming were used by the railroads to diminish the costs of the carrier at rest.

- The mini steel mill, by substituting scrap for iron ore, reduced the heating process from several steps to one step.

- The introduction of chemical knowledge enabled the lumber industry to convert previous waste material (roots, bark, leaves, twigs, and sawdust) into a host of new products.

- Products such as Kool-Aid and Tang eliminated the need to deliver bulky water through the distribution channels of retail customers.

- The use of the scanner, the abandonment of green stamps, and the offering of fewer coupons considerably reduced the problem of slow checkouts in the supermarket.

- The Polaroid camera, invented by Edwin Land, made one-step picture taking and developing a reality.

- The innovations of ambulatory care, small surgical centers, maternity motels, and diagnostic clinics partially curtailed heavy hospital expenses.

- New telephone competitors exploited digital technology (optical wiring, computers, and cable) to establish new and cheaper networks.

- Entrepreneurs in the brokerage industry introduced new techniques for handling paperwork and recognized the importance of the pension and institutional investors as key customers.

- Productivity in the automobile industry was greatly enhanced by outsourcing and just-in-time inventory techniques.

■ Warehousing and distribution costs in discount retailing were drastically reduced by computer programming with real-time information techniques and by making manufacturers accountable for prompt delivery.

In exploring the tactic of incongruity, Drucker did not wish to convey the impression that a business had only one major vulnerability. In a complex business system, it might be possible to identify additional vulnerabilities in the various functional areas. Moreover, he cautioned there was no guarantee of eliminating or modifying a high-cost pressure point, but he was confident an attack on the vulnerability would usually result in improvement.

Demographics

Drucker asserted that population trends were the least risky of all the entrepreneurial sources of opportunities. Use of demographics was a sound tactic for deciphering opportunity, because population trends are illustrations of converting the recent past into a concrete future: "They are unambiguous. They have the most predictable consequences."[11] It is possible to assume, by projecting a long-term demographic birthrate trend, that all the people who will be joining the workforce two decades from now have already been born. "Changes in demographies are, of course, always the most reliable index, for the lead times of population changes are both thoroughly known and inexorable."[12]

In identifying demographic opportunities, the entrepreneur was reminded to grasp the relationship between aggregates and components. Drucker indicated aggregates were significant in capturing the big picture of the nation's population, but only components, specialized demographic areas, had entrepreneurial relevance: for example, "absolute population is the least significant number, age distribution is far more important."[13] It was the job of management not only to accept the factual patterns of these changes as reality but to break down the configurations into specific components of opportunity.

Drucker noted that General Robert Wood, CEO of Sears Roebuck in the 1920s and 1930s, was the first executive to comprehend the entrepreneurial impact of population trends as sources of innovation. Reportedly, he kept a copy of the *Statistical Abstract of the United States* on his desk during the day and by his bedside at night. One of the trends he noticed in thumbing through the voluminous statistics was the migration to suburbia in the 1920s. Attributing the shift chiefly to the increasing use of the automobile, he exploited the trend by adding suburban stores to catalogues as a major vehicle of the company's merchandising strategy. Complementing this innovation, he also saw an opportunity for insuring cars and founded Allstate, one of the most successful companies in insurance history. Wood later recognized the significance of seeing the demographic impact of the automobile as a major opportunity when he noted that although Sears made every mistake in the book, it saw the importance of the automobile in revolutionizing American lifestyles.

According to Drucker it was important for managers to identify data on age distribution, educational patterns, and geographical mobility. For him, the key to age distribution was identifying the dominant cohort, that is, the largest and fastest-growing age segment. For example, shortly after World War II, the major cohort became the baby boomer generation born during the years 1947 to 1957, which foreshadowed a doubling of the population. By assuming that this dominant group was also the first generation born into affluence, managers could predict dramatic consequences in such areas as child rearing, education, jobs, career choices, and spending habits.

More specifically, in tracing the chronological path of the baby boomer generation with its massive population increase, it was possible to anticipate such major social trends as an expansion of infant care services, explosion of educational facilities, rapid growth of entertainment innovations for teenagers, unprecedented rise of college enrollments, precipitous increase in careers for knowledge professionals, rapid growth of housing units to satisfy demands of family formation, and widespread emergence of family vacation travel. And as the baby boomers now enter their fifties with their families raised, they will be more concerned with leisure activities and, in the next decades, with health care in preparation for old age.

Leaving the realm of sociology, Drucker stated that managers, after examining the data, would have to investigate the specific meaning and relevant impact for their individual firms. They really had little choice in this because "demographic pressures are so great and irreversible that they render futile any policy that tries"[14] to resist them.

Drucker provided a sampling of entrepreneurially minded companies that had responded successfully to demographic realities, not only deciphering the impact of demographic opportunities but also converting them to economic results:

■ Kimberly-Clark introduced disposable diapers, and Gerber initiated nutritional innovations in baby foods.

■ Pepsi-Cola, recognizing the baby boom in its initial stage, provided real competition to Coca-Cola to such a degree that *youth generation* and *Pepsi generation* became synonymous terms.

■ Melville detected the pattern that teenagers buy several pairs of shoes a year, but unlike their parents, they buy for fashion and not for durability.

■ Holiday Inn and Club Med introduced unique innovations for travel and vacations for the new, affluent middle class.

■ Many developers recognized that young couples, when purchasing a house, bought according to future expectations and saw present incomes as a purchasing restraint. For example, they included such accessories as rugs and light fixtures as part of the mortgage to be paid over a long period of time.

■ The Brunswick Corporation took bowling from a seedy, delinquent, and youthful activity to a respected form of family and social entertainment by marketing it as an activity rather than a product.

■ In the late 1950s, the large urban banks belatedly adopted the marketing concept (in banking an innovation of A. P. Giannini) and introduced new credit instruments for financing homes, automobiles, and other appurtenances of the affluent society.

■ Citicorp took advantage of the abundance of college-educated women by aggressively recruiting them for managerial positions.

■ After the demise of most of the leading national magazines (such as *Life* and *Look*), the number of specialized and regional magazines increased, reflecting the country's ethnic and regional diversity and newly discovered leisure and hobby activities.

■ Mattel and Toys "R" Us took advantage of the new disposable income of the youth market by manufacturing and distributing a massive assortment of toys and games.

Industry and Market Structure

Upheavals in marketing and structural trends were always important sources of innovation but were difficult to identify in the early stages because they could be extremely deceptive. They usually started undramatically and often went unnoticed. But as they gathered momentum it was impossible not to pay attention to their consequences. Drucker described the long- and short-term interactions this way: "Whoever exploits structural trends is almost certain to succeed. It is hard, however, to fight them in the short run and almost hopeless in the long run. When such a structural trend peters out or when it reverses itself (which is fairly rare), those who continue as before face extinction and those who change fast face opportunity."[15]

One difficulty with the tactic of taking advantage of changes in industry and market structure was the inability of established firms in a given industry to recognize competitors as a threat to their survival. Assuming their safe position was impregnable, they were so frozen in time that they did not realize that in being out of touch they might soon be out of luck. Drucker commented on the myopia and arrogance of such misplaced managerial confidence that "indeed, industry and market structures appear so solid that the people in an industry are likely to consider them foreordained, part of the order of nature, and certain to endure forever. Actually, market and industry structures are quite brittle. One small scratch and they disintegrate, often fast. When this happens, every member of the industry has to act."[16]

It was this failure to recognize the fragility of market structures that paradoxically gave newcomers, those without inside knowledge and experience, an entrepreneurial advantage. Outsiders had a different perspective. Instead of seeing confidence as the part of the old managerial guard, they suspected insecurity. Instead of industrial placidity, they visualized turbulence. Instead of depicting consumer complacency, they imagined unmet customer needs. Instead of idealizing an unassailable stability from outside perils, they saw opportunities. "A change in industry structure offers exceptional opportunities highly visible and quite predictable to outsiders," observed Drucker. "But the insiders perceive these same changes primarily as threats. The outsiders who innovate can thus become a major factor in an important industry or area quite fast, and at relatively low risk."[17]

Drucker remarked it was relatively easy, particularly for an outside competitor, to pinpoint cracks in the established industrial edifice by recognizing signs of potential disturbance. He identified four symptoms for outsider opportunity that were usually the result of insider miscalculation: (1) failure to revise mission statement and organizational design when the industry's revenues doubled over a short period of time, (2) indifference to the fastest-growing segment of the new growth (this tendency to defend the obsolete provided the competitors with beachhead opportunities), (3) inability to visualize that a convergence of technologies previously considered separate was a sure sign of an industrial mutation, and (4) failure to alter basic industry character for a long period of time (making it a safe conjecture that the industry was ripe for a structural shakeout).

Drucker noted several industries (steel, coal, aluminum, automobiles, electronics, watchmaking, stock brokerages, and department stores) that had ignored the aforementioned symptoms of structural change and lost opportunities that were literally right under their noses. Equally important was the emergence of former noncompetitors who filled the vacuum by introducing new innovations and irreversible changes in traditional industrial structures (see the accompanying box).

Drucker commented on such leading examples of the industry and market structure tactic as these:

- Nucor and other mini steel mills rejected the obsolete technology of the large, vertically integrated steel companies.

- The technology of the digital watch was developed by Fairchild and Seiko but ignored by Bulova and other leaders in the watch industry.

- Merrill Lynch, General Electric, and other nonbanks created new financial instruments and credit facilities at the expense of the major banks.

- Eating out by two-income families in restaurants and at fast-food shops was not seen as a threat to supermarkets until they had lost a considerable share of the family food budget.

- Specialty boutiques, such as The Gap and Limited, seized on the changing consumer style preferences before the department stores recognized that change as a structural trend.

- Donaldson, Lufkin & Jenrette recognized the inability of small-size brokerage houses to meet the needs of institutional investors.

- Microsoft refused to accept the proposition that the future of the information industry resided more in hardware than software.

- Procter & Gamble's entry into the paper industry challenged the marketing assumptions of traditional manufacturers.

- Wal-Mart was not viewed as a major competitor by Sears Roebuck, which ignored the discounter's revolutionary merchandising techniques in employee training, customer service, and inventory control.

- The health maintenance organizations (HMOs) discovered innovative ways of delivering patient services that had hitherto been considered the province of established hospitals.

- Sprint, MCI, Rolm, and other noncompetitors recognized that the merging of commercial media and converging of telephonic technologies would mark a breakthrough in the sacred monopoly of AT&T.

Drucker informed us that the chief lessons in understanding the changes in industry and market structure are that there is no absolute way of satisfying the customer in a mass market, that trends are more qualitative than quantitative, that the haughty not-invented-here attitude inhibits innovation, and that noncompetitive outsiders have an advantage of fresh perception and of not having to undergo the painful process of unlearning the so-called conventional wisdom.[18]

Creative Imitation

According to Drucker, the military strategy of Confederate general Nathaniel Forrest, being "fustest with the mostest,"[19] was the most popular and celebrated tactic for a successful entrepreneur. At the same time, he considered this pioneering approach the greatest gamble because of the large stakes involved in creating a new market. It was particularly risky to originate an innovation because there was little room for error if the entrepreneur was not correct the first time. It was "very much like a moon shot: a deviation of a fraction of a minute of the arc and the missile disappears into outer space."[20] Although there had been many pioneering success stories, most bold and aspiring entrepreneurial ideas had disappeared into oblivion. Perhaps the most notable and consistent practitioner of being "fustest with the mostest" had been the Swiss pharmaceutical firm Hoffman LaRoche. It counted three major break-throughs: vitamins in the 1920s, sulfa drugs in the 1930s, and tranquilizing muscle relaxers in the 1950s.

As a footnote to discussing being first on the scene, Drucker downplayed the importance of the creative "Eureka!" discovery. Imagination, of course, was part of the process, but the major part of success was due to serious prob-ing and hard work in implementing the idea. He also cautioned that a suc-cessful pioneer should avoid acting as a monopolist and raising the price. His best model for this policy of resisting the temptation to raise prices was Alfred Nobel, czar of the dynamite cartel, who over the years consistently lowered prices to keep out competitors.

As a counterploy or feasible alternative to the disadvantages of "fustest with the mostest," Drucker suggested *creative imitation*. He conceded the term sounded contradictory because "what the entrepreneur does is something somebody else has already done. But it is 'creative' because the entrepreneur applying the strategy of 'creative imitation' understands what the innovation represents better than the people who made it and who innovated."[21]

In essence, the creative imitator acted on the assumption that the new innovation might be successful, but if it were only approximately correct, there was substantial room for improvement. Typically, the gap between incomplete and full success encountered by the pioneer came about because the original innovation was product driven rather than market driven. The originator's emphasis on technology was missing an ingredient for total success: it lacked attention to satisfying customer expectations. It was the unique talent of the creative imitator to exploit this marketing vacuum by "perfecting or position-ing the new product or service" so that it fulfilled these expectations. In effect, Drucker stated that creative imitation satisfies a demand that already exists rather than creating one: "By the time creative imitators go to work, the mar-ket has already been identified and the demand has already been created."[22]

He offered two outstanding examples of the imitator successfully improv-ing on the original innovation. IBM, for example, did not break new techno-logical ground in responding to Apple's personal computer. IBM's first personal computer was a solid product, but the real added value IBM created lay in establishing convenient distribution centers, providing excellent employee training programs, and guaranteeing first-rate service. Johnson & Johnson did not discover acetaminophen as a painkiller; it had been around for years as an over-the-counter drug. However, Johnson & Johnson reformulated it and promoted it as a safe, universal painkiller under the brand name of Tylenol. Within a couple of years it dominated the market.

Of course, if the pioneer did everything right the first time, the door was closed because there was no opportunity for improvement. But Drucker reiterated that because technological companies tended to be product driven rather than market driven, they were typically vulnerable to the creative innovator.

Moreover, creative imitation was not the exclusive domain of high-tech industries. A prime example of creative imitation in retailing was Wal-Mart. Sam Walton and his colleagues had an obsession with seeking improvement by visiting their competitors' stores. They not only liberally borrowed competitors' innovations but added consumer value to them by providing features that were missing in the original product or service.

Entrepreneurial Judo

Entrepreneurial judo was a tactic in which the innovator used the strengths and weaknesses of an opponent to the innovator's own advantage. Drucker considered it a skillful ploy for obtaining, at the outset, a modest market standing in an industry. It "aims first at securing a beachhead, and one which the established leaders either do not defend at all or defend only halfheartedly."[23] The newcomers have to make themselves distinct.

Taking a page out of the military manual, Drucker saw entrepreneurial judo as an offensive weapon geared to take the enemy by surprise. He believed it to be one of the least risky tactics because competitors who occupied a dominant market position rarely expected an assault on their established excellencies and successful habits. He also used the analogy of the successful criminal who confidently thinks he will never be caught but who inevitably betrays himself when the police discover he leaves the same signature on every crime. Similarly, many businesses with a leadership position display a pattern of bad habits, making them vulnerable to alert competitors. Moreover, despite frequent warnings of the dangers of bad habits, both the criminal and the business executive turn a deaf ear on reforming these threatening habits.

Drucker reported that the corporate cultures of many successful businesses revealed a modus operandi of persistent and inbred traits that were an open invitation for newcomers to diagnose attractive opportunities. In many respects these corporate behavior patterns resembled the actions of a cartel or a monopoly. Some of the major flaws, dissonances, and common miscalculations were these: taking an NIH (not invented here) attitude, creaming the market, holding a mythical belief in quality, adhering to the delusion of premium pricing, and maximizing rather than optimizing profits.[24]

The NIH syndrome assumed that no new idea had any substantive value unless it originated under the umbrella of the established corporate leadership. Drucker used the transistor as an illustration of this introspective attitude toward innovation. In the 1950s, there was an acknowledged consensus in the popular and scientific journals that the invention of the transistor would shake the basic technological foundation of the electronics industry. It was at once realized that the transistor was going to replace the vacuum tube, especially in consumer electronics. Everybody knew this, but nobody did anything about it, and especially not GE, RCA, Sylvania, and the other electronics giants. They immediately rejected the transistor because it was invented by Bell Labs, an outsider separated from the mores and customs of the electronics industry. They thought it inconceivable that any substitute product could replace the impregnable technological superiority of the vacuum tube. In addition they could not imagine how the highly esteemed engineering quality of the vacuum tube could be surpassed by the ridiculously cheap and common raw material in the transistor: "Compared to [vacuum tubes], they thought silicon chips low grade, if not indeed beneath their dignity."[25]

Then Sony, a little-known Japanese company, seized the opportunity by purchasing a license for the transistor from AT&T for $25,000. Then, through a combination of shrewd marketing, rigorous quality control, and product design improvement (especially miniaturization), Sony brought out the first transistor radio in less than two years and captured leadership in the world market within five years.

Drucker emphasized that the transistor was not an isolated example of entrepreneurial judo. Taking advantage of the tenacious complacency and the egregious bad habits of U.S. electronics manufacturers, the Japanese continued to surprise the Americans. They repeated their success in radios with television sets, digital watches, handheld calculators, copiers, and tape recorders.

The U.S. electrical manufacturers were also guilty of endorsing the myth of quality. Their belief in product superiority was based on the delusion that quality was what the supplier put in rather than what the customer paid for. These manufacturers believed that because their vacuum tubes cost a lot and required great skill to produce, the customer was buying technology. In applying the tactic of entrepreneurial judo, the Japanese proved that customers were actually purchasing performance and value added for less cost.

Drucker singled out Xerox as a potential case study of a successful innovator that believed such questionable practices as creaming the market, premium pricing, and maximizing rather than optimizing profits were sources of corporate strength. Actually these perceived strengths were fundamental weaknesses because they opened a wide window of opportunity for the competition to apply entrepreneurial judo. In creaming the market for higher profit margins, the company concentrated chiefly on the big corporate users, enabling the Japanese to establish a beachhead at the low end of the market and then later expand upward and outward to other segments. Similarly, premium pricing was self-defeating because higher margins should be the result of lower costs, otherwise the opportunity to enter the market becomes too tempting for competitors. Drucker asserted that both creaming and premium pricing in a mass market were violations of elementary economics and entrepreneurial management.

Finally, Drucker accused Xerox of resting on its laurels and acting as a monopolist by maximizing rather than optimizing profits. In attempting to satisfy every single user through the same product and service, Xerox allowed competitors to clone its copiers at a much lower cost and to create new pockets of specialized demand.

To parry such thrusts of entrepreneurial judo, pioneers had to act quickly on early success, avoid taking on the role of a monopolist, and recognize that industry structures would change rapidly as a result of breakthrough innovation. Conversely, Drucker advised newcomers challenging the leader that they had to go beyond simply cloning products and providing lower costs. They had to innovate by adding value to the product and improve consumer satisfaction. But before making these unique contributions they must do their homework, applying the following prescription: "To use the entrepreneurial judo strategy, one starts out with an analysis of the industry, the producers and the suppliers, their habits, especially their bad habits, and their policies. But then one looks at the markets and tries to pinpoint the place where an alternative strategy would meet with the greatest success and the least resistance."[26]

The Ecological Niche

Drucker briefly characterized the ecological niche tactic as taking an opportunity that aimed at partial control but not market dominance, focused on corporate anonymity rather than celebrity status, and explored areas where others were unlikely to compete. He discussed two variations of the tactic: (1) tollgate and (2) specialities.

Tollgate. Essentially, the tollgate strategy was directed at obtaining a monopoly position in one small aspect of a business system. Three examples were given by Drucker of this capacity of the entrepreneur to impose a toll on a critical segment of the process—the development of an enzyme that proved indispensable for a cataract operation on the eye, a blowout protection cap that was used as a safety device in the drilling of oil wells, and a sealing compound that was critical in the manufacture of tin cans. In each instance, because of the stringent requirements connected with the larger process, it was easy to assess the risk of not using the product: "The risk of losing an eye, losing an oil well, or spoilage in a tin can—must be infinitely greater than the cost of the product."[27]

Because the tollgate tactic was predicated on the narrow premise of the entrepreneur's possessing a crucial core excellence for the performance of a total process, Drucker cautioned that it was fated to be a static business. Despite its knowledge impregnability, it was from the outset a mature business incapable of expansion. As a captive of a larger business process, its survival depended on the economic viability of the system it was servicing.

Specialties. In surveying the relevance of specialties as an ecological niche, Drucker indicated that the most appropriate time to take advantage of this tactic was in the early stage of an industry's growth, when the inside entrepreneurs did not have the time, money, or knowledge to develop special competencies in certain technologies. This opened the door for outsiders. Moreover, "the business that establishes itself in a specialty skill niche is therefore unlikely to be threatened by its customers or by its suppliers. Neither of them really wants to get into something that is so alien in skill and in temperament."[28]

In the automobile industry, Drucker described how a number of companies (little known outside the field) were able to develop new techniques that were genuine innovations. They included Delco in batteries, Bosch in electronic systems, Bendix in brakes, and A. O. Smith in mainframes. However, businesses that relied on specialty skills also had vulnerabilities: a tendency to have tunnel vision, total dependence on somebody else to bring the product to the market, danger of the specialty becoming universal, and fragility in the face of major technological changes in the environment.

Structural Entrepreneurship

Drucker did not include mergers, acquisitions, and alliances under the umbrella of entrepreneurial tactics, but because they reflect some of the characteristics of risk and opportunity, it is plausible to place them in that category. In making sense of mergers, Drucker emphasized that it is a fallacy to start with numbers. He learned this uncompromising rule as a young man, from a senior investment banker who told him: "Mr. Drucker, you are starting out with the financial figures. That's wrong: One ends with them. You are talking of a marriage. One does not marry a girl without a dowry. But one first investigates her ancestors. First comes the ancestry. Then comes the girl. Finally, the dowry. The only thing that's negotiable is the dowry."[29]

Accusing most architects of mergers and acquisitions of failure to look beyond what they quantify, he remarked that too many mergers "resembled the marriage of two cripples who become twice as old, twice as bureaucratic and twice as undynamic."[30] To avoid a facade of quantitative face-lifting, he counseled it was more prudent to assume that there were no "easy businesses." It was wrong, he asserted, for managers to arrogantly adopt an acquisition policy based on the proposition that they could manage all types of businesses no matter how varied and complex.

Drucker briefly expressed his approach to mergers and acquisitions in these guidelines:[31]

- Begin with the compatibility between the corporate cultures of the partners.

- Refuse to undertake a merger where there is no empathy or understanding of the businesses.

- Recognize that a real synergy depends on a common core or technological and marketing unity.

- Make it an imperative that the acquiring company has respect for the products and markets of the acquired firm.

- Disregard the rhetoric of the miracle of synergy and remember that trust and results depend on hard work and systematic effort.

- Remember that it is a fallacy that all mature businesses are capable of an annual 10 percent growth and 15 percent return on investment.

- Accept the fact that one cannot buy management; the acquiring company must integrate competent people from the acquired company into its top management structure.

- Adopt a hands-off policy for a six-month period to enable the merged partners to understand themselves and their problems.

- Judge performance of the acquisition or the merger by total business objectives and principles rather than by a single financial yardstick.

Drucker also observed that although mergers and acquisitions grab the headlines in the business press, the tactic of alliances, joint ventures, and partnerships was playing a heightened role in the entrepreneurial process. For small and medium-sized companies, the tactic of alliance enabled them to enter the global arena and to compete against the corporate giants. In publishing, for example, smaller firms have flourished more than the corporate giants by demonstrating their flexibility to benefit from close relationships with outside vendors and establish workable relationships with freelance professionals.

Drucker noted that large corporations had always had alliances with vendors in areas outside the business's core competencies. The purpose in the past was to avert increased inside bureaucracies and to obtain outside points of view. Among the areas that came under these informal alliances were advertising, public relations, printing, security, cafeteria services, and training. Drucker observed that these outsourcing arrangements were also important because these areas of corporate activity chiefly offered only dead-end jobs, ones from which people could not rise in the managerial ranks.[32]

Unlike these traditional alliances resulting from make-or-buy corporate decisions, the more recent alliances take the form of a joint enterprise between two independent partners. According to Drucker, the joint enterprise venture has become one of the most convenient ways to fuse multitechnological relationships, joining companies with different types of knowledge. In describing the new configuration of intercorporate relationships, he wrote: "Large computer makers buy into small software houses; large electronics manufacturers buy into small designers of specialty chips; large pharmaceutical companies buy into genetics start-ups; large commercial banks buy into bond traders or underwriters. More and more, such alliances are also the way to get access to people with the know-how. The many research pacts between American universities and large European, Japanese (and American) businesses are good examples."[33]

Drucker acknowledged that joint enterprise alliances were structurally fragile and had a high probability of failure, but their track record of failures was no higher than that of mergers and acquisitions. Joint venture alliances had to overcome the strains of cultural differences, which produced a difficult working environment at the onset of the relationship, but the real crisis came with the attainment of entrepreneurial success. At this stage a real conflict emerged because each partner wanted to control the offspring. For example, when the alliance has performed well, the goals of the partners often become incompatible. Once the firm has developed into an adolescent, one partner might be reluctant to have the adolescent grow up.

To prevent any disintegration of the joint enterprise after achieving success, Drucker urged a contractual agreement at the outset that incorporated these guidelines: think through the objectives of the "child," agree on the principles of management and the people assigned responsibility for performance, and establish methods for the resolution of conflict.

Most managers assumed that the chief cause of alliances was the need to generate trade and investment. Drucker saw this factor as secondary to the critical need to pool knowledge, and where this resource was obtained was irrelevant. He listed two reasons for his lack of optimism in the ability of executives to conduct successful alliances in the global economy. First, there was the misunderstanding about the reasons for alliance creation. Second, there was little managerial experience in handling joint venture alliances.

CEOs, particularly from large corporations, knew little about the complexities of an alliance: because they were so used to "giving orders," few realized it was quite different working with a partner: "In an alliance or a joint venture, you have to begin by asking, 'What do our partners want? What are our shared values and goals?' Those aren't easy questions for somebody who grew up at GE or Citibank and is now at the top or near the top of a huge worldwide enterprise."[34]

The Transformational Business and the Breakthrough Innovation

The combined needs for continuing improvement in the traditional business and for adaptive improvement in the transitional business were integral parts of entrepreneurial change—and were basically self-apparent. But why did management also have to concern itself with the new and different transformational business? Drucker found it necessary for two reasons. First, it was a reality of the current accelerating epoch of turbulent change that every management had to respond to a destabilizing social, cultural, and economic environment. Second, when the typical business was confronted with these upheavals, it typically refused to acknowledge them. The transformational stage of a business had a uniquely different dimension of risk and opportunity than either the traditional or transitional business phases did. The latter two aspects of the entrepreneurial process were concerned with strategies based on empirical principles of organizing knowledge in a systematic fashion. The transformational stage focused on breakthrough innovation, on creating new knowledge as the centerpiece of entrepreneurial opportunity. Operating in the realm of uncertainty, where there were no facts only expectations, management faced the unprecedented challenge of organizing ignorance. A successful knowledge-based breakthrough innovation called for a redefinition of corporate mission, a new design structure, a qualitative shift in research philosophy, and a revision of the corporate culture's policies for staffing, reward, and promotion. Moreover, the fulfillment of the lofty aim of inventing the future through purposely planned change resulted in radically new forms of customer values and substantially different core competencies for the business.

Drucker labeled the scientific and technological opportunities that symbolized business transformation the *superstars* of innovation. He made this designation because, just like the stars in the theater and the sports realm, they received most of the money and publicity in the innovation process. Given the celebrity status of the knowledge-based opportunities, they differed from the typical innovation in that they were temperamental, unpredictable, and hard to manage. As with popular artists in the cultural world, there was a price to pay for the eccentricities and idiosyncrasies of superstars, but it was well worth it when they produced results.[35]

In addition to these obstacles, superstars made inordinate time demands on the entrepreneur: "Superstars are very precious, very expensive and very flighty. But the most substantial difference in managing knowledge-based innovation is primarily one of time. With all of the other sources, the innovator is likely to have a substantial amount of time during which he's left alone. With knowledge-based innovation you are immediately in the spotlight and have far more competition and very little room for making mistakes."[36]

In the business enterprise, managers had to deal not with talented person-alities but with endless pressures, unknown circumstances, and unanticipated events. But when successful, the knowledge-based opportunities not only cre-ated novel products but in many instances entire new industries. High-tech and scientific breakthroughs meant more than a textbook genuflection toward evaluating the future; they transcended prediction by focusing on actually inventing the future. They energized the vision and promoted most of the excitement in the nation's entrepreneurial economy.

Just as there were no accepted methods for the programming and care of artistic superstars, Drucker contended there were no experts in the minister-ing of knowledge-based innovation. He felt therefore that those who studied business had no choice but to consider what was known and unknown about the transformational process so that they could attain an understanding of and a degree of accountability for this unique type of innovation. With this goal in mind he sought out businesses' major features and strategies for coping with the competitive future.

In his analysis of the transformational business, Drucker listed several putative characteristics that posed major challenges for translating the break-through idea into reality. Among the three most significant were (1) the long time span, (2) the convergence of knowledge, and (3) a high casualty rate.

Long Time Span

According to Drucker, a common denominator of all knowledge-based dis-coveries was the long time span during which costs had to be absorbed, with-out any corresponding revenue, before the product reached the marketplace. Because there is no acceptable method for doing market research on the gen-uinely new, "knowledge-based innovation has the longest lead time of all in-novations. There is, first, a long time span between the emergence of new knowledge and its becoming applicable to technology. And then there is another long period before the new technology turns into products, processes, or services in the marketplace."[37]

Drucker did not profess to know the precise reason for this time lag phe-nomenon but suggested a clue might be found in the history of science. He alluded to the studies of history scholar Thomas Kuhn, who stated it took sev-eral generations before the acceptance of a new scientific paradigm received an endorsement from the scientific community. For example, he used the transitions from an Aristotelian to a Newtonian to an Einstein worldview as his models for understanding the lack of acceptance.

In a comparable vein Drucker calculated that it took roughly a generation for a discovery or an invention to attain successful commercial performance. To support this hypothesis, he described a number of illustrations. Among the most prominent were Paul Erlich's sulfa drugs; Charles Kettering's redesign of Rudolf Diesel's original engine; Buckminster Fuller's Dymaxion House, which had no receptivity until the concept was used for the construction of concert tents and sports arenas; and the two-decade period of gestation before Lee De Forest's audio tube became an indispensable feature of the radio industry.

Drucker's favorite illustration of the time lag between discovery and commercial success was penicillin. Alexander Fleming, a Scottish biochemist, accidentally made the discovery in the 1920s, but it languished in scientific journals for more than a decade. In the 1930s, Howard Florey, an Australian scientist, reformulated it and rejuvenated it as a potential marketable product. This goal, however, was not realizable until the hazardous trials to determine the proper dosage could be carried out, largely on hospitalized British troops during World War II. Finally, it took the manufacturing talents of Pfizer, a pharmaceutical company, to master methods of manufacturing the drug in massive quantities in the immediate postwar years. It was only after a generation of trial and error, therefore, that penicillin became the catalyst for the antibiotic revolution, which completely transformed the research and marketing foundations of the pharmaceutical industry.

The time lag for an effective breakthrough innovation existed beyond technical and scientific products. In diagnosing social innovation, Drucker noted a similar period of gestation before performance dividends were achieved for such social innovations as the French entrepreneurial bank, the modern university, the research lab, commercial paper, and the county farm agent, all of which have had a great impact on society but have been greatly neglected by economists.

Despite the volcanoes of inventions in the recent past, there has been no substantive reduction of the time factor. Addressing the persistence and tenacity of the time span before commercialization, Drucker remarked: "It is widely believed that scientific discoveries turn much faster in our day than ever before into technology, products, and processes. But this is largely illusion."[38] Because the time span of a scientific and technological breakthrough demanded patient personal commitment and corporate tenacity of purpose, he counseled that entrepreneurs should accept the reality that there is no probability of results in the immediate future.

Convergence of Knowledge

The convergence of different knowledges or technologies into a larger configuration was the second major characteristic of a knowledge-based innovation. The entrepreneurial talent to perceive the interaction of specialized disciplines and then to integrate their relevance into a marketable pattern was a feature of many successful innovations. To illustrate the characteristic, Drucker provided a number of examples. Henry Wallace's discovery of hybrid corn had its roots in the independent work of William Beal, a scientific animal breeder, and Hugo de Vries, a biologist renowned for his studies on Mendelian genetics. Apparently, the two men had no contact with each other, so their studies existed in a state of isolation until Wallace, a former secretary of agriculture under Herbert Hoover, converted their separate contributions into a successful productive and commercial venture. The fathers of modern aviation, Wilbur and Orville Wright, combined the technology of the early gasoline engine with the knowledge of aerodynamics learned from their experiments with gliders and created a new industry. James Gordon Bennett's *New York Herald* used a merger of high-speed printing and the telegraph to become the first cheap newspaper with a mass circulation that satisfied the growing reading thirst of the new mass literacy in the nineteenth century.

Drucker offered the modern computer as a classic clinical case study in the fusion of several distinct knowledges occurring over a long period of time. The six key types of knowledge needed were the binary theorem of mathematics, which reduced the expression of all numbers to series of ones and zeros; the ideas behind the first, primitive computer, constructed by Charles Babbage in the 1830s; the logic and design of the punch card for machine calculators, developed by Herman Hollerith in the late nineteenth century and providing a technique of information instruction and a form of feedback; the audio tube, devised in 1906 by Lee De Forest, an electronic device to meet the power requirement of mass multiplied by acceleration for the movement of information; the discipline of symbolic logic, which allowed people to express all mathematical concepts in numbers, created by Alfred North Whitehead and Bertrand Russell and published in their seminal book *Principia Mathematica* (1910–1913); and finally, the pragmatic and theoretical concepts of programming derived from the experiences in antiaircraft gunnery during World War I. In short the blending of all these diverse knowledges made it virtually inevitable that a modern computer would be constructed shortly prior to World War II as a prelude to the information revolution.

High Casualty Rate

An inordinately high casualty rate was another common denominator of knowledge-based innovation. Because grandiose and glamorous ideas aimed at going beyond incremental improvement, they were less reliable than any other innovation tactic. "Nine out of every ten 'brilliant ideas' turn out to be nonsense," Drucker reported. "And nine out of every ten ideas which, after thorough analysis, seem to be worthwhile and feasible turn out to be failures. . . . The mortality rate of innovations is—and should be—high."[39] Drucker never offered precise figures on the successes of breakthrough innovations but strongly insisted that only a small minority was able to crack the break-even profitability barrier.

In mentioning novel entrepreneurial ideas that were not of the high-tech variety, he implied that there were a larger number of success stories. That is, the more sophisticated and complex an innovative idea the greater the chance that it would wind up in the limbo of oblivion. He also conveyed the impression that when the factor of impact was considered, it was not always easy to draw a neat line of demarcation between the transitional and transformational businesses. Among the celebrated products in this low-tech classification were the zipper, the aerosol can, and the ballpoint pen.

In dissecting the pattern of the brilliant scientific opportunity in its passage to either success or obscurity, Drucker observed that the innovative idea had the feature of intrinsic ambiguity. Rarely making any logical sense, the original concept for the scientific breakthrough defied precise definition because it was impossible to identify the consumer.

It was hardly surprising that Drucker considered the breakthrough opportunity, which aimed at mutating the enterprise into something radically different, a challenge fraught with danger and uncertainty. He listed three ingredients that were an inherent part of the process: (1) a gamble, (2) unpredictability, and (3) nonreceptivity.

A Gamble. Circumstances change so quickly in today's competitive environment that Drucker equated the knowledge-based decision with a gamble, a "coin toss." An entrepreneur, even working with diligence far beyond the call of duty, even with the tenacity of Penelope at the loom and the patience of Job, could not overcome the odds against the probability of high failure. "There is actually no empirical evidence at all," Drucker observed, "for the belief that persistence pays off in pursuing the 'brilliant idea,' just as there is no evidence of any 'system' to beat the slot machines."[40]

This message has been brought home in a humorous vein by comedian Bob Newhart. In one of his monologues he showed how ridiculous Walter Raleigh would have appeared if he had tried to make a case for the potential value and use of tobacco in a proposal to King James I for commercial endorsement. Likewise Abner Doubleday would have appeared an eccentric fool in trying to describe the rules for his new game of baseball to a nineteenth-century toy manufacturer who had never seen the game and who would find the explanation incomprehensible.

Unpredictability. Drucker gave three examples of the futility of prediction, citing the forecasts of three distinguished companies with a reputation for successful innovation. IBM estimated in the early 1950s that only about two hundred thousand computers would be needed by the 1980s. Intel's management thought a mass-produced personal computer would be a waste of time because it believed the only practical use was for keeping a record of the housewife's recipes.

In 1956, Xerox possessed three major research studies on the newly invented copier. It was projected that the market could absorb only three thousand copiers a year. The management of Xerox proved the studies embarrassingly wrong by producing over eighty thousand in six months. Drucker tersely described the Xerox dilemma when predicting consumer usage and value for a genuinely new product: "No one knew that he needed an office copier before the first Xerox machine came out around 1960; five years later no business could imagine doing without a copier."[41]

Drucker admitted he had no satisfactory answer for the failure to predict things that seem patently obvious with the advantage of hindsight. In examining, moreover, the blind spots of some of the most exceptional minds in history, he concluded that their poor prognostication performance hardly inspired confidence for the average mortal. For example, Galileo Galilei refused to accept the principle of atmospheric pressure. William Thomson, the eminent nineteenth-century British physicist, viewed X rays as a hoax because they failed to meet strict standards of measurability. Thomas Edison for over a generation denounced alternating current for its impracticability. Simon Newcomb, a prominent scientist around the turn of the century, flatly declared shortly before the successful experiments of the Wright brothers that a heavier-than-air aircraft was incapable of flight. Ernest Rutherford, considered one of the twentieth-century's great physicists, dogmatically asserted that the creation of an atomic bomb was beyond the theoretical knowledge and engineering capability of modern physics. Vannevar Bush, one of the main participants in the Manhattan Project, which created the atomic bomb, was convinced that it would take almost a century before a space and missile system could be realized.

Drucker speculated that a major discontinuity or a unique event that ruptured a previous trend was never predictable. He indicated, for example, that the discontinuities resulting from Internet technology and the merging of the media in today's economy would pose similar difficulties even to experts in determining things to come. He cynically suggested that the recent rash of mega-multimedia mergers in the information and entertainment industries had little to do with managerial confidence or certainty about future consumer needs but were predicated on the premise that a major technological breakthrough by one company might mean its competitors would face extinction. The competitors are convinced of a radically new future reality but have no idea of its form.

Nonreceptivity. Drucker's final factor accounting for the high casualty rates of a knowledge-based innovation was that except in such rare instances as a cure for cancer, it was not safe to assume the innovation would be immediately received. If the breakthrough opportunity was premature, it would inevitably collapse; the time and the perception must be ripe for an acceptable application. To support this contention about the gap between innovation and utility, Drucker, as was his usual pattern, turned to the historical record: "The greatest inventive genius in recorded history was surely Leonardo da Vinci. There is a breathtaking idea—submarine or helicopter or automatic forge—on every single page of his notebooks. But not one of these could have been converted into an innovation with the technology and the materials of 1500. Indeed, for none of them would there have been any receptivity in the society and economy of the time."[42]

A more specific business example was the telephone, which was viscerally rejected when it was first proposed in late nineteenth-century Europe. For example, a telephone was invented in Germany about the same time as Alexander Graham Bell invented it in the United States. It received a cool reception from the commercial establishment because the telegraph seemed a sufficient tool for business communication purposes. The poor acceptance of the telephone in Britain was blatantly antitechnological. The British did not see any need for the telephone because they already had messenger boys.

In emphasizing the need to recognize the *ripeness* of an innovation, Drucker cautioned it was prudent to pursue a policy of watchful waiting before plunging mindlessly into developing the breakthrough opportunity. The transformational innovation was inherently more powerful than other business tactics and required a unique entrepreneurial attitude that mixed boldness with humility: "All other innovations exploit a change that has already occurred. They satisfy a need that already exists. But in knowledge-based innovation, the innovation brings about the change. It aims at creating a want. And no one can tell in advance whether the user is going to be receptive, indifferent, or actively resistant."[43]

Requirements

Drucker asserted that with all the limiting features of a knowledge-based innovation (a long lead time, the need for convergence of knowledge, and a high casualty rate), it was easy to assume that the breakthrough opportunity was "not predictable, cannot be organized, cannot be systematized and fails in the overwhelming majority of cases."[44] And yet the "bright idea" (whether in its technological or innovative form) was so critical to the dynamics of the entrepreneurial society that it could not be left to chance. Speaking specifically of technology, he reinforced this conviction by commenting: "High technology is tremendously important: as vision setter, pace setter, excitement maker, maker of the future. But as a maker of the present it is still almost marginal, accounting for no more than 10 percent of the jobs created in the past ten years."[45]

As a business moved in the direction of a business transformation, two prime prerequisites needed to be on the agenda: (1) organizing ignorance and (2) entrepreneurial management.

The Need for Organizing Ignorance. In observing the uncertainty and unreliability found in identifying and implementing the breakthrough innovation, Drucker recognized that projecting trends from the recent past mirrored only one dimension of reality. He argued therefore that organizing knowledge was insufficient to create the transformational stage of a business. The practitioner needed a supplementary methodology to convert worthless speculation about the future into prudent preparation. In short Drucker postulated that it was possible to germinate the seeds of a subject matter for which there were only expectations and no facts. He labeled this seemingly contradictory concept "the power of organized ignorance."[46] Contending that management textbooks and executive seminars devoted their exclusive attention to the organization of knowledge, and without denigrating the importance of this approach, he urged that more attention be paid to organizing ignorance—if for no other reason than that there is so much more of it than knowledge.

The basis of his cautious optimism for the validity of organizing ignorance resided partially in the systems approach, a theory that combined many different specialized sciences and technologies into a holistic frame of reference. This multidisciplinary characteristic was a feature of all the new systems industries, such as biogenetics, information processing, telecommunications, and medical technology. Using the systems approach as an entrepreneurial backdrop for the breakthrough opportunity, he suggested that entrepreneurs could take the following steps to organize ignorance. The first step in the systems model consisted of writing down a description of the expectations of the innovative idea; second, spelling out the conditions that had to be fulfilled to make the brilliant innovation successful; third, framing a budget for the anticipated costs of financial and human resources; fourth, considering the key transactional restraints from the outside that would impact the outcome; fifth, establishing a pattern for implementing the opportunity and making it reality; and sixth, providing a feedback mechanism (amid all the destabilizing effects of the innovation) to monitor the progress and measure the results of the innovation in an organized fashion.

Because it was impossible for Drucker to use the scientific method to confirm his hypothesis that such a convoluted and circular process would work, he used anecdotes to give it greater plausibility, describing a number of scientific innovations whose development mirrored his method of fusing components of ignorance into a successful configuration: the compilation of the chemical table of elements, the conquest of polio, the discovery of the DNA molecule, the invention of the atom bomb through the Manhattan Project, and the development of the intercontinental ballistic missile program by means of an ingenious organization of resources. Each of these breakthroughs had its unique features, but the missile program was a special case for showing how managers overcame a daunting scientific challenge. The managers of the project had to juxtapose into a meaningful configuration four separate areas of both theoretical and engineering ignorance: missile guidance, reentry, fuel, and warhead. The risks were so monumental that no private enterprise had the resources to tackle it.

Examples of breakthrough innovation in the business realm were far less dramatic. Drucker nevertheless considered that these innovations followed a similar model of imagining a future vision for which trends did not exist and then working back to the present to systematically translate the original idea into a commercial reality. Among the most successful outcomes, in which the opportunity resulted in not only a new product but the emergence of a new industry, were the airplane, plastics, transistors, penicillin, and copiers.

An acknowledged breakthrough not of the high-tech variety was Henry Ford's vision of manufacturing an affordable mass-produced automobile for the average worker. Ford based his brilliant marketing strategy on the assumption that an expanding market and not just price alone was the key to the successful creation of demand. He transformed the cottage industry that had been making automobiles singly, as rich men's toys, into the nation's largest consumer industry and stimulated a great social revolution in manners and mobility in the first half of the twentieth century.

The main message of Drucker's conceptual analysis of organizing ignorance was that innovators should not focus on predicting the future but on imposing themselves entrepreneurially on the future by creating a uniquely new type of knowledge that was economically applicable. In short, in all his examples, Drucker emphasized that the key question was not what the future should look like. That was a problem for social and political reformers. The concern of the business innovator was to produce purposeful change by creating new consumer value that at the same time contributed to the business's economic results.

In any event, organizing ignorance was for Drucker an indispensable tenet of the transformational business. He found the topic so enthralling, frustrating, and fascinating that he hoped to crystallize his thoughts into a book. Because he never got around to the challenge, he placed the topic in his long file of books he wished he had written but had never had the time to complete.

The Need for Entrepreneurial Management. Drucker looked upon entrepreneurial management as a supplementary aspect of the managerial task of coping with uncertainty and change. It differed from the textbook description of management in that it entailed an artistic attitude, one that expressed a conscious dissatisfaction with the current state of affairs and assigned a priority to creating new types of consumer demand.

When successful, entrepreneurs were what Drucker called the *silent revolutionaries* of society. He was not certain their practices were teachable, but he was convinced they were learnable. He added that even though there was no rigorous and codified set of rules, there was such a thing as *entrepreneurial inference*, which qualified as a theoretical insight even when the practitioner was unaware of any formal theory. Drucker divided the concept of entrepreneurial management, particularly as it related to the knowledge-based opportunity, into two categories: (1) economic and (2) structural.

Economic. Under the economic rubric Drucker especially stressed that the relevance of scientific and technological products did not depend on their novelty or technological ingenuity but on the market test. Moreover, the innovations had to have consumer acceptance today and not in some distant future. Too frequently scientists avoided this principle, assuming that a product or service would sell merely because they already knew the conditions of success. Comparing this Silicon Valley attitude with that of Benjamin Franklin's adage about inventing a better mousetrap, Drucker stated that scientists failed to answer the key entrepreneurial question, "what makes a mousetrap 'better,' or for whom?"[47]

Drucker often reiterated that opening up the frontiers of technological and scientific knowledge had entrepreneurial significance only to the extent that it created value by meeting intangible consumer satisfactions or solving consumer problems. To support this point, he mentioned, for example, that Werner Siemens, the nineteenth-century German scientist, saw beyond his invention of the generator and paved the way for the electric apparatus industry. Similarly, Thomas Edison invented the electric lightbulb at about the same time that Joseph Swan, an Englishman, invented a functional lightbulb, but Edison also concentrated on a power station and distribution system for cheap electricity, leading Drucker to remark that "Swan, the scientist, invented a product; Edison produced an industry."[48]

These nineteenth-century examples had relevance in today's world. If scientists were blinded by the brilliance of their scientific achievements and ignored consumer utility, if they did not carefully write down their expectations and then monitor them against reality, then the results would be purely academic and intellectual.

Structural. Drucker examined the structural aspects of entrepreneurial management from two major dimensions: (1) the multidisciplinary function and (2) the role of top management. First, he considered it mandatory that executives adopt a holistic perspective toward the entrepreneurial challenge by focusing on opportunities that might change the corporation into a new type of enterprise. This systems approach was especially germane in organizing research and development projects, because "except in very young technologies such as biogenetics, the technology-driven approach is becoming unproductive. We increasingly need a 'business-driven' R&D strategy."[49] The successful innovations were being carried out by cross-functional teams from marketing, manufacturing, and finance, who participated in research from the very beginning.

Second, arguing that the tasks of entrepreneurial management demanded a great deal of professional autonomy and structural decentralization, Drucker rejected the idea that such management was a super-function of top management. Because the command-and-control design of top management was no longer applicable, entrepreneurial management had to promote an atmosphere that encouraged and rewarded successful innovation. Instead of making entrepreneurial decisions by administrative fiat, CEOs had to function well with limited participation and power. In short, "a top management that believes its job is to sit in judgment will inevitably veto the new idea. It is always *impractical.* Only a top management that sees its central function as trying to convert into purposeful action the half-baked idea for something new will actually make its organization—whether company, university, laboratory, or hospital—capable of genuine innovation and self-renewal."[50]

The prime responsibility of the CEO remained the decision to formulate the corporate mission, for without a clear statement of purpose there could be no effective performance. But beyond that mandate entrepreneurial management meant stimulating the spirit of change throughout the organization.

Of course, any top management can damage and stifle entrepreneurship within its company. It's easy enough. All it takes is to say "No" to every new idea and to keep on saying it for a few years—and then make sure that those who came up with the new ideas never get a reward or a promotion and become ex-employees fairly swiftly. It is far less certain, however, that top management personalities and attitudes can by themselves—without the proper policies and practices—create an entrepreneurial business, which is what most of the books on entrepreneurship assert, at least by implication. . . . It requires a good many people who know what they are supposed to do, want to do it, are motivated toward doing it, and are supplied with both the tools and continuous reaffirmation. Otherwise there is only lip service; entrepreneurship soon becomes confined to the CEO's speeches.[51]

Conclusion

The treatment of the transitional and transformational dimensions of the business enterprise centered on a response to Drucker's two key strategic questions for the systematic management of change: What will the business be? and What should the business be? The function of innovation is the distinctive trait in which the transitional and transformational stages differ from the existing business.

Specifically, the transitional business concentrates on adaptive innovation by doing different things to meet unmet customer needs. If the venture is successful, it improves but does not radically alter the core knowledge competencies of the business. The innovation practiced in the transformational business is purposely planned change with the goal of creating a new business mission and competency base.

Both the transitional and transformational phases of the business focus on diagnosing opportunities, but each organizes its approach with a different set of tactics.

Drucker offered two methodologies for improved entrepreneurial results for the transitional business. First, he provided a methodology for diagnosing risk and opportunity, and he suggested a structural design for innovative meetings and the concept of dual budgets to make the organization more receptive to entrepreneurial thinking. Second, he offered a list of specific proposals and guidelines for converting opportunities into concrete results. They included handling the unexpected, analyzing business incongruities, identifying vital demographic trends, examining the pattern of industry structure, and understanding the significance of creative imitation.

Because the transformational business deals with the breakthrough knowledge innovation, Drucker was less expansive in describing specific tactical approaches. The difficulty with the breakthrough innovation is that it has a longer time span, a higher casualty rate, heightened marketing complexity, and convergent technologies—all of which discourage concrete proposals for results. Drucker did introduce, however, the concept of organizing ignorance, and he illustrated how it was possible to create the new when facts were virtually nonexistent. He cited such scientific examples as the chemical table of elements, atomic energy, the conquest of polio, and the discovery of DNA molecules.

Drucker conceded that all of his principles and guidelines for managing change systematically were abstractions unless implemented by managerial talent. The final segment of this study will discuss the way he addressed this challenge of executive effectiveness.

PETER DRUCKER

PART THREE

ON EXECUTIVE EFFECTIVENESS

CHAPTER TWELVE

MANAGING IN THE KNOWLEDGE SOCIETY

Thirty-one years ago Drucker coined the terms *knowledge society* and *knowledge worker*, introducing these insights in his 1968 work, *The Age of Discontinuity*.[1] In the interim the phenomenon of knowledge in contemporary society has been one of his central concerns. Specifically, in demonstrating the interaction between knowledge and society, he probed such topics as the role of technology, social impacts, and knowledge characteristics, which all were major forces in shaping the new educational environment in the United States—the world's first broad-based knowledge society.

Technological Roots

Drucker viewed the legacy of technology, rooted in the misty dawn of early history, as the foundation of today's knowledge society. Technology represented man's continual efforts by artificial means to transcend his natural vulnerabilities and to gain greater control over his environment. Through his toolmaking capacity, the human being demonstrated his superiority over animals by achieving countless technological triumphs to improve his material condition. Equally important, technology was the prime catalyst of work and worker expectations, whether the work was muscular, mechanical, or mental. "Technology is not about things: tools, processes, and products," Drucker commented. "It is about work: the specifically human activity by means of which man pushes back the limitations of the iron biological law which condemns all other animals to devote all their time and energy to keeping themselves alive for the next day, if not for the next hour. . . . We might define technology as human action on physical objects or as a set of physical objects characterized by serving human purposes. Either way the realm and subject matter of the study of technology would be human work."[2]

Moreover, man had the ability to accumulate an arsenal of functional techniques and build up a storehouse of utilitarian information, which could be converted into socialized knowledge because of the human capacity for communication and passed on to future generations. It was misleading, Drucker pointed out, to construe separate technological inventions as coming together in an isolated additive synthesis; each new technological input contributed to organic changes in the environmental configuration. Technology did not operate in a vacuum, but stimulated an interaction between man and his environment. All technology creates change, and any major technological invention produced a revolutionary change in society. For example, the railroad interconnected the cities and towns of a vast continent. The automobile created a mobile America. The typewriter, the first technology widely used by females outside the home, provided women with an independent income and probably did as much for women's emancipation as Susan B. Anthony and all the suffragettes combined. Without air-conditioning, the southwestern Sun Belt would probably have found economic growth too challenging. The electronic medium of television, with its feature of both sight and sound participation, had undermined the appeal of the linear, fragmented sport of baseball and had made football and other sports more attractive to the spectator. Whereas radio was an indispensable tool in Hitler's rise, he probably couldn't have been elected dogcatcher using the medium of television. It would have exposed him for the neurotic he was. At the same time, it would be difficult to imagine the election of Washington, Lincoln, and Jefferson, because of their absence of personal magnetism and lack of dramatic style, which are so highly valued by television audiences. Moreover, television often paves the way for different kinds of charismatic incompetents to gain influence.

According to Drucker, technology was the engine of change, and knowledge (information in action) was its fuel. The pace of all change therefore was mirrored in the sophistication of available tools and the quality of knowledge present at a given point in history. For example, in the long history of technology, Drucker identified three turning points that immutably shaped the historical process. The approximate dates of these significant revolutionary breakthroughs, which radically and irreversibly altered the environment, were 6000 B.C., A.D. 1750, and A.D. 1950. After each date new social systems were created, novel institutions emerged, and innovative patterns of work evolved.

Each of the three technological revolutions was characterized by a unique source of energy that provided the impetus for growth and shaped the nature of work. The first technological revolution, which marked the shift from nomadic to sedentary society, was the introduction of new agricultural techniques and the development of writing. It was the technological epoch of the longest duration and least change, lasting from 6000 B.C. until A.D. 1750, and was distinguished by the application of human energy to a rich variety of relatively primitive tools.[3]

Around the middle of the eighteenth century, the second technological revolution erupted on the historical scene with an explosion of new mechanical inventions, the most celebrated of which was the steam engine. Drucker pointed out, however, that these new inventions owed little or nothing to theoretical science. Most of the inventors were amateur tinkerers with no formal scientific education. Throughout the nineteenth century, machines became increasingly sophisticated, resulting in the mass production society. Toward the end of the century the introduction of organized research, most notably in the fields of chemistry and electricity, fostered many new discoveries. Drucker cited the astonishing statistic that from 1856 to 1914, "a new invention, leading almost immediately to a new industry, was made on average every fourteen to eighteen months."[4]

If the mythical Rip Van Winkle had arisen from a century of slumber that had started in 1850, he would have difficulty convincing himself that he still lived on the same planet. The engine of technology, fueled by the exponential increase of scientific knowledge, had promoted economic results when guided by an adventurous group of entrepreneurs and a new breed, professional managers. A new environment was created with countless new industrial products. It would require volumes to capture the full scope of this technological change, but among the products and services unfamiliar a century earlier, the following stand out clearly: electric light, subways, elevators, telephones, the telegraph, phonographs, photography, central heating and plumbing, skyscrapers, processed food, coal tar (used in countless synthetic drugs), hundreds of electrical robots for the home, refrigerators, automobiles, air-conditioning, suspension bridges, motion pictures, radios, televisions, typewriters, diesel engines, watches, advances in medicine and public health, the mechanization of agriculture, new energy sources, oceanic cables, airplanes, and breakthroughs in military technology.

Drucker's explanation for the astonishing output of innovation during this period was based on his insight that historically the introduction of a tool preceded its theoretical verification. For example, the lever was used for centuries before Archimedes developed a scientific formula to explain its operation. Eyeglasses were in existence in medieval times, but it was not until the eighteenth century that Sir Isaac Newton and Gottfried Wilhelm Leibniz gave us the theory of optics. It took about seventy-five years before William Thomson, 1st Baron Kelvin, provided a theoretical explanation of thermodynamics for James Watt's steam engine. And it took several decades before a theory of aerodynamics could satisfactorily explain why the Wright brothers' flying machine actually flew.

Drucker argued that throughout the era of Western civilization, technology and science had been uncoupled. Because technology (the art of doing) focused on utility and science (the art of thinking) concentrated on metaphysical abstractions, they had only the most coincidental and distant contact with each other. It was not until the last half of the nineteenth century that the technological and scientific streams interconnected, resulting in an explosion of new knowledge.

Drucker left no doubt that he considered technology the dominant partner in this encounter: "It would be claiming too much to say that technology established itself as the paramount power over science. But it was technology that built the future home, took out the marriage license, and hurried a rather reluctant science through the ceremony. And it is technology that gives the union of the two its character; it is a coupling of science *to* technology, rather than a coupling of science and technology."[5]

In any event, the merger paved the way for the German innovation of the research laboratory and Thomas Edison's contribution of systematic invention. In Edison's search for an electric light source, for example, the features of technology and research were combined under one roof through practicing the following steps: (1) defining a need (a reliable economic system of converting electricity into heat); (2) establishing a clear goal (a transparent container in which resistance to current would heat a filament to white heat); (3) identifying the major stages and the critical pieces of work to be accomplished (the power source, the filament, and the container); (4) getting feedback through continual monitoring of performance (for example, Edison found he needed a high vacuum rather than an inert gas as the environment for the filament, which in turn altered research on the container); and (5) organizing the work (each major segment was assigned to a group of professional specialists).

Although Edison's brilliance was the indispensable common denominator, he could not have pulled off the achievement alone. He needed the assistance of many professional minds from various scientific disciplines. Edison's genius consisted less in the invention of the lightbulb (others had also produced such bulbs), but in his vision of creating a new system. With the introduction of the power station and his concept of electricity as a new form of energy and heat at a low cost, the growth of the electrical industry was assured.[6]

The third technological revolution had its inception with the advent of the modern commercial computer around 1950. The uniqueness of the computer as a tool resided in the fact that it transcended the muscle and mechanics of previous technologies. Essentially it was not only a tool that was an extension of the brain with its power of calculation but, with the introduction of the transistor (a miniaturized computer on a chip), it was also a tool into which it was possible "to build intelligence." As a result, Drucker saw a qualitative shift occurring in work and human expectations: "Human nature has not changed much over recorded history. But the skills and the knowledge of people, their work and their jobs, their expectations—and also their life spans and their health—do change, and can change very rapidly. In no area, not even in technology, have the changes of the last thirty years been greater than in the work force; and in no area will the changes be greater—or come faster—in the remaining years of this century than in the work force—its composition, its working habits, its working life."[7]

An unprecedented form of mental energy, the third technological revolution produced an informational and knowledge explosion. So immense has been the cultural metamorphosis that it is difficult to capture it with any precision. Sociologists and economists have cited voluminous statistics documenting the rise of new high-tech industries, emergence of new academic disciplines, plethora of scientific journals, change in structural employment, geographical shifts in industry, escalation of research and development budgets, and education revolution, to cite a few changes.

Social and Economic Impacts

Although the third technological revolution is scarcely more than a generation old, it has produced more accelerated and substantive change than all previous technology combined. Among the most noteworthy of these mutations are the shift from literacy to knowledge and from craft to credentials, the postponed entry into the workforce, the proliferation of professions, and the movement from physical and visible to informational and invisible resources. If taken singly, each of these cultural discontinuities constitutes a major rupture with the past. Taken collectively and as they interact in combination, these new realities represent a silent social revolution. Drucker characterized this unprecedented transformation, based on the application of knowledge to performance, as the major force shaping contemporary society. Because of the significance of each qualitative factor, a brief elaboration is in order.

From Literacy to Knowledge

According to Drucker, literacy was the chief intellectual prerequisite of the machine-dominated second technological revolution. As long as the worker was equipped with the essential reading skills to understand the instructions on the machine, this was considered by the business community as more than sufficient to run an industrial economy. For the majority of the population, the high school diploma was the exception; it was deemed ornamental chiefly because of the dominance of "the self-made man" mentality and its corollary bias of a strong strain of anti-intellectualism in U.S. society. Indeed, prior to World War II, it was a source of constant amazement to foreign observers that so many Americans took parochial pride in the fact that fourteen presidents of the United States never graduated from college.

Drucker pointed out that in the old industrialism the focus was on things and products. In the new industrialism the emphasis was on ideas and information. One distinction between the old and new technology, for example, was the altered status of the Ph.D. degree in the business world. In the late forties at General Motors, Drucker learned that senior vice president Alfred Bradley concealed his doctorate, because it would have been embarrassing to have it recorded in the company's personnel files. Today, General Motors would treat a talented Ph.D. like a head of state.[8]

According to Drucker, the increase in production in the third technological revolution was explained not by machinery but by the installation of knowledge into the design of work. As a result, "for the first time in human history, we can employ large numbers of educated people productively."[9] Theoretical knowledge had in fact become the sine qua non of society's economic system, with the skills of literacy taken for granted. In the previous industrial society of mass production, a scattering of professionals (lawyers, accountants, and engineers) was adequate for staff support purposes, and their elimination from the economic scene would have had only marginal impact on business results. Professionals today account for a minority of the workforce, but without the contributions of educated knowledge workers the economic system would come to a grinding halt.

From Craft to Credentials

The craft tradition of learning, which stressed drill and repetition for the training of skills, was a historical legacy. It was enhanced and supplemented by an apprentice system that had served as the major vehicle for transmitting information in the seven thousand years of civilized man's recorded history. In an information-poor environment characterized by slow change and economic scarcity, the craft and apprentice models were adequate in meeting the demands of a tradition dominated society. However, in the postindustrial reality, the craft model and apprentice skills were vulnerable to knowledge onslaughts. Since World War II, the automation of mechanical processes had reduced millions of previously skilled and semiskilled workers to the status of machine tenders.

Prior to World War II, the college degree was considered a badge of aristocratic privilege or at least a mark of gentility. Moreover, it was deemed socially insulting to export any utility from the academic degree. Only for a minority entering the limited professional scene was it considered a necessary credential. After the war the attitude toward educational credentials began to change. Drucker commented that in particular, "the G.I. Bill of Rights—and the enthusiastic response to it on the part of America's veterans—signaled the shift to the knowledge society."[10] The G.I. Bill was the most spectacular and daring venture in the history of education. With over 2,332,000 veterans availing themselves of higher education, it was the largest and most successful single investment in human resources ever undertaken. In subsequent years, largely as a result of its impact, approximately 50 percent of the college age group attended some form of higher education institution. And the college degree had now become the passport of entry into the job market.

The increased ratio of knowledge workers to semiskilled craft workers had become a permanent structural feature of postindustrial society. Because of their dead-end prospects for higher-paid, challenging jobs, Drucker saw that the craft workers now held a position similar to that of the alienated industrial proletariat of the past century. In the previous economy, dominated by manufacturing, the wage of the craft worker had been the key economic index determining the standard of living. In the knowledge society an intellectual *salariat* assumed dominance over the manual and service proletariat. "Now," Drucker said, "there is practically no access to a middle-class income without a formal degree, which certifies to the acquisition of knowledge that can only be obtained systematically and in a school."[11] For example, in 1940, there were 845,000 coal miners and only 111,000 professors in the United States; by 1970, the number of miners had dwindled to 164,000 whereas the number of college professors had risen to 551,000.

Despite the economy's remarkable achievements during the explosion in educational credentials, Drucker had certain misgivings. "It's easy to fall into the trap because degrees are black-and-white. But it takes judgment to weigh a person's contribution."[12] He questioned the value of hiring exclusively on the basis of credentials as a proxy for competency and capability. Apropos of this excessive emphasis on credentials, he cynically stated that "if the increased educational credentials of the sixties for entrance into the workforce continues unabated, a person would not be able to pick up a broom without a Ph.D."[13]

Postponed Workforce Entry

Drucker pointed out how the unprecedented impact of prolonged schooling radically altered young people's time of entry into the workforce. Comparing the qualitative requirements of manual and knowledge work, he noted that person at the machine understood more about the job than anyone else. But this was not knowledge; it was experience. In contrast, the knowledge worker was paid for concepts learned in school, which the company hoped would be converted into performance. Or, to express the difference in another way, the semiskilled "worker serves the machine." In knowledge work, "the machine serves the worker."[14]

The postponed entry into the workforce necessitated by the need to acquire more knowledge was best illustrated by Drucker in comparing the widening gap between chronological and cultural age. He defined the former as biological age and the latter as the social age or the time in which a person entered the workforce and became financially independent. For example, the gap between the two age segments was relatively closed during the second technological revolution, when young men entered the workforce in their middle and late teens. Because most of them were financially independent at an early age, they started raising families almost immediately after commencing employment. In today's knowledge society, educated youngsters start work in their early twenties. Those aspiring to advanced professional degrees may be in their mid or late twenties before they no longer rely on their parents for disposable income.

Extended schooling, accompanied by deferred entry into the workforce, has become an irreversible social reality, and Drucker has also pointed out that despite the absence of a large segment of youngsters from the job market, that belated entry has been achieved without any loss of national productivity. In making a choice to become knowledge professionals, young people in their late teens and early twenties have been forced to make economic trade-offs. Instead of earning money, gaining practical experience, and contributing socially to national wealth, they have invested their time and money to acquire professional skills, concepts, and credentials in the hope of converting their learning power into future earning power. At the same time, they have different status expectations than their parents and grandparents.[15] The modern knowledge worker wants a career and not just a job, insists on responsibility to match the authority of knowledge, wants the opportunity to work smarter and not harder, and demands knowledge challenges with knowledge pay.

Proliferation of Professions

In the recent past most professional work was individual and independent, occurring outside the framework of large organizations. After World War II, that scenario changed dramatically, most notably in ending the previous isolation of knowledge professionals. According to Drucker, it became increasingly difficult for a knowledge professional to earn a living without membership in an organization.

The knowledge and organizational revolutions also dramatically expanded professionals' employment choices. Drucker cited, for example, professionals in the discipline of mathematics, who in the past were limited almost exclusively to teaching. Today mathematicians enjoy a wide range of employment options in business, science, government, and high-tech systems industries.[16] However, Drucker also stated that this abundance of choice might itself be a problem: "There are so many choices, so many opportunities, so many directions that they bewilder and distract the young people."[17]

The seeds of knowledge also germinated countless new disciplines necessary for the operation of modern industry. Most of the professional job listings in the *New York Times* and the *Wall Street Journal* are for positions of such esoteric variety that no futurologist could have predicted them a generation ago. The older professions of medicine, law, and engineering have spawned new areas of knowledge and specialties, making it almost impossible to incorporate all of them into traditional academic degree programs. Because knowledge is self-generating, it begets new knowledge with astonishing velocity; consequently, there is no end in sight for the exponential growth of information. Every knowledge discipline has grown so extensively and explosively in the proliferation of intellectual diversity that the vision of holistic unity eludes us. As mentioned earlier, Drucker personally reconciled the difficulty of achieving a vision encompassing the whole and integrating the business survival approaches of systems theory and social ecology: "When it comes to the job itself . . . the problem is not to dissect it into parts or motions, but to put together an integrated whole."[18]

From Physical to Informational Resources

Physical raw material formed the foundation of resource inputs in the old industrial society. For example, one primary rule of thumb for factory location, as outlined in all the old geography and business textbooks, was the proximity to natural raw materials and a cheap labor supply.

In contrast Drucker spoke of how knowledge created a new resource reality: "The world is becoming not labor intensive, not materials intensive, not energy intensive, but knowledge intensive."[19] In postindustrial society, the invisible resources of knowledge and information have replaced physical assets as the main factors of production. For example, plant locations for knowledge businesses (brain factories) have increasingly made propinquity to a major university the decisive factor in determining the site of their operations. It is no accident that the new high-tech systems businesses (communications, drugs, computers, biogenetics) have moved their facilities close to such university centers as MIT, Harvard, Princeton, Stanford, and the University of Texas, to cite a few of the new "regional knowledge capitals" of the country.

In the traditional industrial society, the cost of knowledge was a negligible component for any business. In today's economy, knowledge, or mental capital, is the central economic resource and consequently the major cost. Drucker assigned the economic textbook formulation of production to a residual position: "The traditional *factors of production*—land . . . , labor, and capital—have not disappeared, but they become secondary."[20]

Drucker never subscribed to the popular view that the problem of poor productivity was caused by the incompetency of the average blue-collar worker. In addition to the fact that the ranks of blue-collar workers were declining, techniques were available to measure their productivity with precision. Poor productivity was due to the failure to obtain improved results from accountants, lawyers, computer specialists, market researchers, and a whole cadre of knowledge workers.

In order to achieve the goal of greater professional contributions from knowledge workers, Drucker suggested a new perspective in which knowledge specialists would be seen as assets and not as expenses. The more knowledge a job has, the more capital needed. American management had to see the worker as an asset and not as a cost burden. "Knowledge work, unlike manual work, cannot be replaced by capital investment. On the contrary, capital investment creates the need for more knowledge work."[21] Because professionals were overadministered and undermanaged in most large corporations, a serious gap existed between capital investment and performance. Concomitantly, it was the task of top management to encourage knowledge workers to contribute to total corporate results. Educators and executives therefore had no choice but to reexamine the assumptions of executive development and determine what was known about knowledge as a unique resource and a new economic value.

Drucker was among the first social commentators who recognized that the challenge of knowledge productivity was unprecedented and that little was known about it. He indicated that perhaps one of the few valid assumptions available was that knowledge equaled authority: "Knowledge employees cannot, in effect, be supervised. Unless they know more than anybody else in the organization, they are to all intents and purposes useless."[22]

In distinguishing the major philosophical and structural differences between the old mechanical model of industrialism and the new paradigm of postcapitalism based on knowledge foundations, Drucker offered these observations:

- Because information does not degenerate into heat or friction (or at least shows only a minimum amount of decay), it is the first form of energy that is virtually exempt from the second law of thermodynamics.

- Human strengths are no longer confined to the rigidity of the assembly line; with the microprocessor, it is possible to reprogram the manufacturing process.

- A mechanical system is structured around faster speeds, higher temperatures, and heightened pressures; the energy input must increase substantially to achieve productivity as the system grows larger. On the other hand, a flexible informational system of productivity does not need more energy or raw materials. It substitutes data for both.

- Mechanical systems require huge size; a knowledge system miniaturizes size and explodes information.

- Expenditures in a mechanical system are considered social overhead; in an information-based economy they are viewed as capital investment.

- Transition from the second to third technological revolution represents a shift from high entropy and low inefficiency to low entropy and high efficiency.

- The mechanical model resembles a skeleton, and an information-based system is similar to a biological entity. The former has a closed system of communication with an abundance of quantitative measurement. The latter is open ended with an emphasis on qualitative measurement.

Knowledge Characteristics

Based on the proposition that knowledge is a unique form of mental capital, Drucker identified five major concepts in order to improve his understanding of this new resource: (1) storability, (2) measurability, (3) mobility, (4) impermanence, and (5) responsibility.

Storability

According to Drucker, information and data were storable commodities, but knowledge was not conducive to inventory. He made the distinction this way: "For the intellectual, knowledge is what is in a book. But as long as it is in a book, it is only 'information,' if not mere 'data.' Only when a man applies the information to doing something does it become knowledge."[23] Consequently, knowledge (information in action for results) was not an item purchasable from a commercial vendor, as physical raw materials were; it existed only between the two ears of an individual.

Measurability

In manual work the workers were called *hands*, implying productivity was measurable through a whole host of statistical tools and engineering techniques. This also implied that a doubling of manual workers would automatically result in the doubling of labor productivity. However, the problem of measurement for the new knowledge economy presented a different challenge. On the one hand Drucker recognized the inadequacy of simply counting the number of shoes or any other article produced. On the other hand, calculating the productivity of knowledge presented its own difficulties. "Knowledge, especially advanced knowledge, is always highly specialized. By itself it produces nothing."[24]

According to Drucker, the quantitative tools of measurement were not adequate because knowledge is intangible and therefore qualitative. For example, it was conceivable that there was such a thing as an average day's work for manual labor, but this was not possible in knowledge work. It was possible that a knowledge worker might be most productive when he or she was apparently doing nothing. With knowledge workers it was absurd to imagine an additive synthesis for improved productivity. "Two mediocre knowledge workers," he observed, "do not produce twice as much as one first-rate one. They do not even produce as much as one mediocre knowledge worker. In all probability they produce nothing—they just get in each other's way."[25]

Mobility

A further complication that operated against any precise measurement of knowledge as a unique resource was its unhierarchical character. Commenting on this egalitarian feature, Drucker wrote, "No knowledge ranks higher than another; each is judged by its contribution to the common task rather than by any inherent superiority or inferiority."[26] In Frederick Taylor's analysis of the manual worker's productivity, he assumed not only that there was an average worker and an average day's work but that there was one correct method of doing things. Drucker rejected these norms of standardization for knowledge work, because although "there may be 'one best way,' . . . it is heavily conditioned by the individual and not entirely determined by physical, or even by mental, characteristics of the job."[27] In the reality of the postindustrial world, traditional measurements of costs and performance made no sense. Drucker argued that in evaluating the performance of knowledge workers, there are new parameters. The tools of measurement have been replaced by judgment, and "there is a difference between a judgment and a measurement. Anybody with a ruler can measure Suzie's height, except operation research people who will use engineering standards of plus or minus 20 percent. A judgment is effective only when exercised by people with knowledge. A measurement requires only a stick."[28]

Impermanence

In the old industrial order the worker could assume that what he had learned would last a lifetime. Because experience was the critical factor, no craftworker thought of reaffirmation and renewal. A contrary condition occurs in postindustrial society. By its very nature, according to Drucker, knowledge destabilized the environment. And the greater the knowledge the greater the vanishing of yesterdays' assumptions and certainties.[29] Moreover, unless knowledge concepts were continually applied, improved, and challenged, they tended to evaporate quickly. Physical skills, although they could become rusty, could be quickly restored and refurbished.

Given the reality that knowledge obsoleted rapidly, professional specialization required constant renewal and rejuvenation. This reaffirmation imperative demanded that executives face the challenge of lifetime learning. Maintaining that management must be prepared to jettison everything it knows, Drucker contended that executives are now forced not only to learn and relearn continuously but also to unlearn in the process of development.

One recognition of this need for retooling the foundations of knowledge specialization has been the huge amount of money spent by corporations on education and training programs. Many of these corporate education budgets exceed those of large universities; executives now not only have to face the reality of learning, unlearning, and relearning in the process of development, but they can no longer assume that their specialization will remain the same throughout their careers.

Responsibility

Despite their many great insights, Frederick Taylor and Elton Mayo did not recognize that to improve productivity, it was important to "ask the people who do the work." Taylor considered workers "dumb oxen," and Mayo viewed them as "immature" and "maladjusted."[30] Because knowledge workers played such a minuscule role in the industrial system of this earlier era, both men assumed correctly that they had a marginal effect on productivity. If Taylor and Mayo had had the opportunity to study knowledge work in depth, they would have discovered, according to Drucker, that the specialists contributed nothing directly to the product yet their expertise was indispensable for business results.

However, specialized work had to be integrated into the task of contributing to customer value or it was meaningless.[31] And Drucker strongly emphasized that in integrating knowledge no specialized discipline was superior to any other. There was, therefore, no jurisdiction in knowledge work because every discipline that interacted with the task had to be studied and brought together. This accounted for the increased importance of knowledge teams.

Drucker asserted that knowledge is power; therefore, like all power, if it was not endowed with authority and responsibility, it quickly became arrogant and corrupting. Drawing on the legacy of Western political theory, he indicated that knowledge has always been a principle of action, in which a person must take responsibility for making things understood. The big difference was that in the past there were so few knowledge professionals, but in today's economy the educational revolution has created a mass market of careers for knowledge workers.

Given this reality of an abundance of specialized professionals and the imperative that knowledge demands accountability, Drucker contended that the principles of worker supervision found in most textbooks were irrelevant. In effect the only person a knowledge worker could manage was himself or herself. Moreover, Drucker took the position that in a knowledge organization, a manager who used power to force people to obey was actually a petty tyrant and a weak leader.

Although Drucker candidly conceded the intrinsic difficulty of calculating the contribution of knowledge workers, he argued that there was a great deal of evidence available for improving professional effectiveness. This had been the main theme of *The Effective Executive* (1967), his pioneering work on the subject. The main conclusion he reached with regard to the contribution and responsibility of knowledge workers was that the nature of performance has changed drastically. In the past, workers were viewed as hands who had to be worked increasingly harder. In a knowledge society, because the mind is something requiring development and application of concepts and ideas, the task is to make employees work smarter rather than harder. The key to business results is employees' "learning how to learn"; this was the foundation for making mental skills productive.

He also emphasized that knowledge without skill is unproductive. Only when knowledge is used as the basis for a skill does it become productive. In essence this meant that knowledge does not operate in a vacuum but demands continual practice. To achieve results, therefore, the knowledge worker's effectiveness depends on focusing on contribution not effort, output not input, performance not technique, and responsibility not activities.

Work and Working

The seminal contribution of Frederick Taylor, the founder of scientific management, was his pioneering effort on the philosophy and nature of productive work. Aside from pointing out that many past laboring techniques were invalid, he demolished the myth that working harder was more advantageous than working smarter. Notwithstanding Taylor's great innovative impact on the nature of work, however, his primary concern was the objective measurements of the individual task rather than general performance. As a result he neglected such nonquantitative elements as the achievements, fulfillments, and expectations of workers.

This vacuum of the social aspirations of workers was partially filled by sociologist Elton Mayo in his famous Hawthorne studies after World War I, which examined the working attitudes of the labor force. His insights demolished the myth of economic man and established the significance of informal group relationships in the job and the worker's need for individual attention.

According to Drucker, Taylor clearly recognized the objective factor of work, whereas Mayo saw the subjective significance of working.

In further crystallizing the distinction between the two key concepts of work and working, Drucker viewed work as basically external, quantitative, visible, and divisible, whereas the dynamic of working involved personal status, power dimensions, and perceptual elements—all directed at an individual's social position and fulfillment within the framework of communal group relationships. Pointing out that both work and working were crucial in understanding the demands of the employee, he emphasized the need to balance worker's productivity with a sense of personal satisfaction.

Because the literature on the logical analysis of work and the more subjective interpretation of working was highly specialized and academically fragmented, Drucker argued for the need to incorporate "the result focused" aspect of work and the human dimensions of working into a more comprehensive configuration. In order to organize the information about working so it could be used as the background for executive effectiveness, he selected the following five crucial dimensions of working: (1) physiological, (2) psychological, (3) social, (4) economic, and (5) power.

Physiological Dimensions

Drucker derived two major lessons from the countless experiments on the physical aspects of working. First, regardless of the passion involved in practicing a craft or a profession, as a person got tired, the positive results and personal satisfaction diminished. "The human being is not a machine and does not work like a machine."[32] Second, a corollary of this insight was that all jobs are intrinsically boring to a large extent. "For any one task and any one operation the human being is ill-suited. . . . He gets fatigued."[33] Consider, for example, the performance of any skilled professional. What looks simple to the outside observer is the result of years of ceaseless practice—much of it fatiguing, tedious, and boring.

From his early exposure to the automobile and other manufacturing industries, Drucker learned that there was a price to pay for the efficacy of mass production. The assembly line fostered physical stress and deterioration in the worker. The strengths of machinery depended on drill, routine, and repeatability—all of which were physically and mentally counterproductive for the individual. The assembly line produced "engineering misfits" because it was unable to develop human capacities of perception and imagination. In short Drucker viewed the assembly-line worker as a machine tender who found it physically impossible to escape from the pace and rhythm of the machine. Essentially, the assembly line was an inefficient system of engineering because it could not reconcile the dilemma of good machine productivity coupled with poor human engineering in terms of satisfaction for the worker.[34]

Drucker was convinced of the vulnerability of the assembly line largely because it was physically debilitating and mentally demoralizing. As he saw it, assembly-line jobs were suitable only for morons. It was only a question of time, he concluded, before the senseless and mindless work on the assembly line would be replaced by a superior and rational technology.

Where manual work was inflexible, knowledge work was diverse. The job structure of the former required uniformity; the latter demanded variety, with a wide latitude for changing the pace and rhythm of the task. Equally important, knowledge work had to have far more autonomy, precisely because it could not be designed *for* the worker. It could only be designed *by* the worker.[35]

Psychological Dimensions

Avoiding the historical debate about whether working is a curse or a blessing, Drucker saw it as a human necessity. Like George Bernard Shaw, he visualized a permanent two-week vacation as a form of living hell. He also believed that working was an extension of personality in which a person defined himself and measured his worth or humanity: "To make a living is no longer enough. Work also has to make a life."[36]

Motivation was a lever for improved productivity, a process whereby managers attempted, through job satisfaction, to enhance this fulfillment of individual human needs and simultaneously meet the production targets of the organization. The presence of such evocative words as *process, stimulation, needs,* and *fulfillment,* however, suggested that the consensus definition of motivation was subject to varied and debatable interpretations. Drucker often compared the psychologist's pursuit of the goal of unlocking the key to motivation to the search for the Holy Grail. He also found the semantical disputes on the meaning of motivation similar in vigor and intensity to the search for the proof of the existence of God by medieval theologians.

The importance of motivation as an energizing force in the achievement of human results was never denied by Drucker. He questioned, however, the ability of psychologists to transform their approaches into the reality of improved performance. (Because industrial psychologists have considered motivational theory an indispensable approach to worker achievement and satisfaction, a more detailed critique of their views is presented in Chapter Thirteen.)

Social Dimensions

According to Drucker, every working unit in an organization represented a sociological subculture. Their job, for most people, was their one important communal relationship outside of the narrow family unit. Within the bonds of a working group could be found these characteristics: an access to social status, structural linkages and relationships among different people, and a place for individuals to master and express their skills. The social factor, Drucker found, had assumed an added meaning in industrial society as compared to its agrarian predecessor. Because in a farming society everybody had a similar occupation, status was based on one's origins. But in an industrial society, it is based on what one does for a living. Consider a modern individual moving into a new neighborhood; the first question raised by people is not who the person is but what the person does for a living. Is he a doctor, lawyer, mechanic, accountant?[37]

For years Drucker urged that management recognize the need for industrial citizenship. He pointed out that although the family was the only true natural unit, the work group was similar in that it required a form of social bonding, but without the basic requirements and emotional demands of family obligations. To stress the importance of the work group as a socializing catalyst in fulfilling people's needs as social animals, he frequently cited the experience of retired people. They did not miss the work per se but missed the contacts, gossip, and personnel changes in the organization. These memories of social relationships interested retirees the most.

Economic Dimensions

Society's transition in its economic history from a barter economy to an industrial system with a pattern of cash payment for labor, introduced an economic component into the working configuration.[38] Monetary wages for the exchange of work became a significant economic reality in Europe and the United States in the nineteenth century. And this introduction of wage paying as a formal economic activity also created what Drucker labeled the capital versus wage fund dilemma, which he described as the conflict between the future survival needs of the firm and the employee's requirement for a decent standard of living. In short an emphasis on the wage fund meant a higher proportion of the profits went to the worker, but an emphasis on the capital fund meant a greater investment for tomorrow by the firm. In the trade-off between the use of financial resources for the firm's future job needs and for today's economic benefits for the worker, the wage fund was viewed as immediate income for the worker but as a necessary cost for the firm. Moreover, Drucker explained, the worker was disinterested in the financial future of the firm: "A financial stake in the business must always remain a secondary interest to the worker, compared to his job."[39] In effect the job for the worker was not only a source of income, it was the foundation of his economic existence.

Once, fifty years ago in *Concept of the Corporation* (1946), Drucker had thought that the granting of industrial citizenship, through which the firm would assure predictable salaries and other survival benefits, would be an adequate solution to the capital versus wage fund dilemma. In recent years, however, the increasing pressures for benefits and automatic salary increases as entitlements, along with global competition, have put too much pressure on the capital fund for corporations to offer such assurance to employees. He considers that the problem of allocating funds between capital and wage funds, a dilemma reflected in today's conflict between employee downsizing and shareholder value, will continue to be one of the great challenges for capitalism in the twenty-first century.

Power Dimensions

Except perhaps among solitary artists working on their own, power vacuums are contradictions of the requirements of the working world. As soon as people congregated for the purpose of work, the need arose for a framework of informal government, mirrored by rules and regulations. Without this political dimension of power, nobody would have the legitimate authority to schedule tasks, design work structures, distribute economic rewards, and assume responsibility for appraisal.[40]

One task of management has been to harmonize the tension between the corporation's quest for short-term profits and the demands for loyalty from knowledge workers. Drucker viewed this problem as the move from management of personnel as a "cost center" and a problem to leadership of people.[41] In addressing this challenge, he was the first (in *Concept of the Corporation*) to point out the power ramifications and the political dimensions of management. Because of its control of the employee's livelihood and career, the enterprise was a governmental as well as an economic and social institution. Moreover, without the consent and loyalty of employees and their resulting acceptance of the managerial mandate of power in enforcing the rules of the workplace, illegitimate power and anarchy would result. "Those who argue that the organization is without tensions and conflicts are romantics," he remarked, and he concluded there will always be a need to justify power through legitimate authority. On this point of the political dimension of corporate power, Drucker severely criticized top managements for their obscene and unjustified perks, stock options, and salaries, seeing these as acts of blatant irresponsibility.[42]

Conclusion

To Drucker the most troublesome issues, both intellectually and pragmatically, in managing the knowledge society were the one-dimensional explanations of work and working. An obstacle to understanding executive effectiveness was that advocates of a monistic theoretical discipline preached dogmatism. For example, Marxists saw reality only through the prism of economic determinism. Psychologists viewed everything from the aspect of the behavioral sciences. Sociologists looked upon employee status and function as the key to understanding. Political scientists considered institutional power the underlying rationale of corporate effectiveness. Rejecting the "fallacy of a dominant dimension" and calling for a multifaceted approach, Drucker contended that work and working was a human activity involving the whole person, with its own logic and dynamics. He argued that the "dimensions of working—the physiological, the psychological, the social, the economic, and the power dimension—are separate. Each can—and, indeed, should—be analyzed separately and independently. But they always exist together in the worker's situation and in his relationship to work and job, fellow workers and management."[43]

The next two chapters describe some of Drucker's views on the limitations of behavioral science and leadership theory and also the realities of managerial work as Drucker has seen them and his prescriptions for improving executive effectiveness.

CHAPTER THIRTEEN

APPROACHES TO EFFECTIVENESS

Drucker examined improved effectiveness from four points of view: (1) the thoughts of cynics and guerrillas, (2) the theories of behavioral science, (3) the discipline of ethics, and (4) the concepts of leadership. This chapter discusses his reactions to the cynics and guerrillas, the behavioral scientists, and the discipline of ethics. Leadership requires a chapter to itself and is examined in Chapter Fourteen.

Cynics and Guerrillas

Largely because it has left no literature, the cynical school of managerial effectiveness can be treated briefly. An anti-intellectual approach, it claims that all theory is bunk and all alleged principles of practice are suspect. In addressing the question of whether exceptional managers are born or made, the cynics endorse as true only the first proposition. Henry Ford was a classic, but hardly an isolated, example of the indispensable man practicing micromanagement by refusing to delegate authority to others.

Drucker was appalled by the arrogance and anti-intellectual character of this position, and he pointed out two concrete obstacles to its usefulness—the law of probability and the principle of succession. First, he noted that there were many examples of short-run success by managers who believed that after God created them he threw away the mold. But given the forces of change and competition in an entrepreneurial economy, the odds were against their sustained success over the long run. Moreover, as a firm expanded and complexity increased, managerial omniscience faded—the laws of probability rejected the notion that one person could be excellent in all functions and all circumstances.

Second, the individual who saw the business exclusively as a lengthening shadow of himself was bound to ignore the problem of succession. He would be constitutionally unable to see the business in terms of perpetuity because, equating his supposed indispensability with immortality, he would see the search for a replacement as a futile exercise.

The guerrilla approach to improved productivity was more an attitude than a direct frontal attack. According to Drucker, it was a satirical indictment of the pomposity of academic theorists, the hubris of executive skepticism, the insouciance of bureaucratic administrators, the pretentiousness of charismatic leaders, and the myopia of businessmen. The chief representatives of this genre are Robert Townsend *(Up the Organization)*, Shepherd Mead *(How to Succeed in Business Without Trying)*, C. Northcote Parkinson *(Parkinson's Laws)*, Lawrence Peter *(The Peter Principle)*, and Scott Adams *(The Dilbert Principle)*.

Drucker considered the guerrilla writers to be intellectual terrorists, who worked assiduously to undermine the questionable assumptions of conventional wisdom in the field of management. He found them amusing but not helpful in promoting executive effectiveness. Moreover, he thought that a focus on constantly telling others what is wrong results in an essentially barren and sterile exercise that does not address the issue of executive results.

Behavioral Science

In considering the role of the behavioral sciences from the angle of possibly improving executive performance, Drucker focused his critique on four main topics: (1) neglect of the productivity factor, (2) one-dimensional view of human nature, (3) power and morality, and (4) the mirage of motivation.

Neglect of the Productivity Factor

Drucker failed to discover any major correlation between human relations research and productivity. He found that the bulk of research activity, instead of concentrating on actual business results, centered on the validation and confirmation of the hypotheses proposed by the psychologists.

In asserting that human affairs were conducted imperfectly rather than with wisdom, Drucker deplored the dependence on untested assumptions, the fascination with neatly designed symmetrical models divorced from experience, and the tendency to leapfrog from abstraction to abstraction at the expense of concreteness. One reason for this palpable weakness in industrial psychology was the restricted and single-minded focus of the discipline. Behavioral scientists viewed the enterprise exclusively in terms of human satisfactions. Drucker disagreed, contending that the human element was only one of the firm's survival areas, which also included marketing, finance, and innovation. Only a few industrial psychologists were exceptions to Drucker's lack of admiration for the profession; among them were Abraham Maslow, Chris Argyris, and Frederick Herzberg. Although he often vigorously disagreed with their positions, he applauded their efforts to dissect the interaction between theory and practice by examining results.

Drucker admitted that most modern psychologists produced provocative and challenging concepts; however, these concepts were so intrinsically theoretical that it was impossible to convert them into meaningful business principles. Making this uncharitable point in a rather crass fashion, he told an interviewer:

> You know, starting the Nobel Prize in Economics was a fundamental misunderstanding, because economics has to do with policy and not with knowledge. Psychology has to do with insight and vision and not with knowledge. Neither is a science. . . . I don't think a Nobel for psychology makes any sense. Look, in physics and chemistry, the recognition is based directly on the judgment of your peers. But in economics and psychology, what you really recognize is the impact on the laity. That's why the stature of a great psychology can't depend on the judgment of peers, because they'll choose somebody who fed sex hormones to tapeworms and turned them into lesbians.[1]

On several occasions, Drucker conceded that the behavioral sciences were all to the good if they helped the practitioner to understand himself and others. In giving this bland endorsement, however, he failed to cite any concrete examples. Moreover, he made the point that psychology had no monopoly in providing understanding of the human condition. For example, he cited the genius of Shakespeare and Dickens in portraying characters and the dilemmas of human nature with far greater depth than the leading members of the behavioral science discipline.[2]

In discussing its failure to bridge the gap between theory and performance, Drucker severely criticized popular psychology for its infatuation with fads and gimmicks. He seriously questioned the value of such proposed panaceas as Theory X and Theory Y, managerial grids, decision-making trees, role-playing games, assertiveness training, assessment centers for fast-track executives, assignments structured around personality traits, creativity centers, brainstorming, sensitivity training, consulting therapy, and transcendental meditation. According to Drucker there was no evidence that these academic endeavors enlarged the frontiers of knowledge, much less contributed to specific results.

Contending that logic without the test of experience was untenable, he strongly complained that the compulsion on psychologists to *publish or perish* was geared to the interests of academic mandarins rather than to the needs of the potential beneficiaries of psychological research, the professional practitioners.[3] In essence, business academics felt that by emulating their colleagues in the liberal arts, they would earn more scholarly respect in the university for their disciplines. The implication was that scholarship would be considered contaminated, no longer genuine, if it could be labeled useful and pragmatic. Drucker, however, accused the profession of irresponsibility in rejecting practice for panaceas, dismissing fundamentals for gimmicks, sacrificing substance for style, and ignoring profitability performance for abstract and arcane research. He firmly insisted that without consideration of results, there could be no meaningful human relations function in the firm.

Drucker also observed that the publish-or-perish imperative often seemed mainly a vehicle for full employment for academic psychologists. For example, a novel panacea would appear in the business journals. Then a few months later other academics would attack the innovation as nugatory and illusory. Shortly after the old fad became an intellectual corpse, a new idea would became fashionable, only to quickly suffer the same fate as its predecessors.

The research of the behavioral scientists with their elegant equations, impressively packaged models, and promised solutions was cleverly and brilliantly conceived, but it suffered from the low correlation between pseudo-knowledge and specific effectiveness. The chasm between research and effectiveness increased as academics isolated themselves in abstractions, far from the travails of the operating practitioner.[4] And the brilliant intellectual achievement was next to worthless when the industrial psychologist refused to translate it into action. Drucker was reminded of the comment of Catherine the Great to Diderot: that which looks so astonishingly simple on paper loses its substance when put to the test of results. In the classic confrontation between the scholar and the doer, the former tended to adopt an aura of superiority by parading his or her learning. As psychologists focused on behavior to the neglect of results, the outcome was the breeding of arrogance, forcing Drucker to advise the practitioner that it was foolish to put up with the pompousness of academic experts.

What surprised and fascinated Drucker was that hardheaded businessmen who prided themselves on the notion that they were only interested in "what works" were the sponsors of a large part of the psychological research. Perhaps it was the fear of missing a golden intellectual breakthrough or simply peer group pressure that prompted executives to support so many senseless projects. Observing how managements were attracted to psychological fads and panaceas, Drucker became convinced that it was a myth that only the young were susceptible to peer group pressure.

Many consulting psychologists thought their role was to be catalysts in a process that allowed executives to arrive at a comfortable consensus by reconciling personality differences. In Drucker's mind this chimerical quest for getting along by going along was nonproductive. Moreover, he thought that the emphasis on personality traits and the removal of personality conflicts in the organization was a misdiagnosis of reality.

He also did not believe that these consultants had a distinguished track record when it came to employee selection. A great deal of time and money had gone into employee selection using such means as search committees and head hunters. Perhaps these consultants were better than doing nothing—but not much better than doing nothing. The delegation of power to consulting psychologists in the CEO succession process in particular seemed totally ineffective and an abdication of managerial responsibility. He suggested a more valid way of handling the promotion and selection process was to undertake some form of internal market research by asking employees to identify the star performers in the organization and then ascertaining why these individuals performed so brilliantly over average executives.[5]

In Drucker's mind the most disturbing aspect of popular psychology was its creation of a new secular priesthood that claimed it could alter personality in the direction of human perfectibility. The shibboleth of this new trend was the endless search for the discovery of the "real me." The goal was to attain, through a variety of therapeutic methods, greater personal self-esteem and mastery of human relations in the workplace. This idyllic and progressive path to human perfectibility was considered the potential solution to both personal and organizational problems. Drucker was totally skeptical of this quixotic objective,[6] and remarked: "Contrary to everything that modern psychologists tell you, I am convinced that one can acquire knowledge, one can acquire skills, but one cannot change his personality."[7]

These secular attempts at human reengineering "all promise 'consciousness-raising' and non-religious conversion resulting in a 'changed person.'"[8] However, Drucker thought fallacious the belief that such sessions could produce positive, permanent, and healthy outcomes. If the Almighty had wished to create such perfectly intelligent human beings, he would have done so. Drucker pointed out that

> An old gibe defines a "changed person" as a drunkard who does not hit the bottle for a whole week after taking the pledge at the temperance meeting. It pretty much fits the pop-psychological pseudo-revivals.
>
> A month after the great personality change wrought by a week with a T-group, the New Adam likely had again become the Old sinner—just as nasty, intolerant and uncaring as before (though perhaps a little more self-righteous). And while lasting positive effects were few, there often was long-term, sometimes irreversible, damage.[9]

Believing that the basic personality profile of an individual had been formed by the age of five, he accepted that only God had the power to make revisions after that point. Rather than support the consciousness-raising techniques of psychologists, he worked within the framework that the human being was a specimen of neither perfect rationality nor perfect irrationality but an imperfect combination of both. He thought it was the height of folly to devise a perfect theory for human change—then it would only be necessary to wind up a mechanical man to do productive tasks.

As long as these modern forms of brainwashing received the support of top management, Drucker was positive that belief in magic had not ended with the Druids and alchemists. However, in rejecting the road toward human perfectibility, he gave an affirmative to the path toward human improvement (a topic that will receive fuller treatment in subsequent chapters).

One-Dimensional View of Human Nature

Drucker expressed a rigid rejection of absolutes, regardless of their content. It was hardly surprising, therefore, that he was fiercely against the endorsement of any theory of human nature that assumed people are all alike. Cataloguing individuals according to prescribed types could result only in a dull and boring psychology. And, as discussed earlier, he thought that considering psychology a science was an academic hang-up. He praised Freud and other great psychologists not for their scientific principles but for their vision and insights that enabled individuals to have a different perception of themselves and the people around them.[10]

In this connection he also gave little credence to that popular psychological rage of the sixties—packaging human nature into X and Y personality types. Theory X assumed that people were inherently lazy and were incapable of motivation except through fear. Theory Y assumed employees were self-starting, diligent, ambitious, and capable of directing and motivating themselves.

Deriding such an overwhelming simplification of human nature, he did not believe that people had Theory X and Theory Y personalities. Neither Theory X nor Theory Y was all right or all wrong. Reality dictated that confining people to narrow personality profiles was a senseless approach because it was possible to discern "different human natures which behave differently under different conditions."[11] He contended, for example, that to assume under Theory X that many people did not want to work was to be defeated at the outset. It was the manager's job to make work productive and the worker an achiever—this included everybody. It was also a mistake to assume that Theory Y personalities did not require a tremendous amount of mature self-discipline. Theory Y makes extreme demands, and not everybody is adult enough to accept them.[12]

Despite the rhetoric that was flowing from the young about autonomy and freedom, managers had to be careful in adopting such a permissive premise: "People, especially the young, think that they want all the freedom they can get, but it is very demanding, very difficult to think through who you are and what you do best."[13] Because character is a human and not a psychological trait, he argued that humans would always act as humans—unpredictable and indeterminate—and forever would defy the mandates of social and psychological engineering.

Further complicating any deciphering of the human condition was the fact that people, regardless of supposed personality types, react differently under altered circumstances. Drucker found it puzzling that in one situation a person might sabotage something for one reason or another and in other situations perform proficiently. On this point he remarked: "We . . . now know that individuals can acquire the habit of achievement but can also acquire the habit of defeat. This again is not compatible with either the Theory X or the Theory Y of human nature."[14] Moreover, his observation that human uniformity was a fallacy had been reinforced by his early consulting experience: "Of the scores of executives whom I met during my work with General Motors, no two were alike. The main impression that has remained with me is of the diversity of personalities, characters, and idiosyncrasies, in complete contrast to the myth of 'the organization man.'"[15]

Drucker observed that it was the height of folly to slot people into jobs on the basis of personality profiles rather than defined tasks. Because humans participated in many different roles in their lifetimes and careers, each person manifested many different types of personality characteristics. He also felt it was a mistake to design a position around personality because that would inevitably lead to favoritism and conformity. In the final analysis it was the purpose of the job that determined how people would act.

Finally, Drucker ridiculed and dismissed any intellectual quest to design a one-dimensional rationale of human nature, for two major reasons. First, not only was not enough known about human nature, but all attempts to classify people into types ignored the crucial traits of character and integrity. It was not possible to acquire these trustworthy features; either a person had them or he did not. And "character is more important than abilities. That of course isn't learned at an early age."[16] He reasoned that the absence of integrity meant the ultimate destruction of all work, whereas an employee of average competency but with moral values was unlikely to damage the organization. Second, in the real world there was no such element in the human spectrum as an "effective personality."[17] The one common denominator of effective people was that they got things done.

Power and Morality

Drucker found it remarkable that moral tenets were ignored in the literature of popular psychology. In the treatment of power, there was the implicit assumption that the end justified the means and might made right. Equally disturbing, the treatment of power and morality in the business journals was predicated on untested hypotheses, monistic explanations, abstract absolutes, and unverified assumptions about managerial realities. To make their descriptions more impressive and convincing, the scholarly articles were presented in precise quantitative and mathematical form, leading Drucker to quip, " 'Scientific' is not synonymous with quantification—if it were, astrology would be the queen of sciences."[18]

Drucker suggested that it was the penchant of the behavioral scientists for overadministering the employee and undermanaging the productivity of work that forced these scientists to ignore the moral norms of right and wrong. Instead, the emphasis was on treating adults as children and using deceptive techniques of coercion to gain control. The outcome of this amoral attitude was a paternalistic psychology embodying subtle elements of manipulation.

Interspersed throughout his writings, Drucker offered the following criticisms, which constitute a bill of indictment on the ethical shortcomings of industrial psychology:

- It fosters the mindless use of and unjustified faith in testing to predict employees' future performance.

- It structures jobs around personality rather than meaningful contributions.

- It defines jobs rigidly, implying that they are some sacrosanct form of organizational natural law.

- It sorts people into personality profiles in order to make the prophesies of psychological testing self-fulfilling.

- It compels executive spouses to undergo assertiveness training programs to adjust them to the canons of corporate culture.

- It is insensitive to the unintended and harmful side effects of the application of interventionist techniques to individuals.

- It results in companies that have training programs rather than training policies and placement programs rather than career paths for their employees.

- It preaches the slogan that people are our greatest resource but in practice ignores that premise by underutilizing and restricting the capabilities of the human resource.

- It fails to distinguish between the equality of opportunity and the equality of results.

- It is arrogant in proclaiming its ability to spot "crown princes" for top management positions.

- It is insistent on training people who either cannot learn from such training or who reject it.

The tools and practices of coercion (see the accompanying box) violate organizational trust and teamwork—two fundamental moral imperatives for professional work. Paraphrasing the advice of Saint Augustine, Drucker counseled that no mundane institution deserved total allegiance and that every member of an organization required a private life. He reiterated these guiding organizational concepts by insisting that employers had no moral or legal right to demand absolute loyalty; they should require only an honest day's work and a commitment to contribution. Additional demands were unjustified and an invitation to the abuse of managerial power. Unequivocal in his endorsement of the principles of employee privacy, he stated: "Company-ordered psychological seminars . . . are . . . an invasion of privacy that is not justified by any company need. They are morally indefensible. And they are bitterly resented. . . . Hence anything that goes beyond asking for the specific performance for the sake of which the employee is on the payroll is usurpation and illegitimate."[19]

Drucker insisted there was something inherently unnatural about the psychological campaign for constant remedial and coercive therapy. He felt coercive control rejected the more realistic axiom that human beings desired to be human beings and that this simple fact was what human relations was all about. In his mind, when managers exceeded the power required to perform necessary tasks, the inevitable outcome was tyranny. The corrupting element in power became immediately evident when power meant perks and privileges for the superiors holding control and passive loyalty and obedience for the inferiors lacking it. Equally important, he indicated that the outcome, when executives played amateur psychologists, was the impression that "the manager is healthy while everybody else is sick."[20]

Drucker considered the pervasive misuse of psychotherapy techniques throughout the corporate world a violation of the traditional rules of morality and power, commenting that "if we applied the FDA rules of safety to psychotherapy there would be not one panacea on the market."[21] Discussing sensitivity training, one of the most popular therapeutic remedies of the 1960s, Drucker opted for what was for him the height of vitriolic sarcasm: "I'm one of those very simple people who believe that one is not entitled to inflict damage on the living body. For the weak, the lame, the defenseless, the shy, the vulnerable, this is a very dangerous thing. The real sadists, the wolves, tear the little lambs to pieces. The casualty rate is unacceptable."[22]

Drucker believed that psychotherapeutic T-groups were morally unjustified because they were tantamount to dissecting the human body while it was still alive. But equally unacceptable were *consciousness raising* sessions to enable the individual to find the "real me." Drawing upon the wisdom of the philosopher Martin Buber, Drucker equated the search for the "real me" through the vehicle of sensitivity training with a quest for selfish egoism devoid of mutual obligations. T-groups did not communicate because they focused on the "I" and not the "Thou."[23]

According to Drucker, a psychological philosophy that viewed man as an instrument to be controlled rather than an independent moral being was one that also assumed that those who wielded the power were omniscient. He compared this psychological despotism to the doctrine of enlightened despotism in the political sphere. Because both the political and psychological variations of despotism depended for implementation on the creation of philosopher-kings, he predicted a similar fate of inevitable failure for the latter: "Psychological despotism cannot work any more than enlightened despotism worked in the political sphere two hundred years ago—and for the same reason. *It requires universal genius on the part of the ruler.*"[24]

The political tyrant was chiefly interested in the control of the body, but Drucker pointed out that consciousness raising carried out through despotic techniques was an insidious form of "brainwashing": "Under this new psychological dispensation, persuasion replaces command." Emphasizing the dangers of mental manipulation, he added: "To use psychology to control, dominate, and manipulate others is self-destructive abuse of knowledge. It is also a particularly repugnant form of tyranny. The master of old was content to control the slave's body."[25]

Drucker feared that the situational ethics of human relations were replacing the principles of right and wrong. Breaking with the traditional ethics of Western civilization, with its emphasis on individual responsibility, the new elastic ethics of doing one's own thing preached the love of humanity but at the same time found it difficult to love the individual. Similarly, he thought psychologists practiced an insidious form of self-righteousness when they paradoxically exempted themselves from responsibility for their own behavior but were insistent in holding everybody else responsible for his or her own behavior.

Drucker conceded that modern managers had to know a great deal more about themselves and others than they presently did. But in a world of accelerating change and complexities, they also had to have knowledge about countless other disciplines. He further reminded managers of their need to be action focused, rather than allured and overfascinated with introspection. If carried too far, such introspection could endanger the survival of the enterprise. Indeed, "any manager, no matter how many psychology seminars he has attended, who attempts to put psychological despotism into practice will very rapidly become its first casualty. He will immediately blunder. He will impair performance."[26]

In Drucker's mind, the success of a business depended on a unique idea. At the same time, the business mission should also be bolstered by a "sense of right purpose." And the pursuit of wrong purpose was more deleterious to the health of the organization than the inefficient search for a moral purpose. In a similar vein, he urged executives to subscribe to a behavioral science that eschewed unnecessary controls, encouraged responsibility and self-discipline, and avoided the abuse of power.

Mirage of Motivation

Drucker's evaluation of motivation will be more understandable against the backdrop of a summary of his harsh criticisms of the behavioral sciences. These criticisms included the failure to correlate results with heightened theoretical expectations, a disdain for the useful and practical, sterile techniques in evaluating human nature, the inane notion that people are all alike, the proposition that personal fulfillment is more important than organizational achievement, an obsessive concern with control and manipulative techniques, an absence of spiritual values, a fascination with meaningless quantitative models, and the simplistic search for a mythical "real me." These and other severe indictments of the psychological community did not endear Drucker to the educational establishment. And such criticisms partially explain why his reception was much greater in the business than in the academic community. However, given his belief that the purpose of professional knowledge was to increase the effectiveness of the practitioner, Drucker was largely indifferent to the lack of admiration from the scholarly community.

In considering the topic of motivation, he expanded on his previous criticisms and frequently repeated his attacks on the psychologists for what he considered their shallow and irrelevant evaluations of the human condition. Consider, for example, his candid and curt denunciation of five decades of motivational investigation: "And despite all the research done on motivation in the last 50 years, we really so far know very much about how to quench motivation and very little about how to kindle it."[27]

Drucker was convinced that motivational psychologists ignored in their experiments the distinction between the quantifiable *what* and *how* of human activity and the metaphysical *why* of human meaning. The former concerned itself with substance, but the latter resisted concreteness. In delineating the distinction between the *is* and the *ought to be,* he expressed the notion that the observable had its limits and was of little help in the examination of complex intangible phenomena.

In discussing the relationship between what went on in the mind (a "black box") and recognizable behavior, he gave this example: "If little Johnny hits Suzie in the head with a rock, the act is overt. But the motivation is in the black box, and Johnny is just as unable as anybody else to peer into that black box."[28] Given the inability to look into the mystery of the mind, Drucker thought that the voluminous research on the why of motivational drives was fundamentally flawed. Faced with the dubious assumptions of motivational psychologists, he asserted that never have so many contributed so much massive quantification of human conduct with so few qualitative results.

Drucker went as far as to maintain that there had been no major substantive intellectual breakthroughs in our understanding of employee motivation since the Hawthorne study of seventy years ago. Everything in the interim had been a footnote on Elton Mayo's pioneering innovation. He expanded satirically on the superficiality of research in the motivational segment of professional psychology: "There are only two kinds of books on which a publisher never loses money: cookbooks and books on motivation. And for the same reason. They are bought by people who can't do either."[29]

If the enormous literature on motivation were simply a question of mental gymnastics and scholarly irrelevance, Drucker would have considered it a harmless pursuit among members of the academy for intellectual recognition. What troubled him, however, was the motivational psychologists who did not admit their ignorance and who claimed their techniques had the capacity to alter the human psyche. As described earlier, he felt that the perfectibility of human nature was the great illusion of modern psychology.

Drucker also challenged a favorite assumption of psychologists that the dysfunctions of organizational life had their roots in personality defects among professionals in the executive suites. These psychologists' arrogant belief in their capacity to remedy defective personalities produced, in his judgment, a secular priesthood of sorcerers and shamans. Because he considered the hypothesis that personality problems caused corporate problems a flawed one, leading inevitably to a misdiagnosis of human and organizational reality, he offered a more sober evaluation of alleged human differences.

Reflecting on his extensive experience with organizations, Drucker reported it was a misconception of reality when clients complained to him that they had personality problems with their employees. He found that personality problems were in fact rare, largely because organizations were usually tolerant of diverse personalities. And he added parenthetically that too much attention had been paid to the subject of stress as a manifestation of pathology. Making the point that needs were satisfied by results and not hard work, he took exception to much of the literature, contending that most of the stress alluded to was in fact an illusion—it was not really stress if a person did not feel it directly—it was simply hard work.

Drucker's objections to most of the claims of motivational theorists notwithstanding, he recognized the prime importance of motivation in the fact that no project could succeed without strongly committed and dedicated individuals. And the higher the achievement bar of performance was raised, the greater the requirements for motivational drive.

Drucker's argument was not with the significance of motivation but with psychologists' attempts to program motivation into people. He did not know anybody who had the wherewithal to motivate people in a systematic fashion to produce satisfactory results. He suggested that a sounder and simpler alternate approach would be to encourage greater self-motivation through giving individuals responsibility. Personal involvement did matter, because outer success was rare if inner commitment was not present. However, many of the activities connected with motivational management actually seemed to make it difficult for people to work effectively, and Drucker observed that "having nothing to do except make sure that other people work is not managing—it is busyness."[30] The real challenge of executive effectiveness was to create conditions for growth so that individuals could motivate themselves. Yet this goal was currently untenable because of the unbridgeable gap between the theoretical tenets of motivational psychology (however well intended) and the realities of practical application.

Drucker felt it astonishing that the behavioral scientists paid so much attention to the factor of motivation when the real problem was "not to motivate people but to keep from turning them off. The quickest way to quench motivation is not to allow people to do what they've been trained to do."[31] His insight was that study should be devoted to those activities of mismanagement that hamper performance. Unlike the nuances of psychology, he argued, this was an area managers knew something about because they confronted it on a daily basis. As a result of his extensive consulting experience, which had exposed him to hundreds of organizations, he observed a plethora of pathologies that smothered motivation and contributed to nonresults. They included such practices and procedures as ill-designed jobs, unfair compensation plans, poorly conceived training programs, irrational work rules and regulations, encrusted corporate cultures, invasions of employee privacy, and failures to communicate objectives, to cite only a few.

The century-old carrot-and-stick solution for motivating employees was based on a combination of judicious intimidation and selected rewards. Drucker had never been enthusiastic about it even for the old industrialism, and he considered it a major source of demotivation for the knowledge workers of postindustrial society. The work and working dynamics of the new information age were based on the movement of concepts and ideas rather than the making and moving of things. This new economic order emphasized reciprocal relationships of trust and obligation between management and employees.[32] Fear was incompatible with the responsibility and self-direction needed for knowledge work, because "if misused to drive, disciplinary devices can cause only resentment and resistance. They can only demotivate."[33]

If the "stick of fear" destroyed motivation because it lacked power and credibility, the lure of the carrot was even more motivationally debilitating in professional work. Drucker rejected the assumption that it was possible to manage knowledge workers. Because knowledge now equals authority, he deemed it totally imprudent to assert that one can manage the work of knowledge people. And the fact that everybody was asserting it in books did not make it true.

Accordingly, traditional motivational techniques, using the incentive of the materialistic carrot of rewards, were completely at odds with contemporary organizational reality. Drucker looked upon this mercenary approach as a manipulative way of providing psychological security but said it could not promote genuine professional motivation: "Responsibility cannot be bought for money. Financial rewards and incentives are, of course, important, but they work largely negatively."[34] For example, magnificent salaries, luxurious working conditions, regular promotions, and privileges might have symbolic significance, but they can be disillusioning when it comes to motivation because "nothing creates dissatisfaction faster than a big title, a lot of money and only donkey work to do. It destroys your hope because where else is there to go."[35]

Drucker further contended that salary increases were not considered badges of merit but were looked upon as a yardstick of comparison with one's peers, and "there is no more powerful disincentive, no more effective bar to motivation, than dissatisfaction over one's pay compared to that of one's peers."[36] English philosopher Thomas Hobbes (1588–1679), in *Leviathan,* presumed that life was a brutal social existence consisting of a joyless quest for power and a war of all against all,[37] a view that places satisfaction over accomplishment in the economic steeplechase of materialism. Drucker, however, observed that when economic satisfaction is used as a primary motivator, "the increment of material rewards capable of motivating people to work has to become larger. As people get more they do not become satisfied with a little more, let alone with less. They expect much more."[38] He compared money used as a motivator to a heroin addiction because it wore off quickly and required larger and larger doses for ephemeral satisfaction: "This also means that the social side effects of the carrot are reaching toxic proportions. A potent medicine always has side effects; and the larger the dosage, the greater the side effects."[39]

Summary

In *The Practice of Management* (1954), Drucker raised the question of whether or not personnel management was bankrupt. He answered: "No it is not bankrupt. Its liabilities do not exceed its assets. But it is certainly insolvent, certainly unable to honor, with the ready cash of performance, the promises of managing worker and work it so liberally makes."[40] He added that most of what passed for human relations was so mechanical and barren that it could be dispensed by mail. If it were not for the unions, he wondered if personnel departments were at all necessary.

Drucker accused the industrial psychologists of operating under such misguided assumptions as confusing the principle of analysis with the principle of action, divorcing planning from doing, emphasizing fire fighting over fire prevention, focusing on fear and manipulation as substitutes for pride and professionalism in motivating the workforce, concentrating on the passive goals of employee happiness and satisfaction instead of fostering peak performance, practicing psychological despotism under the rhetoric of caring for the workforce, and overstressing the potency of financial rewards to the exclusion of other motivational factors.

Even more important than the use of questionable techniques was the dubious moral philosophy that said material fulfillment and personal security were genuine substitutes for continued learning and development: "We committed a great crime," Drucker said. "We upgraded the income, the social status, and the job security of people without upgrading their competence. It's like bringing a baby raccoon into the house and making a pet out of it, then when it becomes big, you throw it out into the wilds to fend for itself."[41]

Finally, Drucker viewed the psychologists' efforts as concentrating on the manual worker in order to improve productivity, but this was yesterday's worker. Totally lacking was the vision necessary to emphasize the importance of the knowledge worker.

The Ethical Dimension

Drucker's blistering indictment of popular psychology for its lack of moral fervor might readily suggest he would have great expectations that the discipline of ethics would fill this spiritual vacuum in managing the human resource. He indeed recognized the importance of understanding the meaning of right and wrong as an indispensable feature of executive decision making and effectiveness. At the same time, he severely attacked the contemporary discipline of ethics on two grounds: (1) the inadequacy of the currently popular *business ethics* and (2) the fallacy of philosophical rational absolutes.

Business Ethics

The current rage for university courses and executive seminars, the saturation of journal and magazine articles, and the packed attendance at lectures by leading philosophers on the topic of business ethics have not contributed much to executive effectiveness in Drucker's view. Indicating that he derived little from such articles and discussions, he confessed that "he learned more [about ethics] as a practicing management consultant than he did when he taught religion."[42]

Drucker found that the new business ethics lacked the spiritual values that induced passion and commitment. Failing to comprehend the need for a special ethical code for commerce, he viewed such a code as a new species of casuistry, the seventeenth-century political ethic that called for separate moral responsibilities for the ruler and for the ruled. As Drucker pointed out, Blaise Pascal (1623–1662) and many others demolished the intellectual validity of political casuistry on the grounds that this practice failed to establish universal ethical norms—norms applying to both the rich and powerful and the impoverished and the weak—the hallmark of all ethical theories since the time of Plato.[43] All the great moral scholars in the Western tradition had their disagreements over what the specific content of a moral philosophy should be and whether the roots of its authority were to be based on the divine, on human nature, or on the needs of society. But all authorities agreed that there should be only one set of ethics, one set of rules, and one code of individual behavior that was the same for everyone.[44]

Equally important, Drucker considered the contemporary business morality as a specious justification of the power of those in control and a similarly specious mandate for their position of authority. He predicted that just as political casuistry resulted in political despotism, modern business ethics would suffer the fate of psychological despotism. Moreover, if a choice had to be made in a business crisis, executives would select spiritual bankruptcy over economic bankruptcy.

Drucker feared that two dangerous extremes could arise from current business ethics. The first was that management could exploit its power by exerting its control over employees and at the same time enrich itself with stock options, perks, and obscene salaries. At the other end of the corporate spectrum, Drucker thought it possible for a situation to emerge in which the employer had all the obligations and the employees all the rights. He found both scenarios distasteful, but because of the moral laxity of business ethics, both were logical outcomes.

Because it had divorced itself from mainstream historical ethics, Drucker considered business ethics "ethical chic." He objected not only to the way business ethics viewed the morality of right and wrong and its rejection of the axiom of universality but also to its failure to recognize cultural differences in the global arena.[45]

Rational Absolutes

Its derivation of a moral code from rational absolutes was Drucker's other major complaint about modern ethical philosophy. The norms of all the nineteenth-century rational ethical systems were determined by society, resulting in a sacrifice of individual autonomy and moral choice. Drucker included in this criticism the general will of J.-J. Rousseau, the categorical imperative of Immanuel Kant, the historical dialectic of Georg Hegel, the greatest good for the greatest number of Jeremy Bentham, and the economic determinism of Karl Marx.

Drucker traced this flight from the spiritual toward a focus on the mundane to the eighteenth-century Enlightenment. In effect, modern philosophers substituted for the old religious, otherworldly trinity (God the Father, God the Son, and God the Holy Ghost) a worldly trinity (Nature, Reason, and Progress). In adopting secular salvation as the intellectual foundation of contemporary thinking, ethical philosophy of the nineteenth century was formulated on the deification of nature and the denaturing of God.

According to Drucker, the separation of the rational from the spiritual meant that the philosophical analysis of ethics was based on the question, Why did society exist? to the exclusion of the existential question, Why did the individual exist? Because the focus was only on society, Drucker concluded that the outcomes could only be rational absolutes. Philosophically, this analysis could lead only to subjective relativism and ultimately to totalitarianism.

By analyzing right and wrong on the basis of social existence, an absolutist rational, ethical philosophy could contribute to improved behavior in the individual, personal integrity, and civic virtue, but it could not give satisfactory answers to the deeper questions of life and death. Moreover, Drucker rejected the optimistic assumptions of the modern philosophers that were based on a belief in human perfectibility and irreversible social progress. He believed that it was quixotic to prescribe the creation of a heaven here on earth, reducing human beings to a mechanistic response of historical forces.

Drucker turned to the ideas of the Danish philosopher Søren Kierkegaard (1813–1855), who had punctured the naive optimism of rational philosophy and shown how it sacrificed human freedom and moral choice. Essentially, he demolished rational absolutism as a source of ethics by introducing the question, Why did the human exist? As long as mundane social existence was more important than the individual human spirit, Kierkegaard stated that it was inescapable that the outcome would be a negative concept of individual existence. In that outcome, "there is, in short, no human existence, there is only social existence. There is no individual, there is only the citizen."[46]

Kierkegaard centered his main arguments on the simultaneous tensions between two types of time: temporal and eternal. The former was concerned with time spent on earth and the latter with the hereafter. The demarcation point between the two categories of time was death. At that point, in temporal time, the individual vanished and only society remained. However, in eternal time, the individual continued to exist and society was nonexistent. "In eternity only the individual exists. In eternity each individual is unique, he alone, all alone without neighbors or friends."[47] In short, the need to be a social animal was a necessity in temporal time, but was forbidden in eternity.

The rational philosophers' view of the human species as headed for irreversible progress and irrevocable perfection was to Kierkegaard a view of humans reduced to a set of statistics. In their neglect of the factor of death, the rational philosophers failed to give real meaning to either life or death.

Whereas his philosophical opponents were satisfied that humankind was moving inexorably in the direction of an earthly paradise, Kierkegaard pessimistically interpreted humanity as being a condition of tragedy that was filled with "fear and trembling." Because rationalism was not the answer, Kierkegaard could see no alternative to the simultaneous tensions between temporal time and eternity except to equate the latter with "the sight of God." Hence, the answer for him was "a leap to faith."[48]

Kierkegaard played an important role in shaping Drucker's rejection of absolute rationalism and his acceptance of transcendental core beliefs in formulating his own ethical approach, with three key interacting features: (1) the universal value system of the Judeo-Christian tradition, which rested on monotheism, accountability to a higher superior being, and natural laws (this value system might not be provable, but it was discoverable); (2) the role played by conscience as an inner gyroscope in determining right and wrong; and (3) the unique circumstances of a particular ethical decision.

To convey the concept that the mundane was subject to the mandates of the sacrosanct, Drucker called on the ethical philosophy of Saint Bonaventure (1221–1274), who attributed the source of all knowledge to the divinity. Drucker commented: "I must admit that I am not quite sure how cost accounting, or the study of tax loopholes, or brand marketing, will lead back to the Source of All Light, let alone to the knowledge of Ultimate Truth. But I am quite sure that the spirit of Saint Bonaventure's short sentence [about the source of all knowledge] must animate all we do if management is to have results."[49]

The three interacting features Drucker identified serve as the foundation for ethical decision making. Thus there are no simplistic answers for complex moral questions. Drucker did, however, provide a number of suggestions that might help managers in thinking through ethical dilemmas:

- The problem of ethical responsibility is one of moral values and moral education. There is no separate ethics of business nor is one needed.

- The most difficult ethical problems involve not right versus wrong but right versus right.

- Greek tragedy is always a conflict between right and right. Conflict between right and wrong is better put on the stage as a farce.

- Traditional ethics, regardless of school, looked for the right response to a given situation. We need an ethics today that concerns itself with the problems of creating the right situation.

- Economic interests are divisible, whereas political and religious beliefs are not. One can always split an economic difference in two, and although half a loaf is better than no bread, half a child, as King Solomon long ago perceived, is no good at all. The same goes for half a religion, half a philosophy, or half a political principle.

■ The Hippocratic principle of *primum non nocere* ("first, do no harm") continues to be an essential guideline for all professional conduct.

■ The law can handle the rights and objectives of the collective, but ethics is always the matter of the person, the right actions of individuals.

■ The ethics of prudence, a major tradition in the West, demands of individual leaders that they shun actions that cannot easily be understood, explained, or justified. They have an ethical obligation to give the example of "right behavior" and to avoid the example of "wrong behavior."

■ The ethics of prudence does not spell out what right behavior is. It assumes that what is wrong behavior is clear enough—and if there is any doubt about a behavior, then it is questionable and to be avoided.

■ Society needs a return to spiritual values, for it needs compassion. It needs the deep experience that the "Thou" and the "I" are one, which all higher religions share.

■ Totalitarianism is the final result of science without morality.

■ On the one hand, men of strict and virtuous conscience deserve our admiration for their support of unpopular causes. On the other hand, because their conscience refuses to compromise with power in any form, they change nothing, move nothing, and accomplish nothing. Power often corrupts, but the impotence of "pure dissenters" produces casualties instead of results.

■ A basic ethical guideline is to ask the question: When you look at yourself in the mirror the next morning, will you like the person you see?

■ Integrity may be hard to define, but lack of integrity is of such seriousness that it should disqualify an individual for a managerial position.

■ Power and wealth impose moral responsibility.

■ Because knowledge is no longer considered a social ornament but a form of power, the central moral problem of modern society will be the responsibility of knowledge workers.

■ Whenever a man's failure can clearly be traced to management's mistakes, in conscience he has to be kept on the payroll.

- What shocks young graduates is that the top executives do not feel entitled, let alone compelled, to act according to their consciences.

- Stock options reward the executive for doing the wrong thing rather than encouraging right behavior. Instead of asking, Did we make the right decisions? the manager is asking, How did we close today? He is mixing business and personal interests.

- The excessive executive pay phenomenon is not economically significant, but it has a moral impact. The problem in the United States is that executive pay rises even when profits decline.

- Twentieth-century man has achieved the knowledge to destroy himself both physically and morally. This new absolute has added a new dimension to human existence.

- The Confucian ethic is the most durable and successful of all moral traditions. It is a universal ethic in which the same rules and imperatives of behavior hold for every individual. There are five basic relationships of interdependence, which for the Confucian embrace the totality of human interactions in civil society: superior and subordinate, father and child, husband and wife, oldest brother and sibling, and friend and friend. For example, for a Confucian, sexual harassment is clearly unethical behavior because it injects power into a relationship that is based on function. This makes it exploitation.

- Confucianism asserts that interdependence demands equality of obligations. Children owe obedience and respect to their parents. Parents, in turn, owe affection, sustenance, and, yes, respect to their children. In the ethics of interdependence, there are only obligations, and all obligations are mutual.

- In the current version of business ethics in the United States, one side has all the obligations and the other side has all the entitlements. This is compatible neither with the ethics of interdependence nor with a universal code of ethics. It corrodes the bond of trust that ties superior to subordinate.

- If there ever is a viable ethics of the organization, it will have to follow the key Confucian concepts: clear definition of fundamental relationships, focus on right behavior rather than on avoiding wrongdoing, emphasis on behavior rather than motives and intentions, and optimization of each party's benefits, to enhance trust and harmony.

- Start with what is right rather than what is acceptable.

CHAPTER FOURTEEN

LEADERSHIP AND THE JOB OF THE EXECUTIVE

Drucker traced the conceptual roots of leadership in Western civilization to biblical times. In its traditional definition, leadership was generally viewed as a process in which a superior person induced a group to pursue the goals established by him. Pointing out that the subject of leadership had been examined by the best minds in the history of political theory, Drucker compared the newer definitions to preaching salvation without the need for prayer and good works. They presented all sorts of variations, depending on the demands of the audience, such as the charismatic leader, the relationship leader, the heroic leader, the participative leader, and the virtual leader—not to mention the ideal leader, who was a combination of Caesar, Charlemagne, Napoleon, and Churchill. It amazed Drucker that corporations had recently been paying huge fees to create "the one-minute leader" and seeking to unlock the mysteries of leadership in twelve easy lessons.

He further noted that a growth industry in leadership training had emerged in the past two decades, offering people the opportunity to master leadership techniques, most of which had been around for centuries. If motivation was the panacea buzzword of the managerial 1960s and 1970s, leadership was the cynosure for management during the 1980s and 1990s. The products of this growth industry included conferences, seminars, audio-

and videocassettes, along with a voluminous number of how-to books and articles.

Drucker of course never underestimated the significance of leadership, considering it a crucial element in the management process. He indicated that without leadership, organizations would disintegrate into ambiguous anarchy or mindless bureaucracy: "The manager is the dynamic life-giving element in every business. Without his leadership the 'resources of production' remain resources and never become production."[1] His criticism of the recent popular leadership literature centered on its shallow assumptions and simplistic approaches to a complex historical problem.

In this chapter I look first at the analysis Drucker made of leadership and then at the actual job of the executive.

Analysis of Leadership

Drucker's analysis of leadership addressed two major categories. The first, which received a great deal of attention in the popular literature, focused on the concept of the *indispensable man* and the issue of management succession. The second was the concept of *followship* and the crucial ingredients of integrity and trust—none of which he thought received the attention they deserved.

Indispensable Man

Drucker detected a fundamental flaw in the proposition of modern leadership theory that the leader is the indispensable man. The same concept was popularized under the label of the charismatic leader. The prototypical portrayal of the charismatic leader depicted a person with inexhaustible energy, imposing physique, superior intelligence, magnetic personality, and extraordinary technical skills. Drucker described these attributes as not the gifts given to mortals but a prescription for the ideal of a philosopher-king. Regulations were an intrinsic part of all organizations, but the charismatic leader transcended all rules in that he made the rules. He substituted dictatorship for substance, and thus Drucker viewed charisma as a form of misleadership, typified by a Hitler, Stalin, or Mao: "Indeed, charisma becomes the undoing of leaders. It makes them inflexible, convinced of their own infallibility, unable to change."[2]

Drucker saw charisma as an unstable and unreliable guide for directing institutions. Rejecting the unrealistic concept of the philosopher-king, he stated that "no organization can depend on genius; the supply is always scarce and unreliable."[3]

The concept of charismatic leadership raised a debate on whether great leaders are born or made. The champions of the indispensable man approach acknowledged only the first proposition. In their view, in effect, God had graced the charismatic leader at birth with a special combination of genes and chromosomes. Because it was impossible to replicate this model of genius (God having thrown away the mold), the only alternative was to gratefully accept divine benefits. In Drucker's judgment the charismatic approach ran counter to the laws of probability. His own experience led him to conclude that great leaders were neither born nor made. They were self-made. To substantiate this point, he pointed out that "Eisenhower, George Marshall, and Harry Truman were singularly effective leaders, yet none possessed any more charisma than a dead mackerel."[4]

Drucker did, however, offer an interesting insight on how changing circumstances altered the pattern of business authority and leadership. In the old industrialism people were dependent for their security on paternalistic rule, which was based on a combination of status, birth, property, charisma, and power. However, because the source of authority in the new industrialism is knowledge, the capitalists might still possess the tools of production but the knowledge workers now own the means of production. Of course, because both sides need each other, some form of a partnership is necessary. Employee loyalty can no longer be taken for granted; management has to earn it.[5]

In a knowledge society, therefore, it is a misinterpretation of reality to assume that the job of top management, the brain function of the business, rotates around the orbit of a single person. Instead, in today's world of mutual and pension funds, in which the property atom has been irreversibly split, the modern chief executive officer, enveloped in the network of managing and being managed, has become another employee. The power of his title has also been diminished. His title is a concession because he can be bought and sold like other employees. He has even less of a name socially when he leaves, unlike the old business tycoons of more enduring wealth and power.[6] Different types of management teams, not single individuals, are now required to meet the demands of knowledge work. In short, everybody is needed, but nobody is needed too much, because 90 percent of corporate activities are not rooted in top management.

According to Drucker, people were believing in a modern-day version of the fairy tales in which everybody lives happily ever after when they assumed that all problems would disappear once the charismatic leader arrived on the scene with his magic wand. In reality, placing excessive expectations on the ability of some providential savior has counterproductive and negative impacts, leading to institutional rigidity and disintegration. "Reality is . . . always the master," Drucker commented. "It will not subordinate itself to the promises, the programs, the ideologies of the charismatic leader."[7]

Succession

The ultimate defect of charismatic leadership mentioned by Drucker is its attitude toward succession. Drucker viewed the interaction between an institution and its outside environment as a flux between past and present. One of the major themes in his works was this relationship between continuity and change—succession was a bridge linking the two time spans. Because the institution must be capable of perpetuating itself, it had to be able to survive the tenure of one person's rule.[8]

Noting that a philosopher of the logical positivist school of thought would not dignify succession as a problem because it lacked visible concreteness, Drucker took pains to point out that succession might appear to be a metaphysical abstraction in the short run, but in the long run its impact was anything but intangible. Although the question of succession did not lend itself to immediate measurability, measurable results would appear, for better or for worse, many years later.[9] On one occasion he ridiculed the supposedly indispensable executives who would not resign, remarking, "The only way to get rid of incompetent management at the very top is a heart attack." Then he added, "But it usually strikes the wrong person. It is not reliable."[10]

Even when the arrangements for succession are conducted under supposedly objective rules and tested procedures, Drucker cynically noted that uncertainties are involved. Because the choice defied precise calculation, a touch of divine guidance is always necessary. Recalling the quip of the humorist Will Rogers that every time the United States elected a president, everybody prayed to God that providence had not forgotten the country, Drucker suggested the same plea for divine inspiration is required for lesser top management jobs.

Mesmerized by his own egotistical self-image and seeing the organization as his extended shadow, the charismatic leader is likely to be blind to the succession problem. In the event that this leader is compelled to make a succession selection, he is likely, Drucker indicated, to pick an obsequious number two man. Usually this means the appointment of a courtier who has never assumed direct responsibility for a substantive decision and therefore a person ill prepared for the encounters of changing external circumstances. What particularly alarmed Drucker about the selection process for succession was that in too many business corporations it was left to the judgment of one person, a practice rejecting the need for alternatives. Actually Drucker thought it the height of folly and the epitome of egoism for a chief executive officer to pick his or her own successor. Without a consideration of other candidates the decision was bound to be incorrect. Top management could not create leadership, at best it could only create the conditions that prepared for it.[11]

Followship

The popular infatuation with such prototypes of leadership as the charismatic leader, the indispensable man, the great man, and in history, the hero as the single fulcrum of historical understanding had obscured the critical factor of followship. According to Drucker, leadership would indeed be a barren and sterile intellectual concept if one did not consider the significance of followship. Without constituents' consensus, there would be no leadership. Drucker posed the critical interaction of the two this way: "To lead, one must follow because it is only from the viewpoint of the follower that we can reflect on the basis of followship, which when turned around becomes the essence of leadership."[12]

Drucker observed a startling imbalance between the voluminous literature on the techniques and traits of leadership and the almost complete silence on the attributes of followship. A major exception to literature that emphasized leadership as opposed to followship was *The Education of Cyrus the Great,* written by the ancient Greek historian Xenophon, which Drucker considered the single best book on leadership in general and followship in particular.[13] Nevertheless, Xenophon's work did not receive the attention accorded to the work of another great Greek historian, Thucydides, the author of *The Peloponnesian Wars.* In that study the Athenian leader Pericles was described in terms of glowing personal traits of leadership. Possessing charm, poise, wisdom, magnetism, strength, and foresight, he was the ideal charismatic leader.

In contrast, Xenophon depicted Cyrus, the Persian leader, as chiefly concerned with mundane and undramatic tasks of organizational performance. Included in Xenophon's list of leadership obligations was detailed examination of such unexciting techniques and topics as fundamentals of military science, negotiation skills, conduct of meetings, appraisal criteria, promotion guidelines, importance of duty, responsibility and example, role of specialization, relationships with allies, and the fundamentals of communications. The Cyrus described by Xenophon remains a model of bridging the gap between preaching and doing, between professed beliefs and behavior, and between deeds and words.

The Pericles depicted by Thucydides, a deified paragon of charisma, apparently paid little attention to concrete performance and displayed no concern for the concept of followship. Because he was considered indispensable, he had little need to be answerable on these points. Xenophon's Cyrus, on the contrary, viewed leadership as a form of systematic and disciplined activity that required thinking through objectives and harmonizing his goals with those of his constituents. Recognizing that leaders were more than celebrity puppeteers who make their subjects dance to their tune, Drucker found Xenophon's analysis of leadership more probing and relevant than Thucydides'. The great lesson he learned from Xenophon was that performance and not personality was the key to leadership.

Reiterating that in a knowledge organization the needs of the participants and the goals of the institution are no longer dependent exclusively on one man and calling egoism an inappropriate guide to action in modern information-based organizations, Drucker referred to his consulting experience to document the importance of sound relationships with colleagues. Effective leaders he had known never thought "I"; they had trained themselves to think as part of a team.[14]

Drucker expressed admiration for institutions that have endured for long periods. Organizations that have achieved longevity did not do so by accident. They satisfied the goals of their constituents by reconciling and balancing the tensions between continuity and change. One such organization has been the Roman Catholic Church. Drucker ascribed its institutional durability not so much to creating great men as to allowing ordinary men to do outstanding things. By rendering respect to the rank and file of the priesthood, Drucker said, it captured the essence of followship: "It is an old saying that the most astonishing feat of that most successful organization, the Catholic Church, is that it obtains the best leaders from the worst raw material."[15]

Drucker of course recognized that leaders had different temperaments and that all needed the basic skills, tools, and techniques necessary for effectiveness. But without the crucial allegiance and consent from their constituents, these other assets became meaningless: "The only definition of a *leader* is someone who has *followers*. Some people are thinkers. Some are prophets. Both roles are important and badly needed. But without followers, there can be no leaders."[16]

Integrity and Trust

It is a safe assumption that no management consultant has rivaled Drucker's longevity in the field. For more than five decades he has met innumerable leaders from business, church, military, academic, health, and countless other social organizations. In that interim he failed to discover a uniform profile of leadership traits. Instead, he encountered a wide spectrum of executive characteristics and such extremes of human polarity as vanity and humility, brilliance and dullness, impulsiveness and deliberativeness, gregariousness and remoteness, and boastfulness and self-effacement.[17] He compared the quest for a consensual set of leadership traits to the hopeless search for the unicorn, stating that " 'leadership personality,' 'leadership style,' and 'leadership traits' do not exist."[18]

He was dogmatic, however, in insisting on integrity as the one absolute trait of leadership. This characteristic might not lend itself to an easy definition, but its absence should disqualify a person for a management position. In amplifying this point, he wrote: "Trust is the conviction that the leader means what he says. It is a belief in something very old fashioned, called 'integrity.' . . . Effective leadership—and again this is very old wisdom—is not based on being clever; it is based primarily on being consistent."[19] Without integrity, leadership disintegrates into a farce. Because leadership depends on trust, Drucker suggested three areas in which integrity is especially crucial—(1) crises, (2) legitimacy, and (3) ethics.

Crises. According to Drucker the crisis was the one predictable event common to all organizations. In times of common peril it was imperative that there be somebody around whom everyone trusts to make a decision. He compared this person to the captain of a ship who had to take charge in an emergency. A period of great danger was not the time to call a committee meeting. On such an occasion even a poor decision was better than no decision.[20]

Whereas integrity, the ability to convey and inspire trust, was the one common denominator of all effective leaders, a sure symptom of misleadership was the absence of this sense of trust. People could be fooled by manipulation and trickery in many things but not in things that demanded trust. Moreover, Drucker stressed, unlike the development of other managerial skills, trust could not be taught or learned. If a person did not bring integrity to the job, he would never be able to earn or claim it.[21]

Legitimacy. Trust in the leader not only provided the cement for followship but was the basis of institutional legitimacy. Trust mirrored in the consent of followers was the foundation of authority. There was no other effective way to justify power over other people; they had to agree to accept authority as the basis for implementing leadership tasks. Trust was the reason constituents voluntarily submitted to commands rather than practiced the ancient art of sabotage. This fact compelled the leader to rely on persuasion rather than dictatorial techniques of power. Instead of relying exclusively on force the judicious leader recognized that it was impossible to control events. Indeed a sure sign of misleadership was a leader's failure to see the limits of power. Effective leaders, observed Drucker, knew that they did not control the universe. Only misleaders, the Stalins and Hitlers, suffered from this delusion.

Ethics. Drucker contended that people followed most enthusiastically when they were convinced of the ethical correctness of what they were doing. Of course this occasionally occurred in business when the employees or salespeople believed that the product their company produced was of the highest quality. Drucker thought that one of the great strengths of the nonprofit organization was the belief of volunteers that they were accomplishing something morally good. He cited such examples as the teacher who believed he was a change agent producing learning in the child, the activist citizen who saw the building of neighborhood and community as a noble venture, and the cleric who visualized himself uplifting the spiritual life of others. These illustrations confirmed that ethical standards were necessary if a leader were to convey a sense of meaningful mission instead of appearing to spout the deenergizing rhetoric of good intentions.[22] Claiming that the temptation to do good was dangerous when managerial competence was deficient and the prospect for results problematic, he emphasized that the focus should be on converting good intentions into results. To reinforce this responsibility, he recalled the "old saying that good intentions don't move mountains; bulldozers do."[23]

Drucker was acutely aware that the failure to fulfill good intentions created disenchantment and disillusionment among employees. But even more dangerous was executive hypocrisy. For example, managers were preaching that people were a company's greatest asset yet in reality violating the social contract between company and employee. Drucker had in mind the recent rash of mindless corporate *downsizing*, which he feared might upset the stability of the enterprise system. He argued that management was placing the cart before the horse in the timing of most downsizing. Because downsizing decisions have a major impact on corporate morale, a policy is needed at the outset of strategic planning rather than as an afterthought to an economic crisis. He caustically remarked, "There is an old saying among surgeons that the worst surgeon is the one who amputates without making the diagnosis and that's what downsizing, in most cases, has been."[24]

He conceded that there was a need for downsizing because years of overstaffing and overadministration by management had created a crisis. But the response to the crisis was greedy and selfish, with management dismissing other corporate values and its own sense of integrity for economic gain. Without any evidence of real performance, top managements were enriching themselves with high salaries, huge bonuses, obscene stock options, and questionable perks and at the same time discharging employees with reckless abandon. The result was an inevitable rise of employee disloyalty and community hostility. Commenting on this form of executive sadism as a quintessential form of misleadership, Drucker wrote that "a lot of top managers enjoy cruelty, but the financial benefit they get for layoff is morally and socially unforgivable, and we'll pay a nasty price."[25]

Drucker did see one note of hope. He observed that many managements of excellently run firms refused to follow the immoral short-term strategy of economic greed. In adjusting to the realities of the pension and information revolutions, they were meeting the challenge by pursuing a partnership with their employees. "They have defined the task, concentrated work on it, defined performance, made the employee a partner in productivity improvement and the first source of ideas for it, and built continuous learning and continuing teaching into the job of every employee and work team."[26]

It was Drucker's hope that schools of business would share in the partnership process, working to improve the relationship between the individual and the corporation by stressing the study of leadership. Especially important in this study was the recognition that the humanities had a role in helping people to focus on values and commitments.[27] Because essential values and convictions required lucid communication skills, Drucker saw that "the leader's first task is to be the trumpet that sounds a clear sound."[28] Although communication and human relations skills were important, Drucker viewed them as ancillary to integrity of character. Continuing to consider integrity the indispensable keystone of leadership, he wrote:

> The final proof of the sincerity and seriousness of a management is uncompromising emphasis on integrity of character. This, above all, has to be symbolized in management's "people" decisions. For it is character through which leadership is exercised; it is character that sets the example and is imitated. Character is not something a man can acquire; if he does not bring it to the job, he will never have it. It is not something one can fool people about. The men with whom a man works, and especially his subordinates, know in a few weeks whether he has integrity or not. They may forgive a man a great deal: incompetence, ignorance, insecurity, or bad manners. But they will not forgive his lack of integrity.[29]

The Executive Job

Drucker's severe indictment of the behavioral scientists for their failure to improve effectiveness might lead one to the conclusion that he could see only the negative in their work. This impression would be misleading. Nevertheless, his chief complaint against academic theorists was their assumption that executive work was theory-driven rather than task-focused, therefore implying that it was simple rather than difficult.

Drucker argued that effectiveness was critical for the executive job because the starting focus of that job should be end results and not input data and techniques. One advantage executives had in focusing on results was their years of experience. They had direct familiarity with the problems and opportunities connected with productive performance.[30]

Claiming it was a mistake to underestimate the importance of the experiential factor, Drucker stressed the significance of understanding the actual job. "The focus has to be on the job. The job has to make achievement possible. The job is not everything; but it comes first. If other aspects of working are unsatisfactory, they can spoil even the most achieving job—just as a poor sauce can spoil the taste even of the best meat. But if the job itself is not achieving, nothing else will provide achievement."[31]

Drucker was astonished that executives, especially young ones, failed to realize the importance of job selection and to analyze potential jobs. He observed that many chose a job for such superficial reasons as a slightly higher salary, convenient commuting, or the promise of rapid advancement and other attractive perks. Moreover, he told them, "the probability that the first choice you make is right for you is roughly one in a million. If you decide your first choice is the right one, chances are that you are just plain lazy."[32]

Drucker urged young people to consider their strong points and limitations to see if they were suitable to a firm's corporate culture. Among some of the factors worthy of examination in job analysis were one's compatibility with handling pressure, facility for meeting deadlines, preference for working alone or in groups, talent for either analysis or perception, and receptivity to change.

Drucker's main emphasis was that one evaluates one's capacities or the lack of them not just to acquire greater understanding, assurance, and confidence but to recognize the responsibility of managing oneself. "Management texts stress managing others. Few talk of managing oneself. But managing others is always 'iffy.' Does it really work? One can, however, always manage oneself, or at least try."[33]

For knowledge workers, Drucker indicated that "when it comes to the job itself, however, the problem is not to dissect it into parts or motions, but to *put together an integrated whole.*"[34]

Four Components

On the assumption that the essence of effectiveness rotates around the job, Drucker analyzed it from the perspective of four distinctive components: (1) purpose, (2) performance, (3) motivation, and (4) practice.

Purpose. The significance of purpose was addressed in covering the fundamentals of management, but it also deserves special attention with respect to executive effectiveness. According to Drucker, it was not a given that executives would automatically take the path of effectiveness. In fact, cloudy objectives from top management hampered employees' capacity to get the right things done and contributed to general organizational incompetency. The failure of IBM and success of Microsoft in interpreting the future of the computer were illustrations of contrasting interpretations of purpose in the data-processing industry. IBM defined the purpose of the mainframe computer as primarily providing memory, that is, data storage, which led the firm to the conclusion that the industry was hardware driven. Microsoft interpreted the purpose of the computer differently. It viewed the computer itself as a brainless commodity and the computer's purpose as running software; thus the market was driven by software.

Drucker added that too frequently people inside and outside an industry looked upon top management's strategic decisions as articles of faith rather than conveyors of meaningful strategic purpose. For example, few experts had expected the competitive victories of British Airways over Pan Am, Sony over RCA, Honda over General Motors, Nordstrom over Macy's, Komatsu over Caterpillar, and General Electric over Westinghouse. It was the miscalculation and misunderstanding of purpose that made it futile for executives in the losing companies to direct their talents and skills toward effectiveness.

Drucker was adamant that management needed a meaningful mental model of the firm's purpose in order to communicate tomorrow's vision and energize today's work assignments.[35] It was a clear sense of mission that separated successful executives from mediocre ones. Success was not based on superior talent or intelligence but on applying talent and intelligence to the right things, whereas executives in unsuccessful firms applied their talent and intelligence to the wrong things and asked the wrong questions.[36]

In fact, if managers were forced to do things that did not conform to the company's mission, it was best not to do them effectively. An organization could stand a good deal of waste and nonproductive effort providing it had a relevant strategic answer to the question, What is the business? However, the opposite was never true: good work in the pursuit of wrong purpose was always more damaging than bad work in the pursuit of the job objectives.

Performance. *Executive performance* was defined by Drucker as the consistent ability to produce quantitative and qualitative results over a long period of time in a variety of assignments. Because the real test of executive competency was productivity, the focus of contribution should be on measuring the job results of the assigned task and not the personal attributes of an individual.[37] The job of getting the right things done was for Drucker a life of activity, which he personally considered equal, if not superior, to the life of intellectual reflection. He had little use for pseudo-idealism, which he believed usually increased in direct proportion to one's distance from the problem. For him, talking a good job was a form of egregious irresponsibility, which he equated with having to raise the neighbor's children. Moreover, he was never able to see a positive interrelationship between potential and performance. Too many people paraded their learning without any tangible achievement in justifying their paycheck.

Motivation. Drucker compared the attitude of many of the motivational theorists discussed in the previous chapter to that of "an atheist who prayed to God that he would have a best-seller."[38] At the other extreme existed the complete denial of motivation, exemplified in the person who had no professional pride in the achievement after completing a task and who invoked the deity only to thank God it was all over and there was one day less to go for a pension.

According to Drucker, the job is neither a quest for human perfection nor a center of disillusionment. Rather than a biblical curse or an idyllic blessing, the job is a crucible for accomplishment. In answering the question of who motivates the motivator, he replied that the person motivates himself or herself by having positive feelings toward the job and possessing a sense of pride about the products and services of the corporation. He visualized the job not as a search for personal identity but as the avenue to self-development.

Self-improvement on the job means translating the concepts of continuity and change into reality. Drucker amplified the dual tasks of improving traditional executive skills and increasing receptivity for accepting new challenges. Effective self-development must proceed along two parallel streams. One is improvement—to do better with what you already know. The second is change—to do something different. Both are essential.[39] Drucker believed that the study of executive failures was useless in examining the sources of motivation. The key to motivation was to examine models of excellence and try to understand what it was that they did that other managers failed to do as a matter of performance. Failures helped to identify the things that should not be done, but successes provided the incentive for motivation and results.

Practice. In viewing the job as a learning process, Drucker suggested that the key to effectiveness was practice. And as with any practice, job practice did not come automatically but could be acquired through constant learning. This meant the chief challenge for managing the job was to enable ordinary people to do extraordinary things. This ability came about by inculcation of good habits rather than dependence on individual flashes of brilliance. Contending that practice was a commitment that had little to do with the inheritance of natural gifts, Drucker observed that "if effectiveness were a gift people were born with, the way they are born with a gift for music or an eye for painting, we would be in bad shape. For we know that only a small minority is born with great gifts in any one of these areas. We would therefore be reduced to trying to spot people with high potential of effectiveness early and to train them as best we know to develop their talent. But we could hardly hope to find enough people for the executive tasks of modern society this way."[40]

Drucker also opined that job practice would suffer from misdirection if the knowledge professional did not share in the design of the job: "[Effective executives] do not start out with the assumption that jobs are created by nature or by God. They know that they have been designed by highly fallible men."[41] Moreover, because all knowledge jobs by definition are infused with power, responsibility must accompany this power. Drucker considered it unacceptable for knowledge workers to exempt themselves from accountability for whatever reason: "The assertion that 'somebody else will not let me do anything' should always be suspected as a cover-up for inertia. But even where the situation does set limitations—and everyone lives and works within rather stringent limitations—there are usually important, meaningful, pertinent things that can be done."[42]

Drucker once confessed that all his books on human relations grew out of his observations and encounters with the skilled and talented practitioner. He conceded that management had elements of a profession and of a science but that it was fundamentally a practice that focused on applications more than concepts. For example, an outsider viewing expert professional performance in any field (music, sports, surgery) might conclude that it was a simple and easy exercise; yet in actuality, excellent achievement is based on perseverance.

"Effectiveness, in other words, is a habit; that is, a complex of practices."[43] In essence, effectiveness is learnable by synthesizing imaginative insights with practical experience on the job. It was only too common that many brilliant people never learned this lesson because they failed to realize "that the brilliant insight is not by itself achievement."[44] Performance, he stated, would not simply develop if it were left to its own devices: "The only things that evolve by themselves in an organization are disorder, fiction and malperformance."[45]

Realities

Drucker was firmly convinced that the job is the locale for improving effectiveness, but he also realized that the job has pervasive conditions that interfere with productivity. Prior to executives applying their skills, he thought it advantageous for them to understand the operating environment of the workplace. For one thing the job is not a tabula rasa, enabling the manager to start from scratch. The executive has to take cognizance of the claims of the past with its legacy of prior decision making, the various perceptions of individual colleagues, the heritage of an established corporate culture, the traditional appraisal system of promotion and rewards, and the firm's basic strengths and weaknesses—to cite a few of the many restraints on performance.

As a result, organizations and humans have one thing in common. Both display a gap between potential and performance. In the most successful managements Drucker saw a higher correlation of performance to resources than in those of mediocre firms, but the chasm was always present. In raising the question, Why are excellent executives in such short supply and why is mediocrity the rule? Drucker responded that most executives allowed the organization to cloister their skills and smother their talents. This was the main reason why marginal executives were in the majority and excellent managers were the exceptions.

According to Drucker, an organization with a weak and distrustful corporate culture created bureaucratic routines that hampered people from doing what they were trained for. He added that misallocation of resources was the norm and not the exception in organizational life, offering the insight that incompetency was in universal supply.[46] In making this acerbic assertion about weak managerial performance, he did not imply that executives were stupid but that normal organizational activities programmed them for inefficiency. Left to its own devices the pattern of operations for a typical executive was devoted toward nonresults. He also observed that the difference in performance between brilliant and mediocre executives had little to do with intellectual talents but could be traced to the former's refusal to be mired in administrative details. Once the executive allowed the flow of events to dictate what was important, then his activities would be dissipated in fruitless operations.[47]

In extensively surveying the vulnerabilities affecting executive performance, Drucker selected two major categories on which to focus: organizational pathologies and individual activities.

Organizational Pathologies. Combined with the pitfalls of everyday routine executive operations were a plethora of organizational pathologies that exacerbated the quest for improved effectiveness. Despite the fact that mediocre executives actually were just as intelligent as effective ones, they frittered their energies by becoming deeply enveloped in these internal conditions of nonperformance. As a result, they worked harder and harder, but they worked to no avail on the wrong things. Instead of being consumer oriented and entrepreneurial minded, they were superior arsonists. Moreover they expected accolades for putting out their fires.[48]

As mentioned in Chapter Six, the financial controls of an organization, even a knowledge organization, are not devised for detecting certain defects, including the misuse of resource allocation, the misappropriation of intellectual property, and the costs of not doing. This set of circumstances forced Drucker to candidly conclude that organized stupidity is a difficult thing to overcome. Wrapped up in a cocoon of nonresults, executives could foresee only the unimportant things.

Drucker assembled a list of intangible but very real organizational pathologies—all of which are counterproductive:

- Emphasis on the past over the future and the urgent over the important

- Stress on procedures over policies, which confuses input with output

- Tendency to seek consensus over results and to favor good intentions over meaningful objectives

- Undue emphasis on specific controls, which invariably leads to loss of general control

- Concern with costs alone, which results in smothering opportunities

- Proclivity for doing things right, which obscures the need for doing the right things

- Propensity toward working harder at the expense of working smarter

- Tendency to consider promotions more important than achievements

- Resistance to change, which dilutes the entrepreneurial function of innovation

- Preference for administration and bureaucratic activity, which fosters demotivation over motivation

- Concern with personality differences and power plays, which blurs the focus on productivity

- Temptation to quantify the indefinable and the immeasurable

- Existence of an appraisal system that rewards routine activity over meaningful performance

- Failure to recognize that the creative tensions of turbulence are not the same as irremediable conflict

---

Individual Activities. *Operating trap* was the term designated by Drucker to capture the individual realities executives have to overcome for improved effectiveness. This trap has four major components: (1) the activist factor, (2) the time element, (3) the nonsoloist dimension, and (4) the information and communications system.[49]

Activist Factor. Drucker commented that a major characteristic of executive work was continual activity, involving incessant doing. The necessity to prepare reports, meet deadlines, contact customers, confer with colleagues, negotiate with employees, listen to customer complaints, and respond to government regulators meant that any executive neglecting these routine functions would not be around for long. He noted that when he first observed businesses, before World

War II, carbon paper limited reproduction of typewritten documents to four or five copies. But since the arrival of the photocopier, executives have been inundated with reports, enough to blind even the eyes of speed readers. Tidal waves of paper have multiplied the factor of handling, an invitation to waste. Executives have further exacerbated the problem by drowning their colleagues in additional streams of memos.

Time Element. Drucker considered time the executive's single most precious resource. However, time is inelastic; once gone, it is gone forever. In addition, in the normal course of business routing, time is clearly not the executive's own—time belongs to the organization. Because the concept is that managers are managing and being managed at the same time, inevitably management is a time-consuming process.[50]

The opportunity in management for cross-fertilization of business talents means that the whole of management performance is greater than the sum of its parts. But a price is paid for this joint performance. The operating pattern encompasses constant contacts and dealings with other people, and that means encounters with different temperaments, different knowledge backgrounds, and different value systems, all of which hamper individual effectiveness. In short, Drucker acknowledged the principle that people are a corporation's greatest asset but saw that it is also necessary to recognize that a price is exacted for their presence. This is especially true with respect to the time consumed in the task of harmonizing human relationships with the challenge of obtaining results.

Nonsoloist Dimension. Drucker observed that many types of professional work are performed in virtual isolation. He cited the doctor in an office, the teacher in a classroom, the lawyer preparing a brief, the artist in a studio, and the novelist at a typewriter. In these secluded environments the guidelines of accountability and responsibility are set basically by the individual professional. In the corporate universe of interdependence it is impossible for an executive to operate under the soloist assumption that he can do his own thing. Drucker pointed out how difficult it was to identify who made the greatest functional contribution—the accountant, the research scientist, the production engineer, or the marketing expert. Each professional contributed something distinctive to the whole, but no single professional specialty dominated.

In other words a parochial vision of specialized work made no sense for those who had a direct or indirect contact with the customer. The countless duties and multiple demands of managerial work clearly ruled out the mediating role of a philosopher. In the nature of things, doing more often than not took precedence over thinking. In addition there were the inevitable crises which rolled in like the fog. Although it was impossible to predict the inevitable emergencies encountered during a typical day, there was no doubt that their solutions usually required cooperative action by many participants. It was a myth that most managers were long-term systematic planners cerebrating in an ivory tower.

Information and Communications System. According to Drucker, torrents of trivia and deluges of data were apt to swamp the effectiveness of any executive. And the larger the organization, the greater the flood of reports, regulations, policies, and procedures. Drucker pointed out that as a result of the new technology, information has become exponential but communication has become regressive. As a result of this miasma of confused data, reflection is short-changed and ignorance prevails over knowledge. Thus, as discussed at length in Chapter Eleven, Drucker thought one essential task was "what might be called 'Organizing Ignorance'—and there is always so much more ignorance around than there is knowledge."[51]

Job Management

In a 1963 speech he gave to a group of research executives, Drucker reinforced his insight that the job constituted the key focus for the improvement of executive effectiveness. He regarded his comments as fundamental common sense, but to his surprise, these experienced executives considered them innovative. Really they were new discoveries only to the extent that they had been largely unrecognized by most managers. This experience was the genesis of his book *The Effective Executive.*[52]

Many of Drucker's insights about executive effectiveness are taken for granted today. But it was Drucker, nearly two generations ago, who first introduced the theme in a systematic fashion into management literature. Drucker realized that commonsense principles were usually more preached than practiced, but he also found very little evidence that these principles were even being preached. The challenge lay in narrowing the gap between concepts and results, and over the next generation Drucker expanded on many of his guidelines for effectiveness.

Following are some of the more notable guidelines that Drucker advanced to meet the realities of an information-based society:

- Managers no longer can rely on command-and-control authority; they face the unprecedented situation of neither controlling nor being controlled.

- With the increase of outsourcing, managers will increasingly have to work with people who are not employees but outsiders.

- Small companies are creating most of the nation's jobs, and these jobs have almost as much security as those in large corporations.

- Every professional job requires continual learning.

- The word *report* should be stricken from the management vocabulary. Information is replacing authority.

- Plans are only good intentions unless they are converted into hard work.

- The term *empowerment* should be replaced with *responsibility*.

- People rather than money develop a business or an economy.

- Knowledge exists in action and not in hardcover books.

- The individual has to depend on himself or herself for career development. The old career stepladder built by the company is gone, and managing a career is now more like climbing vines—and you bring your own machete.

- Managers must beware of creeping credentialism. It is easy to fall into this trap, because degrees can be viewed in black and white but performance requires judgment.

- Managers no longer manage a workforce. They manage unique individuals for whom there are no averages.

- Power comes from transmitting information, not by hiding it.

- Technology abounds, but no one has yet invented a "work-saving machine" or a "thinking" one.

Conclusion

In essence, Drucker viewed the executive job as sharpening corporate vision, generating improved performance, stimulating motivation, and serving as a platform for practice. Despite his insistence on the importance of the job, he also warned that the job was not an absolute. The job should never become so addictive that the person did not have a life of his or her own.

In dealing with executive effectiveness, Drucker purposefully avoided the approaches of the behavioral sciences and formal leadership theories. He focused on the job as the center of implementation. The roads to improvement were practice and commitment but underlying them were such basic components as contribution, which entailed specific individual results; abandonment and concentration, which involved the elimination of wasteful activities and the concentration on a few key priorities; time management, which concerned itself with the systematic use of a manager's most important resource; emphasis on individual strengths, which meant that results never emerged from weaknesses; proper communication, which was essential to performance; and decision making, which was necessary for understanding risk and opportunity analysis.

The following chapters describe how Drucker analyzed these critical factors of executive effectiveness and how he proposed guidelines for executive improvement against the background of organizational realities.

CHAPTER FIFTEEN

CONTRIBUTION, COMMITMENT, AND CONCENTRATION

Drucker was the first scholar to recognize the knowledge revolution would produce a transformation of organizational design and a radical change in the nature of executive contribution and responsibility. With respect to organizational structure, he specifically pointed out such changes as the shift in the resource of information from scarcity to abundance, the fact that multiple organizational levels were becoming vulnerable and redundant, and the way that the factor of knowledge was diluting the command-and-control design. Based on his six decades of studying organizations and their qualitative structural trends, he was convinced that assuming responsibility for the impact of the information was the greatest task facing management in coming years, chiefly because it was an unprecedented challenge.

This chapter describes the commitment and the sense of contribution that should be inherent in the job if executives are to be effective. It then moves on to the executive task of choosing areas of concentration and of abandonment.

Contribution and Commitment

Contribution and commitment are of particular import in three areas of executive effectiveness: (1) improving performance and undertaking self-development, (2) making the change from span of control to span of relationship in management practice, and (3) understanding team concepts.

Performance and Self-Development

Drucker felt it mandatory for executives to become acutely aware of the sea change from making and doing things to handling concepts and ideas if they were going to manage responsibly for results. One methodology that had been proposed to meet the challenge of exponentially increasing information was *participative management*. According to this democratic proposal for individual autonomy, executives would pursue their own agendas and disregard the limited reality of job descriptions and positions contained in the organizational chart. It was Drucker's position, however, that the organizational chart would be drastically modified but would not disappear. Moreover, he viewed participative management as a form of chaos management leading to organizational anarchy.

Drucker felt the organizational chart would have to be maintained for two basic reasons. First, the inevitability of emergencies in any institution meant that critical decisions had to be made in times of peril. As mentioned, Drucker considered it worse to make no decisions than to make the wrong decisions. Without a trusted person at the top to make these critical decisions, there would be a condition of anarchy. Second, an ineradicable feature of all jobs was that everyone sooner or later ran into trouble, in which case the person required a superior to assist him or her out of the difficulty.

To clarify the concept of the knowledge revolution and the transition from a mechanical model to an organic one with an analogy, Drucker contrasted the static anatomy of a skeleton, representing the traditional structure, and the biological design of a nervous system, mirroring the information-based organization. He specifically noted that the skeleton inhibited the flow of information but that a biological system enhanced the open-ended movement of information.[1] In contrasting the mechanical features of a skeleton with the dynamic elements of a central nervous system, Drucker pointed out that mechanical features had "high entropy and low efficiency" whereas dynamic features had "low entropy and high efficiency." A low entropy system was more efficient because it relied on information rather than physical inputs, making it structurally smaller and less cumbersome.

One advantage of an organization based upon information like an open-ended central nervous system was that it was more amenable to innovation.

Conversely, innovation was difficult in the traditional organization because it had a middle management staffed to a point of redundancy. This meant that the decision-making process needed to adapt to change was reduced to a snail's pace. Drucker further elaborated on the inflexibility and rigidity of the organization designed as a pyramid. It is geared for the defense of the status quo, and "the reason is straightforward: it turns out that whole layers of management neither make decisions nor lead. Instead, their main, if not their only, function is to serve as 'relays'—human boosters for the faint unfocused signals that pass for communication in the traditional preinformation organization."[2]

Drucker hypothesized that the transformation from closed, hierarchical structures to open-ended designs characterized by the free flow of information called for a major revision of executive commitment, contribution, and responsibility. He emphasized that the typical compartmentalized job descriptions, based exclusively on functional activity, were no longer applicable guides for evaluating results. For one thing, traditional departments "won't be where the work gets done."[3]

Postulating that knowledge now creates authority, he insisted that the new criteria of executive performance include such results as converting information into applied action, recognizing the need to participate in teams, and most important, taking personal responsibility for individual growth. Arguing that self-development was intrinsically inner directed, Drucker wrote: "Self-development may require gaining new skills, new knowledge, and new manners. But above all, it requires new experience."[4] To achieve results in these new endeavors, he advised executives that they were no longer servants of the machine but servants of the task.[5] Moreover, doing the same thing during an interim of thirty years, a pattern characteristic of the command-and-control model, produced only stale routine experience and not development. Because the needs of the organization and the challenges of managers will be different tomorrow, development is a necessity. The only choice is between developing them properly or not developing them.

From Span of Control to Span of Relationship

In ruling out hierarchical design with its many levels of organization, Drucker also eliminated its central feature, the span of control. This ancient feature of military and ecclesiastical institutional design was based on the principle that at each level the superior would have anywhere from six to twelve subordinates reporting to him. Drucker criticized the span of control principle on two structural grounds: "In the first place, the principle of the span of control is rarely cited properly. It is not how many people report to a manager that matters. It is how many people *who have to work with each other* report to a manager."[6] Second, the principle assumes that the major focus is downward, but control of subordinates is only one dimension of the executive's job.

As a more relevant construct than the span of control, he substituted the *span of relationship*, which more realistically defined the person's place in the organization and served as a more meaningful catalyst for improved production and communications. Drucker stipulated that the span of relationship principle fulfilled one of the main goals of organizational theory. In the context of effectiveness, he wrote that the fact that the executive is in an organization "means that he is effective only if and when other people make use of what he contributes. Organization is a means of multiplying the strength of an individual."[7]

Drucker also questioned the traditional definition of management, including the span of control concept, when he observed that the principle that the manager was responsible for the work of others was no longer satisfactory.[8] In his judgment, this downward orientation for the majority of executives was reflected in focusing on efforts over results and being concerned about what superiors "owe" them, and not in making a commitment to contribution.

Revising the Job. According to Drucker, the increased need for mutual interaction and information flow called for a revision of old job descriptions. For example, not only did corporate titles lose their previous significance but once the performance of the task took priority, then the factors of junior and senior, male and female, young and old, credentials and lack of credentials became irrelevant in the search for solutions. Drucker emphasized the span of relationship in knowledge work by defining an executive as someone who does not focus on the restrictive assumptions of managing others or rely on titles as symbols of authority: that is, he is someone who refuses to act as a subordinate himself.[9]

Drucker's evaluation of the executive's job was not based on empty rhetoric. He argued that in the future the role of the supervisor would be increasingly redundant once it was recognized that knowledge equaled authority. Because knowledge work cannot be controlled, responsibility can no longer be confined exclusively to paternalistic superiors. In short, once information has become the main factor of production, "No one can direct [the knowledge worker]. He has to direct himself. Above all, no one can supervise him. He is the guardian of his own standards, of his own performance, and of his own objectives."[10] Recently, Drucker advanced some of the reasons for this proposition, remarking that "the knowledge workers must know more about their job than the boss does—or what good are they? The very definition of a knowledge worker is one who knows more about his or her job than anyone else in the organization."[11]

The core content of jobs also changed once the focus was on contribution to the whole rather than confined to work done for separate departments. Because there was no jurisdiction in knowledge work, everything that interacted had to be studied together. In knowledge work, specialization was still vital, but it was the means and not the end. Drucker succinctly captured the essence of span of relationship for the knowledge worker when he emphasized that only people are specialized; tasks and problems never are.

Drucker declared it a farce to assume that executive jobs were anointed because they had natural origins. They were essentially artificial constructs designed by fallible individuals. A job was a response to the need to fulfill a necessary corporate function. There was no divine mandate in the organizational creation of accountants, lawyers, engineers, market research people, and other specialists. Moreover, in order for people to make a qualitative contribution beyond the routine aspect of the job, more was required than routine and passive adaptation, because task and teamwork broke down functional and territorial values. In short, a job was shaped and formed by mortals, and only they could dignify it.

Drucker maintained that a professional specialty per se contributed nothing to overall results: "The effective work is actually done in and by teams of people of diverse knowledges and skills."[12] Instead of a limited and linear functional approach, he called for a systems point of view in which the whole was greater than the sum of the parts. For example, once the purpose of the business centered around the customer, departmental functions immediately required a larger focus.

As pointed out earlier, Drucker viewed an understanding of the job as the starting point of effectiveness. It was imperative therefore that the person understood what he or she was being paid for and the area of direct responsibility. The worst mistake was to follow yesterday's design pattern by defining the job around personality traits, because "if the job is designed for an individual rather than for a task, it has to be restructured every time there is a change in the incumbent."[13]

Of course this does not mean a neglect of the functional dimension of the job. As was so often the case in attempting to create a more meaningful perspective, Drucker resorted to one of his favorite analytical themes—the reconciliation of continuity and change. In pointing out the need to integrate traditional organizational capacities with the efforts to meet the challenges of the information organization, he said: "There is much more to the self-development of an executive than his training in effectiveness. He has to acquire knowledges and skills. He has to learn a good many new work habits as he proceeds along his career, and he will occasionally have to unlearn some old work habits."[14]

The critical feature in merging the fundamentals of functional specialization with an innovative attitude was the need to build "upward responsibility" into the job of each subordinate.[15] That is, to achieve greater accountability and contribution, organizations did not move people to the top—individuals moved themselves to the top. Although sound human relations formed the foundation of executive effectiveness, Drucker also cautioned that the emphasis should be directed toward the end of productivity and not simply placed on the means of getting along with people. He purposefully singled out *sincerity* as a flawed and useless trait, considering it deceptive and the hallmark of the demagogue. He thought Hitler had been probably the most sincere man of the century.[16]

Drucker equated good human relations with performance and contribution, not with cultivating sincerity and other superficial and redundant traits: "Executives in an organization do not have good human relations because they have a 'talent for people.' They have good human relations because they focus on contribution in their own work and in their relationships with others. As a result, their relationships are productive—and this is the only valid definition of 'good human relations.'"[17]

Conversely, the neglect of smooth human relations with others in the organization could destroy corporate performance. However, because solid and meaningful human relationships required work and attention, Drucker urged that the number of an executive's contacts be kept to a minimum. A large group was not conducive to contribution because trivial and inconsequential contacts inhibited meaningful communications and promoted feuds, frictions, and other problems.[18]

Working with the Tridimensional Pattern. Assuming that the span of relationship concept interacted tridimensionally, Drucker separated it into three distinct categories: *downward*, which concentrated on overseeing subordinates;

lateral, which emphasized the importance of contacts with peers; and *upward,* which focused on contributing to the performance of the boss. He considered all three as vital, but in terms of qualitative results, the lateral and upward were more important than the downward.[19]

With regard to specific implementation for all three segments, Drucker offered the following guidelines: managers needed to focus on achievement over promotion, recognize that the purpose of tools is to gain control over limitations, be aware that cooperation with others should take precedence over symbolic leadership, see maximization of individual contribution as synonymous with organizational results, and not limit measurement of performance solely to engineered standards and quantitative contribution.

Appraising performance is a significant step in reengineering the job in an information-based organization. Drucker granted that contribution was difficult to measure, but at the very least, he thought, it could be sensibly judged and continually improved.[20] *He offered these suggestions to managers for shifting from span of control to span of relationship:*

- Be aware that effectiveness demands a commitment to understanding the job and does not depend on brilliance.

- Replace superficial activity with substantive results.

- Substitute the word *accountability* for *empowerment.*

- Define results through meaningful measurement and appropriate feedback.

- Place the focus of authority and responsibility on the task.

- Take responsibility for defining information needs and do not wait for an information specialist to determine them.

- Understand that the danger of designing a job so it is too small is that small jobs inhibit learning and growth.

- Recognize style as packaging and not meaningful contribution to results.

- Do not make the organization your entire life; you become defenseless against the inevitable disappointments.

- Act on the assumption that what is right is a more important consideration than who is right.

- Recognize that human relations not based in the spirit of good performance are actually poor human relations.

- Focus on future action rather than a postmortem and a record of what has already happened.

Downward Relationships. Executives without exception claim that people are their firms' greatest resource; however, in practice they look upon people not as a resource "but as problems, procedures, and costs."[21] Largely because the downward approach to executive effectiveness represented yesterday's conventional wisdom of supervising subordinates in hierarchical organizations, it continued to receive most of the attention in the textbooks. Drucker maintained that the result of this overemphasis on the downward approach resulted in executives who overmanaged activities and undermanaged contribution. He argued that focusing exclusively downward made no sense in the world of knowledge professionals. Moreover as the knowledge revolution continued to gain momentum, many new knowledge specialties were being added to the older ones, further complicating the problem of managing the knowledge asset more effectively. Drucker was uncompromising in his insistence of autonomy for professional employees and his postulation that the knowledge professional should be responsible for the design and direction of the job. Because the fountainhead of authority was not at the top but at the bottom in the minds of specialists, "You can train these workers, work on their specifications, retrain them, transfer them, and reward them, but in their job you cannot supervise them."[22] Drucker also implied that because of the subordinate's up-to-date schooling in his discipline and the fact that as his superior moved up the corporate ladder he had to unlearn his specialized function, it was reasonable to assume that the subordinate probably knew more about the content of the specialty than his superior. Indeed, Drucker insisted that subordinates worth their salt should know more about the subject matter than the boss. "Unless they know more about their specialty than anybody else in the organization, they are basically useless."[23] Of course this endorsement of the premise that knowledge equals authority did not mean that the superior-subordinate relationship was abolished. The organizational chart still made its claims in order to ensure cohesive organizational stability. Because somebody with formal authority had to be accountable for each department's performance, complete individual freedom was out of the question.

Consequently, in order to bridge the gap between the needs of the organization and of the individual in a knowledge organization, Drucker proposed a partnership between superiors and subordinates. He also offered a number of prescriptions for the superiors in order to lubricate and implement the mutual dependency arrangement:[24] recognize the need to give respect and self-esteem to the person and the craft, study and design the job so that the objectives are mutually agreed upon and understood, specify the expectations of tasks, provide the necessary tools for performance, set a good example, communicate the corporate mission, establish standards for performance, enable the person to perform against stated objectives, stress that what matters is not creativity but the capacity to do, provide an opportunity for the development of potential, and create an atmosphere where good people can grow. Some might consider these guidelines a shorthand form of motivation. Drucker rejected any such notion, arguing that these principles demanded serious work and had nothing to do with the manipulative tools and techniques of motivation found in the textbooks.

Drucker thought that the role of young professionals in the superior-subordinate relationship also posed a potential concern. They represented the majority of knowledge workers in the corporation, but there was a low correlation between their quantitative factor of cost and qualitative element of results. In most cases he viewed these young employees as technicians with high expectations for automatic promotions but without a sense of managerial commitment. He also detected a feeling among them of being intimidated by the status and titles of superiors, the remnants of the command-and-control organizational design. Drucker addressed the problem of the superior-subordinate relationship involving these younger professionals from three aspects: (1) sense of impotence, (2) need to overcome restraints, and (3) irrational expectations. He also suggested some guidelines.

• *Sense of impotence.* Drucker observed that the perceived powerlessness of young employees gave them a feeling of hostility toward their bosses and of indifference toward the corporation. This factor of frustration among subordinates was exacerbated by their belief that they did not do things to the world, the world did things to them. He concurred that the young were right when they protested the tendency of the organization to view them as a tool or as a piece of machinery. But, he added, they were wrong to blame the organization for their alienation and disillusionment. Instead, they ought to conceive of the organization as their particular tool of contribution and advancement.

• *Need to overcome restraints.* Drucker never accepted the myth of organization man, which said the large corporation stifled initiative and encouraged conformity. It was his contention that this was the case only when young people allowed themselves to be curtailed by bureaucratic procedures.

Drucker used the nineteenth-century Indian civil service of the British government as an illustration of outstanding youthful administrative performance and saw its structure as a precursor of the flat design so typical of the information-based organization. Consisting of approximately one thousand civil servants, it effectively administered the entire Indian subcontinent. This number was a tiny fraction of the multitudes in the bloated Confucian mandarin bureaucracy who were administering government in China at the same time and who displayed a track record of corruption and malperformance.[25]

Except for monthly reports to a political secretary, individual district officers of the Indian civil service administered large geographical territories with complete autonomy. Living in complete isolation from superiors and peers, they enforced political regulations, adjudicated property disputes, made legal decisions, conducted archaeological surveys, participated in irrigation projects, and handled countless other infrastructure and governmental details.[26] The most informative thing for Drucker was that these civil servants were very young men with recent liberal arts degrees but without any knowledge of accounting or other functional disciplines. He looked upon the absence of certified, functional credentials as irrelevant. More important to him was that the young viceroys performed because of their commitment to learning and concentration on growth.

Considering it specious, he refused to accept the argument that some organizational "they" (whoever these mythical they were) hampered performance. A person possessing this mind-set of using excuses would always be a subordinate, one who slavishly complained that the organization sabotaged his or her effort at contribution.[27] For Drucker, alibis were always poor substitutes for achievement. Despite the inevitable limitations on performance in any organization, there existed important and pertinent opportunities for those young executives willing to accept the challenges.

• *Irrational expectations.* Drucker attributed to inexperience the penchant among the young to talk a good game theoretically and yet fail to meet the standards of high professional behavior. He thought the situation similar to

Aristotle's complaint about the difficulty of teaching political philosophy to the young. Because young people had no experience, they undervalued it, and at the same time they overvalued theory and methodology. Drucker believed that the only thing wrong with young executives was that they had stupid expectations. These expectations were of course not criminal, but they were unrealistic. During their education they were taught that management was a rational activity, and then they discovered that the boss did not practice the management he preached.[28]

Most of the specific details of effectiveness treated in Part Three of this book apply to executives at all ages. Drucker did, however, suggest a few guidelines directly applicable to the young:

- Discover before the age of thirty the thrill of accomplishment by displaying one piece of outstanding work that you thought was beyond your capacity. You should also learn that it is possible to survive failure. Without a setback before the age of forty-four, you are unlikely to recover from later career disappointments.

- Rather than resent good manners and consider them hypocritical, you should cultivate them. Good manners are the lubricating oil that smooths out friction and encourages trust.

- Refuse to stay in an institution that is corrupt or that no longer offers challenges for growth.

Upward Relationships. Upward relationships can also be described as managing the boss. Bosses have not had warm and friendly coverage in the media and arts in the United States. They have been pilloried by novelists, condemned by labor leaders, scorned by journalists, caricatured as villains by cartoonists, satirized by humorists, reviled by psychologists, described as philistines by intellectuals, depicted as minor despots by historians, ignored by the social elite. Even the term *boss* reflects a pejorative connotation when raised in U.S. society. As a result of these negative images, suspicion and distrust were cast like shadows on the integrity and effectiveness of all bosses. Moreover, managing the boss was a neglected subject in the management literature. Because the downward focus was taken for granted, it was deemed presumptuous to trespass beyond that supervisory boundary line. Drucker, however, postulated the challenge of managing the boss as a key to executive effectiveness.

The carrot-and-stick philosophy that dominated the business world until the arrival of the knowledge revolution also contributed to the derisive portrait of business bosses. According to Drucker, this manipulative and controlling doctrine of managing by fear had a lingering legacy. Without wishing to explore the merits of the past portrayal of bosses in U.S. business, he called for a reappraisal in light of the realities of the information revolution and the need to create a new profile of the boss as someone with opportunities for executive effectiveness. Part of this new appraisal was a recognition that contrary to legend, the boss was neither a monster nor an icon: "The effective executive accepts that the boss is human (something that intelligent young subordinates often find hard)."[29]

Drucker suggested that in managing the boss for improved performance of both the subordinate and superior, the aspiring subordinate should consider the value of (1) supporting the boss's success, (2) using the boss as a resource, (3) having a variety of bosses, and (4) fostering a cooperative spirit.

• *Supporting the boss's success.* Drucker declared that all evidence has confirmed that a subordinate is unlikely to have a successful career if the boss is not also successful. It followed logically, therefore, that it was in the best interest of a subordinate to contribute to the boss' achievement and to see the boss as an ally. Indeed it was imperative "to realize that it is both the subordinate's duty and in the subordinate's self-interest to make the boss as effective and as achieving as possible."[30]

• *Using the boss as a resource.* According to Drucker, once the boss was seen as a specific resource, then the executive task was to develop that asset by obtaining improved results. It followed that the boss must be treated like any other resource—he must be developed. Among some of the prerequisites for accomplishing this objective were showing proper respect for the person and his position, establishing an atmosphere of trust and cooperation, overrating him rather than undervaluing him, and assuming that he has had certain talents and accomplishments in his career or else he probably would not be in his current position.

In obtaining a clearer understanding of the boss as resource for mutual performance, however, subordinates were not to tamper with the boss's personality. Drucker was dogmatic on this point. He considered it the greatest piece of counterproductive effrontery to try to change one's boss to fit a particular image. Instead of playing the role of an amateur psychologist, he said it was best to stick to the more pragmatic premise that the boss was an asset and opportunity for improved performance. Claiming that a resource had to be accepted for what it was and not the way one wanted it to be, he wrote: "The subordinate's job is not to reform the boss, not to reeducate the boss, not to make the boss conform to what the business schools and management books say bosses should be like."[31]

• *Having a variety of bosses.* Drucker contended that exposure to many types of bosses should be the norm in the career of any aspiring executive. One vital thing the executive would learn is that no two bosses are the same. For example, in his consulting career, where he had witnessed thousands of effective bosses, Drucker had found there was no common denominator in executive traits. At one extreme, some senior executives were stern, austere, severe, and introverted. At the other end of the top management spectrum, some were warm, sensitive, gregarious, and extroverted. Between these two contradictory poles were countless combinations and permutations of characteristics, most of which had little to do with performance. Except for the trait of integrity, whose absence could destroy relationships and performance, personality traits were singularly unimportant, in Drucker's assessment, as long as there were results.

Dismissing bluntly as counterproductive any reliance on changing personalities and manipulating psychological traits, Drucker introduced a more feasible methodology for managing the boss that called for an understanding of the boss's modus operandi. This understanding started with an acceptance of the fact that each boss is sui generis. Therefore, it is necessary to study and monitor every boss individually with respect to work habits and time allocation, strong points and weaknesses, needs and wants, and objectives and priorities. Knowledge of these and other operating factors in the configuration of a boss's activities enables the subordinate to increase his effectiveness and focus his energies on results.

For example, Drucker suggested one should determine in the communication process whether the boss is more verbally or quantitatively oriented. If he is comfortable only with numbers, then even the most elegant written proposal will fall on deaf ears. In the same vein it is practical to discover whether the boss is an average reader or a speed reader. If the former, it will be a sound tactic to confine and tighten written communications to one condensed page. If the person is a speed reader, a written communication, as long as it is meaningful, can be voluminous. Again the important point is that it is the responsibility of the subordinate to understand as many as possible of the operating practices of each boss so that they can be converted into productive opportunities.[32]

• *Fostering a cooperative spirit.* Perhaps most important of all in seeking improved mutual performance, a confrontational and adversarial stance with a boss must be altered to one of cooperation and flexibility. Drucker contended that converting the boss to a partner was not nearly as difficult as most people thought (see accompanying box).

To supplement his hypothesis that bosses could be converted to partners, Drucker proposed a number of striking insights:

■ Don't try to hide problems; it is like hiding an elephant under the rug.

■ Respect his time; remember he has a boss, too.

■ Don't complain he does not give you enough time; considering his pressures he probably gives you too much.

■ Disregard meaningless contacts and sycophancy. Keep in mind the old adage: "One should not go near the prince unless he calls." At the same time, don't hide.

■ Ask the boss, What do I do that helps you? and What do I do that hampers you?

■ Ascertain the things he finds difficult to do.

■ Determine the form of communication he finds most satisfactory for ideas and reports.

■ Avoid surprises—the fewer the better, because there are no pleasant surprises.

■ Present a clearly defined problem and indicate you want to become part of the solution.

■ Indicate interest in identifying and working on opportunities as well as problems.

■ Identify the key areas in which he needs support.

■ Establish ways in which you can ease his routine burdens.

■ Recognize that when you are brash and confrontational in discussing issues, you are threatening the bonds of trust and confidence.

■ Use the instrument of the *management letter*—explain what you propose to do over the next six months, what you are specifically going to do to meet these objectives, and how you will evaluate your performance six months later through feedback and measurement. Give the letter to your boss and then ask: Am I right? Is this what you expect of me?

Drucker frequently remarked that the best formula for personal success was to work for a boss who was going places. Students and clients agreed with this statement, but typically there was also this rejoinder, "How do you manage the boss who is unmanageable?" The gist of Drucker's response was, How do you define *unmanageable,* and have you really tried? He allowed for only one exception to the responsibility for managing the boss. This was the situation in which the superior clearly lacked character. In this case, he advised, particularly when the person was young enough, that the subordinate seek a transfer to another department or move out of the company entirely.

Lateral Relationships. The dimension of lateral relations encompassed interactions with colleagues from other functional areas who were neither superiors nor subordinates. Drucker depicted these formal and informal lateral relationships as significant factors of mutual dependence in the exchange of information for joint performance. At the same time, he cautioned that "the common weakness of many organizations is, by and large, the lack of adequate concern for, and adequate work on, sideways relationships."[33]

In detailing the pattern of these lateral relationships, he stressed that they were not routine, casual encounters to be taken for granted but contacts in which executives met specialists outside the executives' own operating, functional areas to achieve joint results. He found that people tend to be incredibly ignorant about specialties other than their own. In the knowledge organization especially, "Now nobody knows what others do, even within the same organization. Everybody you work with needs to know your priorities. If you don't ask and don't tell, your peers and subordinates will guess incorrectly."[34] The prime factor in overcoming this communication problem and harmonizing these lateral relationships was that each professional specialist had to make his or her knowledge understandable to others in the organization. In the Tower of Babel confusion of organizational life, the task of comprehending the context and content of jobs was not a simple exercise. In this situation of mutual dependence among different professionals, in which no single knowledge was superior and in which everyone confidently understood his own specialty, each person erroneously assumed that his specialty was equally understood by his colleagues. To illuminate just how untrue this latter assumption can be, Drucker suggested that executives try the exercise of explaining their job to their teenage son or daughter. They should then be prepared for a glazed look of disbelief.

Drucker was convinced that solving this communication problem and integrating the task of contribution were impossible if left to the information specialist, the personnel professional, or the communications officer. These corporate authorities reminded him of academic philosophers. They had a proclivity to talk about things they didn't fully understand and to make it appear that the lack of understanding was the fault of the person receiving the message. Of course Drucker's main point was to dramatize the folly of all experts who attempt to oversimplify complex subjects in which they lack the authority of knowledge. He thought specialists had an arrogant and exalted estimation of their disciplines. Moreover, they often displayed possessiveness and secretiveness about their knowledge and were reluctant to answer their peers' requests for information. Either they responded in a jargon that only they understood or they insisted that colleagues learn their specialty. According to Drucker, such pompousness was totally unacceptable because it froze relationships at the outset. In today's knowledge society, with its plethora of disciplines, it was the height of folly to expect one person to learn another's discipline when looking for relevant information. On the contrary, the specialist's job was to make himself understood and gain the ability to illuminate his specialty to others against the background of experience.[35]

In Drucker's estimation, technological tools are of small use in smoothing professional conflicts and information exchanges among peers. For example, in many ways he viewed the use of the computer as the "application of advanced techniques to meaningless statistics," with the result that the manager was confronted with reams of computer output yet remained hopelessly uninformed.

Consider, for example, the marketing manager who requests an information report from the accounting department for feedback on the company's product line. To include a copious list of all items would present an abundance of irrelevant computer-generated data. Because about 80 percent would fall into a middle-range category, it is assumed that there is probably little the manager could do to improve the overall business performance in the short run.

Drucker suggested that the marketing executive asked the wrong question. Instead of requesting a voluminous report on the full product line, he should have specifically asked the accountants to identify the 10 percent star performers and the 10 percent clinkers. These more meaningful figures would enable top management to allocate resources more effectively by supporting the top performers and withdrawing resources or possibly eliminating the marginal performers.

To avoid a plethora of redundant data, Drucker suggested two tactics: (1) outline the pattern of mutual dependence in the organization on the back of a postcard and (2) keep relationships to the necessary minimum. Both these steps demanded thinking through the span of communication throughout the organization, focusing on these questions: Who depends on me? and Whom do I depend on for relevant information?[36]

In order to put the span of relationship concept into practice, Drucker said, managers needed to enlarge their skills on two levels. First, the professional executive would have to think through the purpose of his job. For example, engineers asked about the nature of their job typically answered quality control. But Drucker contended that this answer did not go far enough. It made no sense to turn out high-cost quality products unless they also met customer needs. To focus just on quality and not customer requirements was not talking quality; it was exposing incompetence. "Good quality is cheap," Drucker commented, "it is poor quality that is expensive."[37]

Second, although the professional might not be proficient in organizational disciplines other than his own, he had to understand the essentials of these other disciplines. If the engineer had sought guidance from his marketing and accounting colleagues he might have avoided misdiagnosing the nature of his job. Drucker attributed the failure to understand the problem of cooperative relationships as the big obstacle for joint performance. It was a mistake to believe that those you worked closely with were mind readers. Even though your needs were apparent to you, it was wrong to assume that they were obvious to your colleagues.

Furthermore, executives should avoid asking colleagues from other departments, What can you do for me? That was the wrong question. More appropriate was this set of questions: What information do I need to do my job? When do I need it? In what form? And from whom should I be getting it?[38] Drucker insisted that in promoting effectiveness among peers, executives had to reconcile the power of information with the fallibility of its users. It was not a challenge to be met with gimmicks but demanded persistent attention and patient work to attain corporate results.

Drucker offered no panacea to improve interactions with peers but formulated a series of questions to help executives coordinate the span of relationship and improve mutual effectiveness:

- Who has to use my knowledge to be effective?

- What way does he or she depend on me—for information, feedback, productivity, approval?

- Whom do I depend on for similar things in order to be effective?

- What do I do that helps me do what I am being paid for?

- What do I do that hampers other people?

- What do others do that helps me, and what do they do that interferes with my work?

- When, where, and in what form do people require information from me?

- After a decision has been made, who has to know that it has been made, and what people are required to make it effective?

Drucker concluded that a central common denominator of people who achieve in knowledge organizations was the ability to build up trust by raising certain specific questions (listed in the accompanying box). He observed that in his consulting experience, when executives raised these questions with peers, the first, surprising response usually was, "Why didn't you ask me these relevant questions earlier?"

Although developing systematic relationships among peers was originally intended as a top management tool of productivity, it was useful to all knowledge professionals concerned with improving relationships. In order to build up trust and applied knowledge throughout the organization, Drucker recommended that the CEO set up, for the want of a better word, a series of *relationship meetings*. In outlining the framework of these open-ended informal conferences, Drucker suggested that each member of the top management team be expected to meet at least once a year with knowledgeable professional people in the organization and say to them: "I'm not here to make a speech or to tell you anything, I'm here to listen. I want to hear from you what your aspirations are, but above all, where you see opportunities for this company and where you see threats. And what are your ideas for us to try to do new things, develop new products, design new ways of reaching the market? What questions do you have about the company, its policies, its direction . . . its position in the industry, in technology, in the marketplace?"[39]

Team Concepts

According to Drucker, an institution is defined by its tasks, and in an information-based organization these tasks are more and more frequently handled by knowledge professionals. In successful information-based organizations the command-and-control design had become increasingly irrelevant, the number of corporate tiers had been incrementally eliminated, and the traditional superior-subordinate relationship had been drastically revised. In making a contrast between the traditional and the knowledge organizations, Drucker envisioned the symphony orchestra as perhaps the best model of the so-called *flat* organization: "In some modern symphonies, hundreds of musicians are on stage together and play together. According to organization theory, there should be several 'group vice president conductors' and perhaps a half-dozen 'division VP conductors.' But there is only one conductor—and every one of the musicians, each a high-grade specialist, plays directly to that person, without an intermediary."[40]

Although Drucker recognized that the team was becoming the dominant design of the future, he saw little impressive empirical evidence on the performance and nature of teams in the management literature. He recommended that a circumspect attitude be taken about their usage, contending that a team was not a panacea for all tasks. For example, there was no need to create a team to do something an individual could do as well or better. Cautioning that the operation of a team task force would alter the traditional nature of executive work, he wrote: "Teams, by contrast, demand, above all, very great self-discipline from each member. Everybody has to do the team's *thing*. Everybody has to take responsibility for the work of the entire team and for its performance. The one thing one cannot do on a team is one's own 'thing.'"[41] He further argued that it would be prudent to analyze just how much we know about the conduct and characteristics of teams.

Drucker evaluated teams from two major viewpoints: (1) structure and (2) commitment.

Structure. He commenced his structural analysis of teams by defining them as organizational tools, and just as there is no perfect organization, there is no perfect team. Each kind of team has its own uses, requirements, strengths, and limitations, and one of the main reasons for misapplication of teams is "the mistaken belief" among executives that there is only one kind of team. Using a sports metaphor, Drucker depicted three kinds of teams—baseball, soccer, and doubles in tennis.[42]

The distinguishing element of a baseball team is that the players play on the team but do not play as a team. A major example of this kind of team in business was the traditional Detroit automobile design team. Designers rarely saw marketing people and never consulted them. The strengths of the baseball team design are the capacity of each member to concentrate on clear goals, the ability of each member to measure himself against certain standards, the opportunity for individual training, and the freedom to tolerate *stars* within the ranks. Most of the business literature has focused on this design because it had been applied advantageously to the one-product firm. Along with its strengths, Drucker noted its concomitant weaknesses: "But the baseball team is inflexible. It works well when the game has been played many times and when the sequence of its actions is thoroughly understood by everyone. That is what made this kind of team right for Detroit in the past."[43]

The two most prominent examples of the organizational team analogous to the football team are the symphony orchestra and the emergency hospital room unit as its members rally around a patient in shock in the middle of the night. "On this kind of team, too, all players have fixed positions. The tuba players in the orchestra will not take over the parts of the double basses. They stick to their tubas. In the crisis team at the hospital, the respiratory technician will not make an incision in the chest of the patient to massage the heart. But on these terms the members work *as* a team. Each coordinates his or her part with the rest of the team."[44]

The actual operations, however, are closely controlled, and "there is no such permissiveness. The word of the coach is law. Players are beholden to this one boss alone for their orders, their rewards, their appraisals, their promotions."[45] Without strong direction, the musician would only be making noise and the football player would be walking around the field in a mindless, uncoordinated fashion.

In discussing the symphony orchestra, Drucker pointed out that all instruments play different parts but they rarely play in unison. Again, except for the conductor there are no bosses: for example, "the first violin is not even the boss of the other violins." At the same time, a critical distinction between an orchestra and a business is found in the score, because "in the orchestra . . . the score is given to both players and conductor. In business the score is being written as it is being played."[46]

The tennis doubles team was the final conceptual leg in Drucker's triangular structure of team design. In an organization this team is not always literally a two-person affair, but it is small, limited to approximately five to seven members. In this design, "the members have to be trained together and must work together for quite some time before they fully function as a team. There must be one clear goal for the entire team yet considerable flexibility with respect to the individual member's work and performance. And in this kind of team only the team 'performs'; individual members 'contribute.'"[47]

Commitment. Because its precepts have been cited in previous pages, the concept of commitment requires only reidentification. Suffice it to say executives working with teams have to assume greater responsibility, sharpen their skills in working with others of different backgrounds and temperaments, and learn the techniques for working on more than one type of team. And because teams cannot be developed overnight, trust and the value of teamwork must be constantly endorsed and reinforced.

Most important, commitment depends on identifying the team's purpose and then designing the most appropriate team to complete the designated task. Drucker called the selection of the proper team a risky task and also warned against the danger of creating a hybrid composed of parts of different teams.

To accomplish results a team has to reconcile the inevitable conflict of diverse temperaments among its members, which means that the role of the team's leader takes on added importance. In the following passage, Drucker captured the essence of this leadership role: "Because the 'players' in an information-based organization are specialists, they cannot be told how to do their work. There are probably few orchestra conductors who could even coax one note out of a French horn, let alone show the horn player how to do it.

But the conductor can focus the horn player's skill and knowledge on the musician's joint performance. And this focus is what the leaders of an information-based business must be able to achieve."[48]

Summary

Without a focus on contribution and commitment, the concepts of working harder and working smarter are both futile. The information-based organization calls for a structural shift from the span of control to the span of relationship, a revision of the executive job based on greater accountability, a reevaluation of the concept of leadership, and the introduction of teams as fulcrums of trust.

In stating that teams were inevitably replacing the hierarchical tiers of traditional organizations, Drucker did not view them as good or bad, desirable or undesirable. He was simply realistically observing that teams had become major facts of organizational life. He warned that any management starting a team for the first time should recognize that it was an extremely difficult task because it demanded the toughest learning challenge—the unlearning of old habits and skills. Stressing that the free-flow, information-based organization was not permissive, he pointed out that it required a high degree of self-discipline on the part of team members. Finally, the selection of the right type of team was of critical importance because the wrong one would destroy both commitment and concentration. The team design had to conform to strategy and not the other way around.

Abandonment and Concentration

Drucker noted that it was a universal characteristic of all large organizations to have a superabundance of superfluous activities alongside its productive tasks. The former needed pruning, and the latter needed to be nourished and supported, because a business could not have enough of them. He also contended there was an iron law of organization with respect to activities; namely, that addition was the norm and subtraction was the exception. As a result the typical organization was likely to be loaded down with yesterday's promises and commitments. But managers must be willing to eliminate noncontributing institutional dead weight, understanding that "it is always amazing how many of the things we do will never be missed."[49]

Abandonment

Confronting the realities of hyperacceleration of change and unprecedented social complexity, Drucker declared that managers must prepare to abandon everything they know.[50] He was brashly dogmatic regarding the elimination of things that were choking and stifling performance. Executives had no choice but to confront the irrefutable proposition that without systematic and purposeful abandonment, they would be overtaken by events. Applying a biological metaphor to input-output analysis, Drucker pointed out that "by now most of us have learned the hard way that dieting off fat is a good deal more difficult than not putting it on in the first place. Excess costs are excess fat."[51] So uncompromising was he on the principle of systematic abandonment that he elevated it to the status of a moral imperative. He viewed putting precious resources into yesterday as not only criminal but sinful. For those activities whose immediate elimination were not feasible, he suggested that at least executives should "stop pouring in further resources and efforts."[52]

Drucker suggested that executives answer a number of commonsense and pertinent questions to help themselves achieve improved productivity through systematic abandonment:

- Am I spending dollar time on penny jobs that should not be done at all?

- Am I a victim of the illusion that what always fails must eventually succeed?

- What are the things that I am doing that I do not understand?

- Do I spend significant time learning things that I should not be doing at all?

- Do I worry about what will happen tomorrow rather than correct what I spoiled yesterday?

- Can I wait six months to fill a job vacancy caused by death, resignation, or retirement to see if the position is still needed?

- Does it make sense to farm out all activities that do not offer the people working in them an opportunity to advance into senior management levels?

- Why not substitute the term *job performance* for *job enrichment* in all training and development programs?

- What are the few high-priority tasks that should be considered the province of staff work?

- What are the levels of management that actually manage nothing?

- Is there any reason to honor a request for additional people in the budget of a department that has done a poor job?

- Have I explored contracting out all work that does not relate directly to revenue results?

- Is there any excuse for having an executive vice president, a group vice president, or any other titled executive when there is no correlation between the title and performance?

- If I were starting all over again, would I want to continue to do a specific activity?

- What are the activities that have ceased to be productive?

- What one ineffective thing am I doing today that I will drop tomorrow?

- What risk do I take if I do nothing about a particular activity?

- In my professional routine, how do I distinguish efficiency from effectiveness, the urgent from the important, problems from opportunities, and procedures from policies?

- Does it make sense for me to conduct another study for a project that has failed several times?

- If I have to do the wrong thing, is there any reason I should do it efficiently?

- What am I doing to eliminate paperwork from my professional routine?

- What would happen if I did not have access to a particular piece of paper?

- Why is the wastebasket the only indispensable tool of management?

- Why is it best to handle a piece of paper only once?

- What procedural activities consuming more than thirty minutes can I safely eliminate?

- Should I candidly admit that the things I am postponing I am actually abandoning?

- What would happen if somebody else took care of a specific activity?

- If all of these queries make sense and are so obvious, why am I not doing anything about them?

Concentration

Drucker asserted that abandonment and concentration were opposite sides of the same coin. By abandoning unproductive activities, executives could increase their effectiveness by concentrating on result areas. One common denominator discovered by Drucker among ineffective executives was that they worked harder but failed to work smarter. More specifically, the average executive said yes to all requests, elevated accommodation to an obsessive virtue, and was incapable of establishing objectives of his own. But "you have to learn to say 'no' when the temptation is to do good. The secret of effectiveness is concentration on the very meager resources you have where you can make a difference."[53] Drucker further observed that the mediocre manager usually had his door open for casual visitors and responded, like a robot, to everything that arrived in the mail. Caricaturing these practices, Drucker remarked that working on one's in-box was tantamount to working on the goals of others.

Drucker attributed a great deal of the blame for these misdirected activities to top management for encouraging, whether consciously or unconsciously, administrative policies that diffused the principle of concentration. Among some of these certain prescriptions for ineffectiveness were creating jobs that were widow makers, giving a competent individual more and more additional chores to do, pairing a mediocre performer with an excellent one, and designing a job that called for incompatible temperaments within one person.

According to Drucker, one irrefutable sign of an effective manager was the ability to escape the temptation to get excessively involved in activities or to participate in too many activities. He observed: "We rightly consider keeping many balls in the air a circus stunt. Yet even the juggler does it only for ten minutes or so. If he were to try doing it longer, he would soon drop all the balls."[54]

Alluding to the probability principle of Vilfredo Pareto (1848–1923), which showed it was uneconomical for managers to devote the same amount of time and attention to the inconsequential that they allocated to the critical, Drucker argued that effective executives were the ones able to spend their time focusing on the vital rather than the trivial. And he suggested that a good formula for being opportunity centered was to attempt things that nobody else was doing, in which case even an achievement of 1 percent on something meaningful would result in contribution.

Drucker insisted that the ability to concentrate was not a matter of employing mechanical reflexes but involved a deep commitment to act rather than react. When an executive was no longer entrapped by the inconsequential, he had a greater chance of making the correct choice of priorities: "Concentration—that is, the courage to impose on time and events his own decision as to what really matters and comes first—is the executive's only hope of becoming the master of time and events instead of their whipping boy."[55]

In an insight contrary to conventional wisdom, Drucker did not consider creativity an ally in the quest for improved performance. "Creativity," he commented, "if by that is meant undirected, unstructured, untutored, and uncontrolled guessing, is not likely to produce results."[56] Brainstorming and other techniques proposed by psychologists to stimulate ideas might actually confuse the concentration process by producing an excessive host of options, and the proliferation of ideas was the least of the problems encountered in developing executive effectiveness. In fact, Drucker said he had never encountered organizations or executives who did not have more ideas than they could use: "No organization which purposefully and systematically abandons the unproductive and obsolete ever wants for opportunities. Ideas are always around in profusion."[57]

Creativity in that form of "undirected, unstructured, untutored, and uncontrolled guessing" usually amounted to an excuse for doing nothing. The real challenge was the implementation of the imaginative idea. Looking upon creativity cynically as a boon to internal public relations within the organization, he saw it as a form of intellectual showmanship posing as contribution, a display of individual brilliance substituting for accountability, and an idyllic abstraction sacrificing reality—all of which reflected a managerial ego trip resulting in inertia and nonperformance.

Drucker organized the principle of concentration on two main levels: (1) professional and (2) tactical.

Professional. Drucker recommended that every executive attain intellectual competency in at least one functional discipline. This professionalism, or ability to understand one area in depth, had for Drucker a moral dimension in that it gave the manager an appreciation of the rigors involved in mastering the foundation and complexity of a discipline. He believed that in a knowledge society of countless functions it was personally reassuring for an individual to carve out a niche of core competency in a particular specialization. He visualized this expertise as a fulcrum for continued intellectual growth, a lever for increasing the knowledge of colleagues in the organization and producing economic results, and a springboard for understanding how a specialty is integrated into the whole.

Tactical. According to Drucker, a common denominator of effective executives that distinguished them from average executives was tactical concentration, the ability to select a few meaningful tasks above and beyond their routine duties. He also singled out the superstars of such concentration, the monomaniacs. These were the individuals who were paragons of performance because they aimed high, looking to achieve distinction and excellence in one major innovative endeavor. For Drucker, the monomaniac was the apotheosis of the concentration principle. During his consulting career he had learned that the most outstanding executive performers were those who left a legacy of one or perhaps two genuine accomplishments. These singular successful contributions earned them a reputation for superiority over other competent rivals in the competition for top management jobs.

The monomaniacal approach of concentrated dedication to a challenging project was no guarantee of winning the trophy of success. In fact, Drucker cautioned that the laws of probability argued otherwise. Nevertheless these were the people who were not afraid of undertaking high-risk opportunities that the typical person with multifaceted interests avoided. And when they were successful, the quality of their impact was likely to be incalculable in its contribution to core corporate strengths and shaping of institutional destiny.

In *Adventures of a Bystander,* Drucker depicted the brilliance and idiosyncrasies of many friends and acquaintances he had encountered in his career to that point. Buckminster Fuller and Marshall McLuhan, two former associates at *Fortune* magazine and cultural icons of their generation, were described as quintessential monomaniacs:

> Bucky Fuller and Marshall McLuhan exemplify to me the importance of being single minded. The single-minded ones, the monomaniacs, are the only true achievers. The rest, the ones like me, may have more fun; but they fritter themselves away. The Fullers and the McLuhans carry out a "mission"; the rest of us have "interests." Whenever anything is being accomplished, it is being done, I have learned, by a monomaniac with a mission. Bucky spent forty years in the wilderness, without even the Children of Israel to follow him. Yet he never wavered in his dedication to his vision. McLuhan spent twenty-five years chasing his vision until it captured him. He too never wavered. And when their time came, both had impact.[58]

As discussed in Chapter Nine, for the implementation of concentration Drucker also drew inspiration from the medieval philosophical concept known as Occam's razor, which he explained as advocating avoidance of too many assumptions, too many ifs and wherefores, and too many dependencies on untested quantification. He also thought Occam's razor should be applied to achieve simplicity in the selection of tools and techniques. He discovered, for example, that too many managers picked an elephant gun to chase sparrows. At the other extreme, too many managers used slingshots against tanks. The real challenge was to evaluate the purpose of each tool and its end results. He remarked: "Information specialists are toolmakers. They can tell us what tool to use to hammer upholstery nails into a chair; we need to decide whether we should be upholstering the chair at all."[59]

From Drucker's writings and lectures over the years, it is possible to assemble a variety of insights that illuminate ways to think about concentration. In the following list they are framed as questions for improving executive effectiveness:

- What have I done in the last three to five years that has made a contribution?

- What are the things that should come first, and what others not at all?

- When you have 186 objectives, nothing gets done. Always ask, What's the one thing I want to do?

- What is the one thing that I, and only I, can do, and if done well makes a difference?

- Why is it better to be 1 percent correct in addressing the right problem than 100 percent correct on the irrelevant one—particularly when no one else is working on it?

- Am I reacting to other people's priorities by responding immediately to everything that arrives in the mail?

- Why not aim high for a qualitative achievement rather than ride on the conventional bandwagon?

- What would I be doing if I only had six months to live?

- What would I like people to say about me at my retirement dinner?

- How would I write my own obituary?

Summary

Combined with its opposing twin, the principle of abandonment, concentration ranked high on Drucker's list of indispensable diagnostic tools for improved executive effectiveness. Failure to use abandonment and concentration was a certain predictor that a manager would be overwhelmed by the operating details of the job and denied the opportunity of contributing to corporate results. Executives who diligently practiced systematic concentration were likely to be looked up to as models of excellence and case studies to be emulated by others in the organization. Drucker also visualized ability to concentrate as a criterion for evaluating the future prospects of managerial candidates. But most important, he saw concentration as a significant part of individual growth and self-development.

Conclusion

Drucker viewed executive effectiveness as resting on fundamental principles of common sense and not some secret mystery. It centered on the integration of three central ingredients—contribution to the mission of the organization, concentration on key tasks, and commitment to professional standards of performance. Interacting together, each of these three intangibles propelled, stimulated, and energized the other. The difficulty, as Drucker analyzed it, was that none of these three critical components was teachable or learnable.

However, in the exemplary performance and results of successful executives, it was possible to discern principles of effectiveness that if not teachable were learnable. And if these guidelines for executive effectiveness were translated into organized work, then the foundations for the managerial development of contribution, commitment, and concentration could be nourished and developed. This was Drucker's aim in discussing such tactics as designing the job; structuring assignments; considering measurement; understanding teams; and focusing on relationships with subordinates, superiors, and peers. There were no guarantees, but at the same time, through proper habits, it was feasible to expect improvement. Supplementing the discussion so far of these principles, the next two chapters continue the theme of systematic executive work by discussing such topics as time management, executive strengths, communications, and decision making.

CHAPTER SIXTEEN

TIME, STRENGTHS, AND COMMUNICATION

In the Chapter Fourteen discussion of the realities of organizational life, the disruptive factors that hampered executive performance were mentioned. Drucker specifically cited such obstacles as the misallocation of time, the focus on weakness, and the misapplication of communication techniques. In this chapter I will describe how Drucker neutralized these negative aspects and converted them into opportunities for the systematic improvement of executive effectiveness. He introduced into the management literature many pioneering insights on the use of time, concentration on strengths, and the role of communications in a knowledge organization.

Time Management

Until Drucker inserted it into the corpus of management theory, the topic of time management had been relegated to self-help books, the most celebrated being Benjamin Franklin's *Poor Richard's Almanac*. After the publication of *The Effective Executive* (1967), Drucker was astonished to see the enormous popular, scholarly, and managerial interest in the topic of time management.

Characteristics

Living in a state of duration, we tend to underestimate the elusiveness of time. This was an insight Drucker learned from Saint Augustine, who said, "Time can only be perceived and measured while it is passing."[1] Another important concept Drucker derived from Augustine's *Confessions* was that there are no facts in the future, only expectations. One passage that impressed him said, "Future things are not as yet; and if they are not as yet they are not; they cannot be seen; yet foretold they may be from things present, which are already and cannot be seen."[2]

Drucker characterized time as a unique resource that a company cannot buy, create, or invent. Everybody is allocated only a certain share, which is irretrievable, ephemeral, irreversible, and unstorable: "The supply of time is totally inelastic. No matter how high the demand, the supply will not go up. There is no price for it and no marginal utility curve for it. Moreover, time is totally perishable and cannot be stored. Yesterday's time is gone forever and will never come back. Time is, therefore, always in exceedingly short supply."[3]

Drucker considered time the most important of all resources and indispensable for executive performance, for unless time gets managed, nothing gets done. He viewed this proposition as the sine qua non of professional activity, yet he was astonished that so few executives grasped its significance for producing results. For example, in the case of a salesman there is a constant relationship between the time he has available for calls and the number of calls he actually completes.

Drucker cautioned that handling time more effectively is not a matter of waiting for an epiphany. Executives have to recognize that in the reality of daily lives, before they can organize their time more effectively, they have to cope with all sorts of restraints:

> The executive's time tends to belong to everybody else. . . . Everybody can move in on his time, and everybody does. There seems to be very little any one executive can do about it. He cannot, as a rule, like the physician, stick his head out the door and say to the nurse, "I won't see anybody for the next half hour." Just at this moment, the executive's telephone rings, and he has to speak to the company's best customer or to a high official in the city administration or to his boss—and the next half hour is already gone.[4]

More specifically, Drucker drew on an episode from his consulting career to illustrate how one executive was able to neutralize interruptions and capture precious disposable time:

> A former client taught me a trick for obtaining a chunk of disposable time. He told his secretary he did not want to be disturbed for the next two hours in order to have uninterrupted time with me unless, of course something important comes up. The secretary asked him to define "importance." He told her only if three people called, the President of the U.S., his wife, or the CEO of the corporation. After closing the door, he said: the President of the U.S. rarely calls me, my wife has more sense than to call; therefore unless my CEO should call, we will have a solid two hours together.[5]

Tactics

Shortly after the publication of Drucker's *Effective Executive,* a veritable volcano of books and articles exploded on the management scene, focusing on guidelines for handling time. The emergence of this embryonic subdiscipline in turn produced a cadre of time management specialists. A number of authorities acknowledged their debt to Drucker for his original insights on the topic. He remarked that, providing executives had the will and commitment to apply the findings of the now ongoing research on the subject, time management represented the most verifiable segment of scholarship in the field of managerial effectiveness.

As described in Chapter Fifteen, a chief distinguishing feature between mediocre and talented executives is that the former spend their time randomly, whereas the latter know how to spend their time productively. Drucker also found that the improved performance displayed by excellent executives is not a natural gift but a matter of systematic attention to using time wisely. Apropos of this point, he once observed that if you want to get things done, get a busy man to do them. It was paradoxical but true that people who apparently had the least time were usually the most productive.

Consequently, for understanding the fundamentals of time management, Drucker suggested we look at the ways very competent people handle time. Digging into the vault of his consulting experience, he observed that on the one hand this minority of managerial practitioners realized that Socrates' sophisticated admonition to "know thyself" was replete with metaphysical complexity. On the other hand, they saw that knowing one's time was a more mundane principle that was both understandable and controllable for the ordinary human being. As Drucker put it: "The analysis of one's time . . . is the one easily accessible and yet systematic way to analyze one's work and to think through what really matters in it. 'Know Thyself,' the old prescription for wisdom, is almost impossibly difficult for mortal men. But everyone can follow the injunction 'Know Thy Time.' "[6]

Drucker's writings and lectures reveal a host of practices and guidelines for managing the precious resource of time for improved results. The following are among the most prominent of what he considered commonsense observations:

- Effective executives make a periodic record of how they spend their time.

- The basic rule for effectiveness is to write down what you expect to happen for a crucial task or activity and then, through feedback, evaluate the performance.

- Arrange for flexibility of time in your planning schedule.

- Remember, everything takes more time than expected.

- Avoid using paperwork as a cover-up and a crutch for personal insecurity.

- Successful completion of important assignments requires big blocks of time devoted to concentration.

- Executives need to systematically prune the timewasters from their daily activities.

- Dispense with Monday morning staff meetings; they violate the psychological law that one can always slow down but one cannot usually speed up.

- Identify the tasks that take more than an hour a week, and see if they can be done in half the time.

- Do not use your most productive and energetic time of the day to accomplish routine and procedural things.

- Start meetings on time and be punctual for appointments; this gives you the feeling of better control of the situation.

- Important things cannot be accomplished with the intermittent use of short spurts of time; they require big blocks of uninterrupted time—consider using the short periods of time for review purposes.

- Trusting to memory is hazardous; write down what you expect to happen with respect to product innovation.

- Apply a diagnostic technique to resolve problems. When you cannot find a feasible solution, stop and save time by redefining what the problem is all about.

- Avoid unnecessary travel by using available media tools (fax, e-mail, conference calls, cellular phones, and so on).

- Attempt to restrict routine affairs (opening mail, scanning newspapers and magazines, handling correspondence, and routing telephone messages) to a special segment of the day.

- Establish a procedure for acquiring a block of time to work on opportunity projects; this will increase your probability of results.

- Arrive at the office a half hour early to plan the day's agenda and accomplish a few things without the normal office interruptions.

- To obtain a better grasp of time as a financial asset, calculate, based on your salary, the hourly worth of your time.

- Continually ask, What do I have to learn today to keep learning for tomorrow?

- Be aware that one cannot travel and hope to work effectively; this is an especially important consideration in the jet age, when travel has become a substitute for thinking.

- To find timewasters, ask of all activities, What would happen if I were starting from scratch? Would I still be doing them?

Meetings

Meetings and procrastination were two challenges for improved time management that Drucker thought called for special attention. The downside of meetings was the low correlation between having a meeting and getting things done. Drucker recommended that executives avoid calling an excess of unproductive meetings in the following ways: recognizing when corporate meetings have lost their original purpose and have become encrusted in bureaucratic routine; understanding that in order to satisfy executive egos, meetings tend to breed like jackrabbits; concluding that meetings have become counterproductive when they absorb more than 25 percent of an executive's time; and determining when meetings have become a form of martyrdom for those compelled to attend them.

Drucker continually emphasized the significance of the old adage that nobody controlled the universe. This was a frank recognition of the restraints of time in which executives could get things done. Warning against an abundance and high expectations of meetings, he noted that "there is nothing less productive than the attempt to cram more productive effort into time than it will comfortably hold."[7] Equally counterproductive was the tendency for officials to leave a meeting in a state of harmony and good feeling but without any sense of direction or program of action. Donald Keogh, former president of Coca-Cola, revealed how Drucker drove this point home to him: "He would tell me after each session—don't tell me you had a wonderful meeting with me. Tell me what you are going to do on Monday that's different."[8] Because work did not get done and results were not achieved at misdirected meetings or excessive meetings, they were a sign of organizational mismanagement: "As a rule, meetings should never be allowed to become the main demand on an executive's time. Too many meetings always bespeak poor structure of jobs and the wrong organizational components. Too many meetings signify that work that should be in one job or in one component is spread over several jobs or several components. They signify that responsibility is diffused and that information is not addressed to the people who need it."[9]

It was hardly surprising, given Drucker's preachments on systematic abandonment, that he called for reducing the number and the size of meetings: "Few of these committees would ever be missed. And they would do a better job in less time if they had three instead of seven members."[10] Nevertheless, despite his often severe criticisms of meetings and committees, he indicated that they had an important plus side when used as vehicles for improved communication and effectiveness. Even in this case, however, they were productive only when their purpose was made clear. For example, it was imperative to determine at the outset the reason for calling a meeting. Was it to seek opinions on new projects? Was it to announce a directive without calling for any discussion? Was it to obtain feedback on earlier decisions? Was it to request new methods for satisfying the unmet needs of customers? Was it to receive complaints and suggestions from employees in order to improve company morale? Was it to acknowledge and congratulate individual subordinates' performance through a show-and-tell exercise? Was it to propose a potential decision and ask for alternatives? Depending on the meeting purpose, the meeting agenda could be of infinite variety.

Drucker singled out two issues for particular consideration—the two-person meeting and the practice of restraint in calling meetings. Of all types of meetings, Drucker selected the two-person meeting as the most difficult in which to achieve meaning and accomplish results. In order for it to succeed, Drucker advised a few minutes of casual chatter to ease the social tensions. He also advised that the one-on-one meeting demanded more intense preparations on objectives and more detailed homework on content than a larger meeting did.

Because of their potential for debilitating effects and negative impacts, Drucker urged great restraint in the calling of meetings. If managers felt the temptation, he strongly advised that they should resist it. If they nevertheless felt compelled to introduce a new meeting into the organizational routine, he insisted that before doing so they eliminate an old meeting. (As with all Drucker's suggested guidelines, these were not to be seen as formalized rules but as a basis for thoughtful judgment. The goal was not pursuing the ideal but seeking the possible.) Finally, to facilitate the smooth operations of meetings, he urged that they should be started punctually, conducted courteously, attended only by people who have something to contribute, and ended at the announced time.

Procrastination

It was debatable, Drucker argued, whether we were living in the best of times or the worst of times, but he was certain that it was the only time we had. Looking at procrastination from this point of view, he saw it as the greatest thief of time and the most obvious impediment to achieving results.

In any discussion of time, Drucker said, it was crucial to address procrastination, the normal human propensity to postpone to tomorrow what should be done today, to talk about intentions rather than work toward results, and to delay actions until ideal conditions prevail. All these factors contributed to lost opportunities, exacerbated emotions, produced psychological fears, and generated unnecessary pressures. Equating procrastination with the fine art of staying apace of yesterday, he observed that postponement resulted in physical fatigue and psychological anguish that made the job seem increasingly difficult the more it was put off.

Drucker realized that simply sermonizing on the ways procrastination inhibited action was useless. His recipe for avoiding these pitfalls of procrastination in the first place invoked an alliterative triad of steps: definition, delegation, and deadline. The executive needed to define the problem or the task, delegate accountability to a specific person along with responsibility for the specific thing to be accomplished, and establish a firm deadline for completion. The definition ensured a sense of purpose, the delegation identified who was going to do the actual work, and the deadline substituted action for inertia.[11]

To offset the perils of procrastination, Drucker's greatest single antidote was "to start." Then, by doing a little bit on a regular and consistent basis, even the biggest project would diminish in size. Moreover, in commencing a task some degree of accomplishment was inevitable, and this achievement reduced the element of fear and apprehension. Drucker was convinced that a sure sign of a consummate professional was the capacity for "getting started." However, he also worried that a robotic concern with the principles of time management could destroy the human side of executive effectiveness. It could lead to the sacrifice of family responsibilities, the neglect of friendships, the forfeiture of hobbies, and the loss of the satisfaction of serving others through voluntary activity. Drucker considered this too big a price for pursuing a successful career.

Moreover, a virtue could disintegrate into a vice if the rigorous control of time created a workaholic. Drucker concluded there were few more pressing issues in effectiveness than the proper management of time, but when taken to extremes it violated the moral tenet that everybody needed a private life.

The Principle of Capitalizing on Strengths

As part and parcel of his consulting routine, Drucker was always certain to raise this question with clients: "What is unique about your institution?" Typically, the top management response was predictable: "We have very good people in our organization." He came to wonder, if every company he encountered had only strong people, where were the weak and incompetent people?[12] Therefore, without intending to be insulting or irreverent, his next question was, "Good for what?"[13] He asserted that the word *good*, without a relevant reference, was meaningless. He knew that the statement "We have good people" was pure rhetoric, but he also knew that it was possible to identify a company's outstanding people and then to examine their work habits and contributions. The self-delusion of executives amazed him in that, not having gone beyond the rhetoric in order to investigate the actual performance, "they see strengths where none exist and weaknesses where there are none."[14] Similarly, executives made the common mistake of failing to learn from their successes.[15] In seeking out the most competent people in an organization, Drucker's method was an illuminating form of internal market research. He simply asked people to name their outstanding colleagues and spell out the accomplishments that made these colleagues different from the average practitioners.

Drucker hypothesized that no company had an advantage over any other in recruiting from the general employment pool. As soon as a company reached the size of six employees, it was selecting from the same source as everyone else and thus competing with everyone else. It was a myth therefore that one could find better people; there was no such thing. Considering the term *good people* an empty shibboleth, divorced from reality, Drucker pondered the rationale for paying so little attention to the more pertinent point of good for what? One reason he proposed was that in diagnosing a firm's human resources, personnel specialists had a paradoxical penchant for favoring disease over health in their assessment, for seeing weaknesses rather than strengths. Calling for a redressing of this negative approach, he stated that "the task of an executive is not to change human beings. Rather, as the Bible tells us in the parable of the Talents, the task is to multiply performance capacity of the whole by putting to use whatever strength, whatever health, whatever aspiration there is in individuals."[16]

As mentioned previously, the accounting model was another factor in the failure to evaluate the strengths of human resources because of its inability to measure performance. Accountants might know the cost of knowledge workers, but they did not know what they were worth. Moreover, in the traditional accounting method, intellectual property was viewed as an expense rather than as an asset. Pointing out the need to incorporate mental capital into an activity accounting model, Drucker argued for a sharper understanding of the knowledge worker human resource. Accounting was not the only function that neglected human strengths; personnel management confused analysis with action and equated fire fighting with results.[17]

Drucker was unashamedly dogmatic and took an absolutist stance on the proposition that human performance capability depended on strengths and not on weaknesses. Of course weaknesses had to be acknowledged and neutralized, but they were incapable of creating results. In his consulting work he followed the principle of avoiding any discussion of what his clients could not do, emphasizing instead what they were capable of doing and what it made sense for them to do.

Because the only purpose for hiring people was to produce results, employees should be paid only in consideration of their strengths, not their weaknesses.[18] But in reality, the opposite was often the case. The organization had a proclivity to focus on human defects, to criticize and harp on the negative aspects of individuals, to see people as threats rather than opportunities, and to esteem the potential of credentials instead of competency. Conversely, "the effective executive makes strength productive. He knows that one cannot build on weakness. To achieve results, one has to use all the available strengths—the strengths of associates, the strengths of the superior, and one's own strengths. These strengths are the true opportunities. To make strength productive is the unique purpose of organization. It cannot, of course, overcome the weaknesses with which each of us is abundantly endowed. But it can make them irrelevant. Its task is to use the strength of each man as a building block for joint performance."[19]

At the same time, Drucker realized a danger in an analysis conducted exclusively through the positive prism of strengths. If it overestimated human capacities, it might seem to endorse the myth of human perfectibility. To dramatize the need to avoid excessive human expectations, he recalled a passage in Fyodor Dostoyevsky's *Brothers Karamazov,* in which the Grand Inquisitor accuses Jesus of overestimating human capacity for spiritual strength and of setting standards so high that they can be met only by a small group of the elect.

Without compromising on his basic position that only strengths produce results, Drucker recognized that in order to capitalize on strengths, it was also necessary to take into account the symbiotic relationships between human talents and frailties.[20] In acknowledging the pervasiveness of human imperfections, he was willing to tolerate bad habits with one exception—character weakness.

In implementing the principle of capitalizing on strengths, such cosmetic features as age, gender, ethnicity, credentials, and personality traits were irrelevant. The only consideration, Drucker said, was the bottom line of meritocracy. He also maintained, however, that there was a correlation between great strengths and weaknesses in an outstanding performer. It was necessary to accept the fact that "strong people always have strong weaknesses."[21] In short, the person with no major flaws was unlikely to have major strengths; he or she was usually a predictable mediocrity. Distrustful of the person who never made a mistake, Drucker wrote: "The better a man is, the more mistakes he will make—for the more new things he will try."[22]

The Corporate Milieu

In his analysis of obtaining results by capitalizing on strengths, Drucker used a dual approach, exploring the corporate setting and individual improvement. As previously mentioned, he described a clear organizational purpose and the ability to communicate core institutional competencies as the foundation for meeting the challenge of results.

But a clear mission and able professionals alone were insufficient. Before the organization could manage these strengths, it had to provide an atmosphere where good people could grow, flourish, and contribute. In order to eliminate factors contributing to organizational frictions, Drucker offered various admonitions. A number of them appeared in Chapter Fifteen, including the following: don't thoughtlessly give strong people additional things to do; don't create jobs so onerous that the person has no private life; don't combine a weak performer with a strong one and hope to obtain positive results; don't design the job around the person rather than the task; don't show concern for methodology if the results are there; don't believe that the wedding of two severely handicapped individuals will produce a healthy offspring; don't try to fill a job that calls upon its occupant to exercise widely different temperaments, and don't assign the ablest people to yesterday's problems rather than tomorrow's opportunities. All of these misdirected practices are certain prescriptions for producing a corporate climate of inefficiency and diluting individual strengths. Once again, in Drucker's judgment the statement that "people are our greatest assets" was empty rhetoric as long as employees were actually treated "as problems, procedures, and costs."[23]

Drucker viewed a company's appraisal system as its single most important instrument of control because it mirrored the real values of corporate culture by telling people how they were perceived and how they were rewarded by management. Unfortunately, most methods of employee evaluation did little to enhance the individual's self-esteem and promote effectiveness because they focused on behavior rather than results, concentrated on personal likes and cosmetic dislikes at the expense of contribution, stressed incompetence to the neglect of competence, and emphasized vices over virtues.

Drucker remarked that most appraisal forms seemed the products of "abnormal psychologists." In effect, they forced the superior to look for the subordinate's shortcomings as though he or she were on a treasure hunt for dysfunctional characteristics.[24] Because of the factor of human judgment, it was illusory to think that there could be a perfect appraisal system. Nevertheless, one could hope for a system that was reasonably fair. Any assessment that gave priority to standards of pathology over health, however, was not only unfair but was bound to be counterproductive. He thought it an appalling violation of policies dominating principles when there was only an evaluation yardstick for what was wrong and none for what was right.

Drucker strenuously objected to assessment policies that relied on designing personality profiles, conducting complex mathematical models of efficiency, filling out redundant questionnaires, predicting future "crown princes," applying narrow engineering and quantitative standards of measurement, and probing personal idiosyncrasies. Rejecting these doubtful methodologies of assessment, he suggested the key question was, Is the person "more or less" a competent performer? He also declared that "there is no magic to good staffing and promotion—just hard work and disciplined thought."[25]

Drucker offered a modest proposal of his own for evaluation. He said it was far from complete and foolproof but it had the advantages of being positive and simple. It required the evaluator to think through four basic questions: What has the person done well in the past? What is it likely that he or she will do well in the future? What support in training techniques and necessary tools does the individual need to do well in the future? If I had a son or daughter, would I want them to work for this person?[26]

A humorous barb in the 1970s at the conventional appraisal system was the popular Peter Principle, which postulated that everybody gets promoted to his or her level of incompetency. Drucker not only failed to endorse it but missed its humor because it considered weakness more important than strength. He criticized the Peter Principle as both immoral and stupid. It was stupid because it assumed that people who had performed in three or four assignments would suddenly stop performing. And it was immoral because it was the supervisor who had made the mistake.[27] His recommended antidote when a person was promoted beyond his capacity was for the executive to admit frankly and candidly that the promotion was a mistake and to resolve not to make a similar mistake in the future. Parenthetically, the person he cited as the ideal model for assuming responsibility for promotions and demotions was one of his great executive heroes, General George Marshall.[28]

Drucker urged management to accept the fact that excellent people would always be in short supply. As he saw it, the rules of probability dictated that in any organization, 10 percent of the people would be outstanding, 80 percent would display various degrees of competence, and the other 10 percent or so ought to pay the company for the privilege of the job. The task of top management was to identify the outstanding individuals but also to give everybody the opportunity to display his or her talents.

In addition, management should terminate directionless promotion processes. Turning to an insight he derived from Bernoulli's theorem, Drucker asserted that in the event a certain job had defeated two or three competent men or women for whom a manager originally had high expectations of success, then the rule was don't look for another candidate. It was best to conclude that the job made no sense. It was obviously designed not for a human but for a mermaid or a unicorn.[29]

Prototypical appraisal forms, displays of executive omniscience in the selection process, and facile explanations such as the Peter Principle not only failed to measure performance properly but also completely neglected the factor that people go through varied stages of development and have alternative responses to different situations. For example, it troubled Drucker that people who had never been given a real opportunity to perform were often labeled as misfits and nonentities. These so-called losers had been known to blossom suddenly in crises and to reveal hidden talents when thrust into a situation where their strengths could become effective.

One of Drucker's more incisive insights for capitalizing on strength concerned the ratio of performance between excellent and mediocre executives. He believed that there was a fixed ratio, a *performance gap,* between outstanding and average performers and that if the performance of the elite were raised it would elevate the performance of the others. In short, because moving the mass was difficult, it was easier to get results by concentrating on the elite.

As a corollary, it was also unlikely that outstanding performers would learn much from average executives. However, Drucker argued, it was possible for mediocre executives to model themselves after excellent ones. Essentially, this meant learning what the excellent ones did that the rest failed to do at all:

"Don't ever try to learn from other people's mistakes. Learn what other people do right."[30]

Drucker was a staunch advocate of equality of opportunity. At the same time, he recognized that the laws of probability did not dictate equality of results. The outcome was the rise of an aristocracy of talent, meaning, in effect, that high-level competence was antiegalitarian. This was why successful performers must be assiduously studied rather than ignored.

In dealing with clients, Drucker constantly conveyed the message that the gap between the elite and the average could be easily closed with a little effort. For example, as suggested earlier, rather than focus on sales education and training in a discipline where few solid principles existed, it was sounder to eliminate redundant paperwork, senseless meetings, and unnecessary travel so that each salesperson's number of calls could be increased. Through this procedure the performances of both the stars and the average salespeople would increase the overall results.

To fortify his contention that the elite elevated the performance of the average, Drucker cited illustrations from such various disciplines and activities as heart surgery, organ transplantation, athletics, use of the marketing concept and of activity accounting, and entrepreneurship. In these and other areas, once the breakthrough trail was blazed by the original knowledge pioneers, the average practitioner also quickly improved his or her performance by emulating the innovation.

Individual Improvement

The corporation was the crucible of strengths, but it was only meaningful insofar as it allowed individuals to express and implement their skills and talents. As Drucker repeatedly remarked, the organization is a means to an end, not an end in itself. And throughout history well-managed institutions have owed their longevity to following two basic rules: first, allow individuals a private life of their own, and second, avoid the temptation of trying to change the personality of the institutions' members. Too few individuals, however, take advantage of this autonomy by seeing the institution as a tool for their achievement.

Even more surprising to Drucker was that people seldom paid attention to their strengths. When asked, "Do you know what you are good at?" and, "Do you know your own limitations?" executives responded in an evasive and hesitant manner. For example, Drucker reported, people either "look at you with a blank stare or they often respond in terms of subject knowledge, which is the wrong answer."[31] In determining strength resulting from functional experience, Drucker asserted it was a myth that thirty years of doing the same thing contributed to individual strengths and personal development.

Drucker believed strongly that a secret for identifying strengths was a system for ascertaining the things a person was particularly good at. In achieving success, one then exploited these talents and activities: "Self-development means making oneself better in what one is already good at. It also means overcoming unnecessary limitations, bad habits, lack of skills, and lack of knowledge, and not worrying about the things one cannot be good at."[32]

The failure of executives to realize the significance of strengths and weaknesses was a certain prescription for ineffectiveness. It meant, in effect, that they would overlook such elements as the equation of performance with strength, the role of personal core competencies in producing results, and the fact that strong people also have major weak points. They would believe the myth that a person can be proficient in everything, they would not be aware that worrying about things one can't control is a waste of time, and they would succumb to the hubristic belief that it is possible to predict the performance of employees.

Drucker commented briefly on three other factors that influenced managing an individual's strengths: (1) empowerment, (2) multiple talents, and (3) physical rhythm.

Empowerment. Drucker found the popular term *empowerment* distasteful; he preferred the term *responsibility.* With this in mind he raised a number of questions that could convert insights into strengths, such as: Do you really enjoy the job? Do you see it as a challenge for growth and contribution? Do you have the temperament to cope with pressures? Can you function when things are rough and confused? Do you absorb information more readily by reading or listening? Are you aware of your facility for applying certain talents? From these questions strengths emerged easily for those people with natural skills and talents, and also weaknesses they had never suspected.[33]

Multiple Talents. Because some people attained certain skills effortlessly, they labored under the illusion that other skills would be obtainable with equal facility. It was as a result of such unfounded confidence, for example, that the comedian was tempted to play Hamlet and the violin virtuoso to play the drums. Objecting to the quixotic goal of creating universal geniuses, Drucker was more concerned with the pragmatic task of encouraging ordinary people to perform extraordinary things. Recognizing that no two people had the same configuration of strengths, managers had to accept the responsibility "to make people capable of joint performance, to make their strengths effective and their weaknesses irrelevant."[34] In this way, everybody in the organization contributed, but each contributed differently.

Physical Rhythm. The physiological aspect of capitalizing on strengths was understood by only a small minority of effective executives. These were the ones who were aware that each individual has a different metabolic system and therefore different needs for accomplishing tasks. For example, some people work more proficiently in an isolated setting, whereas others need constant contact with colleagues. The period of the day is another factor in individual physical rhythm; some people are better workers in the evening whereas others prefer the morning. Once again, Drucker stated, it was the individual's responsibility to monitor his biological clock to see if the job was suitable to his physical makeup and to ascertain his best time of day for effectiveness.

Drucker proposed a number of specific guidelines for managing strengths and neutralizing weaknesses:

- List your major contributions over the last two or three years.

- Consider the specific things for which the company is holding you accountable.

- Seek ways to identify your weaknesses and make them irrelevant.

- Determine what you cannot do, as well as what you can do.

- Look for demanding assignments that will make a difference.

- Aspire constantly to maintain high standards of performance.

- Examine the best in yourself before exploring the best in other people.

- Ask the Good Lord to give you the strength to change what you can change and to keep your mouth shut about things you can't change.

- Avoid the false pride of contending you are a great judge of human nature and admit that it is impossible to predict how people will perform.

- Do not fear strong colleagues or ambitious subordinates.

- Don't resent talent; surround yourself with it.

- Allow excellent performers to display and teach their strengths.

- Get good people out of yesterday.

- Ascertain whether you are better at working with ideas or people.

- Be very economical with praise. It should be meaningful—not as in the case in which all first graders receive a gold star. One praises so that it is not forgotten.

- Be among real doers of the world; don't waste time criticizing others and making them look bad.

- Regard manners as the outward manifestation of a sympathetic regard for the feelings of others.

- Realize that civility is not a substitute for genuine empathy but that it does keep human relations from freezing up.

- Display courtesy; it is the cheapest form of fuel and should be used lavishly.

- Determine whether your talents and skills coincide with your temperament.

- Bear in mind that the greater a person's strengths, the stronger his or her concomitant weaknesses.

- For spiritual strength, think on the great existential questions: Who am I? Where am I going? What is life all about?

Communications

Communications was a topic that Drucker touched on often throughout his writings. With regard to its impact on executive effectiveness, his analysis focused most prominently on five issues: (1) diagnosis, (2) information technology, (3) paucity of clarity, (4) lack of perspective, and (5) perception.

Diagnosis

An important part of Drucker's consulting repertoire was to ask managers what they considered the major problems of their institutions. Invariably, communications found itself on the top of almost every corporate list. Despite this generally acknowledged recognition of the importance of communications, what astonished Drucker was that so little systematic attention was given to understanding and diagnosing the communication problem. The typical executive seemed to believe that communication consisted of little more than a bundle of basic skills that could be acquired from quick courses in speed reading, remedial writing, and elocution.

Drucker never underestimated the importance of skills and content in the communication process, but he maintained that confining attention narrowly to the supply side could only cloud comprehension of that process. He stated that content (what is said), technique (how it is said), and timing (when it is said) could either help or hamper effective communications. However, even when content, technique, and timing were perfectly organized, they would produce only static and noise unless the demand side of communications (the person to whom the message is being delivered) was taken into account. Answering the old riddle about the tree falling in the forest, Drucker maintained that there was no sound unless somebody actually heard and perceived it.[35]

A central feature of Drucker's thought on communications was that here, ends take priority over the means. As a result, an emphasis on the supply side of communications was a weak foundation for effectiveness. Information was inert until applied subjectively and selectively in a systematic fashion; therefore the key to effective communications was the recipient and not the sender. "For centuries we have attempted communication 'downward,'" Drucker declared. "This, however, cannot work, no matter how hard and how intelligently we try. It cannot work, first, because it focuses on what *we* want to say. It assumes, in other words, that the utterer communicates. But we know that all he does is utter. Communication is the act of the recipient."[36]

The added problem of miscommunication has been exacerbated in the recent past as face-to-face communications declined and were replaced by more abstract communications. According to Drucker, the exponential increase in information has taken place without a commensurate increase in effective communications, when "the more information the greater is the need for functioning and effective communication. The more information, in other words, the greater is the communications gap likely to be."[37]

Drucker attributed this deterioration in communications to the downward emphasis of the evokers rather than to the recipients. Effective executives needed to learn to communicate upward and laterally as well as downward. They needed to be more aware that "communication . . . always makes demands. It always demands that the recipient become somebody, do something, believe something."[38]

Drucker asserted that the historical roots of the downward approach to communication were traceable to the tenacious concept of command, which had held sway throughout the many centuries. In acknowledging the strength of the *one-way command* approach, he indicated that it was the most orderly and efficient of all methodologies, but because of its rigor, it also was totally devoid of understanding. That is, it could be thought of as a stimulus based on drill and repetition to elicit a given response, whereas communications could establish a shared understanding between the sender and the recipient.

The carrot-and-stick technique for the reinforcement of commands seemed the most manipulative to Drucker. He sidestepped the issue of whether the carrot or the stick was the more efficient tool for results, saying he was happy to allow the psychologists to debate that controversial issue. He did observe, however, that in the short run the stick produced more immediate results. Therefore, if very little time was available, the use of the carrot was inappropriate. To illuminate this principle he cited the example of the little boy who accidently puts his hand on a hot stove. Any attempt to provide positive reinforcement is futile, because there is no time available to explain the theory of heat. The only alternative is to slap the child. At the same time, in situations calling for lasting results managers need the positive reinforcement of the carrot.

In analyzing the one-way command communications methodology, Drucker researched the background of military training. Using the regimented routine of army drill as an illustration, he presupposed two elements in its composition. First, the response to an order was indelibly built into the mind of the individual recipient. Second, the response had to be unambiguous and immediate, because instant action was required. For example, when the sergeant gave the order to fire, he did not have time to teach the theory of ballistics. He expected an automatic pulling of the trigger. Parenthetically, Drucker postulated that the one-way command had relevance for all institutions during times of emergency. In the case of a fire or other common peril, the rule was that to prevent harm to people you needed command and not understanding.

In probing the ramifications of communicating by command, Drucker found that the method was exceedingly limited by the number of verbal commands typically learned. Throughout military history, for example, the number ranged from about twenty-five in the Roman legions to about a hundred in the polyglot army of Austria-Hungary, although the Gurkhas from Nepal, professional mercenaries who campaigned for the British Empire, managed to function with one hundred and twenty five signals or commands (and in English rather than their native language).

The basic difficulty of the command approach to communications for the corporation is its inflexibility. This rigor was especially evident in the downward communication techniques of the assembly-line system of manufacturing, where the managers, the brains, passed orders down to the workers, the hands. Consisting of executive fiats from the top or a series of orders composed of nothing but "don'ts," commands must be limited so that the proper behavioral reflexes can be produced. As for its use as a communications tool, Drucker concluded that the communicator was not being heard because that person was addressing himself or herself to things that people were incapable of hearing, much less understanding. The command mode is especially ineffective as a communications tool in an information-based organization in which the professional recipients are more responsive to understanding, because most messages are directed upward and laterally.

Information Technology

As discussed earlier, Drucker interpreted technology as a catalyst that changed the nature of work, increased production, affected social trends, and altered organizational structures. It would therefore be surprising indeed if Drucker had failed to examine the effect that computers, fax machines, e-mail, and smart telephones, to name a few recent devices, are having on the communication process. After examining the relationship between the quantity and quality of their output, he was, however, less than enthusiastic about the contributions of these new technological tools.

Because he thought the information explosion was producing an exponential increase in data but a regression in communication, Drucker viewed it from the angles of (1) its paucity of clarity and results and (2) its lack of perspective.

Paucity of Clarity

Drucker pointed out that it was important to celebrate the achievements of information technology, but not at the expense of failing to understand the difference between information and communication. For example, the proliferation of new information technologies and resulting mechanization of communication would exact a price. In the transmission of information, there would be an accompanying loss of incidental and informal face-to-face communications. In explaining the confusion created by the way data were blacking out communications, he posited an inverse ratio between information and communication: "Yet communications has proven as elusive as the Unicorn. The noise level has gone up so fast that no one can really listen any more to all that babble about communications. But there is clearly less and less communicating. The communications gap within institutions and between groups in society has been widening steadily—to the point where it threatens to become an unbridgeable gulf of total misunderstanding."[39] Another price arising from the data overload was a neglect of attention to results.

Drucker advised that the information explosion required serious study and reexamination of the fundamentals of communications theory. The abundance of information changes the communications problem and makes it more urgent and less tractable.[40]

A key reason for the gap between the potential and the performance of the new information technology has been that companies look at the technology through a rear view mirror. As Drucker commented: "So far, most computer users still use the new technology to do faster what they have always done before—'crunch' conventional numbers."[41] When he wrote these words in 1989, he indicated that there was nothing unusual in this technological lag characteristic of new inventions but that in the future the numbers would have to be crunched differently to meet the new challenges in activity accounting, inventory control, market research, and manufacturing productivity.

Lack of Perspective

Drucker saw that managers' perspective on the relationship between communications theory and the new information tools was bankrupt. First, at one extreme, the vast majority of executives displayed their data illiteracy by overreacting to the new tools and techniques of the information revolution. They were like children in a candy store who could not resist the temptation to gorge and overindulge themselves heedlessly.

Second, at the other extreme, a new breed of management scientists were convinced by their mathematic models that a solid scientific discipline had been discovered. Drucker thought they had deified their conclusions on the omniscience of quantification. They were so fascinated with the speed and memory capacity of the computer that the reliability of the information being produced was largely ignored. Pointing out this dichotomy between the overwhelming abundance of data and the poor quality of information, he observed: "At present the computer is the greatest possible obstacle to management information, because everybody has been using it to produce tons of paper. Now, psychology tells us that the one sure way to shut off all perception is to flood the senses with stimuli. That's why the manager with reams of computer output on his desk is hopelessly uninformed."[42]

In examining the purpose and perspective of the computer, the main tool of the information explosion, Drucker took a more analytical position. He viewed it technologically as an extension of the brain, playing the role of a power station that provided energy for mental and informational tasks, just as the electrical power station provided energy for mechanical tasks. It was a magic moron capable of performing only those tasks that humans had programmed for it. He saw it as both a threat and opportunity, but also as something to be managed: "the computer makes no decisions; it only carries out orders. It's a total moron and therein lies its strength. It forces us to think, to set the criteria. The stupider the tool, the brighter the master has to be—and this is the dumbest tool we have ever had."[43]

Perception

Drucker did not propose a solution for the inadequacy of communications theory as it related to executive effectiveness, but he did argue that a clearer understanding of *perception* would occupy a central place in any future synthesis. In his conception of perception he visualized it as a matrix consisting of three major interacting components: experience, expectations, and involvement.

In treating the factor of experience, he reiterated the importance of the evoker taking cognizance of the recipient as the foundation of the communication process. Moreover, perceptual experiences took primacy in communication over information. In making a distinction between information and perception, he stated: "Information is indeed conceptual. But meaning is not; it is perception."[44] Because effective communications hinged on the capacity to reach others in a comprehensible manner, the logic of information and the quantity of objective data had to be transcended by the subjective quality of perception. Because of the limitations of the tools and techniques of communication, demand assumed priority over supply, otherwise noise and static would contaminate the entire communications process. In short, a requirement of a successful message was that it had to be conveyed in terms of the recipient's language, intellectual capacities, and general experiential background.[45]

Closely associated with experience was the component of expectations, which dealt with how the message had to fit into the receptivity of the recipient. Drucker fused the essence of both recipient experience and recipient expectations of the communication process when he stated: "*Communication is expectation.* We perceive, as a rule, what we expect to perceive. We see largely what we expect to see, and we hear largely what we expect to hear. That the unexpected may be resented is not the important thing—though most of the work on communications in business and government thinks it is. What is truly important is that the unexpected is usually not received at all. It is not seen or heard, but ignored. Or it is misunderstood, that is, mis-seen or mis-heard as the expected."[46]

Finally, Drucker asserted that sound communications required involvement. Without the recipient's commitment to action and results, communication would be reduced to empty rhetoric. Essentially, the communication of knowledge created the executive responsibility to make sense of it and to convert it into performance.

Acknowledging the insights he had derived from Plato's *Phaedrus*, Drucker postulated that it was perception that made communication possible for the recipient. In emphasizing further the importance of the interaction between concept and percept, he suggested that the Cartesian proposition, "I think, therefore I am," would take on greater communication significance if it were supplemented by the further proposition, "I see, therefore I am."[47] He argued that "percept and concept in the learner, whether child or adult, are not separate. We cannot perceive unless we also conceive. But we also cannot form concepts unless we can perceive. To communicate a concept is impossible unless the recipient can perceive it, that is, unless it is within his perception."[48]

Drucker offered a number of principles and insights about perception as it applies to the communications process:

- Perception is limited to what the recipient is capable of receiving.

- A person needs a mental vision of the individual he or she is trying to influence.

- Figures are often more compelling than the power of reasoning.

- If a person defines a situation as real, it is real in its consequences.

- The whole person comes with the process; one cannot communicate a word.

- The more information is increased, the greater the need to grasp perceptual reality by constantly redefining incomplete messages.

- The quest for certainty is wrong; start off with what should be conveyed in order to make sense.

- Communication and information are different and indeed largely opposite—yet interdependent. Whereas communication is perception, information is logic.

- The most dangerous illusion of all is to think that the recipient has only one role and one reality.

- The focus should not be on what you consider important but on what the recipient considers important.

- Don't try to find out why a person is wrong, but attempt to find out what he is trying to say; he might be right, who knows?

- Perception is multidimensional, but people still see only one of these dimensions at a time.

- Perception is limited by physiological factors: for example, the eye and the ear have different capabilities.

- You can't cram a great deal of material into a voice channel. In a good speech one gets one good idea across.

- Accept the fact that other people see things differently.

- Listening is important, but it is one dimensional. Its success relies on the manager understanding the value system of those below him.

- Hearing is natural; listening must be learned by making sense of what we hear.

- People have to receive communications and that is up to them; the sender has no control over it.

- The individual, and not nature, aggregates facts, events, and numbers.

- Information presupposes communication.

- The avowed aim of sensitivity training is not communication but awareness. The focus is on the "I" and not the "Thou."

- The assumption that what is obvious to you is also obvious to everyone else is a mistake.

- Perception is experience. This means that one always perceives a configuration. One cannot perceive singular specifics; they always become part of a total picture.

- Difficulty in communicating can often be overcome by changing not what we say but how we say it.

- Executives see the organizational inside clearly but the outside poorly.

- Effective executives establish channels of communication throughout the organization.

- In dealing with issues of public relations, top management messages will often have to be complex but should not be complicated.

- The organization's communications bottleneck is usually at the top of the bottle.

- The fewer the data needed, the better the information.

Summary

Drucker's interest in communications was more polemical than philosophical. It disappointed him that communications theory was in a state of disarray. Among the experts in linguistics, psychology, anthropology, sociology, and philosophy, there was little agreement and certainly no consensus. In effect, everybody was his or her own communications specialist. Drucker's main concern, therefore, was how communications affected the practitioner. His emphasis was on its importance in the arena of managerial effectiveness. He thought that by focusing on the futility of the downward approach, the key role of the recipient, the impact of technological change, and the role of perception greater understanding and pragmatic insights would emerge to assist executives. Finally, he hoped he had raised the right questions.

Conclusion

Time management, capitalizing on strengths, and communication clarity were considered by Drucker to be three of the most indispensable skills of effective management. His analysis of these elements came with many suggestions for achieving results. Because his major concern was improving the performance of the practitioner, he considered two major proposals crucial for capturing the spirit and standard of professional management. They are practice and commitment. The first stressed the development of good habits and the elimination of poor habits. The second emphasized a focus on action and results.

Drucker used parables to bring these two principles to life. In considering practice he tells the story of the professional musician who was once asked why he had to practice five to six hours a day. He replied that if he stopped for one day, he recognized the difference in the quality of his music. If he stopped for a week, the critics recognized the decline. And if he stopped playing for a month, the public recognized the inferior quality of his performance. In addressing the theme of commitment, Drucker tells of the three masons who were asked the reason they were working. The first responded that he was making a living. The second replied that he was refining the techniques of his craft. And the third answered that he was building a cathedral! The moral of these secular parables was that without practice and commitment, individual prescriptions for effectiveness would lose their meaning and degenerate into manipulative gimmicks. The job of management was not a sinecure, and if it were to evolve into an accepted profession someday, practice and commitment would be the building blocks of its responsibility.

CHAPTER SEVENTEEN

THE DECISION-MAKING PROCESS

Drucker looked upon decision making as the heart and soul of management practice. He considered the skill in making effective decisions as the catalyst of virtually all organizational decisions. But he especially indicated the impact of successful decisions on institutional identity and corporate culture and emphasized its role in enhancing other executive skills.

The topic of decision making indirectly permeated the entire corpus of his writings. Without claiming to be exhaustive in covering all of Drucker's ideas and perspectives on the subject, in this chapter I address the essence of his thought in two major areas: (1) misconceptions about decision making and (2) the nature of the process. I also summarize the decision-making guidelines and insights that appear in his writings. Before I probe these specific areas, however, a brief treatment of his general ideas on the rudiments of decision making is in order.

General Ideas

Drucker noted that decision making has been a human activity since the dawn of history. He also pointed out that man, because of his large human brain, is the only animal equipped to perform this imaginative task. At the same time, despite many centuries of endless small and large decisions by countless people, we know very little about the actual process. Prior to recent times, a decision was considered by the average business practitioner to be more or less an intuitive and subjective choice. Aside from the static principles found in formal logic, with its analysis of fallacies and exploration of syllogisms, there was little systematized thinking on the subject. Drucker looked upon logic as an academic exercise in mental gymnastics that provided interesting explorations into the nature of syllogisms but was silent about actual risk taking and results. He explained the absence of organized attention to decision making in business history by observing that in an environment of relative equilibrium and under conditions of social simplicity, the businessman in the past had no reason to accord a high priority to such study. Because dramatic and turbulent inputs of change were few, the businessman looked upon the enterprise as an extension of himself. Once his business was successfully launched, all he had to do was to react automatically to minor changes in the economic system. Innovation, or the decision to undergo purposeful change, was not a part of his intellectual vocabulary. Moreover, the relatively small size and uncomplicated knowledge base of the corporation of the past meant that business decisions were assured the luxury of a time cycle with a relatively long duration.

The early twentieth century witnessed the rise of mass production and mass marketing and the emergence of the large corporation with its separation of ownership and control. These events also created the phenomenon of professional management, which Drucker labeled one of the most revolutionary innovations of the twentieth century. Despite the fact that professional management implied that experience alone was no longer adequate for executive effectiveness and that a more sophisticated understanding of knowledge breakthroughs in specialized functions was needed, little attention was devoted to decision making as an independent intellectual activity. At the same time, statisticians overrationalized the decision-making process with their stress on models and formulas, and psychologists oversimplified it with their focus on the techniques of role-playing, creativity, decision trees, and game simulation.

It was the arrival of the computer on the business scene shortly after World War II that led to the organized exploration of decision making. Drucker signaled the significance of this new invention by pointing out that all previous technological tools had either muscular, mechanical, or sensory characteristics but that the computer was unprecedented in functioning as an extension of the human brain. In keeping with his finding from technological history that the tool preceded the theory, Drucker hinted that as we understood the computer more, it was likely that we would also acquire more knowledge of the theoretical ramifications of decision making.

As described in Chapter Twelve, Drucker illuminated his hypothesis that hardware invention preceded scientific explanation with many historical illustrations, including the lever, eyeglasses, and the steam engine, all of which were employed for many years before they were accorded a satisfactory and scientific rationale. Consequently, it is hardly surprising that he visualized the computer, the tool that was figuratively an extension of the mind, as an avenue for opening up new vistas into the mysteries of decision making.

Drucker also detailed how the new discipline of management science had developed a number of new mathematical techniques for improved decision making, such as PERT (program evaluation and review technique), linear programming, regression analysis, queuing theory, and operations research. In addition to these concrete tools of applied knowledge, Drucker also noted the recent investigations into the philosophical nature of decision making, including the provocative works of such scholars as Eric Ashby, Herbert Simon, West Churchman, and Kenneth Boulding.

The new techniques and the scholarly investigations were impressive, but Drucker expressed serious reservations about their relevance to the executive who was actually making a genuine decision. He had two major criticisms of the new research literature.

First, he cautioned that despite their promises and expectations, management scientists still focused on improving what is already known rather than on innovation breakthroughs for improved productivity and wealth creation. Second, he argued that it was too often forgotten that it was the task that determined the use of the tool and not the other way around. He warned that excessive fascination with tools and techniques could cloud the distinction between the quantitative (how to do) with the qualitative (what to do). As noted earlier in discussing entrepreneurial strategy, this was especially true of the computer, which focused on internal problems rather than external opportunities.

Tools and techniques, he emphasized, were a supplement to and not a substitute for judgments about risk and uncertainty. And he feared that a singular stress on the tools divorced from meaningful concepts of the interaction between work and working would produce an army of technicians and specialists talking only to themselves, creating a jargon understandable only by themselves, and focusing on scientific validity over applied relevance. Echoing

Georges Clemenceau, the French politician who proclaimed that war was too important to be left entirely under the control of the generals, Drucker said that the study of the computer and the understanding of the decision-making process were too important to be left exclusively in the hands of the management science experts.

Misconceptions

The problem, as Drucker saw it, was putting to work what was already known about operating techniques and theoretical concepts, building this knowledge into a systematic framework for management use. But before integrating theory and practice into a clearer pattern of understanding, it was first necessary to show the errors in some ubiquitous myths surrounding the word *decision*. That is, before trying to fathom what a decision was, it was necessary to understand what a decision was not. To achieve this goal Drucker assembled and examined a number of popular myths. They dealt with (1) the isolated decision, (2) the routine and procedural decision, (3) problem solving, (4) ideas and intentions, (5) positional authority, and (6) forecasting.

Myth of the Isolated Decision

According to Drucker, an isolated decision is as meaningless as an individual speck of sand in the desert. Although much celebrated, the idea that there could be a "flash of insight or Eureka decision" divorced from some past stimulus or background was a misconceived abstraction. Genuine decisions did not lend themselves to such neat fragmentation; "every decision is, of necessity, part of a *decision-structure*."[1] If we examine the major personal decisions in our lives, for example, they do not exist in a vacuum, separated from experiential antecedents. Drucker therefore described decision making as a process that, although it consisted of stages, had no clear-cut beginning or end. What appeared on the surface as a single decision was, upon closer scrutiny, intertwined with such threads as personal perceptions of reality, family values, and social mores, to cite a few of the programmed inputs that determine the choices made by individuals. These diverse backgrounds and experiences helped explain the various responses of managers from different countries in deciding similar problems. In short, "There are really no isolated decisions on a product, or on markets, or on people. Each major risk-taking decision has impact throughout the whole; and no decision is isolated in time. Every decision is a move in a chess game, except that the rules of enterprise are by no means as clearly defined. There is no finite 'board' and the pieces are neither as neatly distinguished nor as few in number. Every move opens some future opportunities for decision, and forecloses others. Every move, therefore, commits positively and negatively."[2]

Myth of the Routine or Procedural Decision

Drucker postulated that the routine, or procedural, response is not, qualitatively speaking, an act of decision making. Being a repetitive act based on some previous policy, it is at best a programmed decision. There was probably a real decision made when the initial corporate policy was designed, but after the original choice became a policy, the response evolved into a conditioned reflex action. That is, once an option has been programmed into the brain, it becomes habit rather than novelty. In a sense a routine decision is a storage or switching mechanism found in the nervous system. In his lectures Drucker cited Hobson's choice as the most celebrated illustration of a procedural decision. Hobson, an English livery owner, permitted the selection of horses in his stable only on the basis of first in, first out, thereby allowing no real choice to his customers. At its inception, the policy of forcing the customers to select the horse that had rested the longest or none at all was a genuine decision, but all selection decisions after that first one became routine.

A similar analogy existed in the corporate area for administering operations. Policies were introduced for such functions as inventory, labor relations, and personnel travel, but once established they became part of the rules and regulations of the institution's corporate culture. Except for a dictated range of limited autonomy, the basic decision-making pattern for executives was one of repetition and routine. Questioning this pattern's substantive features, Drucker contended that a routine decision was devoid of judgmental risk. The executive did not make a genuine decision; he or she just knew the rules.

Myth of Problem Solving

Drucker associated the search for certainty that runs through Western philosophy with a similar quest for assurance in decision making. He noted that it was only the West that had emphasized the logic chopping of scholasticism (in the Middle Ages), the scientific method (in the seventeenth century), rationalism (during the eighteenth-century Enlightenment), and (in recent times) logical positivism. The legacy of this stream of thought in the Western tradition was reflected in the work of management scientists as they sought a methodology of problem solving. They searched for certainty, developing a rigorous and rational methodology that was devoid of emotion and subjectivity. Drucker questioned the philosophical emphasis on certainty, wondering why the known was more relevant than the unknown in the decision-making process. When managers started with the assumption that there was a right answer on the order of two plus two equals four, they inevitably lost sight of what the decision was really all about. It was naive to equate a decision, which was a commitment of existing resources, with a mathematical exercise.[3]

According to Drucker, the theorists' approach to problem solving implied that risk could be eliminated, sought the delusion of a self-fulfilling prophecy, and let the answer supersede the question. He conceded that in mathematical problem solving it was valid to assume that there were right and wrong answers, but in business decision making there were no guarantees. Often problems were never actually solved in a social institution; at best the practitioners grimly survived them. Therefore, Drucker posited that decision making was not the same as finding the right answer. Indeed, as long as there was a right answer, it was not a genuine decision.

Drucker thought the concentration in management science literature on finding the right answer was a disservice to practitioners because it did not assist them to understand the meaning of a decision. Pursuing the right answer was the least important thing in decision making. Moreover, there was nothing more dangerous or useless than finding the right answer to the wrong question. Epitomizing his position, he wrote that a decision "is at best a choice between 'almost right' and 'probably wrong'—but much more often a choice between two courses of action neither of which is provably more nearly right than the other."[4]

Myth of Ideas and Intentions

Drucker equated a decision bereft of action with a fish out of water. Without the component of doing, a decision is relegated to the status of an intention; regardless of the nobility or the brilliance of the concept, it will remain an abstraction if it is devoid of application and results. Ideas without work and responsibility, therefore, are not worthy of being dignified with the label of decisions, because "a decision is only pious intention unless it leads to action. Every decision, therefore, has an *impact stage*."[5]

Decisions are not mental calisthenics or moral preachments; they are a commitment to action by people who have the responsibility to implement them. College bulletins were often used by Drucker as an example of pious platitudes masquerading as decisive truths. Many of them promised to instill wisdom and educate the whole person, along with other rhetorical fancies, but these noble aspirations were completely devoid of feasible feedback or meaningful measurement. Individuals and institutions were similarly rife with pious ideas and intentions divorced from any responsibility, such as ambitious corporate mission statements without the resources for implementation; the certainty of subordinates that they can solve the boss's problems; the belief of experts that they have the ability to solve problems in other functions (that is, to raise the neighbor's children); the committee recommendations that are substitutes for action; the essays of journalists and academicians that purport to solve the nation's economic, social and foreign policies; and the brilliant plans of every sports fan for managing the local major league baseball club.

Another manifestation of an intention rather than a decision is the directive from top management to subordinate. It is sent in the blind belief that it will automatically produce action, but not only is the human animal capable of sabotage, a skill not found in any other animal, but there is a tendency in organizations to camouflage information and delay action through various ploys. Drucker recalled President Harry Truman's recognition of this capacity for organizational inertia in a comment on what his successor, Dwight Eisenhower, would experience: "Poor Ike; when he was a general, he gave an order and it was carried out. Now he is going to sit in that big office and he'll give an order and not a damn thing is going to happen."[6]

Drucker concluded that creation of ideas was rarely an organizational problem. In his experience the difficulty lay in reluctance to implement the ideas. Alibis frequently became a substitute for achievement. Looking upon good intentions as a deceptive form of sincerity and the practice of internal pseudo-public relations, he considered them worthless rubbish, paving materials for roads that had already been paved.

Myth of Positional Authority

Individualism has been considered by social philosophers as such a prime American value that it has been similarly assumed that decisions in corporate life emanated from one person, the chief executive officer. For example, in the usual planning pattern of a large corporation or a government agency, the top manager decided the choice of a problem or opportunity and then delegated a small group of juniors to make a study of it. After a year or two of study the task force presented its report to senior managers who invariably initialed and approved it. Typically, the recommendations of the report were filed for possible future action at some unnamed date. When the appropriate time arrived, they then became the basis of implementation.[7]

These procedures raised a philosophical question in Drucker's mind: Was the actual decision made by top management or by the cadre of juniors who prepared the report and recommendations? There was no clear simple answer to this question. It did reveal, however, that in a world of accelerated change and increased complexity, it was impossible for any top management alone to assemble the information and background for the many problems it encountered. Because juniors were the ones shaping the parameters and content of these long time span decisions, a strong argument could be made that they and not the authorities at the top made the decisions. Of course Drucker also conceded that top management had both responsibility for the initial selection of the problem and the veto power over any project.[8]

In exposing the myth that decisions originated only from the territory at the top, Drucker also showed that decision making was often located with the people in the organization having the relevant information or knowledge. In his lectures he cited such examples as clerks who wrote the initial drafts of decisions for justices of the Supreme Court, congressional staff who researched and wrote legislative bills, executive secretaries who controlled the agenda items for policy meetings, and bureaucrats who acted as information gatekeepers in hierarchical organizations.

Myth of Forecasting

Forecasting in general and statistical forecasting in particular represented the final misconception of decision making on Drucker's list. He described statistical forecasts as the extrapolation of past and present trends into the future, observing that "forecasting attempts to find the most probable course of events, or, at best, a range of probabilities."[9] Because they were based on the past, however, such projections revealed more about the past than the future. Therefore, except for very short time spans, they were unreliable guides for risk and action. Looked at as intellectual calculations, statistical forecasts were harmless abstractions and had little impact. They became dangerous when executives considered them to be future reality and treated them as decisions by acting on them. Given these assumptions, it was hardly surprising that Drucker stated, "We must start out with the premise that forecasting is not a respectable human activity and not worthwhile beyond the shortest of periods."[10]

Drucker felt it was the task of management to create the future, but he thought it the height of arrogance to predict the future. He regarded the new futurology think tanks with suspicion, contending that they revealed more about the perceptions of the individual forecaster than about future events. Moreover, in making their predictions the futurologists neglected discontinuity. They did not factor in the possibility of a unique event, some incident that would alter the pattern of a series and thus destroy the premise of the prediction. In addition, by the time the manager used a statistical forecast, it was part of the past and had already lost any relevance for practice.

Equally important, statistical forecasting was of no help in raising the appropriate strategic question. This question did not ask what the organization should do tomorrow, but what it had "to do today to be ready for an uncertain tomorrow."[11] Consider, for example, that prior to World War II, demographers were predicting zero population growth. The discontinuity of the postwar baby boom made those calculations useless, but company marketers who had acted on the zero growth prediction paid a disastrous price for placing their faith in statistical forecasting.

It was the reality of the unique event that made Drucker distrustful of quantification of forecasts. Forecasts seemed particularly unreliable in social and economic affairs, in which the events that really mattered were incapable of being quantified. He considered that a "good statistician knows this and distrusts all figures—he either knows the fellow who found them or he does not know him; in either case he is suspicious."[12]

Finally, because forecasting implied the decision maker was cognizant of future reality, he thought of his forecast as an actual future decision. Drucker, however, argued that a decision maker could not deal with future decisions, only with the futurity of present decisions: "Decisions exist only in the present. . . . The question is not what will happen in the future. It is: What futurity do we have to factor into our present thinking and doing, what time spans do we have to consider, and how do we converge them to a simultaneous decision in the present?"[13]

As a result of his analysis of forecasting, Drucker's preference was for personal perception rather than statistical analysis in making strategic decisions.

His focus was on selecting those events that had already happened and that could be converted into entrepreneurial opportunities.

Summary

By attempting to understand what a decision was not, Drucker hoped to formulate a clearer synthesis of the decision-making process. He came to define decision making as a process involving a risk-taking value judgment, entailing a number of hypothetical uncertainties, containing specific alternatives, requiring plans for action and implementation, encompassing an ethical component, providing for feedback measurements, and identifying the reversibility or irreversibility of the actual choice. The definition contained so many intangibles interacting together that Drucker would probably be the first to concede that in some ways it was overly simplistic and that like most definitions dealing with complicated concepts it obscured as much as it illuminated.

At the same time, Drucker felt it had the advantage of not containing many of the misconceptions found in the management science textbooks. At the very least, it was devoid of esoteric jargon, complicated theorems, sophisticated models, and unintelligible paradigms—all of which had no relationship to applied knowledge for the practitioner. Moreover, it focused on common sense and not higher mathematics.

As for the hardware of decision making, Drucker had mixed feelings. Initially, he was less than enthusiastic about the computer. Calling it a "magic moron," he implied it was only capable of accelerated addition and subtraction. Subsequently, he conceded that when the computer added the microprocessor, it also gained the potential to move beyond simple computational business tasks to more sophisticated internal applications, particularly in accounting, marketing, research, and manufacturing. According to Drucker, its greatest strength was in providing alternative scenarios for these operations.

Despite these and other examples of applying knowledge for improved results, Drucker felt that the votaries of tools and techniques had overpromised performance in the area of decision making. He was particularly skeptical about the feasibility of artificial intelligence, which implied that the computer might become the master rather than the servant. Meanwhile, until he witnessed a simulated decision successfully implemented, he felt we still had a great deal to learn about the nature of the decision-making process. Based on the assumption that thought should precede calculation, he suggested further investigation into decision making in such areas as cultural ramifications, inputs from other disciplines, principles of probability, classification factors, and experiential guidelines.

Nature of the Process

To do full justice to Drucker's thought on the nature of the decision-making process would require an entire volume. I have elected to analyze three areas that seem to best reflect his philosophy on the topic: (1) the contrast between Japanese and American approaches, (2) the lesson from the medical profession, and (3) decision classification by procedure and strategy.

Contrast Between American and Japanese Approaches

In exploring the differences between managers' decision-making processes in Japan and the United States, Drucker selected the following topics: (1) the right question versus the right answer, (2) the future versus futurity, (3) bottom-up versus top-down emphasis and the group versus the individual, (4) significant versus trivial issues, and (5) the staffing process.

Right Question Versus Right Answer. Drucker commenced his analysis by stating that nobody in the world was as good at making decisions as the Japanese. One reason for their particular ability was that "the Japanese process focused on understanding the problem,"[14] whereas in the West the emphasis was on reaching the answer. In Japan the desired end result is action and behavior on the part of people. This almost guarantees that all the alternatives will be considered. It rivets managerial attention to essentials. It does not permit commitment until management has decided what the decision is all about.

From his years of personal and consulting experience, Drucker recognized the futility of expecting results when solutions precede questions and knew that the most serious mistakes are made as the result of such premature answers. The most dangerous thing in decision making was asking the wrong question. By focusing on the problem, the Japanese method "may come up with the wrong answer to the problem (as was the decision to go to war against the United States in 1941), but they rarely come up with the right answer to the wrong problem."[15]

Drucker emphasized that the Japanese concentration on the problem rather than the solution was a reflection of the Japanese value system, which discouraged people from taking sides on a given issue. He pointed out that the copious note taking of the Japanese was a substitute for immediate debate and a sign they were assiduously studying the problem. The Japanese were also acutely aware that bringing information together through endless discussion (a feature in the U.S. culture) was not a logical process. Drucker was of the opinion that the Japanese are not conceptual people. The access to Japan is not through philosophy or mathematics or constitutions, but only through art and calligraphy. They are totally perceptual.[16]

Future Versus Futurity. In Drucker's view the Japanese and Americans looked at the time span of decisions differently. In the planning process, U.S. managers tended to believe the future had an immediate concrete reality. Drucker, as mentioned previously, insisted this was a myth because decisions existed only in the present; anything else was a pious hope. To put it another way, the Japanese centered their attention on acknowledging the principle that futurity emanates from the effectiveness of today's decision making. The Americans, however, were more concerned with predicting the future. As a result, the Japanese took a more realistic approach to the time span factor, operating on the assumption that long-range planning "does not deal with future decisions. It deals with the *futurity of present decisions.*"[17]

Bottom-Up Versus Top-Down Emphasis and Group Versus Individual. The Japanese practice bottom-up management through their *ringi* system, in which the decision-making process commences with the group at the lowest level and after a consensus is reached there, a formal seal of approval is attached at each senior level of the decision-making process. In addition to fostering clear problem definitions, this bottom-up methodology helps ensure a more effective decision because alternatives are explored, and when the time comes for implementation everybody understands what the decision is all about. Consequently, according to Drucker, "the Japanese . . . spend absolutely no time on selling a decision. Everybody has been presold."[18]

In the United States, with its pronounced emphasis on individualism, the decision making occurred at the top in the form of administrative fiat. Decisions had the advantage of being reached more quickly, but the price paid was employees' lack of understanding about the essence of the choice and the failure to establish foundation for future implementation. In the United States there was also less proclivity to seek alternatives, with the result that the decision maker often became a prisoner of the organization's culture pattern. And in Drucker's view, "a decision without an alternative is a desperate gambler's throw, no matter how carefully thought through it may be."[19]

In the United States, top management participated directly in administering the organization in order to maintain control over the decision-making process. In Japan this strict administrative and operational control has not been needed because responsibility for routine operations is undertaken at the lower levels. When the Japanese reach the point U.S. managers would call a decision, they are in the "action stage."[20] Moreover, "very few CEOs of large [Japanese] companies have any time available for managing their companies. All their time is spent on 'relations,'"[21] even the time spent on internal company business. These CEOs are focused on maintaining appropriate relationships with leading government bureaucrats, politicians, and other prominent members of the business establishment.

U.S. management, with its command-and-control philosophy of organization, looked upon disagreements in the executive suite as a threat to its authority. The absence of any challenge to top management strategy meant executives were not stimulated to use their imaginations about other opportunities. The outcome of this methodology of pseudo-accommodation was a penchant for *feel-good* decisions. Drucker took a dim view of collective approval when it was divorced from serious thinking. The failure to factor into the decision-making equation the element of dissent makes a consensus decision a most dangerous one. Therefore, he asserted that "the first rule in decision making is that one does not make a decision unless there is disagreement."[22] And he recalled how Alfred Sloan of General Motors applied this principle by postponing any proposed decision that was reached by acclamation and was devoid of alternatives.[23]

Significant Versus Trivial Issues. Drucker also noted how group relationships helped the Japanese to arrive at consensus decisions, particularly on important matters: "Their system forces the Japanese to make big decisions. It is much too cumbersome to be put to work on minor matters. It takes far too many people far too long to be wasted on anything but truly important matters leading to real changes in policies and behavior. Small decisions, even when obviously needed, are very often not being made at all in Japan for that reason."[24]

At the same time, he described how the congested system of decision making operating in the United States was forced to focus on the inconsequential; in Western institutions "managers make far too many small decisions as a rule. And nothing causes as much trouble in an organization as a lot of small decisions. Whether the decision concerns moving the water cooler from one end of the hall to the other or the phasing out of one's oldest business makes little emotional difference. One decision takes as much time and generates as much heat as the other."[25] In attempting to demonstrate that the Japanese practice of concentration on the important decisions was not entirely new, he pointed out that a similar concentration was a salient feature of the Roman legal system, in which the magistrates did not trifle with trivial things. He urged U.S. managers to relearn this ancient principle.

Staffing Process. In Drucker's judgment, staffing decisions were the most visible and identifiable to members of the corporation. They were also most unpredictable in terms of their long-term impact. A rough idea of his appreciation of the uniqueness of personnel choices is contained in his comment that "people-decisions are time-consuming, for the simple reason that the Lord did not create people as 'resources' for organization. They do not come in the proper size and shape for the tasks that have to be done in organization—and they cannot be machined down or recast for these tasks. People are always 'almost fits' at best. To get work done with people (and no other resource is available) therefore requires lots of time, thought, and judgment."[26]

In comparing the Japanese and American systems of appointments, Drucker considered the former superior because it more closely approximated the following criteria of staffing effectiveness. Appraisals were conducted slowly and thoughtfully. The search examined a number of qualified candidates and evaluated how their strengths matched the assignment. The methodology invoked feedback from individuals who had worked closely with the candidates. An attempt was made to see if the candidate's temperament was suitable for the position. And it was imperative that a person under consideration understood the nature and objectives of the assignment.[27] Drucker did not find these standards of staffing in the United States. Instead, with rare exceptions, managerial ego worked to make the selection process a self-fulfilling prophecy. This was especially true when the CEO assumed the prerogative of choosing his successor. To allow one person to make such a crucial decision was, in Drucker's opinion, a serious miscalculation.

Nevertheless, in assessing the possible transfer and application of Japanese decision-making principles to the United States, Drucker wrote that "it would be folly for managers in the West to imitate these policies. In fact, it would be impossible. Each is deeply rooted in Japanese traditions and culture."[28] At the same time, he thought it possible to learn from the Japanese success and to emulate those practices that could fit the U.S. culture.

Lesson from the Medical Profession

The discipline of medicine had a special attraction for Drucker. Having several relatives and many friends in the profession, he had stimulating conversations on the history and philosophical nature of medicine. In addition, he lectured to medical groups and consulted with many hospitals, which alerted him to possible cross-fertilization between the practices of medicine and management. There was little doubt, however, that it was on the subject of decision making that he derived major insights from the field of medicine. He observed that medicine's concern with conditions of uncertainty provided beacons of light for applying his multidisciplinary approach to knowledge and that the field of medicine was also instructive for its long professional legacy of interrelating theory and practice. And given a discipline that had three thousand years of mistakes, it would be wise for management not to repeat those mistakes. Realizing that an explanation of medical decision making involved a repetition of many principles, he thought the exercise was worthwhile to give the concepts greater understanding and reinforcement.

Drucker selected five specific categories from the discipline of medicine that he considered most relevant for understanding the nuances of decision making: (1) conducting the proper diagnosis, (2) using feedback, (3) recognizing the interaction between symptoms and meaning, (4) acknowledging the relationship between knowledge and ignorance, and (5) evaluating ethical dimensions.

Conducting the Proper Diagnosis. There is an old aphorism that a problem clearly identified and articulated is half solved, and as discussed previously, Drucker thought defining the problem was the most important part of decision making. This was why he put diagnosis, the appraisal of uncertainty, at the forefront of medical activities that carried a message for managers.

The quest for a feasible diagnosis demanded the testing of several hypotheses concerning the patient's ailment. The practitioner had to avoid simply looking at surface manifestations and making a rush to judgment. Because few prepackaged solutions to medical problems were available, the practitioner used the diagnosis process to eliminate various disease alternatives. The disease selected for treatment temporarily ruled out other possible answers.

Drucker argued that in conducting a proper examination of what the problem was all about, either the medical or the business practitioner always started with opinion rather than facts. Because facts in the early stage of the appraisal are not the crucial factor, he stated that diagnosis preceded computation: "To get the facts first is impossible. There are no facts unless one has a criterion of relevance. Events by themselves are not facts."[29] He also warned about conjecture, about having too many assumptions in the search for a sensible diagnosis and allowing the presence of too many ands, ifs, and buts in the investigation. Once a hypothesis for a diagnosis was established by the practitioner, one did not argue with it. The only sound method was to test it, asking first: "What do we have to know to test the validity of this hypothesis?"[30]

Another principle of medical diagnosis with potential application for business decision making was the degenerative factor of the human body. Drucker implied that the vigor of a company's business excellence was bound to eventually disintegrate and that a competent executive acted decisively when conditions were irreversibly degenerative. In this connection, the diagnostic process taught Drucker the lesson that there were no risk-free decisions. Using the medical metaphor, he cogently made this point by stating, "There is no inherent reason why medicines should taste horrible—but effective ones usually do."[31]

Using Feedback. Feedback was the principle Drucker had in mind when he stated that a solution not tested was a certain prescription for failure, because even the allegedly best decisions had unintended consequences. His two basic rules for feedback were to spell out and write down expectations for the solutions and to provide an organized system for appraising solution outcomes.[32] During the process of decision verification, he specifically warned, the practitioner should not argue with the results. He also insisted that when results did not turn out as expected in a treatment or an experiment, the practitioner should not persist in the same diagnosis. Instead of continuing the original procedure or treatment that was producing no results, a competent diagnostician would drop it and begin a new analysis. The worst possible mistake for the practitioner to make when results did not turn out as expected was to compulsively double the effort based on the initial premise. An effective medical decision maker might make a major diagnosis, but if there were no results, he would candidly admit that he didn't understand the case and turn it over to somebody else. Actually this is a medical illustration of the previously discussed Bernoulli theorem—if at first you don't succeed, it is futile to combat the laws of probability with a mindless continuation of the same effort. Drucker admitted that this was a tough lesson for everybody, including himself, to learn. And it was also sobering, because it confirmed that humans were fallible and not divine.[33]

Recognizing the Interaction Between Symptoms and Meaning. Drucker

advanced the proposition that the patient knows the symptoms but the doctor knows the meaning. This was a reflection of his insight in communications theory that the recipient and not the sender determines the message. He also suggested that this principle has an intellectual connection with the marketing concept in a business and that there is some similarity between a patient's symptoms and a customer's wants. Both patient and customer must be listened to, and practitioners must not complain that the patient did not attend medical school or that the customer is irrational. In this regard the important lesson for any effective decision maker is to avoid the curse of hubris, to understand that people are rational in their own perceptions, and to remember that he or she is not being paid for cleverness and brilliant ideas but for results.

Acknowledging the Relationship Between Knowledge and Ignorance.

Throughout his career Drucker steadfastly maintained that there was always much more ignorance around than knowledge. A corollary of this proposition for medicine was that a good diagnostician was one who believed less in medical knowledge than in medical ignorance.[34] Conjecturing about the relationship of knowledge and ignorance in the medical and business professions, Drucker conceded that both were humbling and complicated disciplines in which to attempt clear understanding. Moreover, one effect of the ceaseless innovations and new technologies was to confirm how little the practitioner actually knew.

In the case of medicine this was Drucker's quaint way of saying that people got well without and despite the doctor. But in an artificial institution such as the corporation, the manager could not count on this human factor of periodicity. The corporation had a degenerative tendency rather than a repetitive tendency. Moreover, even to the degree that there was any regularity in an open social system like the corporation, it was of no operational significance in the decision-making process. Drucker's main point was not to make invidious comparisons between medical and business practitioners, but to reiterate for both decision makers that astonishing advances in ignorance always accompanied the knowledge breakthroughs. Equally important, he wanted to alert practitioners to the reality that ignorance posed a major challenge to those who modeled simulated decisions, and it reinforced the need for risk-taking judgment in the decision-making process.

Evaluating Ethical Dimensions. In dealing with the ethical component, Drucker urged that "one has to start out with what is right rather than what is acceptable."[35] He reasoned that most decisions required compromise, but the degree of trade-off depended on the substance of the problem; that determined whether it was the right or wrong compromise. One kind of compromise was expressed in the proverb that a half a loaf is better than none. Conversely, there was the Solomonic injunction, which was based on the reality that half of a baby is no baby at all. Half a loaf of bread is still nourishment; a divided baby is only a corpse. In this distinction between the material and economic on the one hand and the humane and spiritual on the other, Drucker stated that it was possible to compromise on the former but never the latter.

Moreover, there was one ethical principle that was so compellingly significant that it applied to all professionals. This was the famous Hippocratic oath, *primum non nocere* ("first, do no harm"; or in other words, "when you don't know what to do, be careful what you prescribe").

As mentioned earlier, Drucker had reservations about segmenting ethics into separate categories of subject matter. However, his works do contain many ethical principles and guidelines for decision making (see the list in Chapter Thirteen).

Decision Classification by Procedure and Strategy

Drucker divided the topic of decision making into two main categories: (1) the distinction between a generic and a procedural decision and (2) the quality and timing of a decision.

Generic Versus Procedural Decisions. A generic decision was defined by Drucker as a programmed response to an established policy within an organization. A strategic decision, however, was qualitatively different because it involved a response to a unique event for which no formal rule of policy existed. A strategic approach was inappropriate for handling routine decisions, but it was also incorrect to apply a routine approach to making a strategic decision.

The only exception to this two-dimensional framework was what Drucker called the catastrophe, or "non-recurring emergency." In a crisis such as a fire, flood, or other form of large-scale disaster, people had to immediately drop everything they were doing in order to take care of the present danger. Because catastrophes rarely occurred more than once in exactly the same manner, there was no way to adopt a rule to prevent their recurrence.[36]

In contrast, a recurring crisis was predictable. And because it stood alone, Drucker stated it was possible to view it as an opportunity and to introduce a generic decision into the organization as a method of preventing future recurrences. "A recurrent crisis should always have been foreseen. It can therefore either be prevented or reduced to a routine which clerks can manage."[37]

Qualitatively speaking, the generic decision was not risky and substantive but was based on the ability to know and follow a rule. Because generic decisions have to conform to an established policy or procedure, executives have limited autonomy and restricted imagination in executing them. To illustrate, every business has policies for inventory, pricing, labor relations, recruiting relations, and promotions. The repetitive generic decisions that follow from these policies allow little originality, which led Drucker to speculate that the typical executive made very few genuine risk-taking decisions.

In short, "The first question the effective decision-maker asks is: 'Is this a generic decision or an exception?' 'Is this something that underlies a great many occurrences? Or is the occurrence a unique event that needs to be dealt with as such?' The generic always has to be answered through a rule, a principle. The exceptional can only be handled as such and as it comes."[38]

The strategic decision involves an original response to an unprecedented situation or unidentified new trend for which there is no general rule or policy. Ralph Nader's consumer protest, the environmental movement, the thalidomide side-effect scandal, the global economy, the knowledge worker, the Tylenol tampering case—these have been just a few of the many unprecedented events that have produced entirely new conditions for the business practitioner. Because no generic or standard policies existed, the effects of these novel events and discontinuities in trends created new sets of circumstances that compelled managements to make commitments to new courses of strategic action.

Confusing the need for a generic decision with the need for a strategic decision could lead to disastrous circumstances. For example, the individual who responds in a strategic fashion to every routine or procedural matter would experience stress that could lead to a nervous breakdown. At the other extreme, a generic response to an unprecedented situation could cause severe turbulence and upheaval throughout the organization.

One example of this type of miscalculation occurred in General Motors when its management reacted to Ralph Nader as if he were a typical dissatisfied customer. The company used its traditional public relations technique of sending a form letter to a disgruntled customer. Then it investigated Nader's private life. This was a totally unacceptable, unsuitable approach to use with the man who established the new reality of the modern consumer movement throughout the economy. In short, the routine response of an apologetic form letter might assuage the average dissatisfied customer, but Nader's unprecedented persistence in demanding satisfaction from General Motors resulted in the need for the company to establish a new strategy for customer relations.

Another celebrated example of applying the routine approach to a situation that called for a strategic response took place when the diesel engine was introduced in the railroad industry during the 1920s. Because managers viewed the diesel as a modest technological improvement that would be limited to use with commuter traffic, they agreed in union negotiations to accept a redundant fireman on the diesel engine. After failing to see the diesel as a major innovation that called for a new labor policy, they were stuck with the extra man in the diesel cab for decades.

Quality and Timing. Considering every decision to be like a surgical intervention in a system, Drucker determined the decision's *quality*, whether it was a major shock or a minor tremor, by giving it a priority or a posteriority designation. Priority decisions dealt with the important tasks, whereas posteriority decisions amounted to trivial concerns. In conducting his or her work, a lazy or ineffectual executive was likely to make an excessive number of trivial decisions, because "the normal human reaction is to evade the priority decision."[39] Drucker attributed this weakness of making many senseless decisions to the abundance of tasks, problems, and crises encountered by executives on a daily basis and that increased the pressures of the job.

To avoid allowing job pressures to dominate the making of proper decisions, a choice "therefore has to be made as to which tasks deserve priority and which are of less importance."[40] Drucker warned, however, that simply establishing a priority list was deceptively easy; the difficult thing was deciding which priorities to concentrate on. This process of elimination was, in effect, a method of establishing the posteriorities, the tasks that should be deleted from executive routine. However, the fact was that "setting a posteriority is . . . unpleasant. Every posteriority is somebody else's top priority. It is much easier to draw up a nice list of top priorities and then to hedge by trying to do 'just a little bit' of everything else as well. This makes everybody happy. The only drawback is, of course, that nothing whatever gets done."[41]

Drucker concluded that the secret of selecting a priority depended on the ability to concentrate on a few key tasks and the courage to stick with the choices. In following this method, an executive could have reasonable assurance of focusing on big decisions and avoiding the small ones.

According to Drucker, there were no formulas for the timing of decisions. Timing was essentially a judgment call. Perhaps the most important timing choice was whether to act or not to act on a problem. In effect, if a problem failed to get worse, then inaction was the most feasible alternative, but if the condition were progressively and irreversibly deteriorating, then decisive action was imperative. In selecting the choices for the timing problem, he wrote: "The great majority of decisions will lie between these extremes. The problem is not going to take care of itself; but it is unlikely to turn into degenerative malignancy either."[42]

As was so often the case, Drucker looked to the example of medical experience to test his appraisal. Among themselves, surgeons might disagree on content and diagnosis, but they would agree on one point—a good surgeon did not perform unnecessary surgery. In other words, if there was a high degree of self-correction, one did not interfere. At the same time, it was necessary to recognize another long-tested medical rule of effective decision making: namely, that a degenerative disease will not be cured by procrastination—decisive action is required. Drucker's appraisal of the degenerative dilemma is tersely expressed: "One has to make a decision when a condition is likely to degenerate if nothing is done. This also applies with respect to opportunity. If the opportunity is important and is likely to vanish unless one acts with dispatch, one acts—and one makes a radical change."[43]

Here are some of Drucker's most salient guidelines for effective decision making:

- Figuring out what the decision is all about is the most important component of the decision-making process.

- Diagnosis is a guess, and guesses have to be verified by actual events.

- In a human system you can count on repetition, but in a social system you cannot assume homeostasis; it has genuine uncertainty.

- Don't start off with facts; a decision grows out of dissent and clashing alternatives.

- A decision without alternatives is a gambler's throw, no matter how carefully one thinks it out.

- If you had the decision to do over again, would you make it the same way?

- If the decision doesn't work as presented, do not persist on the same course.

- Remember, there is no way to hide the impact of people decisions; they are eminently visible.

- Make decisions on the highest possible grounds for results and the lowest possible level for implementation.

- Make few priority and qualitative decisions and make them slowly.

- Comfortable and unchallenged decisions are signs of lack of homework.

- Ask what would happen if we did nothing.

- Avoid the temptation to gather more information and set up additional committees as a smokescreen for action.

- Ask what efforts, financial resources, and people are needed to carry out the decision successfully.

- What you are postponing, you are actually abandoning.

- If the results are not there, do not continue.

- The priority decision is the toughest decision.

- When you don't know what to do, be careful what you prescribe.

- Courage rather than analysis dictates the truly important rule for identifying priorities.

- Value decisions are important ones, and they are not easily resolved.

- Managerial games teach the wrong behavior, an unthinking mechanical response, a gimmick response.

- Effective decision makers do not apply halfway efforts. They either act or do not act.

- In making promotion decisions, remember the old adage that every subordinate requires a competent superior.

- It is futile to try to minimize or escape risk; that is why it is important to undertake the right risk.

- A decision should be appropriate to the capacities of the people who have to carry it out.

- Fast personnel decisions are likely to be wrong.

- It is not possible to be effective until you decide what you want to do.

- One successful promotion decision is worth more than a thousand memos.

- Leaders probably don't make decisions or create ideas. Deliberation is what goes on, and that is not decision making.

- If you hear of or see a problem that is solvable by rigorous mathematics—distrust it.

- I have yet to see a decision with respect to distribution channels that was not obsolete five years later.

- Whatever would have been appropriate to do a year earlier is now too late to be done.

- A good diagnostician is not one who believes in medical knowledge but in medical ignorance.

- Trusting in memory is hazardous; write down what you expect to happen from your decision.

- A simulated decision is an elegant example of unreality. I have yet to observe one that has worked in practice.

Conclusion

Drucker pointed out that practice was the single common denominator of performance. Reiterating the theme that one learns from what was done right and not what was done wrong, he viewed practice as the pragmatic pathway to competent performance. It was distinguished by emphasizing learning over teaching, self-discipline over personality traits, substance over style, a focus on improvement over panaceas, and a dependence on average people over a reliance on genius. In short, Drucker viewed management as a discipline that emphasized application over knowledge, practice as a catalyst that increased the correlation between potential and performance, and utility as a catalyst for promoting change.

In dismissing the ideal of perfection, he hoped that his study of effectiveness through systematic work would enable the executive to convert worthless speculation into prudent preparation for performance. Although practicing his principles would not result in perfection, it would contribute to the kind of improvement that enables ordinary people to do extraordinary things. Moreover, the price of perfection is prohibitive; it is more sensible to have attainable goals and reasonable standards of measurement.

Habit, responsibility, and commitment were considered by Drucker to be the prime prerequisites in the development of effective practice. Indeed, practice arrived at its apogee when it was reduced to habit. This was the stage at which an activity becomes second nature, eliminating the person's need to think about how to do it. In short, good habits facilitate performance, and bad habits are impediments that require neutralization or abandonment.

Drucker divided his interpretation of practice into two categories—its quality and the personal skills it required. Under the qualitative category, he called for an implementation of the concepts of effectiveness discussed in the previous pages, including effectiveness through contribution, concentration, time management, capitalizing on strengths, communications, and the decision-making process. His minimum list of individual skills focused on demanding good manners from yourself and others, avoiding the temptation of showing up your colleagues, averting the lavish use of praise, recognizing that everybody is capable of some achievement, forgetting other people's superficial views of you, and ignoring the pretense of unnatural style.

The interrelationship between authority and responsibility is also important, and "it is irresponsible—and lust for power—to assume responsibility in areas in which authority is lacking. For responsibility always goes together with authority."[44] Because of downsizing and restructuring in today's corporate environment, this piece of advice now has added importance. Today's professional is no longer able to count on a predetermined career or the former benefits of managerial education. Nor can he or she assume that there is an automatic promotion ladder; the rungs of the past have been eliminated. In short, executives have to take personal responsibility for developing their own skills and concepts around the axis of practice—the centerpiece of the management process.

One such responsibility is to select tasks worthy of practice. If tasks are incapable of results, they are meaningless. Taking on a task that is intellectually challenging but devoid of results is the action (and error) of a subordinate, not an executive. Doing an inappropriate task is related to the trap of wanting to be right about an issue. But Drucker found that under conditions of uncertainty, getting the right answer was not central. It was better to be approximately wrong about the right question than totally correct about the wrong question.[45]

According to Drucker, today's professionals are neither bosses nor employees, and they are certainly not subordinates because they report rather than take orders. He epitomized their role when he stated that "the business enterprise of today is no longer an organization in which there are a handful of 'bosses' at the top who make all the decisions while the 'workers' carry out orders. It is primarily an organization of professionals of highly specialized knowledge exercising autonomous, responsible judgment. And every one of them—whether manager or individual expert contributor—constantly makes truly entrepreneurial decisions, that is, decisions which affect the economic characteristics and risks of the entire enterprise."[46]

Commitment is the final ingredient in Drucker's matrix of practice. Based on the supposition that people grow according to the demands made upon them, executives must recognize that the job is not a sinecure but a continual quest for higher standards of performance. It is impossible to automatically and magically program potential into results. Instead, one must have the intangible but indispensable feature of personal motivation: that is, "Unless there is personal commitment to the values of the idea and faith in them, the necessary efforts will . . . not be sustained."[47] Commitment also involves being in the arena of action, which means the executive has to expect his share of failure and disappointments while achieving success. Finally, effectiveness has nothing to do with good breaks, prestigious schools, or advanced degrees. Nor is it instantaneous or natural. It requires a commitment to constant renewal that is achieved by acting on the question, What do we have to learn today in order to keep learning for tomorrow?

CONCLUSION

In assigning book review projects to his students, Drucker routinely directed them to address two points. First, evaluate the content of the book and, second, express your opinions on what lessons you have learned from the author. Because the content of Drucker's managerial *oeuvre* has been described in the preceding pages, I will concentrate here on his principal ideas and themes that have impressed me most and have sharpened my managerial outlook.

Compiling a list of pertinent topics to evaluate presents no problem. Scores of themes come to mind. Rather than offer a laundry list, I have selected only those that percolate, permeate, and penetrate the entire body of his writings. They constitute six interacting themes that in my assessment provide the intellectual cement that binds together his managerial thought. They are (1) the systems approach, (2) continuity and change, (3) the challenge of productivity, (4) the role of the practitioner, (5) the moral dimension, and (6) the organization of ignorance. In addition, I comment on Drucker's unique ability to blend analysis and perception. Although it is not a managerial theme in the same sense as the other topics, it carries its own set of lessons.

Systems Approach

Before Drucker embarked on the study of management, there had been many successful achievements by individual business figures who had no systematic training in the discipline of management. Moreover, even as his stature and reputation grew as an authority on management, there continued to be many competent executives who had never read his books. He respected, admired, and learned a great deal from the individuals who were successfully practicing management without a formal theory. At the same time, he compared them to the gentleman in Moliere's drama who was unaware he was speaking prose. Drucker's seminal innovation was to identify practices and results of outstanding individuals and codify their accomplishments and specialized activities into an organized and integrative pattern.

Drucker's theory of modern management did not advocate the introduction of a single new business function. His innovation consisted in combining the major business survival components (profitability, marketing, human relations, and public responsibility) into an integrated whole. In this configuration, corporate survival required that each function contribute at a minimum level of performance. Corporate management, therefore, is no longer seen as a traditional bundle of business specialties but as an interacting discipline capable of being organized for systematic work.

Included in this specific form of top management work are such tasks as providing the company with a purposeful mission statement, organizing for capital and people results, identifying the specific tasks incapable of being delegated to others, and recognizing that tools and techniques are means but never ends.

Once Drucker singled out the creation and satisfaction of the customer as the central principle of corporate activity, he insisted that no firm (not even a monopoly) has complete control of the consumer. Logic compelled him to offer one of his chief operating insights, the importance of the corporation's outside landscape. Inside a business are only efforts, problems, and costs. Therefore meeting and taking advantage of innovative opportunities in the dynamic external realm compelled managers to view this realm as the only source of revenue and results. Drucker also deviated from the traditional view of specialization by introducing the corollary systems principle that people may be functionally specialized but problems never are. Once an issue is identified, it automatically becomes multidimensional.

Continuity and Change

The interaction of continuity and change was the topic of Drucker's first major monograph. As described in Chapter Two, it studied the work of Friedrich Stahl, a nineteenth-century German philosopher, and was published during the Third Reich in 1933. Politically, it advanced the *conservative innovation* thesis that progress involved a dynamic stability between reconciling the legitimate claims of the past with the needs of the future. In large part Drucker attributed the inability to apply the precept of conservative innovation to the rise of totalitarianism in Europe and the stagnancy of capitalism in the free world during the thirties. In the midst of reflecting and writing in the 1930s and 1940s, he gradually came to the conclusion that it was possible to avoid the mistakes and pitfalls of ideological determinism by examining how autonomous social institutions justified their power through contributing to a larger community.

Based on the assumption that knowledge becomes obsolete quickly, his concept postulated that a business had to be managed simultaneously but differently in three dimensions—the traditional, transitional, and transformational. The traditional focuses on managing better what was already known, the transitional concentrates on adapting to new opportunities in the environment, and the transformational seeks an entirely new business direction through purposeful innovation. In responding to these challenges, Drucker raised three provocative operating questions: What is the business? What will the business be? What should the business be?

Essentially, Drucker's analysis of the tension between continuity and change stipulated that if management managed only for today there would be no tomorrow and if it managed only for some distant glorious future and disregarded the past there also would be no tomorrow. He later put muscle on this conceptual skeleton by adding a number of principles and guidelines for implementation, such as concentrating on knowledge excellencies, practicing systematic abandonment, and identifying relevant outside trends for adaptive and breakthrough opportunities. The relationship between continuity and change subsequently became the foundation for his theories of strategic corporate planning and for his focus on the entrepreneurial process.

Challenge of Productivity

Born in the first decade of the twentieth century, Drucker witnessed three major historical models of productivity. Prior to World War I, societies were overwhelmingly agricultural and mirrored a technology based predominantly on muscle. After the war, he observed the social and economic transformation to an advanced industrial system that featured a sophisticated mechanical technology based on "moving people and making things." Shortly after World War II and after his insight that technology was the engine of change and that information was its fuel, he was the first to identify the transition to the knowledge society. In this new society the traditional physical factors of land, labor, and capital have become economically secondary to the invisible mental capital of information, now the major business resource. He also noted that the driving force of productivity in this knowledge economy has been a dramatic shift away from the movement of commodities and manual workers and toward the movement of "data and concepts."

It has been Drucker's contention, however, that the economic system has achieved, after decades of efforts, only marginal gains from the new technological tools and techniques. He has asserted that the main reason full productivity potential has not been achieved by the new technology has been management's focus on improving what was already known rather than concentrating on new and different challenges. He also has criticized the failure of specialists in the organization to ask what relevant information they need from each other to improve their performance and what measurements of productivity are most appropriate. As a result, there has been intrinsic misdiagnosis of how to relate information to productivity tasks. For example, Drucker has cited the recent strategic reengineering policy of downsizing as a symptom of the productivity malaise. Certainly, some downsizing was needed to meet the realities of global competition. He has pointed out, however, that too many managements have made the unforgivable mistake of performing amputation before making a diagnosis.

Drucker has been credited with pioneering insights in activity accounting, particularly in exposing the inability of traditional accounting principles to measure the costs of downtime and of actual corporate worth when the factor of knowledge is taken into account. He has maintained that the real challenge of knowledge productivity will never be realized until managers recognize that the largest expense in a business is not the tangible physical resources but the invisible information resource.

Role of the Practitioner

A common emphasis in all Drucker's managerial writings is that management research and writing ought to contribute to the practitioner's results. Drucker learned early on in his consulting career that if an intellectual concept failed to meet this standard of producing positive performance, it was simply raw and useless information. To reinforce this principle of utility, he punctuated his analyses with pragmatic insights and anecdotal illustrations of successful accomplishments by outstanding executives. Of course, this laser beam concentration on the user of information did not mean Drucker took the responsibility for implementation, for how-to-do. That was the job for which executives were paid. He has visualized his role as a catalyst, one who raises relevant questions and stimulates managers to become action oriented, suggesting how-to-think methods.

Drucker's focus on knowledge in action for results did not heighten his popularity with the academic community. He believed that subjects that could be mastered by experience should not be taught in school. This explains why he gave more credence to experience than to credentials. Except for the physical, or *hard*, sciences, he seriously questioned the value of the Ph.D. and other advanced degrees in preparing for a business career. He did admit that certain hard-core degree programs (in accounting, computer science, real estate, taxation, finance, and statistics) had merit, but only if the student took responsibility for his or her own further learning after receiving the degree.

Drucker's critique of business school higher education has been directed at its philosophy and operational programs. Philosophically, he has adopted the assumption that the primary mission of any professional school is to serve the needs of its client, in this case the business practitioner. However, he has discovered little evidence that the ultimate user of knowledge is at the core of current educational activity. He has also found a mismatch between rhetoric and practice in the way collegiate schools of business prepare students for excellence and educate the whole person. These goals mirror only good intentions; the schools have not established relevant feedback and have contributed neither wisdom nor experience to people confronting business realities. Moreover, in examining college bulletins, he has observed that these business programs, instead of being genuine schools of business administration, are made up of fragmented academic baronies teaching tools and techniques.

On the implementation level, he has criticized the system for a narrowly specialized curriculum that stresses means over ends, promotes a research policy of publish or perish that makes contact with utility remote and accidental, emphasizes accumulating credential credits rather than meeting demanding standards, asks for simulations of real-world decision making, inculcates a delusion that case studies and mathematical models are satisfactory solutions to century-old intractable problems, tends to overrate investigative analysis and dismiss imaginative perception, fails to understand the education students are not receiving (particularly in the humanities), exhibits a proclivity to stress traditional techniques and resist innovation, and manifests a pattern of structural uniformity—all these characteristics enforced by accrediting agencies that foster one way of doing things.

Of course, he has admitted a minority of notable exceptions to his critique. There are some performing schools, successful graduates, and illustrations of outstanding research. Whether these achievements occur because of or despite educational leadership, he has considered a moot point. He has mentioned, however, that one advantage of the Japanese system is its assumption that the student learns nothing in school and that it is the responsibility of management to train people on the job.

In his dissent from the conventional wisdom about educating future business leaders, Drucker has not looked upon himself as a cantankerous contrarian, a dogmatic ideologue, or a radical reformer. As a matter of fact, his harsh criticism has been in large part based on informal market research acquired from his decades of consulting experience with hundreds of corporations and thousands of executives. In identifying the defects of academe, he has pictured himself as an outside social observer who, with a sense of cool detachment, is attempting to raise the right questions for possible improvement.

Because of its deficiencies in methodology and curriculum, Drucker has asserted that the collegiate school of business requires drastic changes in two of its educational approaches. First, it needs to recognize the reality that at present it is possible to teach only concepts and not genuine application. Second, it needs to make its major educational commitment one of helping students in "learning how to learn."

The bulk of Drucker's complaints about business higher education has been that it is completely unsuited for immature students who are totally devoid of practical experience. In order to build a bridge in the direction of experience, he has made several suggestions: postpone entry into college for five years so that students can gain experience on the job, encourage part-time evening school attendance in conjunction with full-time employment, arrange for meaningful internships with corporations, and increase the number of adjunct faculty members with operating experience. In effect, Drucker has been reestablishing the Aristotelian proposition that certain subjects are best learned at a mature stage—and management is one of them.

Moral Dimension

Drucker has examined the moral dimension of management from the angle of institutional legitimacy and individual responsibility. He has especially objected to the fashionable popularity on Wall Street of speculator capitalism and its features of hostile takeovers and "greedy" managerial takeovers. Such actions have been triggered by the assumption that shareholder equity is the only purpose of the enterprise, but Drucker has regarded this monistic objective as an additional obstacle to the corporation's claim to genuine social legitimacy, that is, to the acceptance and consent required for its survival. He thought it extremely dangerous for an institution to subscribe exclusively to the economic value of earnings per share and to ignore its obligations to employees, its need for innovation, and its community accountability. According to Drucker, allowing the stock market to become the arbiter of corporate destiny is a myopic short-term perspective that is intolerable and destined to fail in the long run.

What has irritated Drucker the most about predatory corporate capitalism is the obscene salaries and perks that top managers have bestowed upon themselves without any regard to ethical performance criteria. Judging such practices to be blatantly immoral and reminiscent of the robber baron mentality, he has accused those practicing such greed for greed's sake of violating the norms of professional work.

According to Drucker, the new investor capitalism is contributing to corporations' loss of employee loyalty and allegiance. Because management is unconcerned with employee welfare or security, employees now view themselves as chattels instead of assets. The only choice currently available to them is to pursue their self-interest. Over the years it has troubled Drucker that obsessive loyalty to the corporation deprived the employee of a private life of his or her own. It created a situation in which making a living was considered more important than having a life. As he has viewed the contemporary organizational environment, he has envisaged a Hobbesian war of all against all, in which making a living and having a life are becoming increasingly irreconcilable. Considering the mania and frenzy of mega-mergers as a number-crunching financial game, he has reminded executives that after the fun of a short-term deal is over, they will face the hard and somber task of managing for long-term results. He would not predict the outcome of the current relationship but has been certain that the system will pay a heavy price for such shortsighted and mindless policies. A policy of rapacious corporate gain at the expense of employee well-being has made Drucker increasingly skeptical of "deal making" capitalism. Arguing that a healthy economic institution in a sick society is a contradiction in terms, he has insisted it is a moral institutional imperative to treat employees decently in order to exert genuine leadership and justify business power.

Drucker has pointed out that one visible outcome of both corporate and government failure to respond to key moral questions and create real citizenship has been the loss of the business corporation's position as the only dominant social power. It now has to share social power with other institutions, particularly with what he has called the *third sector*—the not-for-profit voluntary organizations. Not only have they become the employers of the largest single workforce segment in the country but they have become the crucible where individuals put community interest over self-interest.

Organization of Ignorance

Drucker frequently remarked that *Organizing Ignorance* was the one book that he had often started but never finished. This is a reminder that although the body of his work on management is substantial, it represents only one strand in his intellectual firmament. Moreover, when one considers Drucker's seminal concept that the environment outside the business is the source of business results and opportunities, one conclusion must be that there is no way of isolating the study of management from other academic disciplines.

Drucker has offered several explanations for the self-contradictory term *organizing ignorance*. He has contended that given the unprecedented velocity of change and heightened complexity of events, every advance of knowledge is now accompanied by a concomitant increase in ignorance. Equally important, he has argued that the new technological tools for improving the tasks of accounting and management might increase the quantity of information but simultaneously might distort its quality. Because the focus of accounting and management science is on the amassing of internal data, these disciplines have little or nothing to contribute to the information managers really need most for diagnosing external threats and opportunity trends. Consequently, ignorance will always outpace knowledge in the analysis of problems because there is always so much more of it. The commendable pursuit of knowledge, therefore, no matter how brilliant the findings, should be tempered with humility. Many executives, for example, falsely believe that the computer is a divine tool created by God to grant certitude. Drucker has called this faith a delusion, because the Bible reveals that God originally created chaos. The reality of instability and uncertainty of knowledge has been convincing evidence in Drucker's mind that management can never attain the status of the physical sciences. Principles of probability are possible, but developing scientific laws based on controlled and repeatable experiments is out of the question when decision making must take place in a future business landscape where there are only expectations and no facts.

Studying Drucker's managerial thought will not produce the pragmatic or the predictable, but it does provide a perspective for understanding the restraints of both knowledge and ignorance. A guiding principle for him in confronting the turbulence of uncontrollable outside events has been to identify the future that has already happened but whose real impact had yet to be felt. I have already cited many of Drucker's illustrations of corporations that have taken advantage of outside social trends, but it is interesting to identify more of the issues that he believes will have an irreversible impact on the future environment. Among the incipient social and economic forces that require closer managerial attention are the destabilizing upheavals in the international currency markets; dynamic patterns of global demographics; ethnic and terrorist threats to national sovereignty and multinational corporations; surprising achievements by the less developed world in technology transfer, training, and marketing; and the challenge of civilizing the modern city by reconciling the requirements of freedom with the obligations of community.

Blend of Analysis and Perception

Drucker is sui generis. Many social observers are talented in either analysis or perception, but he has been exceptional in both. These skills are indeed distinct. Analysis demands a talent for disciplined investigation and for organizing the content of subject matter. Perception relies on the ability to develop insights and ideas from personal and direct experience. If the pendulum of observation swings too far toward excessive analysis of informational facts, the observer faces the danger of being blinded by data, with the result that he sees nothing. If it swings too far in the other direction and lacks respect for scholarly research, the observer runs the risk of developing perceptions devoid of substance and degenerating into nonsense. Both analysis and perception are important but not in their extreme manifestations. Drucker achieved a balance.

In studying each particular issue, Drucker displayed the probing analytical ability of a historical scholar in investigating and screening background data. By virtue of his curiosity and multiple interests as a journalist, he was also constantly honing his perceptual skills. Translating these analytical and perceptual capacities into reality also demanded writing craftsmanship of the highest order. His prodigious output of books, articles, essays, consulting reports, and novels is testimony to this communication skill and workmanship. He once remarked that writing was his only real talent. People might disagree with what he wrote, but he rarely confused them.

By blending an analytical capacity for separating the wheat from the chaff with a perceptual imagination, Drucker produced a profusion of managerial concepts and ideas. If he did not originate most of the fundamental principles of modern management, he certainly nurtured their beginnings. It is difficult to identify a single major concept to which he has not made a contribution. Consider, for example, such insights as the existence of consumer sovereignty and corporate culture; the systematization of corporate governance; the dilemma surrounding the role of trade unions; the concept of social responsibility; the theory of decision making; the practices of management by objectives, activity accounting, time management, and vulnerability analysis; the significance of the consumer movement; and the growing importance of the multinational corporation, the global supermarket, and the nonprofit sector, to cite a few.

Undoubtedly Drucker's indigenous gifts explain a great deal about his distinctiveness. But surely they are not the whole answer. Consideration must also be given to his career as a critic of Japanese art. Most museum directors are probably not aware that Drucker is a noted authority on business management. And probably still fewer business executives know that Drucker is a leading connoisseur and appraiser of Japanese painting. Because Japanese political theory and social history are decidedly more perceptual than analytical, the implication is clear that his perceptual talents may have been greatly enhanced by his study of Japanese society. His perceptual imagination then sparked many insights on the unique features of Japanese society and business, earning him the title "father of Japanese management."

The closest Drucker has come to providing a structured intellectual explanation of both the multidisciplinary approach to developing ideas that he employs and the interplay of knowledge and ignorance that managers should engage in was his discussion of his theme of social ecology, which focused on our artificial ecosystem as opposed to our natural one.

Rejecting the typical academic design for the social sciences, he argued that economics, sociology, philosophy, and political theory made less and less sense as independent and separate disciplines. And in *The Ecological Vision* (1993), he offered a succinct epitome of his intellectual rationale for integrating diverse subject matter:

When asked what I do, I say I write. Technically this is correct. Since I was twenty, writing has been the foundation of everything else I have been doing, such as teaching and consulting. But when people ask: "What are you writing about?" I become evasive. I have written quite a bit about economics, but surely am not an economist. I have written quite a bit about history, but surely am not a historian. I have written quite a bit about government and politics, but though I started out as a political scientist, I long ago moved out of the field. And I am also not a sociologist as the term is now defined. I myself, however, know very well—and have known for years—what I am trying to do. I consider myself a *social ecologist* concerned with man's man-made environment.[1]

Drucker has realized that the practice of blending different knowledges into relevant configurations has a long way to go before it will be developed into an acceptable theory. However, at least one writer, Theodore Levitt of Harvard University, has lavished high praise on Drucker for his efforts at connectivity and at comprehensively developing the big picture. He has compared Drucker's managerial output with the work of some of the intellectual giants of modern Western civilization. And he has found that "like the styles of Newton, Smith, Marx, Freud, Darwin and others, Drucker's encyclopedic explosion of managerial tasks, responsibilities and practices provides a meaning and casts an illumination on its subject that transcends the subject itself."[2]

NOTES

Chapter One

1. A. Bennett, "Management Guru," *Wall Street Journal* (July 28, 1987).
2. J. J. Tarrant, *Drucker: The Man Who Invented the Corporate Society* (Boston: Cahners Books, 1976).
3. J. Micklethwait and A. Wooldridge, *Witch Doctors: Making Sense of the Management Gurus* (New York: Times Books, 1996), p. 321.
4. R. Poe, "A Walk and Talk with Peter Drucker," *Across the Board* (Feb. 1983), p. 34.
5. Micklethwait and Wooldridge, *Witch Doctors*, p. 64.
6. G. S. Day, *Market Driven Strategy* (New York: Free Press, 1990), p. viii.
7. G. Hamel and C. K. Prahalad, *Competing for the Future* (Boston: Harvard Business School Press, 1994), p. xiv.
8. C. Skrzycki, "The Enduring Peter Drucker," *Washington Post* (May 7, 1989).
9. Micklethwait and Wooldridge, *Witch Doctors*, p. 74.
10. R. Lenzer and S. S. Johnson, "Seeing Things as They Really Are," *Forbes* (Mar. 10, 1997), p. 124.
11. Lenzer and Johnson, "Seeing Things," p. 124.
12. M. J. Kami, *Trigger Points* (New York: McGraw-Hill, 1988), p. 71.
13. P. Truell and L. Gurwin, *False Profits* (Boston: Houghton Mifflin, 1992), p. 184.
14. T. Levitt, "The Living Legacy of Peter Drucker," in T. H. Bonaparte and J. E. Flaherty (eds.), *Peter Drucker: Contributions to Business Enterprise* (New York: New York University Press, 1970), pp. 6–7.
15. Levitt, *Living Legacy*, p. 7.

Chapter Two

1. P. F. Drucker, *Adventures of a Bystander* (New York: HarperCollins, 1978; reprint, New York: HarperCollins, 1991), pp. 9–82 (page citations are to the original edition).
2. P. F. Drucker, *Landmarks of Tomorrow* (New York: HarperCollins, 1959), pp. 147–148.
3. Drucker, *Adventures of a Bystander,* pp. 62–82.
4. Drucker, *Adventures of a Bystander,* pp. 24–61.
5. P. F. Drucker, *The Ecological Vision: Reflections on the American Condition* (New Brunswick, N.J.: Transaction, 1993), pp. 441–442.
6. P. F. Drucker, *Post-Capitalist Society* (New York: HarperCollins, 1993), p. 40.
7. "Career Moves for Ages 20 to 70," *Psychology Today* (Nov.–Dec. 1992), p. 54.
8. Correspondence with the author (Oct. 28, 1995).
9. Correspondence with the author (Oct. 28, 1995).
10. J.J. Sheehan, *German History 1770–1866* (New York: Oxford University Press, 1989), p. 594.
11. Sheehan, *German History,* p. 595.
12. Correspondence with the author (Oct. 7, 1998).
13. M. L. Polak, "Business Should Be Boring," *Philadelphia Inquirer Magazine* (Aug. 30, 1987), p. 9.
14. J. A. Byrne, "Is Research in the Ivory Tower 'Fuzzy, Irrelevant, Pretentious'?" *Business Week* (Oct. 29, 1990), p. 62.
15. Drucker, *Ecological Vision,* p. 135.

Chapter Three

1. L. Steffens, *The Autobiography of Lincoln Steffens* (New York: Harcourt Brace, 1958).
2. H. N. Brailsford, Preface, in P. F. Drucker, *The End of Economic Man* (New York: John Day, 1939; reprint, New York: HarperCollins, 1969), p. viii (page citations are to the original edition).
3. P. F. Drucker, *The End of Economic Man* (New York: John Day, 1939; reprint, New York: HarperCollins, 1969), p. 236 (page citations are to the original edition).
4. Drucker, *Economic Man,* p. 38.
5. J. Ortega y Gasset, *The Revolt of the Masses* (New York: Norton, 1932).
6. Drucker, *Economic Man,* p. 24.
7. Drucker, *Economic Man,* p. 78.
8. Drucker, *Economic Man,* p. 236.
9. Drucker, *Economic Man,* p. 190.
10. Drucker, *Economic Man,* p. 15.
11. Drucker, *Economic Man,* p. 261.
12. P. F. Drucker, *The New Realities: In Government and Politics/In Economics and Business/In Society and World View* (New York: HarperCollins, 1989), p. 30.

Chapter Four

1. P. F. Drucker, *Adventures of a Bystander* (New York: HarperCollins, 1978; reprint, New York: HarperCollins, 1991), pp. 223–224 (page citations are to the original edition).
2. Drucker, *Adventures of a Bystander,* pp. 256, 78.
3. P. F. Drucker, *The Future of Industrial Man* (New York: John Day, 1942), p. 22.
4. Drucker, *Industrial Man,* p. 74.
5. Drucker, *Industrial Man,* p. 128.
6. W. J. Baumol and A. S. Blinder, *Macroeconomics: Principles and Policy* (Orlando: Harcourt Brace, 1997), p. 35.
7. J. Burnham, *The Managerial Revolution* (New York: John Day, 1941).
8. Drucker, *Industrial Man,* p. 128.
9. Drucker, *Industrial Man,* p. 93.
10. Drucker, *Industrial Man,* p. 81.
11. Drucker, *Industrial Man,* p. 34.
12. Drucker, *Industrial Man,* pp. 34–35.
13. Drucker, *Industrial Man,* p. 36.
14. Drucker, *Industrial Man,* p. 37.
15. Drucker, *Industrial Man,* p. 21.
16. R. A. Dahl and C. E. Lindblom, *Politics, Economics, and Welfare: Planning and Politico-Economic Systems Resolved into Basic Social Processes* (New York: HarperCollins, 1953), p. 481.
17. Drucker, *Industrial Man,* p. 80.
18. Drucker, *Industrial Man,* p. 100.
19. Drucker, *Industrial Man,* p. 99.
20. Drucker, *Industrial Man,* p. 297.
21. Drucker, *Industrial Man,* p. 25.
22. Drucker, *Industrial Man,* p. 106.
23. Drucker, *Industrial Man,* pp. 26–27.
24. Drucker, *Industrial Man,* p. 102.
25. Drucker, *Industrial Man,* p. 112.
26. Drucker, *Industrial Man,* p. 117.
27. Drucker, *Industrial Man,* p. 118.
28. Drucker, *Industrial Man,* p. 120.
29. Drucker, *Industrial Man,* p. 121.
30. Drucker, *Industrial Man,* p. 122.
31. Drucker, *Industrial Man,* p. 119.
32. Drucker, *Industrial Man,* pp. 121–122.
33. Drucker, *Industrial Man,* p. 123.
34. Drucker, *Industrial Man,* p. 295.
35. J. Barzun, "A Vision for Free Men," *New Republic* (Oct. 26, 1942), p. 551.

36. A. M. Kantrow, "Why Read Peter Drucker?" *Harvard Business Review* (Jan.–Feb. 1980), p. 79.

37. Kantrow, "Why Read Peter Drucker?" p. 76.

38. A. Smith, "The Shape of Things to Come," *New York Times Book Review* (Apr. 11, 1993), p. 8.

39. P. F. Drucker, *The Ecological Vision: Reflections on the American Condition* (New Brunswick, N.J.: Transaction, 1993), p. 457.

40. For a more detailed treatment of Drucker's views on systems theory and social ecology, see P. F. Drucker, *Landmarks of Tomorrow* (New York: HarperCollins, 1959), pp. 17–60; *Ecological Vision*, pp. 441–447.

Chapter Five

1. Conversation with the author.

2. P. F. Drucker, *Concept of the Corporation* (New York: John Day, 1946; reprint, New York: Mentor, 1972), pp. 15–29 (page citations are to the reprint edition).

3. P. F. Drucker, *Adventures of a Bystander* (New York: HarperCollins, 1978; reprint, New York: HarperCollins, 1991), pp. 256–262 (page citations are to the original edition).

4. Drucker, *Adventures of a Bystander*, p. 1.

5. R. L. Lacey, *Ford: The Men and the Machine* (Boston: Little, Brown, 1986), pp. 283–299; P. F. Drucker, *Managing for the Future: The 1990s and Beyond* (New York: Truman Talley Books, Dutton, 1992), p. 310.

6. P. F. Drucker, "Why Management Consultants?" in M. Zimet and R. G. Greenwood (eds.), *The Evolving Science of Management* (New York: AMACOM, 1979), p. 475.

7. Drucker, *Concept of the Corporation*, p. 71.

8. Drucker, *Concept of the Corporation*, p. 240.

9. P. F. Drucker, *An Introductory View of Management* (New York: HarperCollins, 1977), p. 568.

10. Drucker, *Concept of the Corporation*, p. 79.

11. Drucker, *Concept of the Corporation*, p. 112.

12. Drucker, *Concept of the Corporation*, p. 127.

13. D. Halberstam, *The Reckoning* (New York: Morrow, 1986), p. 334.

14. Drucker, *Concept of the Corporation*, pp. 135–136.

15. Drucker, *Concept of the Corporation*, p. 132.

16. Drucker, *Concept of the Corporation*, p. 171.

17. Drucker, *Concept of the Corporation*, p. 27.

18. R. Hofstadter, *The American Political Tradition* (New York: Knopf, 1948), p. 166.

19. Drucker, *Concept of the Corporation*, p. 86.

20. Drucker, *Concept of the Corporation*, pp. 250–251.

21. Drucker, *Concept of the Corporation*, p. 81.

22. Drucker, *Concept of the Corporation*, p. 81.

23. P. F. Drucker, *Post-Capitalist Society* (New York: HarperCollins, 1993), p. 79.

24. Drucker, *Concept of the Corporation*, p. 83.
25. Drucker, *Concept of the Corporation*, p. 4.
26. J. A. Byrne, *The Whiz Kids: The Founding Fathers of American Business and the Legacy They Left Us* (New York: Bantam Books, 1993), pp. 125, 169–170.
27. Drucker, *Adventures of a Bystander*, p. 267.
28. P. F. Drucker, "The Best Book on Management Ever," *Fortune* (Apr. 23, 1990), pp. 145–150.
29. Drucker, *Adventures of a Bystander*, p. 291.
30. Drucker, *Adventures of a Bystander*, p. 291.
31. Drucker, "The Best Book on Management," p. 148.
32. Drucker, "The Best Book on Management," pp. 145–150.
33. C. N. Parkinson, Foreword, in J. J. Tarrant, *Drucker: The Man Who Invented the Corporate Society* (Boston: Cahners Books, 1976), p. xi.

Chapter Six

1. P. F. Drucker, "Making Managers of Communism's Bureaucrats," *Wall Street Journal* (Aug. 15, 1990).
2. P. F. Drucker, *Post-Capitalist Society* (New York: HarperCollins, 1993), pp. 181–219.
3. P. F. Drucker, "The Coming Rediscovery of Scientific Management," in *Toward the Next Economics, and Other Essays* (New York: HarperCollins, 1981), p. 96.
4. P. F. Drucker, Introduction, in P. Graham (ed.), *Mary Parker Follett: Prophet of Management* (Boston: Harvard Business School Press, 1995), pp. 1–13.
5. P. F. Drucker, *Management: Tasks, Responsibilities, Practices* (New York: HarperCollins, 1973), p. 10.
6. Conversation with the author.
7. M. L. Polak, "Business Should Be Boring," *Philadelphia Inquirer Magazine* (Aug. 30, 1987), p. 9.
8. P. F. Drucker, *The Effective Executive* (New York: HarperCollins, 1967), p. 80.
9. Drucker, *Management: Tasks, Responsibilities, Practices*, p. 399.
10. P. F. Drucker, *Managing in Turbulent Times* (New York: HarperCollins, 1980), pp. 30–38; *The Changing World of the Executive* (New York: Truman Talley Books, Times Books, 1982), pp. 50–54.
11. Drucker, *Changing World of the Executive*, p. 49.
12. P. F. Drucker, *Technology, Management and Society: Essays by Peter Drucker* (New York: HarperCollins, 1958; reprint, New York: HarperCollins, 1977), p. 95 (page citations are to the original edition).
13. P. F. Drucker, *The Frontiers of Management: Where Tomorrow's Decisions Are Being Shaped Today* (New York: Truman Talley Books, Dutton, 1986; reprint, New York: Perennial Library, 1987), p. 9 (page citations are to the original edition).
14. P. F. Drucker, "Business Objectives and Survival Needs," *Journal of Business of the University of Chicago* (Apr. 1958), p. 9.

15. Drucker, *Managing in Turbulent Times,* pp. 68–71.
16. Drucker, *Management: Tasks, Responsibilities, Practices,* p. 17.
17. P. F. Drucker, *The Practice of Management* (New York: HarperCollins, 1954), p. 129.

Chapter Seven

1. P. F. Drucker, *Landmarks of Tomorrow* (New York: HarperCollins, 1959), p. 21.
2. P. F. Drucker, *The Practice of Management* (New York: HarperCollins, 1954), p. 49.
3. Drucker, *Practice of Management,* p. 50.
4. Richman, T. "The Entrepreneurial Mystique" (interview with Peter Drucker), *Inc.* (Oct. 1985), p. 49.
5. P. F. Drucker, "Business Objectives and Survival Needs," *Journal of Business of the University of Chicago* (Apr. 1958), p. 3.
6. J. Micklethwait and A. Wooldridge, *Witch Doctors: Making Sense of the Management Gurus* (New York: Times Books, 1996), p. 73.
7. Micklethwait and Wooldridge, *Witch Doctors,* p. 64.
8. J.J. Tarrant, *Drucker: The Man Who Invented the Corporate Society* (Boston: Cahners Books, 1976), p. 11.
9. P. F. Drucker, *An Introductory View of Management* (New York: HarperCollins, 1977), p. 6.
10. Drucker, *Introductory View,* p. 5.
11. P. F. Drucker, *Managing for Results: Economic Tasks and Risk-Taking Decisions* (New York: HarperCollins, 1964), p. xi.
12. J. A. Byrne, "Management's New Gurus," *Business Week* (Aug. 31, 1992), p. 46.
13. Micklethwait and Wooldridge, *Witch Doctors,* p. 71.
14. Micklethwait and Wooldridge, *Witch Doctors,* p. 321.
15. A. Wooldridge, "Peter Drucker on L.A. Versus San Francisco, Downsizing and Newt the Entrepreneur," *Los Angeles Times* (Feb. 2, 1997).
16. T. Levitt, "A View of 'Management,'" *Business Week* (Feb. 9, 1974), pp. 50–51.

Chapter Eight

1. J.J. Tarrant, *Drucker: The Man Who Invented the Corporate Society* (Boston: Cahners Books, 1976), p. 256.
2. Tarrant, *Drucker,* p. 257.
3. P. F. Drucker, *The Age of Discontinuity: Guidelines to Our Changing Society* (New York: HarperCollins, 1968), p. 66.
4. P. F. Drucker, *Technology, Management and Society: Essays by Peter Drucker* (New York: HarperCollins, 1958; reprint, New York: HarperCollins, 1977), p. 133 (page citations are to the original edition).

5. P. F. Drucker, *Management: Tasks, Responsibilities, Practices* (New York: HarperCollins, 1973), p. 88.
6. P. F. Drucker, "Keeping U.S. Companies Productive," *Journal of Business Strategy* (Winter 1987), p. 15.
7. P. F. Drucker, "The Theory of the Business," *Harvard Business Review* (Sept.–Oct. 1994), pp. 96–98.
8. Drucker, "Theory of the Business," p. 102.
9. P. F. Drucker, *Managing in Turbulent Times* (New York: HarperCollins, 1980), p. 41.
10. Drucker, *Management: Tasks, Responsibilities, Practices*, p. 122.
11. Drucker, *Technology, Management and Society*, p. 130.
12. P. F. Drucker, *Managing for Results: Economic Tasks and Risk-Taking Decisions* (New York: HarperCollins, 1964), pp. 203–208.
13. P. F. Drucker, *Innovation and Entrepreneurship: Practice and Principles* (New York: Harper-Collins, 1985), p. 22.
14. Drucker, *Innovation and Entrepreneurship*, p. 12.
15. Drucker, *Innovation and Entrepreneurship*, p. 150.
16. Richman, T. "The Entrepreneurial Mystique" (interview with Peter Drucker), *Inc.* (Oct. 1985), p. 38.
17. Richman, "Entrepreneurial Mystique," p. 38.
18. Drucker, *Management: Tasks, Responsibilities, Practices*, p. 113.
19. P. F. Drucker, *Managing in a Time of Great Change* (New York: Truman Talley Books, Dutton, 1995), p. 48.
20. Drucker, *Managing in Turbulent Times*, p. 68.
21. P. F. Drucker, *The Practice of Management* (New York: HarperCollins, 1954), p. 37.
22. Drucker, *Management: Tasks, Responsibilities, Practices*, p. 83.
23. Drucker, *Management: Tasks, Responsibilities, Practices*, p. 511.
24. Drucker, *Innovation and Entrepreneurship*, p. 66.
25. Drucker, *Practice of Management*, p. 38.
26. Drucker, *Management: Tasks, Responsibilities, Practices*, pp. 64–65.
27. Tarrant, *Drucker*, p. 255.
28. P. F. Drucker, *The Changing World of the Executive* (New York: Truman Talley Books, Times Books, 1982), p. 67.
29. P. F. Drucker, *Managing for the Future: The 1990s and Beyond* (New York: Truman Talley Books, Dutton, 1992), p. 101.
30. P. F. Drucker, "The Retail Revolution," *Wall Street Journal* (July 15, 1993).
31. Drucker, *Management: Tasks, Responsibilities, Practices*, p. 61.
32. Drucker, *Managing in a Time of Great Change*, p. 111.
33. P. F. Drucker, "The Shame of Marketing," *Marketing Communication* (Aug. 1969), p. 64.
34. Conversation with the author.
35. A. Corbin, "The Impact of Drucker on Marketing," in T. H. Bonaparte and J. E. Flaherty (eds.), *Peter Drucker: Contributions to Business Enterprise* (New York: New York University Press, 1970), p. 151.

Chapter Nine

1. P. F. Drucker, *The Changing World of the Executive* (New York: Truman Talley Books, Times Books, 1982), p. 65.
2. P. F. Drucker, *Managing in Turbulent Times* (New York: HarperCollins, 1980), pp. 18–19.
3. Drucker, *Managing in Turbulent Times*, p. 19.
4. Drucker, *Managing in Turbulent Times*, pp. 20–21.
5. Drucker, *Changing World of the Executive*, p. 76.
6. Drucker, *Managing in Turbulent Times*, pp. 69–70.
7. Drucker, *Managing in Turbulent Times*, p. 29.
8. Drucker, *Managing in Turbulent Times*, p. 30.
9. P. F. Drucker, *The Ecological Vision: Reflections on the American Condition* (New Brunswick, N.J.: Transaction, 1993), p. 103.
10. Drucker, *Managing in Turbulent Times*, p. 13.
11. Drucker, *Changing World of the Executive*, pp. 63–64.
12. P. F. Drucker, *An Introductory View of Management* (New York: HarperCollins, 1977), p. 397.
13. P. F. Drucker, *Managing for Results: Economic Tasks and Risk-Taking Decisions* (New York: HarperCollins, 1964), p. 70.
14. Drucker, *Managing for Results*, p. 105.
15. Drucker, *Changing World of the Executive*, p. 64.
16. P. F. Drucker, "Managing for Business Effectiveness," *Harvard Business Review* (May–June 1963), p. 56.
17. Drucker, *Managing for Results*, pp. 32–34.
18. Drucker, "Managing for Business Effectiveness," p. 56.
19. Drucker, *Changing World of the Executive*, p. 68.
20. Drucker, *Managing for Results*, p. 9.
21. P. F. Drucker, "The New Productivity Challenge," *Harvard Business Review* (Nov.–Dec. 1991), p. 73.
22. H. T. Johnson and R. Kaplan, *Relevance Lost: The Rise and Fall of Management Accounting* (Boston: Harvard Business School Press, 1983), pp. 241–242.
23. P. F. Drucker, "Drucker's Challenge for CMAs," *Managing Accounting Magazine* (June 1995), pp. 12–14.
24. P. F. Drucker, "The Coming of the New Organization," *Harvard Business Review* (Jan.–Feb. 1988), p. 50.
25. P. F. Drucker, *Managing in a Time of Great Change* (New York: Truman Talley Books, Dutton, 1995), pp. 118–119.
26. Drucker, "Managing for Business Effectiveness," p. 59.
27. Conversation with the author.
28. P. F. Drucker, *Innovation and Entrepreneurship: Practice and Principles* (New York: HarperCollins, 1985), p. 151.

29. P. F. Drucker, *Management: Tasks, Responsibilities, Practices* (New York: HarperCollins, 1973), p. 126 (emphasis added).

30. P. F. Drucker, "The New Society of Organizations," *Harvard Business Review* (Sept.–Oct. 1992), p. 95.

31. Drucker, *Managing in a Time of Great Change*, p. 38.

32. P. F. Drucker, *Post-Capitalist Society* (New York: HarperCollins, 1993), p. 164.

33. Conversation with the author.

34. Drucker, *Managing in a Time of Great Change*, p. 291.

35. Drucker, "New Society of Organizations," pp. 97–99.

36. Drucker, "New Society of Organizations," p. 100.

37. R. Lenzer and S. S. Johnson, "Seeing Things as They Really Are," *Forbes* (Mar. 10, 1997), p. 124.

38. Drucker, "New Society of Organizations," p. 100.

Chapter Ten

1. P. F. Drucker, *America's Next Twenty Years* (New York: HarperCollins, 1955), pp. 23–24.

2. P. F. Drucker, *Management: Tasks, Responsibilities, Practices* (New York: HarperCollins, 1973), pp. 797–799.

3. P. F. Drucker, *Innovation and Entrepreneurship: Practice and Principles* (New York: Harper-Collins, 1985), p. 151.

4. P. F. Drucker and I. Nakauchi, *Drucker on Asia: A Dialogue Between Peter Drucker and Isao Nakauchi* (Newton, Mass.: Butterworth-Heinemann, 1997), p. 130.

5. Drucker, *Innovation and Entrepreneurship*, p. 149.

6. Drucker, *Management: Tasks, Responsibilities, Practices*, p. 799.

7. P. F. Drucker, "Management and the World's Work," *Harvard Business Review* (Sept.–Oct. 1988), p. 76.

8. Richman, T. "The Entrepreneurial Mystique" (interview with Peter Drucker), *Inc.* (Oct. 1985), p. 36.

9. Drucker, *Innovation and Entrepreneurship*, p. 151.

10. A. Rutigliano, "An Interview with Peter Drucker: Managing the New," *Management Review* (Jan. 1986), p. 39.

11. Drucker, *Innovation and Entrepreneurship*, p. 19.

12. P. F. Drucker, *Managing for the Future: The 1990s and Beyond* (New York: Truman Talley Books, Dutton, 1992), pp. 340–341.

13. Drucker, *Innovation and Entrepreneurship*, p. 130.

14. R. Poe, "A Walk and Talk with Peter Drucker," *Across the Board* (Feb. 1983), p. 39.

15. Rutigliano, "Interview with Peter Drucker," p. 40.

16. P. F. Drucker, *The Frontiers of Management: Where Tomorrow's Decisions Are Being Shaped Today* (New York: Truman Talley Books, Dutton, 1986; reprint, New York: Perennial Library, 1987), p. 263 (page citations are to the original edition).

17. P. F. Drucker, "This Competitive World," *Harvard Business Review* (Mar.–Apr. 1961), p. 131.

18. Drucker, *Management: Tasks, Responsibilities, Practices,* p. 127; *The Ecological Vision: Reflections on the American Condition* (New Brunswick, N.J.: Transaction, 1993), p. 452.

19. Drucker, *Management: Tasks, Responsibilities, Practices,* p. 788.

20. T. G. Harris, "The Post-Capitalist Executive: An Interview with Peter F. Drucker," *Harvard Business Review* (May–June 1993), p. 118.

21. Drucker, *Innovation and Entrepreneurship,* p. 155.

22. Drucker, *Innovation and Entrepreneurship,* p. 149.

23. P. F. Drucker, *The Changing World of the Executive* (New York: Truman Talley Books, Times Books, 1982), p. 87.

24. G. Gendron, " 'Flashes of Genius.' " *Inc., 18*(7), May 1996, p. 38. (Special issue: The State of Small Business.)

25. P. F. Drucker, *Managing for Results: Economic Tasks and Risk-Taking Decisions* (New York: HarperCollins, 1964), pp. 203–207.

26. Drucker, *Managing for Results,* pp. 206–208.

27. Drucker, *Innovation and Entrepreneurship,* p. 140.

28. P. F. Drucker, "Twelve Fables of Research Management," *Harvard Business Review* (Jan.–Feb. 1963), p. 107.

29. Drucker, *Managing for Results,* pp. 173–192.

30. P. F. Drucker, *Managing in a Time of Great Change* (New York: Truman Talley Books, Dutton, 1995), p. 12.

31. P. F. Drucker, "The New Society of Organizations," *Harvard Business Review* (Sept.–Oct. 1992), p. 96.

32. P. F. Drucker, *The Age of Discontinuity: Guidelines to Our Changing Society* (New York: HarperCollins, 1968), p. xiii.

33. Drucker, *Managing for the Future,* p. 93; *Post-Capitalist Society* (New York: HarperCollins, 1993), pp. 19, 93.

34. Drucker, *Post-Capitalist Society,* p. 46.

35. Drucker, "New Society of Organizations," p. 101.

36. Richman, "Entrepreneurial Mystique," p. 36.

37. Harris, "Post-Capitalist Executive," p. 116.

38. Drucker, *Frontiers of Management,* p. 4.

39. Drucker, *Innovation and Entrepreneurship,* p. 156.

40. Drucker, *Innovation and Entrepreneurship,* pp. 157–158.

41. P. F. Drucker, *Managing in Turbulent Times* (New York: HarperCollins, 1980), pp. 41–42.

42. Drucker, *Innovation and Entrepreneurship,* p. 163.

43. Drucker, *Managing in Turbulent Times,* p. 42.

Chapter Eleven

1. G. Gendron, " 'Flashes of Genius.' " *Inc., 18*(7), May 1996, p. 31. (Special issue: The State of Small Business.)

2. P. F. Drucker, *Innovation and Entrepreneurship: Practice and Principles* (New York: Harper-Collins, 1985), p. 37.
3. A. Rutigliano, "An Interview with Peter Drucker: Managing the New," *Management Review* (Jan. 1986), p. 38.
4. Drucker, *Innovation and Entrepreneurship*, p. 38.
5. Gendron, "'Flashes of Genius,'" p. 38.
6. Drucker, *Innovation and Entrepreneurship*, p. 45.
7. Drucker, *Innovation and Entrepreneurship*, p. 46.
8. Rutigliano, "Interview with Peter Drucker," p. 38.
9. Drucker, *Innovation and Entrepreneurship*, p. 54.
10. Drucker, *Innovation and Entrepreneurship*, p. 57.
11. Drucker, *Innovation and Entrepreneurship*, p. 88.
12. P. F. Drucker, *The Changing World of the Executive* (New York: Truman Talley Books, Times Books, 1982), p. 89.
13. Drucker, *Innovation and Entrepreneurship*, p. 95.
14. Drucker, *Changing World of the Executive*, p. 95.
15. P. F. Drucker, *Managing in a Time of Great Change* (New York: Truman Talley Books, Dutton, 1995), pp. 41–42.
16. Drucker, *Innovation and Entrepreneurship*, p. 76.
17. Drucker, *Innovation and Entrepreneurship*, p. 81.
18. Drucker, *Innovation and Entrepreneurship*, pp. 84–87.
19. Drucker, *Innovation and Entrepreneurship*, p. 209.
20. Drucker, *Innovation and Entrepreneurship*, p. 215.
21. Drucker, *Innovation and Entrepreneurship*, p. 220.
22. Drucker, *Innovation and Entrepreneurship*, pp. 224–225.
23. Drucker, *Innovation and Entrepreneurship*, pp. 230–232.
24. P. F. Drucker, "The Five Deadly Business Sins," *Wall Street Journal* (Oct. 21, 1993).
25. Drucker, *Innovation and Entrepreneurship*, p. 225.
26. Drucker, *Innovation and Entrepreneurship*, p. 232.
27. Drucker, *Innovation and Entrepreneurship*, p. 235.
28. Drucker, *Innovation and Entrepreneurship*, p. 239.
29. P. F. Drucker, "Why Some Mergers Work and Many More Don't," *Forbes* (Jan. 18, 1982), pp. 35–36.
30. Conversation with the author.
31. P. F. Drucker, *Managing for the Future: The 1990s and Beyond* (New York: Truman Talley Books, Dutton, 1992), pp. 287–291; "Why Some Mergers Work," pp. 34–36.
32. Drucker, *Managing for the Future*, pp. 257–262.
33. Drucker, *Managing for the Future*, p. 288.
34. Gendron, "'Flashes of Genius,'" p. 38.
35. Drucker, *Innovation and Entrepreneurship*, p. 107.
36. Rutigliano, "Interview with Peter Drucker," p. 39.
37. Drucker, *Innovation and Entrepreneurship*, p. 107.
38. Drucker, *Innovation and Entrepreneurship*, p. 111.

39. P. F. Drucker, *Management: Tasks, Responsibilities, Practices* (New York: HarperCollins, 1973), p. 792.

40. Drucker, *Innovation and Entrepreneurship*, p. 131.

41. Drucker, *Innovation and Entrepreneurship*, p. 190.

42. Drucker, *Innovation and Entrepreneurship*, pp. 133–134.

43. Drucker, *Innovation and Entrepreneurship*, pp. 126–127.

44. Drucker, *Innovation and Entrepreneurship*, p. 132.

45. P. F. Drucker, *The Frontiers of Management: Where Tomorrow's Decisions Are Being Shaped Today* (New York: Truman Talley Books, Dutton, 1986; reprint, New York: Perennial Library, 1987), p. 51 (page citations are to the original edition).

46. P. F. Drucker, *Landmarks of Tomorrow* (New York: HarperCollins, 1959), p. 28.

47. Drucker, *Innovation and Entrepreneurship*, p. 12.

48. Drucker, *Innovation and Entrepreneurship*, p. 119.

49. Drucker, *Managing for the Future*, p. 271.

50. P. F. Drucker, *The Age of Discontinuity: Guidelines to Our Changing Society* (New York: Harper-Collins, 1968), p. 57.

51. Drucker, *Innovation and Entrepreneurship*, p. 169.

Chapter Twelve

1. P. F. Drucker, *The Age of Discontinuity: Guidelines to Our Changing Society* (New York: Harper-Collins, 1968), pp. 263–267.

2. P. F. Drucker, "Work and Tools," *Technology and Culture* (Winter 1959), p. 30.

3. P. F. Drucker, "The First Technological Revolution and Its Lessons," *Technology and Culture* (Spring 1966), pp. 143–151.

4. P. F. Drucker, *Managing in Turbulent Times* (New York: HarperCollins, 1980), p. 50.

5. P. F. Drucker, *Technology, Management and Society* (New York: HarperCollins, 1958; reprint, New York: HarperCollins, 1977), p. 179 (page citations are to the original edition).

6. P. F. Drucker, "Technological Trends in the Twentieth Century," in M. Kranzberg and C. Purcell Jr. (eds.), *Technology in Western Civilization*, Vol. 2 (New York: Oxford University Press, 1967), pp. 18–19.

7. P. F. Drucker, *The Changing World of the Executive* (New York: Truman Talley Books, Times Books, 1982), p. 145.

8. P. F. Drucker, *Adventures of a Bystander* (New York: HarperCollins, 1978; reprint, New York: HarperCollins, 1991), pp. 259–260 (page citations are to the original edition).

9. P. F. Drucker, "Management and the World's Work," *Harvard Business Review* (Sept.–Oct. 1988), p. 60.

10. P. F. Drucker, *Post-Capitalist Society* (New York: HarperCollins, 1993), p. 3.

11. Drucker, *Post-Capitalist Society*, p. 42.

12. T. G. Harris, "The Post-Capitalist Executive: An Interview with Peter F. Drucker," *Harvard Business Review* (May–June 1993), p. 118.

13. Conversation with the author.

14. Drucker, *Post-Capitalist Society,* p. 85.

15. Drucker, *Age of Discontinuity,* pp. 326–327, 281.

16. Drucker, *Age of Discontinuity,* pp. 273–274.

17. Drucker, *Age of Discontinuity,* p. 274.

18. P. F. Drucker, *The Practice of Management* (New York: HarperCollins, 1954), p. 295.

19. P. F. Drucker, *Managing for the Future: The 1990's and Beyond* (New York: Truman Talley Books, Dutton, 1992), p. 334.

20. Drucker, *Post-Capitalist Society,* p. 42.

21. Drucker, *Managing in Turbulent Times,* p. 26.

22. Drucker, *Post-Capitalist Society,* p. 65.

23. Drucker, *Age of Discontinuity,* p. 269.

24. Drucker, "Management and the World's Work," p. 67.

25. Drucker, *Age of Discontinuity,* p. 290.

26. P. F. Drucker, "The New Society of Organizations," *Harvard Business Review* (Sept.–Oct. 1992), p. 101.

27. P. F. Drucker, *The Ecological Vision: Reflections on the American Condition* (New Brunswick, N.J.: Transaction, 1993), p. 148.

28. Conversation with the author.

29. Harris, "Post-Capitalist Executive," pp. 117–120.

30. P. F. Drucker, "The New Productivity Challenge," *Harvard Business Review* (Nov.–Dec. 1991), p. 77.

31. Drucker, "New Productivity Challenge," pp. 75–77.

32. P. F. Drucker, *Management: Tasks, Responsibilities, Practices* (New York: HarperCollins, 1973), p. 183.

33. Drucker, *Management: Tasks, Responsibilities, Practices,* p. 183.

34. Drucker, *Practice of Management,* pp. 292–293.

35. Drucker, *Management: Tasks, Responsibilities, Practices,* pp. 180–183.

36. Drucker, *Management: Tasks, Responsibilities, Practices,* p. 179.

37. Drucker, *Management: Tasks, Responsibilities, Practices,* p. 187.

38. Drucker, *Management: Tasks, Responsibilities, Practices,* pp. 188–189.

39. Drucker, *Management: Tasks, Responsibilities, Practices,* p. 191.

40. Drucker, *Management: Tasks, Responsibilities, Practices,* pp. 192–193.

41. Drucker, *Management: Tasks, Responsibilities, Practices,* p. 160.

42. P. F. Drucker, "Tomorrow's Restless Managers," *Industry Week* (Apr. 18, 1988), pp. 25–27.

43. Drucker, *Management: Tasks, Responsibilities, Practices,* p. 194.

Chapter Thirteen

1. E. Hall, "A Conversation with Peter F. Drucker," *Psychology Today* (Dec. 1982), p. 62.

2. Conversation with the author.

3. P. F. Drucker, "New Age Sessions Are Same Old Brainwashing," *Wall Street Journal* (Feb. 9, 1989).

4. P. F. Drucker, *Post-Capitalist Society* (New York: HarperCollins, 1993), pp. 204–218.

5. P. F. Drucker, "Getting Things Done: How to Make People Decisions," *Harvard Business Review* (July–Aug. 1985), pp. 22–25.

6. Drucker, "New Age Sessions."

7. M. H. Hall, "The Psychology of Managing Management," *Psychology Today* (Mar. 1968), p. 23.

8. Drucker, "New Age Sessions."

9. Drucker, "New Age Sessions."

10. Hall, "Conversation with Peter F. Drucker," p. 62.

11. P. F. Drucker, *Management: Tasks, Responsibilities, Practices* (New York: HarperCollins, 1973), p. 234.

12. Drucker, *Management: Tasks, Responsibilities, Practices*, pp. 232–234.

13. T. G. Harris, "The Post-Capitalist Executive: An Interview with Peter F. Drucker," *Harvard Business Review* (May–June 1993), p. 118.

14. Drucker, *Management: Tasks, Responsibilities, Practices*, p. 234.

15. P. F. Drucker, *Adventures of a Bystander* (New York: HarperCollins, 1978; reprint, New York: HarperCollins, 1991), p. 263 (page citations are to the original edition).

16. T. Murray, "Peter Drucker Attacks: Our Top-Heavy Corporations," *Dun's* (Apr. 1971), p. 41.

17. P. F. Drucker, *The Effective Executive* (New York: HarperCollins, 1967), p. 21.

18. J. J. Tarrant, *Drucker: The Man Who Invented the Corporate Society* (Boston: Cahners Books, 1976), p. 259.

19. Drucker, "New Age Sessions."

20. Drucker, *Management: Tasks, Responsibilities, Practices*, p. 244.

21. Tarrant, *Drucker*, p. 261.

22. Tarrant, *Drucker*, p. 260.

23. Conversation with the author.

24. Drucker, *Management: Tasks, Responsibilities, Practices*, p. 244.

25. Drucker, *Management: Tasks, Responsibilities, Practices*, p. 244.

26. Drucker, *Management: Tasks, Responsibilities, Practices*, p. 244.

27. P. F. Drucker, "Management: The Problems of Success," *Academy of Management Executive* (Feb. 1987), p. 18.

28. Hall, "Conversation with Peter F. Drucker," p. 62.

29. Hall, "Conversation with Peter F. Drucker," p. 62.

30. Murray, "Peter Drucker Attacks," p. 40.

31. Hall, "Conversation with Peter F. Drucker," p. 62.

32. Drucker, *Post-Capitalist Society*, pp. 62–65.

33. Drucker, *Management: Tasks, Responsibilities, Practices*, p. 237.

34. P. F. Drucker, *The Practice of Management* (New York: HarperCollins, 1954), p. 303.

35. Murray, "Peter Drucker Attacks," p. 41.

36. Drucker, *Management: Tasks, Responsibilities, Practices*, p. 240.

37. W. Kaufmann (ed.), *Philosophic Classics*, Vol. 2: *Bacon to Kant* (Englewood Cliffs, N.J.: Prentice Hall, 1962), pp. 102–103.
38. Drucker, *Management: Tasks, Responsibilities, Practices*, p. 238.
39. Drucker, *Management: Tasks, Responsibilities, Practices*, p. 239.
40. Drucker, *Practice of Management*, p. 287.
41. Hall, "Conversation with Peter F. Drucker," p. 66.
42. P. F. Drucker, "Teaching the Work of Management," *New Management* (Fall 1988), p. 5.
43. Drucker, *Post-Capitalist Society*, p. 99.
44. P. F. Drucker, *The Changing World of the Executive* (New York: Truman Talley Books, Times Books, 1982), pp. 235–236.
45. Drucker, *Changing World of the Executive*, pp. 254–256.
46. P. F. Drucker, "The Unfashionable Kierkegaard," *Sewanee Review* (Oct. 1949), p. 588.
47. Drucker, "Unfashionable Kierkegaard," p. 590.
48. Drucker, "Unfashionable Kierkegaard," p. 591.
49. Drucker, "Teaching the Work of Management," p. 5.

Chapter Fourteen

1. R. Lenzer and S. S. Johnson, "Seeing Things as They Really Are," *Forbes* (Mar. 10, 1997), p. 126.
2. P. F. Drucker, "Leadership: More Doing Than Dash," *Wall Street Journal* (Jan. 6, 1981), p. 14.
3. P. F. Drucker, *Management: Tasks, Responsibilities, Practices* (New York: HarperCollins, 1973), p. 455.
4. Drucker, "Leadership: More Doing Than Dash."
5. P. F. Drucker, *Post-Capitalist Society* (New York: HarperCollins, 1993), pp. 62–67.
6. P. F. Drucker, "The Mystery of the Business Leader," *Wall Street Journal* (Sept. 29, 1987).
7. P. F. Drucker, *The New Realities: In Government and Politics / In Economics and Business / In Society and World View* (New York: HarperCollins, 1989), p. 109.
8. P. F. Drucker, *The Practice of Management* (New York: HarperCollins, 1954), pp. 169–170; *Technology, Management and Society* (New York: HarperCollins, 1958; reprint, New York: HarperCollins, 1977), p. 156 (page citations are to the original edition).
9. P. F. Drucker, *The New Society: The Anatomy of Industrial Order* (New York: HarperCollins, 1950), pp. 210–211.
10. A. Bennett, "Management Guru," *Wall Street Journal* (July 28, 1987).
11. Drucker, *Practice of Management*, p. 159.
12. Drucker, "Leadership: More Doing Than Dash."
13. Drucker, *Practice of Management*, p. 159.
14. Drucker, *Post-Capitalist Society*, pp. 106–109.
15. Conversation with the author.
16. P. F. Drucker, Foreword, in F. Hesselbein, M. Goldsmith, and R. Beckhard (eds.), *The Leader of the Future: New Visions, Strategies, and Practices for the Next Era* (San Francisco: Jossey-Bass, 1996), p. xii.

17. Drucker, Foreword, p. xii.

18. Drucker, Foreword, p. xi.

19. Drucker, "Leadership: More Doing Than Dash," p. 14.

20. Conversation with the author.

21. Drucker, *Practice of Management,* pp. 157–158.

22. P. F. Drucker, "What Business Can Learn from Non-Profits," *Harvard Business Review* (July–Aug. 1989), pp. 88–93.

23. P. F. Drucker, *Managing the Non-Profit Organization: Principles and Practices* (New York: HarperCollins, 1990), p. 59.

24. R. Donkin, "Interview with Peter Drucker," *Financial Times* (June 14, 1996), p. 12.

25. P. Schwartz and K. Kelley, "A Cantankerous Interview with Peter Schwartz and Kevin Kelley," *Wired* (Aug. 1996), p. 119.

26. P. F. Drucker, "The New Productivity Challenge," *Harvard Business Review* (Nov.–Dec. 1991), p. 79.

27. P. F. Drucker, "Teaching the Work of Management," *New Management* (Fall 1988), p. 4.

28. Drucker, "Leadership: More Doing Than Dash."

29. Drucker, *Management: Tasks, Responsibilities, Practices,* p. 462.

30. P. F. Drucker, *The Effective Executive* (New York: HarperCollins, 1967), pp. 21–23.

31. Drucker, *Management: Tasks, Responsibilities, Practices,* p. 266.

32. M. H. Hall, "The Psychology of Managing Management," *Psychology Today* (Mar. 1968), p. 22.

33. P. F. Drucker, *The Changing World of the Executive* (New York: Truman Talley Books, Times Books, 1982), p. 3.

34. Drucker, *Practice of Management,* p. 295.

35. P. F. Drucker, "The Theory of the Business," *Harvard Business Review* (Sept.–Oct. 1994), p. 98.

36. Drucker, "Theory of the Business," p. 101.

37. P. F. Drucker, *An Introductory View of Management* (New York: HarperCollins, 1977), pp. 243–247.

38. Conversation with the author.

39. Drucker, *Effective Executive,* p. 169.

40. Drucker, *Effective Executive,* pp. 20–21.

41. Drucker, *Effective Executive,* p. 78.

42. Drucker, *Effective Executive,* p. 96.

43. Drucker, *Effective Executive,* p. 23.

44. Drucker, *Effective Executive,* p. 1.

45. J. J. Tarrant, *Drucker: The Man Who Invented the Corporate Society* (Boston: Cahners Books, 1976), p. 257.

46. Drucker, *Effective Executive,* p. 18.

47. Drucker, *Effective Executive,* p. 12.

48. Conversation with the author.

49. Drucker, *Effective Executive,* pp. 9–18.

50. Drucker, *Effective Executive,* p. 10.

51. Drucker, *Post-Capitalist Society*, p. 193.
52. Drucker, *Post-Capitalist Society*, p. vii.

Chapter Fifteen

1. T. Murray, "Peter Drucker Attacks: Our Top-Heavy Corporations," *Dun's* (Apr. 1971), p. 41.
2. P. F. Drucker, *The Ecological Vision: Reflections on the American Condition* (New Brunswick, N.J.: Transaction, 1993), p. 347.
3. P. F. Drucker, "The Coming of the New Organization," *Harvard Business Review* (Jan.–Feb. 1988), p. 40.
4. P. F. Drucker, *An Introductory View of Management* (New York: HarperCollins, 1977), p. 348.
5. P. F. Drucker, *Post-Capitalist Society* (New York: HarperCollins, 1993), p. 91.
6. Drucker, *Introductory View*, p. 333.
7. P. F. Drucker, *The Effective Executive* (New York: HarperCollins, 1967), p. 12.
8. Conversation with the author; Drucker, *Effective Executive*, pp. 2–6.
9. Conversation with the author.
10. P. F. Drucker, *Management: Tasks, Responsibilities, Practices* (New York: HarperCollins, 1973), p. 279.
11. P. F. Drucker, "Management's New Paradigms," *Forbes* (Oct. 5, 1998), p. 164.
12. Drucker, *Effective Executive*, p. 66.
13. Drucker, *Introductory View*, p. 332.
14. Drucker, *Effective Executive*, p. 169.
15. Drucker, *Introductory View*, p. 263.
16. P. F. Drucker, *Men, Ideas and Politics* (New York: HarperCollins, 1971), p. 97.
17. Drucker, *Effective Executive*, pp. 63–64.
18. Drucker, *Introductory View*, pp. 333–335; *Effective Executive*, p. 43.
19. Drucker, *Effective Executive*, pp. 53–70.
20. P. F. Drucker "Management and the World's Work," *Harvard Business Review* (Sept.–Oct. 1988), p. 76.
21. Drucker, *Management: Tasks, Responsibilities, Practices*, p. 308.
22. P. F. Drucker, "Professionals' Productivity," *Across the Board* (Nov.–Dec. 1993), p. 1.
23. P. F. Drucker, "The New Society of Organizations," *Harvard Business Review* (Sept.–Oct. 1992), p. 101.
24. Drucker, "Professionals' Productivity," p. 3.
25. P. F. Drucker, *The New Realities: In Government and Politics / In Economics and Business / In Society and World View* (New York: HarperCollins, 1989), pp. 212–213.
26. Drucker, "Coming of the New Organization," p. 48.
27. Drucker, *Effective Executive*, p. 96.
28. P. F. Drucker, *The Changing World of the Executive* (New York: Truman Talley Books, Times Books, 1982), p. 162.

29. Drucker, *Effective Executive*, p. 93.

30. P. F. Drucker, "How to Manage the Boss," *Wall Street Journal* (Aug. 1, 1981).

31. P. F. Drucker, *Managing for the Future: The 1990's and Beyond* (New York: Truman Talley Books, Dutton, 1992), p. 166.

32. Drucker, *Effective Executive*, pp. 93–97.

33. Drucker, *Introductory View*, p. 333.

34. T. G. Harris, "The Post-Capitalist Executive: An Interview with Peter F. Drucker," *Harvard Business Review* (May–June 1993), p. 119.

35. Drucker, *Effective Executive*, pp. 61–63.

36. Drucker, "Coming of the New Organization," p. 49.

37. P. F. Drucker, "Why Automation Pays Off," *Wall Street Journal* (Sept. 30, 1985).

38. P. F. Drucker, "Be Data Literate: Know What to Know," *Wall Street Journal* (Dec. 1, 1992).

39. P. F. Drucker, *Innovation and Entrepreneurship: Practice and Principles* (New York: Harper-Collins, 1985), p. 157.

40. Drucker, *New Realities*, p. 212.

41. P. F. Drucker, "New Templates for Today's Organization," *Harvard Business Review* (Jan.–Feb. 1974), p. 53.

42. Drucker, *Post-Capitalist Society*, pp. 86–87.

43. P. F. Drucker, *Managing in a Time of Great Change* (New York: Truman Talley Books, Dutton, 1995), p. 99.

44. Drucker, *Post-Capitalist Society*, p. 87.

45. Drucker, *Managing in a Time of Great Change*, p. 100.

46. P. F. Drucker, *The Frontiers of Management: Where Tomorrow's Decisions Are Being Shaped Today* (New York: Truman Talley Books, Dutton, 1986; reprint, New York: Perennial Library, 1987), p. 206 (page citations are to the original edition).

47. Drucker, *Managing in a Time of Great Change*, p. 101.

48. Drucker, *Ecological Vision*, p. 350.

49. Drucker, *Managing for the Future*, p. 198.

50. Drucker, "New Society of Organizations," p. 95.

51. Drucker, *Managing for the Future*, p. 201.

52. Drucker, *Management: Tasks, Responsibilities, Practices*, p. 94.

53. J. Flower, "Being Effective: A Conversation with Peter Drucker," *Health Care Forum Journal* (May–June 1991), p. 53.

54. Drucker, *Effective Executive*, pp. 101–102.

55. Drucker, *Effective Executive*, p. 112.

56. Drucker, *Management: Tasks, Responsibilities, Practices*, p. 271.

57. P. F. Drucker, *The Age of Discontinuity: Guidelines to Our Changing Society* (New York: Harper-Collins, 1968), p. 193.

58. P. F. Drucker, *Adventures of a Bystander* (New York: HarperCollins, 1978; reprint, New York: HarperCollins, 1991), p. 255 (page citations are to the original edition).

59. Drucker, *New Realities*, p. 215.

Chapter Sixteen

1. Saint Augustine, Bishop of Hippo, *The Confessions of Saint Augustine* (New York: Modern Library, 1941), p. 256.
2. Augustine, *Confessions,* p. 258.
3. P. F. Drucker, *The Effective Executive* (New York: HarperCollins, 1967), p. 26.
4. Drucker, *Effective Executive,* p. 10.
5. Conversation with the author.
6. Drucker, *Effective Executive,* p. 51.
7. P. F. Drucker, *The Practice of Management* (New York: HarperCollins, 1954), p. 44.
8. R. Lenzer and S. S. Johnson, "Seeing Things as They Really Are," *Forbes* (Mar. 10, 1997), p. 124.
9. Drucker, *Effective Executive,* p. 45.
10. P. F. Drucker, "The New Productivity Challenge," *Harvard Business Review* (Nov.–Dec. 1991), p. 74.
11. Conversation with the author; Drucker, *Effective Executive,* pp. 37–38.
12. Conversation with the author.
13. Drucker, *Effective Executive,* p. 73.
14. R. Poe, "A Walk and Talk with Peter Drucker," *Across the Board* (Feb. 1983), p. 39.
15. P. F. Drucker, "The Information Executives Truly Need," *Harvard Business Review* (Jan.–Feb. 1995), p. 59.
16. Drucker, *Effective Executive,* p. 99.
17. Drucker, *Practice of Management,* pp. 277–282.
18. P. F. Drucker, *Managing in Turbulent Times* (New York: HarperCollins, 1980), p. 65.
19. Drucker, *Effective Executive,* p. 71.
20. P. F. Drucker, *Management: Tasks, Responsibilities, Practices* (New York: HarperCollins, 1973), p. 233.
21. M. Johnson, "Drucker Speaks His Mind," *Management Review* (Oct. 1995), p. 14.
22. Drucker, *Management: Tasks, Responsibilities, Practices,* p. 457.
23. P. F. Drucker, *Managing in a Time of Great Change* (New York: Truman Talley Books, Dutton, 1995), p. 86.
24. Drucker, *Effective Executive,* p. 84.
25. P. F. Drucker, "Getting Things Done: How to Make People Decisions," *Harvard Business Review* (July–Aug. 1985), p. 21.
26. Drucker, *Effective Executive,* p. 86.
27. Drucker, "Getting Things Done," p. 22; *The Changing World of the Executive* (New York: Truman Talley Books, Times Books, 1982), p. 12.
28. Drucker, *Effective Executive,* pp. 89–91.
29. Drucker, *Effective Executive,* p. 79.
30. P. F. Drucker, *Adventures of a Bystander* (New York: HarperCollins, 1978; reprint, New York: HarperCollins, 1991), p. 75 (page citations are to the original edition).

31. T. G. Harris, "The Post-Capitalist Executive: An Interview with Peter F. Drucker," *Harvard Business Review* (May–June 1993), p. 117.

32. P. F. Drucker, "Keeping U.S. Companies Productive," *Journal of Business Strategy* (Winter 1987), p. 15.

33. J. Flower, "Being Effective: A Conversation with Peter Drucker," *Health Care Forum Journal* (May–June 1991), p. 53.

34. P. F. Drucker, *The New Realities: In Government and Politics / In Economics and Business / In Society and World View* (New York: HarperCollins, 1989), p. 229.

35. P. F. Drucker, *Technology, Management and Society* (New York: HarperCollins, 1958; reprint, New York: HarperCollins, 1977), p. 5 (page citations are to the original edition).

36. Drucker, *Management: Tasks, Responsibilities, Practices*, p. 490.

37. P. F. Drucker, *The Ecological Vision: Reflections on the American Condition* (New Brunswick, N.J.: Transaction, 1993), p. 332.

38. Drucker, *Technology, Management and Society*, p. 11.

39. Drucker, *Management: Tasks, Responsibilities, Practices*, p. 481.

40. Drucker, *Ecological Vision*, p. 332.

41. Drucker, *New Realities*, p. 208.

42. Drucker, *Technology, Management and Society*, pp. 174–175.

43. Drucker, *Technology, Management and Society*, p. 174.

44. Drucker, *New Realities*, p. 262.

45. Drucker, *Management: Tasks, Responsibilities, Practices*, p. 487.

46. Drucker, *Management: Tasks, Responsibilities, Practices*, p. 485.

47. Drucker, *New Realities*, p. 264.

48. Drucker, *Technology, Management and Society*, p. 7.

Chapter Seventeen

1. P. F. Drucker, *Technology, Management and Society* (New York: HarperCollins, 1958; reprint, New York: HarperCollins, 1977), p. 139 (page citations are to the original edition).

2. P. F. Drucker, "Long-Range Planning: Challenge to Management Science," *Management Science* (Apr. 1959), p. 145.

3. Drucker, *Technology, Management and Society*, p. 134.

4. P. F. Drucker, *The Effective Executive* (New York: HarperCollins, 1967), p. 143.

5. Drucker, *Technology, Management and Society*, p. 139.

6. Drucker, *Effective Executive*, p. 141.

7. Drucker, "Long-Range Planning," pp. 239–241.

8. Drucker, *Technology, Management and Society*, p. 134.

9. Drucker, "Long-Range Planning," p. 239.

10. P. F. Drucker, *Management: Tasks, Responsibilities, Practices* (New York: HarperCollins, 1973), p. 124.

11. Drucker, *Management: Tasks, Responsibilities, Practices*, p. 125.

12. Drucker, *Management: Tasks, Responsibilities, Practices,* p. 471.

13. Drucker, "Long-Range Planning," pp. 239–240.

14. Drucker, *Management: Tasks, Responsibilities, Practices,* p. 469.

15. Drucker, *Management: Tasks, Responsibilities, Practices,* p. 464.

16. P. F. Drucker, "A View of Japan Through Japanese Art," in *Toward the Next Economics, and Other Essays* (New York: HarperCollins, 1981), pp. 181–202; E. Hall, "A Conversation with Peter F. Drucker," *Psychology Today* (Dec. 1982), p. 64.

17. Drucker, "Long-Range Planning," pp. 239–240.

18. P. F. Drucker, "What We Can Learn from Japanese Management," *Harvard Business Review* (Mar.–Apr. 1971), p. 112.

19. Drucker, *Effective Executive,* p. 150.

20. Drucker, "What We Can Learn from Japanese Management," p. 112.

21. P. F. Drucker, "Behind Japan's Success," *Harvard Business Review* (Jan.–Feb. 1981), p. 87.

22. Drucker, *Management: Tasks, Responsibilities, Practices,* p. 472.

23. Drucker, *Effective Executive,* p. 148.

24. Drucker, *Management: Tasks, Responsibilities, Practices,* p. 469.

25. Drucker, *Management: Tasks, Responsibilities, Practices,* p. 469.

26. Drucker, *Effective Executive,* p. 33.

27. Drucker, "What We Can Learn from Japanese Management," pp. 119–121.

28. Drucker, "What We Can Learn from Japanese Management," p. 110.

29. Drucker, *Management: Tasks, Responsibilities, Practices,* p. 471.

30. Drucker, *Management: Tasks, Responsibilities, Practices,* p. 472.

31. Drucker, *Effective Executive,* p. 157.

32. Drucker, *Management: Tasks, Responsibilities, Practices,* p. 480.

33. Drucker, *Effective Executive,* p. 139.

34. P. F. Drucker, *Landmarks of Tomorrow* (New York: HarperCollins, 1959), p. 28; *Post-Capitalist Society* (New York: HarperCollins, 1993), p. 193.

35. Drucker, *Effective Executive,* p. 134.

36. Drucker, *Effective Executive,* pp. 124–125.

37. Drucker, *Effective Executive,* p. 41.

38. Drucker, *Effective Executive,* p. 123.

39. P. F. Drucker, *The Age of Discontinuity: Guidelines to Our Changing Society* (New York: HarperCollins, 1968), p. 195.

40. Drucker, *Effective Executive,* p. 109.

41. Drucker, *Effective Executive,* p. 111.

42. Drucker, *Management: Tasks, Responsibilities, Practices,* p. 476.

43. Drucker, *Effective Executive,* p. 155.

44. P. F. Drucker, *An Introductory View of Management* (New York: HarperCollins, 1977), p. 292.

45. Drucker, *Introductory View,* pp. 338–339.

46. Drucker, "Long-Range Planning," p. 242.

47. P. F. Drucker, *Managing for Results: Economic Tasks and Risk-Taking Decisions* (New York: HarperCollins, 1964), p. 191.

Conclusion

1. P. F. Drucker, *The Ecological Vision: Reflections on the American Condition* (New Brunswick, N.J.: Transaction, 1993), p. 441.
2. T. Levitt, "A View of 'Management,'" *Business Week* (Feb. 9, 1974), p. 51.

PUBLISHED WORK OF PETER DRUCKER

Books

Friedrich Julius Stahl, Konservative Mtaatslehre & Geschichtliche Entwichlung. Tübingen: Mohr, 1933.

The End of Economic Man. New York: John Day, 1939. (Reprint, New York: Harper-Collins, 1969.)

The Future of Industrial Man. New York: John Day, 1942.

Concept of the Corporation. New York: John Day, 1946. (Reprint, New York: Mentor, 1972.)

The New Society: The Anatomy of Industrial Order. New York: HarperCollins, 1950.

The Practice of Management. New York: HarperCollins, 1954.

America's Next Twenty Years. New York: HarperCollins, 1955.

Technology, Management and Society: Essays by Peter Drucker. New York: HarperCollins, 1958. (Reprint, New York: HarperCollins, 1977.)

Landmarks of Tomorrow. New York: HarperCollins, 1959.

Managing for Results: Economic Tasks and Risk-Taking Decisions. New York: HarperCollins, 1964.

The Effective Executive. New York: HarperCollins, 1967.

The Age of Discontinuity: Guidelines to Our Changing Society. New York: HarperCollins, 1968.

(Ed.) *Preparing Tomorrow's Business Leaders Today.* Englewood Cliffs, N.J.: Prentice Hall, 1969.

Men, Ideas and Politics. New York: HarperCollins, 1971.

Management: Tasks, Responsibilities, Practices. New York: HarperCollins, 1973.

The Unseen Revolution: How Pension Fund Socialism Came to America. New York: Harper-Collins, 1976.

An Introductory View of Management. New York: HarperCollins, 1977.

Management Cases. New York: Harper's College Press, 1977.

People and Performance: The Best of Peter Drucker on Management. New York: Harper's College Press, 1977.

Adventures of a Bystander. New York: HarperCollins, 1978. (Reprint, New York: HarperCollins, 1991.)

Managing in Turbulent Times. New York: HarperCollins, 1980.

Toward the Next Economics, and Other Essays. New York: HarperCollins, 1981.

The Changing World of the Executive. New York: Truman Talley Books, Times Books, 1982.

The Last of All Possible Worlds: A Novel. New York: HarperCollins, 1982.

Concept of the Corporation. (2nd ed.) New York: New American Library, 1983.

Innovation and Entrepreneurship: Practice and Principles. New York: HarperCollins, 1985.

The Frontiers of Management: Where Tomorrow's Decisions Are Being Shaped Today. New York: Truman Talley Books, Dutton, 1986. (Reprint, New York: Perennial Library, 1987.)

The New Realities: In Government and Politics / In Economics and Business / In Society and World View. New York: HarperCollins, 1989.

Managing the Non-Profit Organization: Principles and Practices. New York: HarperCollins, 1990.

Drucker in the Harvard Business Review. Boston: Harvard Business School Press, 1991.

Managing for the Future: The 1990s and Beyond. New York: Truman Talley Books, Dutton, 1992.

The Ecological Vision: Reflections on the American Condition. New Brunswick, N.J.: Transaction, 1993.

Post-Capitalist Society. New York: HarperCollins, 1993.

Managing in a Time of Great Change. New York: Truman Talley Books, Dutton, 1995.

With Nakauchi, I. *Drucker on Asia: A Dialogue Between Peter Drucker and Isao Nakauchi.* Newton, Mass.: Butterworth-Heinemann, 1997.

Management Challenges for the Twenty-First Century. New York: HarperCollins, 1999.

Major Articles

"What Became of the Prussian Army." *Virginia Quarterly Review,* Jan. 1941.

"Meaning and Function of Economic Function Today." *Review of Politics,* Apr. 1943.

"Keynes, White, and Postwar Currency." *Harper's,* July 1943.

"Exit King Cotton." *Harper's,* May 1946.

"Keynes: Economics as a Magical System." *Virginia Quarterly Review,* Oct. 1946.

"Way to Industrial Peace." *Harper's,* Jan. 1946.

"Who Should Get a Raise and When?" *Harper's,* Mar. 1946.

"Henry Ford: Success and Failure." *Harper's,* July 1947.

"Key to American Politics: Calhoun's Pluralism." *Review of Politics,* Oct. 1948.

"Function of Profits." *Fortune,* Mar. 1949.

"The Unfashionable Kierkegaard." *Sewanee Review,* Oct. 1949.

"Are We Having Too Many Babies?" *Saturday Evening Post,* May 6, 1950.

"Care and Feeding of Small Business." *Harper's*, Aug. 1950.

"Mirage of Pensions." *Harper's*, Feb. 1950.

"Labor in Industrial Society." *Annals of the American Academy of Political and Social Science*, Mar. 1951.

"Frontier for This Century." *Harper's*, Mar. 1952.

"How to Be an Employee." *Fortune*, May 1952.

"Myth of American Uniformity." *Harper's*, May 1952.

"Productivity Is an Attitude." *Nation's Business*, Apr. 1952.

"The American Genius Is Political." *Perspectives U.S.A.*, Spring 1953.

"The Employee Society." *American Journal of Sociology*, Jan. 1953.

"The Liberal Discovers Big Business." *Yale Review*, June 1953.

"Today's Young People: More Responsible Than You Were." *Nation's Business*, June 1953.

"Integration of People and Planning." *Harvard Business Review*, Nov.–Dec. 1955.

"America Becomes a Have-Not Nation." *Harper's*, Apr. 1956.

"Business Objectives and Survival Needs." *Journal of Business*, Apr. 1958.

"Marketing and Economic Development." *Journal of Marketing*, Jan. 1958.

"Organized Religion and the American Creed." *Review of Politics*, July 1958.

"Long-Range Planning: Challenge to Management Science." *Management Science*, Apr. 1959.

"Potentials of Management Science." *Harvard Business Review*, Jan.–Feb. 1959.

"Work and Tools." *Technology and Culture*, Winter 1959.

"The Art of Being an Effective President." *Harper's*, Aug. 1960.

"Politics for a New Generation." *Harper's*, June–Aug. 1960.

"The Baffled Young Men of Japan." *Harper's*, Jan. 1961.

"The Technological Revolution: Notes on the Relationship of Technology, Science and Culture." *Technology and Culture*, Fall 1961.

"This Competitive World." *Harvard Business Review*, Mar.–Apr. 1961.

"Big Business and the National Purpose." *Harvard Business Review*, Mar.–Apr. 1962.

"Economy's Dark Continent." *Fortune*, Apr. 1962.

"Japan Tries for a Second Miracle." *Harper's*, Mar. 1963.

"Managing for Business Effectiveness." *Harvard Business Review*, May–June 1963.

"Twelve Fables of Research Management." *Harvard Business Review*, Jan.–Feb. 1963.

"Care and Feeding of the Profitable Product." *Fortune*, Mar. 1964.

"If I Were a Company President." *Harper's*, Apr. 1964.

"American Direction: A Forecast." *Harper's*, Feb. 1965.

"Automation Is Not the Villain." *New York Times Magazine*, Jan. 10, 1965.

"Crash New Year?" *Harper's*, June 1965.

"Is Business Letting Young People Down?" *Harvard Business Review*, Nov.–Dec. 1965.

"The First Technological Revolution and Its Lessons." *Technology and Culture*, Spring 1966.

"How to Manage Your Time." *Harper's*, Dec. 1966.

"Notes on the New Politics." *The Public Interest*, Summer 1966.

"This Romantic Generation." *Harper's*, May 1966.

"Frederick W. Taylor: The Professional Management Pioneer." *Advanced Management Journal*, Oct. 1967.

"On the Economic Basis of American Politics." *The Public Interest,* Winter 1968.

"Worker and Work in the Metropolis." *Daedalus,* Fall 1968.

"Is Technology Credible?" *Technology and Culture,* Oct. 1969.

"Management's New Role." *Harvard Business Review,* Nov.–Dec. 1969.

"The Owner and Future Manager." *Management Today,* May 1969.

"The Shame of Marketing." *Marketing Communication,* Aug. 1969.

"The Sickness of Government." *Nation's Business,* Mar. 1969.

"The Surprising Seventies." *Harper's,* July and Sept. 1971.

"What We Can Learn from Japanese Management." *Harvard Business Review,* Mar.–Apr. 1971.

"How Best to Protect the Environment." *Reader's Digest,* Mar. 1972.

"How to Make the Presidency Manageable." *Fortune,* Nov. 1974.

"Multinationals and Developing Countries: Myths and Realities." *Foreign Affairs,* Oct. 1974.

"New Templates for Today's Organization." *Harvard Business Review,* Jan.–Feb. 1974.

"Managing the Knowledge Worker." *Wall Street Journal,* Nov. 7, 1975.

"Six Durable Economic Myths." *Wall Street Journal,* Sept. 6, 1975.

"Japan: The Problems of Success." *Foreign Affairs,* Apr. 1978.

"Monster and the Lamb." (Excerpt from *Adventures of a Bystander.*) *Atlantic,* Dec. 1978.

"Science and Industry: Challenges of Antagonistic Interdependence." (Adaptation of an address.) *Science,* May 25, 1979.

"Why Management Consultants?" In M. Zimet and R. G. Greenwood (eds.), *The Evolving Science of Management.* New York: AMACOM, 1979.

"Japan Gets Ready for Tougher Times." *Fortune,* Nov. 3, 1980.

"Behind Japan's Success." *Harvard Business Review,* Jan.–Feb. 1981.

"Education: The Crisis Is the Same Everywhere." *Christianity Today,* June 12, 1981.

"Ethical Chic." *Forbes,* Sept. 14, 1981.

"How to Manage the Boss." *Wall Street Journal,* Aug. 1, 1981.

"Leadership: More Doing Than Dash." *Wall Street Journal,* Jan. 6, 1981.

"Why Some Mergers Work and Many More Don't." *Forbes,* Jan. 18, 1982.

"Schumpeter and Keynes." *Forbes,* May 23, 1983.

"Thomas Watson's Principles of Modern Management." *Esquire,* Dec. 1983.

"Business Innovation: Our Entrepreneurial Economy." *Current,* May 1984.

"Getting Things Done: How to Make People Decisions." *Harvard Business Review,* July–Aug. 1985.

"Why Automation Pays Off." *Wall Street Journal,* Sept. 30, 1985.

"The Changed World Economy." *Foreign Affairs,* Spring 1986.

"Japan's Choices." *Foreign Affairs,* Summer 1987.

"Keeping U.S. Companies Productive." *Journal of Business Strategy,* Winter 1987.

"Management: The Problems of Success." *Academy of Management Executive,* Feb. 1987.

"The Mystery of the Business Leader." *Wall Street Journal,* Sept. 29, 1987.

"Business of the Future." *Current,* July 1988.

"The Coming of the New Organization." *Harvard Business Review,* Jan.–Feb. 1988.

"Management and the World's Work." *Harvard Business Review,* Sept.–Oct. 1988.

"Take Me to Your Leader." *Inc.,* Feb. 1988.

"Teaching the Work of Management." *New Management,* Fall 1988.

"Tomorrow's Restless Managers." *Industry Week,* Apr. 18, 1988.

"How Schools Must Change." *Psychology Today,* May 1989.

"New Age Sessions Are Same Old Brainwashing." *Wall Street Journal,* Feb. 9, 1989.

"The New World According to Drucker" (with Niles Howard). *Business Monthly,* May 1989.

"Peter Drucker Asks." *Industry Week,* Mar. 20, 1989.

"Peter Drucker's 1990s." *Economist,* Oct. 21, 1989.

"The Post-Business Knowledge Society Begins." *Industry Week,* Apr. 17, 1989.

"Sell the Mailroom." *Wall Street Journal,* July 25, 1989.

"What Business Can Learn from Non-Profits." *Harvard Business Review,* July–Aug. 1989.

"After Protection, a Time for Risks." *New York Times Magazine,* June 10, 1990.

"The Best Book on Management Ever." *Fortune,* Apr. 23, 1990.

"The Emerging Theory of Manufacturing." *Harvard Business Review,* May–June 1990.

"The Limits of Government." *Design for Arts in Education,* Mar.–Apr. 1990.

"Making Managers of Communism's Bureaucrats." *Wall Street Journal,* Aug. 15, 1990.

"The Third Sector: America's Non Market Counterculture." *New Perspectives Quarterly,* Spring 1990.

"A Better Way to Pay for College." *Wall Street Journal,* May 9, 1991.

"The Big Three Miss Japan's Crucial Lesson." *Wall Street Journal,* June 18, 1991.

"Business of Bureaucracy." *Society,* Sept.–Oct. 1991.

"Don't Change Corporate Culture: Use It!" *Wall Street Journal,* Mar. 28, 1991.

"How to Be Competitive Though Big." *Wall Street Journal,* Feb. 7, 1991.

"It Profits Us to Strengthen Our Profits." *Wall Street Journal,* Dec. 19, 1991.

"Japan: New Strategies for a New Reality." *Wall Street Journal,* Oct. 2, 1991.

"The New Productivity Challenge." *Harvard Business Review,* Nov.–Dec. 1991.

"Our Irritable Friend." (Book review of *The Japan That Can Say No.*) *New York Times Book Review,* Jan. 13, 1991.

"Reckoning with the Pension Fund Revolution." *Harvard Business Review,* Mar.–Apr. 1991.

"Secrets of the U.S. Export Boom." *Wall Street Journal,* Aug. 1, 1991.

"The Accountable School." *Director,* Dec. 1992.

"Be Data Literate: Know What to Know." *Wall Street Journal,* Dec. 1, 1992.

"Beyond the Blue-Collar Worker." *Modern Office Technology,* Dec. 1992.

"Doing Good in Challenging Times" (with Richard Steckel). *Wilson Library Bulletin,* Dec. 1992.

"The Economy's Power Shift." *Wall Street Journal,* Sept. 24, 1992.

"Focusing on the New World Economy." *Modern Office Technology,* Nov. 1992.

"The Future Is Already Around Us." *Modern Office Technology,* Oct. 1992.

"How '90s Changes Will Affect Business." *San Francisco Chronicle,* Mar. 23, 1992.

"The New Society of Organizations." *Harvard Business Review,* Sept.–Oct. 1992.

"Planning for Uncertainty." *Wall Street Journal,* July 22, 1992.

"The Post-Capitalist World." *Public Interest,* Fall 1992.

"Productivity Will Be Challenge of '90s." *San Francisco Chronicle,* Mar. 30, 1992.

"Reflections of a Social Ecologist." *Society*, May–June 1992.

"There's More Than One Kind of Team." *Wall Street Journal*, Feb. 11, 1992.

"Where the New Markets Are." *Wall Street Journal*, Apr. 9, 1992.

"China's Growth Area: The Service Sector." *Wall Street Journal*, Mar. 3, 1993.

"The End of Japan Inc.?" *Foreign Affairs*, Spring 1993.

"The Five Deadly Business Sins." *Wall Street Journal*, Oct. 21, 1993.

"Japan Inc.'s Shaky Future." *Harper's*, July 1993.

"Plan Now for the Future." *Modern Office Technology*, Mar. 1993.

"The Post-Capitalist World." *Current*, Feb. 1993.

"Professionals' Productivity." *Across the Board*, Nov.–Dec. 1993.

"Restructuring Middle Management." *Modern Office Technology*, Jan. 1993.

"The Retail Revolution." *Wall Street Journal*, July 15, 1993.

"Retailing in a Post-Capitalist Society." *Stores Magazine*, Aug. 1993.

"The Rise of the Knowledge Society." *Wilson Quarterly*, Spring 1993.

"Seeking Financial Accountability." *Modern Office Technology*, Feb. 1993.

"Six Rules for Presidents." *Wall Street Journal*, Sept. 22, 1993.

"Tomorrow's Manager." *Success*, Oct. 1993.

"A Turnaround Primer." *Wall Street Journal*, Feb. 2, 1993.

"We Need to Measure, Not Count." *Wall Street Journal*, Apr. 13, 1993.

"The Age of Social Transformation." *Atlantic Monthly*, Nov. 1994.

"The Continuing Feminist Experiment." *Wall Street Journal*, Oct. 17, 1994.

"Five Questions." *Executive Excellence*, Nov. 1994.

"How to Save the Family Business." *Wall Street Journal*, Aug. 19, 1994.

"Infoliteracy." *Forbes*, Aug. 29, 1994.

"The New Superpower." *Wall Street Journal*, Dec. 20, 1994.

"Political Correctness and American Academe." *Society*, Nov.–Dec. 1994.

"The Theory of the Business." *Harvard Business Review*, Sept.–Oct. 1994.

"Trade Lessons from the World Economy." *Foreign Affairs*, Jan.–Feb. 1994.

"A Weak Dollar Strengthens Japan." *Wall Street Journal*, Nov. 22, 1994.

"Deep Beneath a Hurricane-Tormented Sea: Social Currents at Work." *Houston Chronicle*, Jan. 1, 1995.

"From Stalinism to Multiculturalism: Political Correctiveness and American Academe." *Current*, Feb. 1995.

"The Information Executives Truly Need." *Harvard Business Review*, Jan.–Feb. 1995.

Introduction. In P. Graham (ed.), *Mary Parker Follett: Prophet of Management*. Boston: Harvard Business School Press, 1995.

"The Network Society." *Wall Street Journal*, Mar. 29, 1995.

"Drucker's Challenge for CMAs." *Managing Accounting Magazine*, June 1995.

"Noted." *Training*, June 1995.

"Paying Attention." *World Business*, Spring 1995.

"Really Inventing Government." *Atlantic Monthly*, Feb. 1995.

"Rethinking Work." *Executive Excellence*, Feb. 1995.

"Five Years Ago in *The Corporate Board*." *The Corporate Board,* May–June, 1996.

Foreword. In F. Hesselbein, M. Goldsmith, and R. Beckhard (eds.), *The Leader of the Future: New Visions, Strategies, and Practices for the Next Era.* San Francisco: Jossey-Bass, 1996.

"Leaders Are Doers." *Executive Excellence,* Apr. 1996.

"Management Is Not a Technique." *Across the Board,* Jan. 1996.

"Not Enough Generals Were Killed!" *Forbes,* Apr. 8, 1996.

"Management's New Paradigms." *Forbes,* Oct. 5, 1998.

BIBLIOGRAPHY

Augustine, Saint, Bishop of Hippo. *The Confessions of Saint Augustine.* New York: Modern Library, 1941.

Barzun, J. "A Vision for Free Men." *The New Republic,* Oct. 26, 1942.

Baumol, W., and Blinder, A. *Macroeconomics: Principles and Policy.* Orlando: Harcourt Brace, 1997.

Bennett, A. "Management Guru." *Wall Street Journal,* July 28, 1987.

Burnham, J. *The Managerial Revolution.* New York: John Day, 1941.

Byrne, J. A. "Is Research in the Ivory Tower 'Fuzzy, Irrelevant, Pretentious'?" *Business Week,* Oct. 29, 1990.

Byrne, J. A. "Management's New Gurus." *Business Week,* Aug. 31, 1992.

Byrne, J. A. *The Whiz Kids: The Founding Fathers of American Business and the Legacy They Left Us.* New York: Bantam Books, 1993.

"Career Moves for Ages 20 to 70," *Psychology Today,* Nov.–Dec. 1992.

Corbin, A. "The Impact of Drucker on Marketing." In T. H. Bonaparte and J. E. Flaherty (eds.), *Peter Drucker: Contributions to Business Enterprise.* New York: New York University Press, 1970.

Dahl, R. A., and Lindblom, C. E. *Politics, Economics, and Welfare: Planning and Politico-Economic Systems Resolved into Basic Social Processes.* New York: HarperCollins, 1953.

Day, G. S. *Market Driven Strategy.* New York: Free Press, 1990.

Donkin, R. "Interview with Peter Drucker." *Financial Times,* June 14, 1996.

Drucker, P. F. *The End of Economic Man.* New York: John Day, 1939. (Reprint, New York: HarperCollins, 1969.)

Drucker, P. F. *The Future of Industrial Man.* New York: John Day, 1942.

Drucker, P. F. *Concept of the Corporation.* New York: John Day, 1946. (Reprint, New York: Mentor, 1972.)

Drucker, P. F. "The Unfashionable Kierkegaard." *Sewanee Review,* Oct. 1949.

Drucker, P. F. *The New Society: The Anatomy of Industrial Order.* New York: HarperCollins, 1950.

Drucker, P. F. *The Practice of Management.* New York: HarperCollins, 1954.

Drucker, P. F. *America's Next Twenty Years.* New York: HarperCollins, 1955.

Drucker, P. F. "Business Objectives and Survival Needs." *Journal of Business of the University of Chicago,* Apr. 1958.

Drucker, P. F. *Technology, Management and Society: Essays by Peter Drucker.* New York: HarperCollins, 1958. (Reprint, New York: HarperCollins, 1977.)

Drucker, P. F. *Landmarks of Tomorrow.* New York: HarperCollins, 1959.

Drucker, P. F. "Long-Range Planning: Challenge to Management Science." *Management Science,* Apr. 1959.

Drucker, P. F. "Work and Tools." *Technology and Culture,* Winter 1959.

Drucker, P. F. "This Competitive World." *Harvard Business Review,* Mar.–Apr. 1961.

Drucker, P. F. "Managing for Business Effectiveness." *Harvard Business Review,* May–June 1963.

Drucker, P. F. "Twelve Fables of Research Management." *Harvard Business Review,* Jan.–Feb. 1963.

Drucker, P. F. *Managing for Results: Economic Tasks and Risk-Taking Decisions.* New York: HarperCollins, 1964.

Drucker, P. F. "The First Technological Revolution and Its Lessons." *Technology and Culture,* Spring 1966.

Drucker, P. F. *The Effective Executive.* New York: HarperCollins, 1967.

Drucker, P. F. "Technological Trends in the Twentieth Century." In M. Kranzberg and C. Purcell Jr. (eds.), *Technology in Western Civilization,* Vol. 2. New York: Oxford University Press, 1967.

Drucker, P. F. *The Age of Discontinuity: Guidelines to Our Changing Society.* New York: HarperCollins, 1968.

Drucker, P. F. "The Shame of Marketing." *Marketing Communication,* Aug. 1969.

Drucker, P. F. *Men, Ideas and Politics.* New York: HarperCollins, 1971.

Drucker, P. F. "What We Can Learn from Japanese Management." *Harvard Business Review,* Mar.–Apr. 1971.

Drucker, P. F. *Management: Tasks, Responsibilities, Practices.* New York: HarperCollins, 1973.

Drucker, P. F. "New Templates for Today's Organization." *Harvard Business Review,* Jan.–Feb. 1974.

Drucker, P. F. *An Introductory View of Management.* New York: HarperCollins, 1977.

Drucker, P. F. *Adventures of a Bystander.* New York: HarperCollins, 1978. (Reprint, New York: HarperCollins, 1991.)

Drucker, P. F. "Why Management Consultants?" In M. Zimet and R. G. Greenwood (eds.), *The Evolving Science of Management.* New York: AMACOM, 1979.

Drucker, P. F. *Managing in Turbulent Times.* New York: HarperCollins, 1980.

Drucker, P. F. "Behind Japan's Success." *Harvard Business Review,* Jan.–Feb. 1981.

Drucker, P. F. "The Coming Rediscovery of Scientific Management." In *Toward the Next Economics, and Other Essays.* New York: HarperCollins, 1981.

Drucker, P. F. "How to Manage the Boss." *Wall Street Journal,* Aug. 1, 1981.

Drucker, P. F. "Leadership: More Doing Than Dash." *Wall Street Journal,* Jan. 6, 1981.

Drucker, P. F. *Toward the Next Economics, and Other Essays.* New York: HarperCollins, 1981.

Drucker, P. F. "A View of Japan Through Japanese Art." In *Toward the Next Economics, and Other Essays.* New York: HarperCollins, 1981.

Drucker, P. F. *The Changing World of the Executive.* New York: Truman Talley Books, Times Books, 1982.

Drucker, P. F. "Why Some Mergers Work and Many More Don't." *Forbes,* Jan. 18, 1982.

Drucker, P. F. "Getting Things Done: How to Make People Decisions." *Harvard Business Review,* July–Aug. 1985.

Drucker, P. F. *Innovation and Entrepreneurship: Practice and Principles.* New York: Harper-Collins, 1985.

Drucker, P. F. "Why Automation Pays Off." *Wall Street Journal,* Sept. 30, 1985.

Drucker, P. F. *The Frontiers of Management: Where Tomorrow's Decisions Are Being Shaped Today.* New York: Truman Talley Books, Dutton, 1986. (Reprint, New York: Perennial Library, 1987.)

Drucker, P. F. "Keeping U.S. Companies Productive." *Journal of Business Strategy,* Winter 1987.

Drucker, P. F. "Management: The Problems of Success." *Academy of Management Executive,* Feb. 1987.

Drucker, P. F. "The Mystery of the Business Leader." *Wall Street Journal,* Sept. 29, 1987.

Drucker, P. F. "The Coming of the New Organization." *Harvard Business Review,* Jan.–Feb. 1988.

Drucker, P. F. "Management and the World's Work." *Harvard Business Review,* Sept.–Oct. 1988.

Drucker, P. F. "Teaching the Work of Management." *New Management,* Fall 1988.

Drucker, P. F. "Tomorrow's Restless Managers." *Industry Week,* Apr. 18, 1988.

Drucker, P. F. "New Age Sessions Are Same Old Brainwashing." *Wall Street Journal,* Feb. 9, 1989.

Drucker, P. F. *The New Realities: In Government and Politics / In Economics and Business / In Society and World View.* New York: HarperCollins, 1989.

Drucker, P. F. "What Business Can Learn from Non-Profits." *Harvard Business Review,* July–Aug. 1989.

Drucker, P. F. "The Best Book on Management Ever." *Fortune,* Apr. 23, 1990.

Drucker, P. F. "Making Managers of Communism's Bureaucrats." *Wall Street Journal,* Aug. 15, 1990.

Drucker, P. F. *Managing the Non-Profit Organization: Principles and Practices.* New York: HarperCollins, 1990.

Drucker, P. F. "The New Productivity Challenge." *Harvard Business Review,* Nov.–Dec. 1991.

Drucker, P. F. "Be Data Literate: Know What to Know." *Wall Street Journal,* Dec. 1, 1992.

Drucker, P. F. *Managing for the Future: The 1990s and Beyond.* New York: Truman Talley Books, Dutton, 1992.

Drucker, P. F. "The New Society of Organizations." *Harvard Business Review,* Sept.–Oct. 1992.

Drucker, P. F. *The Ecological Vision: Reflections on the American Condition.* New Brunswick, N.J.: Transaction, 1993.

Drucker, P. F. "The Five Deadly Business Sins." *Wall Street Journal,* Oct. 21, 1993.

Drucker, P. F. *Post-Capitalist Society.* New York: HarperCollins, 1993.

Drucker, P. F. "Professionals' Productivity." *Across the Board,* Nov.–Dec. 1993.

Drucker, P. F. "The Retail Revolution." *Wall Street Journal,* July 15, 1993.

Drucker, P. F. "The Theory of the Business." *Harvard Business Review,* Sept.–Oct. 1994.

Drucker, P. F. "Drucker's Challenge for CMAs." *Managing Accounting Magazine,* June 1995.

Drucker, P. F. "The Information Executives Truly Need." *Harvard Business Review,* Jan.–Feb. 1995.

Drucker, P. F. Introduction. In P. Graham (ed.), *Mary Parker Follett: Prophet of Management.* Boston: Harvard Business School Press, 1995.

Drucker, P. F. *Managing in a Time of Great Change.* New York: Truman Talley Books, Dutton, 1995.

Drucker, P. F. Foreword. In F. Hesselbein, M. Goldsmith, and R. Beckhard (eds.), *The Leader of the Future: New Visions, Strategies, and Practices for the Next Era.* San Francisco: Jossey-Bass, 1996.

Drucker, P. F. "Management's New Paradigms." *Forbes,* Oct. 5, 1998.

Drucker, P. F., and Nakauchi, I. *Drucker on Asia: A Dialogue Between Peter Drucker and Isao Nakauchi.* Newton, Mass.: Butterworth-Heinemann, 1997.

Flower, J. "Being Effective: A Conversation with Peter Drucker." *Health Care Forum Journal,* May–June 1991.

Gendron, G. " 'Flashes of Genius.' " *Inc., 18*(7), May 1996. (Special issue: The State of Small Business.)

Halberstam, D. *The Reckoning.* New York: Morrow, 1986.

Hall, E. "A Conversation with Peter F. Drucker." *Psychology Today,* Dec. 1982.

Hall, M. H. "The Psychology of Managing Management." *Psychology Today,* Mar. 1968.

Hamel, G., and Prahalad, C. K. *Competing for the Future.* Boston: Harvard Business School Press, 1994.

Harris, T. G. "The Post-Capitalist Executive: An Interview with Peter F. Drucker." *Harvard Business Review,* May–June 1993.

Hofstadter, R. *The American Political Tradition.* New York: Knopf, 1948.

Johnson, H. T., and Kaplan, R. *Relevance Lost: The Rise and Fall of Management Accounting.* Boston: Harvard Business School Press, 1983.

Johnson, M. "Drucker Speaks His Mind." *Management Review,* Oct. 1995.

Kami, M. J. *Trigger Points.* New York: McGraw-Hill, 1988.

Kantrow, A. M. "Why Read Peter Drucker?" *Harvard Business Review,* Jan.–Feb. 1980.

Kaufmann, W. (ed.). *Philosophic Classics,* Vol. 2: *Bacon to Kant.* Upper Saddle River, N.J.: Prentice Hall, 1962.

Lacey, R. L. *Ford: The Men and the Machine.* Boston: Little Brown, 1986.

Lenzer, R., and Johnson, S. S. "Seeing Things as They Really Are." *Forbes,* Mar. 10, 1997.

Levitt, T. "The Living Legacy of Peter Drucker." In T. H. Bonaparte and J. E. Flaherty (eds.), *Peter Drucker: Contributions to Business Enterprise.* New York: New York University Press, 1970.

Levitt, T. "A View of 'Management.'" *Business Week,* Feb. 9, 1974.

Micklethwait, J., and Wooldridge, A. *Witch Doctors: Making Sense of the Management Gurus.* New York: Times Books, 1996.

Murray, T. "Peter Drucker Attacks: Our Top-Heavy Corporations." *Dun's,* Apr. 1971.

Ortega y Gasset, J. *The Revolt of the Masses.* New York: Norton, 1932.

Parkinson, C. N. Foreword. In J. J. Tarrant, *Drucker: The Man Who Invented the Corporate Society.* Boston: Cahners Books, 1976.

Poe, R. "A Walk and Talk with Peter Drucker." *Across the Board,* Feb. 1983.

Polak, M. L. "Business Should Be Boring." *Philadelphia Inquirer Magazine,* Aug. 30, 1987.

Richman, T. "The Entrepreneurial Mystique" (interview with Peter Drucker). *Inc.,* Oct. 1985.

Rutigliano, A. "An Interview with Peter Drucker: Managing the New." *Management Review,* Jan. 1986.

Schwartz, P., and Kelley, K. "A Cantankerous Interview with Peter Schwartz and Kevin Kelley." *Wired,* Aug. 1996.

Sheehan, J. J. *German History 1770–1866.* New York: Oxford University Press, 1989.

Skrzycki, C. "The Enduring Peter Drucker." *Washington Post,* May 7, 1989.

Smith, A. "The Shape of Things to Come." *New York Times Book Review,* Apr. 11, 1993.

Tarrant, J. J. *Drucker: The Man Who Invented the Corporate Society.* Boston: Cahners Books, 1976.

Truell, P., and Gurwin, L. *False Profits.* Boston: Houghton Mifflin, 1992.

Wooldridge, A. "Peter Drucker on L.A. Versus San Francisco, Downsizing and Newt the Entrepreneur." *Los Angeles Times,* Feb. 2, 1997.

THE AUTHOR

*J*ohn E. Flaherty is professor-in-residence emeritus at Pace University, where he was formerly dean of the Graduate School of Business and chairman of the Social Science Department. He earned his B.A. degree from Union College in Schenectady, New York, and his M.A. and Ph.D. degrees from New York University. Before joining the faculty at Pace in 1950, he taught at Long Island University and New York University.

Flaherty's main research concern has been the interaction between the corporation and society. He is the coeditor of *Peter Drucker: Contributions to Business Enterprise* (with Tony Bonaparte, 1970) and the author of *Managing Change* (1979). Over the past forty years he has consulted and participated in executive training programs with scores of corporations. He now lives with his wife in Convent Station, New Jersey.

INDEX

A

Abandonment, systematic, 104, 149–158; Bernoulli theorem for, 152–154; concentration versus diversification and, 155–158; Drucker's recommendations for, 154–155; executive effectiveness and, 313–315; guideline-questions for, 314–315; implementation of, 152–155; market as criterion for, 149–150; methodologies for, 152–154; of outdated mission, 150–151; of outdated products and services, 149–150; of people, 153–154; resistance to, 151–152; transactional analysis for, 152

Absolutism, rational, 266–268, 269

Academic community: Drucker's reputation in, 16, 176, 260, 377–379; management field status in, 75–76; reception of *Concept of the Corporation* in, 64, 75; reception of *The Practice of Management* in, 81

Academic curriculum: financial accounting and computer science in, 149; in management, 75–76, 377–379

Academic specialization: Drucker's views on, 9, 16; management curriculum and, 75–76, 80, 378; social ecology and, 50; systems theory and, 49

Acclaim for Drucker. *See* Drucker, P.; Reception and reputation

Accounting. *See* Activity accounting; Cost accounting; Financial analysis; Quantitative measurement

Accounting departments, 149

Accounting executives, 73

Acetaminophen, 203–204

Acquisitions: guidelines for, 208–209; as structural entrepreneurship, 208–210

Activity accounting, 146–149, 376–377; Drucker's suggestions for, 148; limitations of, 147–148, 177; transactional analysis and, 146–147; use of, for entrepreneurial management, 131, 147–148

Adams, H., 8

Adams, S., 249

Adaptive innovation, 165–170; defined, 163–164; principles of, 165–170. *See also* Innovation; Transitional business

Administrative details, executives mired in, 286, 287–288, 325

Adventures of a Bystander (Drucker), 6–7, 318

Advertising, as form of preselling, 133

Agar, H., 15

Age, chronological versus culture, 235

Age of Discontinuity (Drucker), 227

Agenda setting, for meetings, 326–327

Aggregates versus components analysis, 141–143, 197

Agrarian society, working in, 245

Alertness, entrepreneurial, 191–192

Alibis, 301, 353

Alienation, 40–41

Alliances: causes of failed, 210; contractual agreements for, 210; cross-border, 183; for small and